Gender, artWork and the global imperative

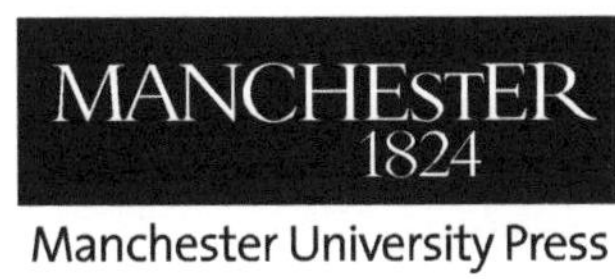

MANCHESTER
1824

Manchester University Press

rethinking
art's histories

SERIES EDITORS
Amelia G. Jones, Marsha Meskimmon

Rethinking Art's Histories aims to open out art history from its most basic structures by foregrounding work that challenges the conventional periodisation and geographical subfields of traditional art history, and addressing a wide range of visual cultural forms from the early modern period to the present.

These books will acknowledge the impact of recent scholarship on our understanding of the complex temporalities and cartographies that have emerged through centuries of world-wide trade, political colonisation and the diasporic movement of people and ideas across national and continental borders.

Also available in the series

Art, museums and touch   Fiona Candlin

The 'do-it-yourself' artwork: Participation from fluxus to relational aesthetics   Anna Dezeuze (ed.)

After the event: New perspectives in art history
Charles Merewether and John Potts (eds)

Photography and documentary film in the making of modern Brazil
Luciana Martins

Women, the arts and globalization: Eccentric experience
Marsha Meskimmon and Dorothy Rowe (eds)

After-affects/after-images: Trauma and aesthetic transformation in the virtual Feminist museum   Griselda Pollock

Vertiginous mirrors: The animation of the visual image and early modern travel   Rose Marie San Juan

Screen/space: The projected image in contemporary art   Tamara Trodd (ed.)

Timed out: Art and the transnational Caribbean   Leon Wainwright

Gender, artWork and the global imperative

A materialist feminist critique

Angela Dimitrakaki

Manchester University Press

Published by Manchester University Press
Oxford Road, Manchester M13 9PL, UK
www.manchesteruniversitypress.co.uk

British Library Cataloguing-in-Publication Data
A catalogue record for this book is available from the British Library

ISBN 978 0 7190 8359 4   hardback
ISBN 978 0 7894 9294 1   paperback

First published 2013

The publisher has no responsibility for the persistence or accuracy of URLs for external or any third-party internet websites referred to in this book, and does not guarantee that any content on such websites is, or will remain, accurate or appropriate.

Typeset in Minion with Myriad
by Toppan Best-set Premedia Limited

Contents

List of illustrations

Acknowledgements

The book is the culmination of many years of absorbing, doubting, testing and re-gaining confidence in a politically meaningful connection between feminism and contemporary art. My journey began with my doctoral research in the late 1990s, with Susan Malvern (to whom I am indebted), and has continued through teaching and writing. Completing this book in 2013, after several years of focused research in conditions of global turbulence, is my way of accepting that the issues preoccupying me in relation to feminist praxis will not go away in my lifetime and will require regular revisiting and revising. I would like to express my gratitude to all those who helped me remain calm in the face of this prospect and who enable and motivate me to keep trying. Thanks are due to my mother, Despoina (the first feminist I loved and fought against), my sister, Christina (an expert in solidarity), and my wee daughter, Alma (the negation of my negation); my students at the University of Edinburgh for occasionally asserting that feminist values can save lives; my colleagues and friends, especially Jenny, Dimitris and Diogenis; Miltos Tsiantis, the best interlocutor on the complex subject of historical materialism I could ever have had; Oskari Kuusela for a lot really, including for demonstrating the persistence of ideology against which feminism is practised. Above all, I remain indebted to the artists, curators and historians whose groundbreaking work inspired this research – in particular Ursula Biemann whose video essays, when I first encountered them in the early 2000s, suggested to me that something was changing; I am grateful to the Royal Society of Edinburgh (RSE), The Carnegie Trust for the Universities of Scotland, and the University of Edinburgh for their financial support; to the series editors Marsha Meskimmon, Amelia Jones and the MUP team for their patience and encouragement; to Mujeres Públicas for the cover photo and all the individuals and organisations that provided images with such generosity. Last but not least, I am grateful to the women who, as au pairs, have supported me in my often impossible double role of migrant waged labourer and unwaged mother: Tuuli, Emmi, Henna, Moona, Emma, Jenna, thank you. In Chapter 2, my discussion of Mare Tralla's *WeeViews* draws on my short article, 'The Global

Art World and Critical Melancholy: Mare Tralla's WeeViews', *Read More* Issue 7 (2008): 3–6, freely available at http://issuu.com/horsecrossarts/docs/read-moreissue-7. Chapter 4 is a slightly revised version of my article 'Materialist Feminism for the Twenty-first Century: The Video Essays of Ursula Biemann', *Oxford Art Journal* 30 (2) (2007), 205–32. I am grateful for the permission to reproduce it here.

Introduction
Capital, gender and the work of art: an intervention of, and in, materialist feminism

On the densely woven histories of women, art, work, capital, feminism

This book is about feminism, art and its histories in the globalised socio-economic paradigm of the early twenty-first century. The exploration of ideas and practices in the pages that follow constitutes an effort to think through the contradictions of this perplexing moment, which feminism must claim as its own. This is because women are proving to be at great disadvantage in the socio-economic processes we understand as globalisation. Not all women of course. If we aim for the big picture, some, very few, women are, or at least appear to be, in a much better position than others. And so globalisation can also be apprehended as an epoch where the exploitation of woman by woman has been realised as a tragic extension of Marx's understanding of capitalism as man's exploitation of man. Let me provide an example. In December 2009 *The Economist* published a special issue on 'Women and Work'. Subtitled 'We did it!' and featuring on its cover a drawing of Rosie the Riveter, a popular American icon during the Second World War when women were urged to (temporarily) take up men's place as industrial workers for the good of the country, the special issue's editorial stated:

> At a time when the world is short of causes for celebration, here is a candidate: within the next few months women will cross the 50% threshold and become the majority of the American workforce. Women already make up the majority of university graduates in the OECD countries and the majority of professional workers in several rich countries, including the United States. Women run many of the world's great companies, from PepsiCo in America to Areva in France. Women's economic empowerment is arguably the biggest social change of our times.[1]

This triumphal statement requires contextualisation. First, articles in the same special issue highlighted an important fact: the entry of women into the formally acknowledged labour force did not become possible through a redistribution of domestic labour between men and women. Nor did it happen because of a welfare state in support of high quality, affordable (let alone free), public childcare. Rather, what primarily permitted American women's flooding of waged labour sites was an army of cheap female domestic servants imported from less privileged societies (in this case, mostly Mexico).[2] Second, most women do not run multinational companies on six-figure salaries. Rather, many work for multinational companies that outsource their production units so that they can hire cheap female labour outside the First World. Third, the white female industrial worker figure, represented by Rosie the Riveter, hardly represents women at work today – and certainly not in a developed economy such as the United States. The entry of women into waged labour is connected with capitalism's transformation into a service economy.[3] Yet the last sentence of *The Economist* quotation above makes an insightful connection: contrary to dominant strands of feminist thinking that underplay the links between economic and social processes, the editorial asserts that an economic fact is translated into, and must be understood in terms of, *social change*. And significantly, the editorial also sees women's position in the economy as central to 'the biggest social change of our time'. Even if women's actual position in the economy is hereby blatantly misrepresented, the link between women and the economy is established as the motor of contemporary social life and its transformation. An emphasis on this link is also claimed in the present study, although it is pursued through attention to the often wayward and experimental practices comprising art and its contexts. Outside the circles of art-world intellectuals, such practices are rarely ever associated with the affirmation or subversion of neoliberal ideology, for instance, or with the boosting of knowledge economies or with the glamorisation of mobility. In this respect, this study attempts to do something new: to investigate how a complex production paradigm, globalisation, typically experienced as 'culture', engages the gendered territories of art and vice versa.

But how is art indeed relevant to all the above? An answer to this question can begin in many different ways. First, the feminist art movement – that should be perhaps renamed as the feminist art and art history movement, since art history played a major role in the movement's claims and direction – illuminated the inseparability of art as a gendered practice from the power relations constituting a gendered society. This movement, focused on art and its histories, took shape in the late 1960s and throughout the 1970s, mainly in the West in interaction with, and as part of, a militant women's movement. Feminist art, like feminist art history, did not provide, and could not have provided, a unified terrain of artistic and social critique because, as in all spheres of human action, ideological divisions in this terrain were deeply connected with women's and feminists' different lives as well as historical process as such. Precisely how second-wave feminism fitted within a broader historical process is a moot point at present. And this has important implications for understanding how feminist art and art history operated within the same historical process. As regards second-wave feminism in general, in recent years there has been the argument that 'the cultural changes jump-started by the second wave, salutary in themselves, have served to legitimate a structural transformation of capitalist society that runs directly counter to feminist visions for a just society'.[4]

Groundbreaking and devastating, this argument, at least as shaped by American feminist theorist Nancy Fraser, does not constitute a charge against second-wave feminism but an astute analysis of its political economy. Irrespective of its motives and intentions, how feminism's second wave operated within a totality of social and economic relations after the Second World War emerged as an urgent issue for feminism at the most recent *fin de siècle*. Feminist art history, and feminist cultural analysis more generally, possessed this way of thinking from early on. Griselda Pollock, a founding figure of feminist art history, and others persistently argued that even when feminist intentions are present, these do not guarantee that a work of art or a cultural practice achieves a subversion, let alone transformation, of gender and related hierarchies.[5] That said, it has been really hard to determine what does, which is partly why the feminist art and art history movement spent much of its energy debating which strategy, realised as art practice and/or theory, would stand the best chance of meeting feminist objectives.

But did all feminists share the same objectives? The short answer is yes *and* no. Whereas all feminists agreed on the objective of ending women's oppression, there was no consensus on what this oppression was an outcome of. This becomes in fact clearer if we look at art. While some feminists merely wished for equal representation of male and female artists (dead or alive!) in art institutions, others saw the very institutions of art as representative of broader structures and ideologies that were inherently oppressive to women (and most men). For these feminists, the problem was not merely access but what one claimed access to. And there were a number of variants within this divided position concerning art as an institution as well as similarly divided positions on other matters. With the benefit of hindsight, we can say today that *only those feminists who claimed access to art's existent institutions met (some of) their objectives*. Of course, their struggle entailed and pressed for institutional reform. For example, they had to convincingly argue that women are just as good artists as men so that collectors and museums would start to buy and show women's work. This was partly achieved, and so we have a number of successful and highly visible women artists today. And the same pretty much happened with female curators. But these reforms did not amount to a new art world. Successful women artists do not necessarily wish for a new art world where their 'success', as defined in a capitalist market economy, might be undermined.

In 2006, Britain's Channel 4 documentary series 'Artshock' presented renowned female artist Tracey Emin investigating which factors in women's lives prevent women artists from securing as good sales as male colleagues.[6] The questions posed by Emin are in fact highly relevant to this study, as they highlight the connection between a woman's so-called life choices (for example, to have children or not) and her success in the environments of paid-for work. But the question for Emin is how women *can* sell, not whether selling and buying in capitalist markets possibly structures women's exploitation and oppression. Indeed, we have witnessed the unstoppable unfolding of an art market where even socially oriented feminist art is ultimately inscribed not as a practice conducive to social justice but as a valuable curiosity, politically correct but preferably shocking, and often exotic – if the work is made by an artist who happens to bear the credentials of cultural otherness. As expected, not all varieties of cultural otherness are welcome by the market as the alpha art institution. Instead, market and institutions subordinate to it are in a position to regulate entry, so that different cultural others can exist in a competitive, antagonistic relationship. One 'benefit' of this is that the entry of this or that cultural other into the institution can assume the guise of political success and be perceived as a privilege that few would oppose. And, as *Third Text* founder Rasheed Araeen has polemically suggested, postcolonial critique and identity politics (with which second-wave feminism was closely allied) had exactly the same fate in the art world.[7]

The bottom line is that we must recognise *feminism as an ideologically divided terrain*, one connected with broader material socio-economic divisions. Arguably, for the sake of a future-oriented solidarity, Fraser's argument underplayed the issue of ideological divisions within feminism and so sees second-wave feminism at large as enabling or at least dovetailing with processes that – today, we know – have deepened most women's oppression (and also men's). This study begins by acknowledging ideological divisions within feminism. It thus sides with a current of feminist praxis, known as materialist feminism, which became particularly important in the early years of second-wave feminism. But as many have observed, after the 1970s materialist feminism receded.[8] This is important to remember when (re)thinking feminist histories, also or perhaps especially in the arts. In short, as postmodernism advanced, materialist feminism lost ground but feminism *did not*, found instead to thrive hand in hand with postmodernism.[9] How can we resolve this absurd equation?

Perhaps we cannot, yet. Such a rethinking of the course of feminist (art) histories can only be achieved if we start reflecting on the kind of feminism we need in the first half of the twenty-first century. Beyond art history's feminist project, materialist feminism is now making an inspiring come-back.

Indicatively, in 2012, the editorial of the first issue of *Lies: A Journal of Materialist Feminism* stated:

> we draw on and participate in multiple traditions of thought and struggle: feminism, Marxism, queer theory, communist theory, and anti-racist theory. We find abstraction useful but we aim to keep our ideas grounded, to see how the contours of thought are also social relationships. We are careful that whatever work or politics our ideas imply is desirable, while not forgetting that an idea is never a brick, and in this way our feminist practice is materialist.[10]

The above excerpt already points to an expanded, exploratory and experimental materialist feminism wishing to leave no stone (or brick) unturned in an effort to understand what exactly constitutes the material terms of gender-based oppression. This study hopes to contribute to this new materialist feminism and, by examining issues that pertain to art, to strengthen its interdisciplinary make-up. The book's thematic and methodological orientation were decided with this in mind, and should, in the first instance, be seen as an attempt to revive the interrupted project of materialist feminism in art history and to highlight the latter's relevance for a rigorous reading of recent developments.

By 'materialist feminism' I mean a feminism that is informed by historical materialism in the broadest sense, stressing an analytical commitment to illuminating the interpenetration of gender hierarchies and capitalism, where such interpenetration is seen to produce material, and not least, ideological effects. The rise of an economic subject in contemporary art supplanting the cultural subjects of postmodernism, as I argue in subsequent chapters, the newly totalising tendencies of contemporary capital and the hugely influential new terminologies emanating primarily from a revitalised Marxist critique of globalisation (often drawing on and updating the lessons of Italian Autonomia from the 1970s) are three reasons that necessitate, in my view, a rethinking of the possibilities of materialist feminism in art history and beyond.[11] And this is indeed underway, precisely because of the exacerbation of social discontent that has accompanied the consolidation of global capital in the 1990s and its regime of 'permanent crisis' from the following decade to date. As put by feminist social theorist and activist Chandra Talpade Mohanty:

> political shifts to the right, accompanied by global capitalist hegemony, privatization and increased religious, ethnic and racial hatreds, pose very concrete challenges for feminists. In this context, I ask what it would mean to be attentive to the micropolitics of everyday life as well as to the larger processes that recolonize the culture and identities of people across the globe. How we think of the local in/of the global and vice versa without falling into colonizing or cultural relativist platitudes about difference is crucial in this intellectual and

political landscape. And for me, this kind of thinking is tied to a revised race-and-gender conscious historical materialism.[12]

Like Mohanty, I consider the exchange between feminism and historical materialism a response to, and an outcome of, historical forces. Ultimately, it is these forces that suggest the focal points of this study as described in the book's title: gender, artWork and the global imperative. The book title does not name 'these forces' as 'capital' (the title's absent guest, whose place at the table no one can dare challenge) in order to enhance the impression of capital's spectral presence – now perceptible, now imperceptible – and its diffusion into and across social, economic and sexual relations. Instead, the title names two other more ambiguous terms, whose relevance to feminist politics in the arts is hereby claimed. I am referring, of course, to the title's 'artWork' and 'global imperative'. Let's begin with the latter, as a prerequisite for understanding the former.

Globalisation has become a colloquial term since the 1990s though it entered the conceptual apparatus of art history a bit later. A declared engagement with globalisation as the defining framework of contemporary art emerged in art history in the first decade of the twenty-first century, with the first reader explicitly focused on the subject appearing in anglophone literature only in 2011.[13] Significantly, art history and cultural analysis more generally witnessed (are witnessing) a lot of confusion as to what globalisation actually means. The word 'global' had become so ideologically dominant in the previous fifteen years as to be constantly appropriated by discourses and research fields under pressure to be updated and 'modernise'. These efforts were premised on the observation that ultimately 'globalisation' is an empty vessel awaiting content.[14] And in many respects these voices were right. Globalisation can be simply described as a process of something spreading around the globe. And yet it is far from accidental that the term 'globalisation' became itself viral on a global scale during a particular phase in the history of capitalism, one defining the closure of the twentieth century. It is not, for example, that the widespread use of 'globalisation' coincided with the spread of patriarchy or socialism around the world. Patriarchy was already there and socialism is nowhere. Globalisation thus refers us to the globalisation of capitalism, to the full encompassing of geographically dispersed human life by capital – an encompassing that required the prior colonisation of world resources during the era of Western imperialism and the discrediting of any alternatives to capitalism. But the era of Western imperialism has gone and Soviet culture, for those who considered it an alternative to capitalism, ended noisily around 1990.

As I write these lines, in 2012, post-Maoist China is the second economic power in the world, fully operative in the global capitalist market. Globalisation cannot therefore be equated with Americanisation, although this impression remained valid for many years because US geopolitical and economic hegemony has been a complex combination of military force and an aggressively exported cultural industry. Yet what is crucial is that the globalisation of capital is *not* a mere geographical condition. Capital is realised as a relationship between human beings and with oneself and globalisation describes, to an extent, the generalisation and ubiquity of this relationship. This is why a feminist art history addressing globalisation *cannot* be equated to a process of representing, in exhibitions or studies such as this one, women's art drawn from all the uneven geographies of capital.[15] In deploying the phrase 'the global imperative' in the book title I intend to raise curiosity: what is the global imperative? To what process or processes does it really refer? Who exercises it or aspires to it? If the global imperative belongs to capitalism, it can also belong to a politics of resistance and emancipation, such as feminism – and to give an example, the quest for transnational feminist solidarity, as flagged up by Mohanty and others, entails just such a global imperative.

There has been a lot of emphasis recently on transnationalism in the arts, also in relation to feminism. But because the art market's structure enacts relationships of competition, as described above, transnationalism has often been translated into a politics of representation and various returns to cultural translation. This study sees a need for a slight but important shift of the terrain. Whereas geography remains one axis of analysis, my aim here is not to represent, say, women's art from across the globe. Instead, in understanding capital's global imperative as transforming women's and men's lives (and not merely their habitus) and feminism's global imperative as exposing how and where this occurs and to what gendered effects, this study focuses primarily on work. More specifically, it focuses on the exchange between art and work – an emerging issue in art-world debates as I was conducting this research from 2007 onwards.[16] The question posed in relation to art as a gendered practice, but one capable also of challenging gender norms, is: what understandings of gender relations does art provide when approached as a form of work? The term 'artWork' is intended to take further feminist art history's partial displacement of the delivered artwork as the exclusive origin of meaning and rethink what 'process-based work' can possibly describe. Yet the artwork is far from irrelevant to this enquiry. For to understand what artists do when they work today in, and with, the sites of gender, one must look at the artworks they make. This, after a long but inevitable detour, brings me to the second answer that the question 'what art has to do with it all?' can receive.

Simply put, art has evolved along with the economy, meaning that it has changed along with capital's connection with the social field. In the past ten years, critics have noted a new 'social turn' in art and have also questioned the hegemony of postmodernism, which provided the dominant paradigm in cultural life from the 1970s to about the mid-1990s.[17] Some theorists have stressed the impact of globalisation on the transformation of art, though there is *no* overarching theory describing and accounting for these changes. Broadly speaking, the social turn in art evident around 2000 is understood to have generated a new emphasis on collaborative artistic practice, a critical engagement with real life and an interest in art's possibility to provide knowledge about the social field. Recent studies have stressed art's dialogical nature, the artists' exodus from the studio and the relocation of their practice in the terrain of social relations, the exchange between documentary techniques and the subjective inscription of social processes, the importance of curatorial work in determining art's meaning and remit of intervention, the fraught relationship between activism, art-making and theory as social praxis as well as a critical revival of cosmopolitanism. Let us consider briefly some of these positions and their relationship with this book's general aims.

Grant H. Kester notes, for instance, that 'a number of contemporary artists and art collectives…have defined their practice around the facilitation of dialogue among diverse communities', further observing that 'the idea that a work of art should solicit participation and involvement so openly…is antithetical to dominant beliefs in both modernist and postmodernist art and theory'.[18] Kester pinpoints the problem as the inability and/or reluctance of a hegemonic art paradigm in the twentieth century at large to deal with a 'collaborative, rather than a specular, relationship with the viewer'.[19] Setting the problem in these terms has important repercussions for feminism as a critical art discourse and practice since, during postmodernism, feminists placed emphasis on a politics of representation that remained largely specular. It is in this context that psychoanalysis was found to be such a useful tool. Many of the practices highlighted in this book suggest precisely *a disruption of a purely specular economy in contemporary art*, but this disruption does not merely – or always – involve the viewer. Instead, it may well involve social actors whose everyday reality constitutes the ground for the work of art – the ground where art does its work – but who may remain distinct from art's 'secondary public', that is those who often experience art as a finished and aesthetically perfected object (or text) in an institutional context.[20] This issue becomes particularly important in critical theorisations of the documentary turn, with which this study necessarily engages – both because the documentary turn is increasingly witnessed in the efforts to chart capital's gendered and classed landscapes and because it has been so visible in art addressing globalisation. T. J. Demos has argued that an exchange between documentary and fiction sustains the primarily aesthetic import of contemporary art whereas Carles Guerra has placed the documentary turn within an expanded pedagogical and epistemic project for contemporary art at present.[21] How a feminist politics is, or can be, realised through these exchanges among aesthetics and a politics of knowledge addressing global space is a question that is raised throughout this book.

In attending to both the broader imagination of contemporary art and feminist concerns, in 2011, Marsha Meskimmon provided a vital insight in addressing this question. Noting the feminist preoccupation with domesticity and the figure of 'home' since the 1970s, she observes that, paradoxically, 'the most nuanced explorations of the domestic in contemporary art tend to be found in work that is decidedly not "local", work that has no intention of staying at home'. She further notes that contemporary works inscripting home, literally and metaphorically, displace 'constructions of "authentic" identity', and, for her, such works 'constitute a form of "being at home" that is simultaneously marked by movement, change and multiplicity. In this way, they participate in a critical dialogue between ethical responsibility, locational identity' and what Meskimmon calls 'cosmopolitan imagination'.[22] The question she poses is: 'What are the ethical and political implications of be(long)ing at home everywhere, of a cosmopolitan imagination that is premised upon an embodied, embedded, generous and affective form of subjectivity in conversation with others in and through difference?'[23] Meskimmon then engages both the legacy of second-wave feminism (the concern with the domestic) and postcolonial critique (the concern with multiple locations and the transformation of identity) to rethink the premises of a contemporary subjectivity that art practice helps produce rather than merely represent. This subjectivity is cast in a positive light: it is about being generous, affective and ethically aware of difference. As such, it should be distinguished from the cosmopolitan subjectivities that a privileged art world produces and recycles, as described, for instance, by Miwon Kwon in her groundbreaking study of contemporary art's right of crossing through social sites.[24] But whether, indeed, it can be distinguished remains a moot point, precisely because, as we find out in many parts of this study, art as the site of inter-subjective relations is also a site of labour – or work, as the distinction is impossible to draw in contemporary capitalism where the Fordist (assembly-line) economy distinction between life as separate from work is unsettled.[25]

Numerous analyses of how we work in the early twenty-first century note the hegemony of immaterial labour (meaning work that does not produce tangible goods and/or is dominated by informatised production) as concomitant with capital's globalisation. Affective labour constitutes a widespread paradigm of immaterial labour, and so we see that the affective turn of contemporary art exists not exclusively in ethical terms, partaking instead in a more general shift of the production relations that give capital its historically specific form in the twenty-first century. Even as the appropriateness of the phrase 'immaterial labour' is questionable, the processes the term refers to have been the main cause for the rise of an economic subject as an effect of diffused economic relations. Contemporary forms of work are, indeed, productive of subjectivity and this is where opinions differ. Whether contemporary labour produces a surplus of social relations that cannot be captured by capital is what divides theories that focus on contemporary relations of production when, at the same time, such relations are largely understood as biopolitical: as extending to, and traversing, all aspects of a social being's life, not just the part that is traditionally understood as work. Contemporary capital is, indeed, a generalised regime of power relations that organise and administer life as productivity that can ultimately generate profit. Materialist feminists, including those associated with Autonomist Marxism, have persistently drawn attention to how women's role in species reproduction and childrearing also produces tomorrow's armies of workers (who will in turn produce the surplus value that generates the capitalist's profit), though *this* kind of essential productivity is purposefully mystified by capital as private and placed outside the regime of labour.[26] Indeed, the reason why feminism associated with Italian Autonomia in the 1970s is revisited today with some urgency is capital's generalised biopolitical rule and the loss of distinction between work and life.[27] And as regards modern art, it is now acknowledged that its cherished values of autonomy, flexibility, privileged non-alienation and round-the-clock creativity (the passion for work) were used at the close of the twentieth century as the blueprint for the highly exploitative regime of globally dominant productivity today. In the words of Brian Holmes, 'the social system had to accept and divert the demands for autonomy, self-expression and meaning; it had to turn these very demands into a new mode of control'.[28] A mode of control that, as Michel Foucault suspected early on and others clarified in greater detail later on, is exercised across all human – and necessarily socialised – activity so that the entirety of life is subjected to the power relations addressed by politics.[29]

The current realisation that we collectively – if very unevenly – inhabit such a biopolitical reality is both good and bad news for feminism. On the one hand, second-wave feminism's call to recognise the personal as political is harder than ever to refute, being of undisputed relevance to women, men and anyone in between or beyond. But on the other hand, contemporary feminism is facing the challenge of explicating how the personal as political continues to be expressed as a gendered reality, as well as sustaining connections with other sites of struggle where gender-based oppression often becomes a secondary issue. This study offers many opportunities to consider art's biopolitical existence at present – opportunities where gender is found to play a crucial role in seeing how the historical avant-gardes' quest for art as life becomes realised today. The generalised biopolitical rule suggests, however, that any such understandings do not just hold meaning for art and its histories

– a condition that has everything to do with art's commitment to forms of experimentation that involve, knowingly or not, the social field.

On when, how and why this book was written

Following on from the above, the writing of this book is part of a wider effort to consider the impact of the expansion of the capitalist mode of production on contemporary art as a gendered practice. I came up with the idea after I became a mother in 2006 in a household where two (female–male), highly educated, commuting, 'immaterial' workers, immigrants to the UK from two Schengen Area countries could share parenthood only during the weekend, and even then we were compelled to keep on 'working' for our formal economy jobs in turns. I submitted the book proposal to the UK publisher in 2009. In the course of writing the book, I became a single mother: the threat of unemployment meant that parting with one's tenured job contract (wherever one could find it) was apparently harder psychologically than breaking with the nuclear family model. I wrote most of the book during a short sabbatical in my home town, Athens – a decision based on the availability of free, family-provided childcare that would make frequent research travel possible. Writing in Athens in the autumn of 2010 meant living through the crushing impact of fresh neoliberal 'structural adjustment' policies, now uniting the edges of Europe (Greece) and Latin America (Argentina), while alternative and mainstream media were registering an emerging student movement in Britain, where I was (and am) employed, rising against the apparent dismantling of higher education by a neo-Conservative government (for example, with the introduction of fees, the pressure to promote IT over humanities courses and emphasis on a more vocational paradigm). Artists, along with other cultural workers, were also becoming vocal about the slashing of public art funding. Whereas only a few years ago mentioning the economy invited charges of economic reductionism, the economy was suddenly all I heard and talked about. In the summer of 2012, when I finally sent the book to the publisher, the economy was still all I was hearing about. The economy is no longer just the economy, and this is partly what urged me to rethink artistic practice in ways that hopefully elucidate such a realisation.

I therefore strive here to attend to artWork that engages with social phenomena associated, in many different and not always transparent ways, with globalisation, as well as with the processes and contexts of art making, including if, and how, a 'global imperative' has transformed the social role of the artist as a gendered individual. Finally, what motivated this study was the need to reflect on the role of feminist politics in mediating such developments. The connections established among different chapters are intended to facilitate a revisiting of the premises of feminist art history, a site of theoretical mediation and political contestation enacted in the 1970s, in an attempt to align feminist critique with recent work in left political theory addressing globalisation but also the demand for a new feminist paradigm in art history as an evolving discipline. Yet by attempting to bring together contemporary art, political theory on the left, the legacies of feminist criticism and the desire of art history to review its critical visions, this study is situated in a complex intellectual space. The latter is defined by major contradictions, of which the following are but a sample.

A prominent contradiction is that questions in the academy and beyond over the viability and necessity of feminist politics are posed right when the expansion of global capitalism has apparently engendered, or rendered visible, a further deepening of the gender gap worldwide, leading to formulations such as 'the feminisation of poverty'.[30] A global terrain of antagonisms was thus exposed where gender plays a structural role. Second, new political theory on the left addressing globalisation is similarly, and rather curiously, also peripheralising the diversity and ideological battles of feminist legacies. Third, the currently increasing demand for politically aware or socially minded art, often including activist art and tactical media, is matched by a relative or complete (depending on context) marginalisation of feminist art histories. In a mainstream context, the excision of feminist histories from the influential discourse around Nicolas Bourriaud's *Relational Aesthetics* is a case in point, of obvious relevance to shaping the canon of (contemporary) art.[31] Fourth, contemporary art criticism is on the verge of producing a new polarisation between a discourse on ethics and human rights and another one taking as its focus the rise of economic subjects, refraining in either case from attending to the implications of this polarisation for the future of feminism, which played a key role in foregrounding art's previous 'social turn' in the 1970s. A fifth difficulty can be observed in anglophone art history's (rather than sociological studies of art) hesitant attendance to the material and ideological condition of global capitalism, despite the past emphasis on various forms of internationalism that, one imagined, could have provided the impetus for a more immediate response to the condition of the global. This fifth difficulty may have something to do with the fact that political theory on the left is rapidly transforming the conceptual terms across disciplines in the humanities. To give the obvious example, terms such as 'immaterial labour', attending to the informatisation of a global labour force, raise a number of issues for the conceptual apparatus of art history as well. At the same time, art history, as much as art criticism, has only marginally negotiated the subtle and not-so-subtle displacements that the transition from the postcolonial to the global implies or, in some cases, necessitates.

Sixth, within the broader spectrum of feminist interventions in art history (including curatorial work) even after the 1990s, there has been a persistent suppression, and even self-repression, of materialist feminism, as a result of which references to 'differences' among women are rendered in abstract terms, associated with so-called 'post-capitalist practices', or are relegated to questions around subjectivity.[32] In relation to this, it must be noted that references to transnationalism do not necessarily claim a rigorous critical space for articulating the material conditions and implications of differences among women. The discourse on intersectionality, ameliorating to an extent the principle of 'difference', is not yet firmly embedded in emerging feminist art histories (at least in the West) and in any event, revisiting and updating the project of materialist feminism in art history can further the debate on the constitutive subjects of a transformative art and theory.[33] And finally, closely connected with the above is the fate of identity politics, where feminist and postcolonial critique had provided two major forces. On the one hand, 'identity' – stretching from the national to transnational formations (for example, in the concept of 'New Europe'), from the activist to the religious, from the consumerist to the terrorist, from class to ethnicity, gender and so on – is visible more than ever before in social and political life. On the other hand, its relevance within contemporary cultural practice is contested. The emphasis in political theory on the left is on alliances that are either tactical (for example, the description of the anti-globalisation movement as 'the movement of movements') or purportedly fostered through the practices of capital as a social relation. With the exception of Amelia Jones' head-on confrontation with the subject in 2012, the response of feminism to this is far from clear, at least in art history.[34] Although a detailed analysis of Jones' argument cannot take place in this Introduction, her position implies a fluid space of soft, potentially mutable identifications – a *queering* in terms of *de-normalisation* of hard-core identity – and her analysis can be read productively alongside Michael Hardt and Antonio Negri's concluding chapter in their *Commonwealth*, where identity may be where radical politics begins but it is certainly not where it is supposed to end.[35]

The previous paragraph offers a general description of the layered theoretical and social paradigm where this study is situated and hopes to intervene. Providing a comprehensive account of practices and theories that might define a feminist response to globalisation was neither a feasible nor a desirable outcome at any stage of researching and writing. Similarly, this book does not intend to 'prove' feminism's relevance to local histories or estimate the arrival time of a transnational feminism. And it substitutes an analytic of race and ethnicity with one of economic positioning. In fact, many (though by no means all) of the examples of artWork presented here involve European artists, theorists, curators, even if this study is about global space and relations. Such an acknowledgement raises questions about how a fragmented and unified cultural space such as Europe, a space so aware of imperial projects, of war and discarded utopias, of the failures of 'development' can be connected to the global imperative of our times. With all this in mind, this study sets out to realise a modest but hopefully useful enterprise, in considering a selection of case studies that illustrate the advances and shortcomings of contemporary art and theory in addressing the unrelenting, gendered exercise of global capital's biopower. Arguably, feminist analysis, attending to the exercise of power in the most intimate areas of life, has a lot to contribute to such a project of resistance, and the proposed study begins its work from this premise.

The first chapter of this study focuses on feminist politics and art history, asking how a dialogue between the two can engage the transition from post-modernism to global capitalism. Here I begin from the hypothesis that although a feminist project in art history became possible in the period char-acterised by a hegemonic postmodernism in cultural production (1970s and 1980s), the gradual association of feminist theory with the fragmentation of the social subject – gendered or other – ultimately suppressed feminism as a politics from the 1990s onwards. An outcome of these developments was the ideological construct of 'post-feminism', which dominated curatorial and artistic practice in the 1990s. Yet since the late 1990s globalisation resulted in a reinvigorated interest in feminism in art, as it became clear that the society of 'flows' of global capitalism thrived on the gender gap.[36] But what defines the rise of a new feminist paradigm? I am arguing that feminism in the twenty-first century must be understood in the context of a wider critical shift from the cultural subject, associated with postmodernism, to an economic subject. Feminist theory's job, also done in, and on, art history, is to shed light on this salient development and reflect on its repercussions for enacted and future struggles. This is why there is a need for a materialist feminist enquiry in art history: because we are faced with something new, because globalisation's material conditions must be understood in order to be meaningfully opposed. In short, the chapter sets out to imagine *how* this move would be possible, what it would mean to locate the struggle to destabilise patriarchy within the struggle to destabilise capitalism in the early twenty-first century. One aim of this chapter is, nevertheless, to reflect on the residual ideologies that hinder the realignment of feminism with, and its reinvestment in, materialism.

The second chapter focuses on post-socialist Europe, a social, economic and cultural space that has a lot to teach about the imbrication of 'transition', capitalism and gender. Overall, this study considers the demise of state-socialist regimes in Eastern Europe as a major event in consolidating the current phase in world capitalism, and in setting out to write this chapter it became obvious that I would have to examine two overlapping areas: first, women artists' reaction to the realisation that the westernisation of Eastern

Europe generated particularly problematic forms of gendered mobility (for instance, prostitution and new forms of arranged marriages). My concern here is the inter-European border and its literal and metaphorical capacity to hyper-sexualise the migrant. Yet the analysis suspends a politics of geography to consider how the artist's gendered labour becomes the site of a sociality where all immediately available positions are orchestrated by capital, not in terms of inclusion and exclusion but in terms of realised and potential assimilation. By following the artWork of Tanja Ostojić and Mare Tralla in particular, we get a glimpse of both the range of strategies explored by the contemporary woman artist in a transitional process that requires her to manage the transformation of her identity as well as how a gendered art practice metabolises into forms of alienated labour constituting self-conscious responses to globalisation.

Second, this chapter discusses the ambivalent and divided exchange with feminism across the art scenes of Eastern Europe. My timing here was fortunate as in 2009–10 Serbian curator Bojana Pejić coordinated the project 'Gender Check', comprising a major exhibition, an exhibition catalogue, a reader on art criticism and gender in the region and a couple of conferences that furthered discussion and debate. Deploying a comparative methodology and focusing its energies on the needs of a regional feminist transnationalism, 'Gender Check' offers itself to further analysis as it marked the turn to a new 'we' in the region's art histories in their ambivalent relationship to feminism – not a 'we' that is in reality a 'them', imposed from elsewhere, but one relying on the reactivation of historical consciousness for present–future use. Yet the discussion concludes by considering the possibilities of not limiting this 'we' to a regional level. One of the prospective benefits of such a move would be the subversion of the logic of exceptionalism and peripheralisation that accompanies the 'transition' speech, embedded in Eastern European art scenes for two decades now. To that effect, the discussion in this chapter constitutes an explicit attempt to review the gendered art histories of Eastern Europe in terms of globally, rather than locally, relevant feminist politics.

The third chapter takes global space as the contemporary woman artist's production site. I attempt to connect the historical category of 'woman artist' with current thinking about capital's organising of production. The 'woman artist', reclaimed by art histories attached to second-wave feminism and radicalised in the latter's political discourses, is here a gendered labouring subject, working in fairly specific conditions. Understood primarily in connection to domesticity until the heyday of postmodernism, the woman artist in the age of global imperatives often works in a social outdoors. But the political economy of this exodus remains unclear – and to begin to unravel the thread of connections, I propose to not see the woman artist as comfortably inhabiting but as *crossing* global space. My discussion therefore focuses on women's journeys and their temporary destinations. In 2008 when I presented the core ideas of this chapter at the Association of Art Historians Annual Conference in London, Nicolas Bourriaud was already elaborating his concept of 'the journey-form'. In 2009 he stated: 'This evolution [of the artist as traveler] can be seen in the way works are made: a new type of form is appearing, the journey-form, made of lines drawn both in space and time, materialising trajectories rather than destinations. The form of the work expresses a course, a wandering, rather than a fixed space-time.'[37] Whereas Bourriaud claimed that today 'what remains of the Baudelairean model of modernism is no doubt this *flânerie*, transformed into a technique for generating creativeness and deriving knowledge', I argued that the trajectories of the woman artist transform this figure into something 'beyond a global *flâneuse*'.[38] But to argue this point, I had to think of the journey not in terms of disembodied 'form' but as a directed movement of corporeal-social materiality – that is, the woman artist – engaged in productive labour. What she produces is primarily art, which, we know, has a market value. The contemporary woman artist shares little with the observation-cum-thrilling-encounter principle identified with modernity's *flâneur*. She shares much more with all those who must travel in order to find work or do their work – for example, the au pairs that help me look after my daughter – in an environment of interdependent mobile workers: my mobility is tied to these other women's mobility.

Starting then with a critical negotiation of second-wave feminism's take on the subject of work, the third chapter moves on to consider women's artistic practice realised today in global space. If anything, the form we can associate with this type of work is capitalism's ubiquitous invention sustaining immaterial labour: the project, a concept dominating our everyday exchanges. Typically a collaborative, research-based, organised, durational affair, the project is indeed the dominant form assumed by much immaterial labour today. Such a narrative must then seek convergences between the woman artist's labour across geographies that complicate any smooth operation of the 'transnational' and recent theorisations of labour. For feminism, two important issues in this analysis are the deflation of private versus public space and work–time versus life–time – as generated by contemporary modes of productivity. To the extent that such an approach to the journey and public space involves the crossing of borders, the situation is quite different from that described in Chapter 2, focused on Eastern Europe. The artists examined here choose to enter bleak landscapes of socio-economic relations in the knowledge, or at least the assumption, that they can exit them. They typically appear to occupy a position of privilege in relation to the sites they enter, although this does not mean that, as women and as artists, they are not caught in relations of power. Important examples in the narration of this relationship between women artists and global space are *Transcultural Geographies* (2003–4), a collective and interdisciplinary project by Ursula Biemann, Angela Melitopoulos and Lisa Parks, activating relationships between spaces and artworks, Jenny Marketou's *Translocal* (1996–2001), Ann-Sofi Sidén's *Warte Mal! Prostitution after the Velvet Revolution* (1999), and Lin + Lam's *Departure* (2004–6).

In contextualising these works, what new methodologies can feminist art history employ in order to situate women artists' crossing of global space politically? Part of the argument in this chapter involves how the institutional demand for a record of artWork actually executed in the field of social relations privileges the artist's affective work on the spectator rather than exchanges actualised in a terrain largely external to the institutions of art. This may bear negatively on the prospect of art contributing to feminist transnational solidarity, as the record may re-enact the division between those who represent and those who are represented. And yet things are not so simple, as such records can equally provide alternative pedagogies. The analysis will consider, among other things, how conflicting demands over documentation – both the documentation of ephemeral art and the documentation of social life – inform these projects, proposing a particularly loaded position for these artists' work.

Chapter 4 is concerned with how contemporary art addresses gendered economies. Specifically, I approach the video essay as an experimental practice that is connected to the claims of a materialist feminism in the twenty-first century. I discuss three video essays by Ursula Biemann that concentrate on the complex ways in which women find their 'place' not at home but in a global capitalist economy. Extending the reflections of the preceding chapter, I concentrate here on case studies that highlight specific aspects of feminism's turn to global space and the concrete expression of this turn in the visual arts. In their engagement with various instances of spatial politics, the video essays pay particular attention to labour relations, migration, the Internet as an economy of desire and human trafficking. I argue that by effecting a shift from patriarchy to global capitalism, Biemann's approach to femininity and the economy between 1999 and 2001 constitutes a major turn in a politically aware contemporary cultural practice, cutting across art, theory and activism. In reintroducing and updating the 'forgotten' potential of a materialist feminist method in the arts, the video essays *Performing the Border*, *Writing Desire* and *Remote Sensing* (all between 1999 and 2001), signalled at the time the end of a naively liberal (post)feminism and the emergence of a feminism responsive to capital's global 'empire' – a term introduced into contemporary political theory in 2000, at the same time that Biemann's video essays were articulating a feminist reworking to Fredric Jameson's 'cognitive mapping' as a methodology addressing global space.[39] The chapter situates this body of work critically with reference to current trends in art and political theory while also elucidating the video essay's complex ancestry across feminist film theory and practice, feminist practices in the visual arts and Marxist debates on the meanings and possibilities of realism. Key terms in this analysis include the 'instrumentality of the author', the 'multitude of femininity' and the 'spectacle of the real'.

Chapter 5 focuses on labour, masculinity and contemporary art's turn to an economic subject. This chapter seeks to extend the feminist analysis of masculinity by negotiating the latter's structural presence in art since the 1990s in ways that, intentionally or not, make apparent the move from a cultural to an economic subject. This is evident in the practice of leading contemporary male artists – from Jeremy Deller and Steve McQueen to Renzo Martens. Like Allan Sekula, Deller and McQueen have featured in their very different practices a traditionally male working-class subject, the miner (Sekula has focused on the stevedore). What are the implications of this investment in the once disappeared (as in outsourced or made redundant) proletariat in a contemporary art seen in glamorous museums and biennials, an art, we might add, dedicated to the production of art tourists' well-being? Whether the image of the rediscovered worker is made to work in the affect factory of the art exhibition is at the core of my analysis. On the other hand, Martens incorporates a deliberately narcissistic, neocolonial image of himself in a daring and devastating critique of relations of exploitation masquerading as charity in globalisation. And yet, the question of masculinity in contemporary art acquires a different meaning once we observe that a number of male artists are seen to engage in morally provocative practices: Dani Marti, for instance, demonstrates that masculinity has a prominent role to play in 'social care' artWork. Of greater concern to some perhaps, global capital has catapulted to fame a generation of 'bad boys' roaming biennials and museums where they reinvent the shock of the new in terms of the morally shocking. Displacing postmodernism has also diminished the visibility of an artist generation where women associated with critical postmodernism were prominent. The analysis considers whether the institutional success of 'bad boys' – including, for example, Artur Żmijewski – is co-extensive with a breach of the pact between capitalism and democracy. Narratives of a playful, 'risky' masculinity in global capitalism bespeak of an aggressively authoritarian, competitive and 'macho' banker-gangster type able to survive and flourish in the bumpy rides of global capital.

The sixth and final chapter opens by reflecting on the relationship between artist and curator. Tanja Ostojić's artWork of embodied critique, bringing forth the gendered aspects of this relationship, provides the initial focus of analysis. Following that, the chapter considers a different site of critique: the rise of all-female artist and curatorial collectives, also connected with women exploring forms of self-empowerment that undermine institutional power or else claim a share of such power. The sixth chapter thus provides opportunities for thinking through the intersection of art, action and activism in relation to a dynamic feminist present. Moving from the deconstructive work of an individual artist to the proliferating eruptions of female collectivism, it involves both art and life in the twenty-first century. The analysis prioritises the renewed interest in sexual politics in the past ten years as manifest in the rise of independent art and curatorial collectives established after 2000: Mujeres Públicas in Argentina, WHW in Croatia, Kuratorisk Aktion in Denmark and MFK in Sweden provide the main examples (a list that could have expanded to the point of becoming a book of its own, should it have incorporated the Spanish Spring of feminist collectives; indicatively, I mention the exemplary Precarias a la deriva, fusing the negations of Situationist International and militant working-class feminism). Across such practices, art or curating may translate into grass-roots feminist action addressing a specific social context and yet one always situated within a global economy. I am particularly interested in elucidating the new terms in which feminism, in the work of such groups and collectives, acquires a political identity as part of a concerted, interactive project of resistance, where positions often must be re-examined from scratch. How do these collectives articulate their relationship to feminism, as past and present? How do they make use of institutional settings and/or other spaces? Do they manage to put forward viable models for the integration of feminism into a broader political landscape or does 'feminism' provide a mere horizon of desire – for example, the desire to keep its legacy into view or the desire of women to exist fully as political beings?

There seems to be no uniform response to, and engagement of, the institution of art by such collectives, whose procedural and tactical identifications may relate to feminism in a number of ways. In any event, past feminism is never the *exclusive* political matrix and springboard for rethinking feminist values, alliances and courses of action now. It is important to acknowledge, for example, that national or regional histories of dissidence and subcultural contexts may well inform the current rise of artist or curatorial collectives. An awareness of a past moment of Western feminism and its questioning of the art institution is rarely translated into local and/or transnational idioms of resistance in the twenty-first century; there seems to be no straightforward transcription of feminist politics over space and time. What this reveals about the circulation, in space and time, of feminist strategies remains to be seen.

A short review of some of the main points presented in discrete chapters concludes the volume as a whole. The primary aim of this review is to think through the current ideological struggles and material conditions shaping a feminist politics in the arts. I do not hope to clarify once and for all how feminism's global imperative meets that of capital but to at least elucidate some aspects of this relationship. This can happen by establishing that, at present, feminism is a way of working creatively together despite capital's sustained efforts at keeping us apart.

Notes

1 See 'Editorial: We Did It!', *The Economist* (30 December 2009), www. economist.com/node/15174489 (accessed 5 December 2010). Available also in print.

2 See 'Women in the Workforce: Female Power', *The Economist* (30 December 2009), www.economist.com/node/15174418 (accessed 6 December 2010). Available also in print.

3 See the chapter 'In the United States: A Political and Economic Sea Change', in H. Eisenstein, *Feminism Seduced: How Global Elites Use Women's Labor and Ideas to Exploit the World* (Boulder and London: Paradigm Publishers, 2009).

4 N. Fraser, 'Feminism, Capitalism and the Cunning of History', *New Left Review* 56 (March/April 2009), 97–117. Here 99.

5 Roszika Parker and Griselda Pollock stated in the early 1980s: 'It is a matter of calculating what effect any particular procedure or medium will produce in relation to a given audience, a particular context and the actual historical moment', R. Parker and G. Pollock, 'Fifteen Years of Feminist Action: From Practical Strategies to Strategic Practices', in R. Parker and G. Pollock (eds), *Framing Feminism: Art and the Women's Movement 1970–1985* (London: Pandora, 1987), 5.

6 Tracey Emin's documentary 'What Price Art?' was aired on 15 March 2006 on Britain's Channel 4. The BBC stated: 'The Turner Prize nominee believes that no matter how acclaimed or successful a woman artist is, her work will almost always sell for less than her male counterparts.' See www.bbc.co.uk/radio4/ womanshour/01/2006_11_wed.shtml (accessed 10 November 2010).

7 R. Araeen, 'A New Beginning: Beyond Postcolonial Cultural Theory and Identity Politics', *Third Text* 50 (Spring 2000), 3–20.

8 R. Hennesy and C. Ingraham, 'Introduction: Reclaiming Anticapitalist Feminism', in R. Hennesy and C. Ingraham (eds), *Materialist Feminism: A Reader in Class, Difference and Women's Lives* (New York and London: Routledge, 1997), 5.

9 C. Owens, 'Feminists and Postmodernism', in H. Foster (ed.), *Postmodern Culture* (London: Pluto, 1985).

10 Editorial, *Lies: A Journal of Materialist Feminism* 1, unpaginated, available at http://liesjournal.info/index.php?/volumes/volume-1/ (accessed 10 September 2012).

11 By Italian Autonomia I refer to the Marxist movement that grew in Italy around the journal *Quaderni Rossi*, founded in 1961. Today Antonio Negri is the best-known theorist associated with the group and broader movement. Autonomia was interested in subverting capitalist labour relations and liberating the worker from the oppression of work (as socially unnecessary labour). Mariarossa Dallacosta and Silvia Federici are among the most prominent feminist thinkers and activists associated with Autonomia, though the relationship has not been smooth. Their radical work is only now, after 2010, beginning to be revisited by contemporary feminists. For a critical analysis of Italian feminism and Autonomia in the 1970s, see P. Cuninghame, 'Italian Feminism, Workerism and Autonomy in the 1970s: The Struggle against

Unpaid Reproductive Labour and Violence' (2008), http://libcom.org/ history/italian-feminism-workerism-autonomy-1970s-struggle-against- unpaid-reproductive-labour-vi. See also N. Dyer-Witheford, 'Autonomist Marxism and the Information Society', *Multitudes Web* http://multitudes. samizdat.net/Autonomist-Marxism-and-the.html (accessed 10 December 2011). See also S. Lotringer and C. Marazzi (eds), *Autonomia: Post-Political Politics* (New York: Semiotext(e), 2007).

12 C. T. Mohanty, *Feminism without Borders: Decolonizing Theory, Practicing Solidarity* (Durham and London: Duke University Press, 2003), p. 229.

13 J. Harris (ed.), *Contemporary Art and Globalization* (Hoboken: Wiley- Blackwell, 2011).

14 The issue of the temporality of globalisation was, for example, debated at the conference 'Global Cultures', organised by the Centre of Modern Studies, University of York, 20 June 2009.

15 I must therefore stress that my deployment of the 'global imperative' as a concept useful to materialist feminism is very different, and almost stands in contrast, to the term's use in the exhibition catalogue by M. Reilly and L. Nochlin (eds), *Global Feminisms: New Directions in Contemporary Art* (New York: Merrell Publishers, 2007).

16 Indicatively, 'Work, Work, Work: A Series of Seminars on Art and Labour' was organised by IASPIS in Stockholm to take place in November and December 2010, as this Introduction was in progress. ' "Mashing Up": Art + Labour, A Public Conversation' was organised by the art magazine *Variant* on 9 November 2010 in Glasgow. See also events and projects cited at the Reading Room of the website for the exhibition ECONOMY, which I co-curated with Kirsten Lloyd in 2013, http://economyexhibition.stills.org/reading-room/

17 C. Bishop, 'The Social Turn: Collaboration and Its Discontents', *Artforum International* (February 2006), 179–85; D. Karlholm, 'Surveying Contemporary Art: Post-War, Postmodern, and Then What?', *Art History* 32/4 (September 2009), 712–33.

18 G. Kester, *Conversation Pieces: Community and Communication in Modern Art* (Berkeley: University of California Press, 2004), 1 and 11–12.

19 Ibid., 11.

20 D. Karlholm, 'Reality Art: The Case of Oda Projesi', *Leitmotiv* 5 (2005–6), 115–24.

21 T. J. Demos, 'Moving Images of Globalization', *Grey Room* 37 (Fall 2009), 6–29; and C. Guerra, 'Negatives of Europe: Video Essays and Collective Pedagogies', in M. Lind and H. Steyerl (eds), *The Greenroom: Reconsidering the Documentary and Contemporary Art 1* (Berlin: Sternberg Press, 2008).

22 M. Meskimmon, *Contemporary Art and the Cosmopolitan Imagination* (Abingdon: Routledge, 2011), 2–5.

23 Ibid., 6.

24 M. Kwon, *One Place after Another: Site-Specific Art and Locational Identity* (Cambridge Mass.: The MIT Press, 2004).

25 Consider, for example, Lewis Hyde's classic distinction: 'Writing a poem, raising a child, developing a new calculus, resolving a neurosis, invention in all forms – these are labors' whereas 'work is an intended activity that is accomplished through the will', in L. Hyde, *The Gift: Creativity and the Artist*

in the Modern World (London: Vintage Books, 2007 [1983]). Hyde argues that 'labors' have their own internal rhythms – but it is precisely that right to autonomy which is lost in a biopolitical capitalist economy, where life and work fuse but the principle of profit rather than social necessity rules.

26 S. Federici, 'Precarious Labour: A Feminist Viewpoint', *Variant* 37 (Spring/Summer 2010). Federici's influential essay was first delivered as a lecture. It was originally published in 2008 and is available at http://inthemiddleofthewhirlwind.wordpress.com/precarious-labor-a-feminist-viewpoint/ (accessed 5 November 2010).

27 See online journal *The Commoner* 15 (Winter 2012), special issue 'Care Work and the Commons' (www.commoner.org.uk/) for a summary presentation of Autonomist feminism in the 1970s and the relevance of these debates in post-2000 left theory and activism.

28 B. Holmes, *Unleashing the Collective Phantoms: Essays in Reverse Imagineering* (New York: Autonomedia, 2008), 19.

29 See S. Binkley and J. Capetillo (eds), *A Foucault for the 21st Century: Governmentality, Biopolitics and Discipline in the New Millennium* (Newcastle: Cambridge Scholars Publishing, 2010). See also M. Lazzarato, 'Biopolitics/Bioeconomics: A Politics of Multiplicity', *Multitudes* (April 2006), http://multitudes.samizdat.net/Biopolitics-Bioeconomics-a (accessed 5 November 2010).

30 Coining the phrase is attributed to sociologist Diana Pearce. See D. M. Pearce, 'The Feminization of Poverty: Women, Work, and Welfare', *Urban and Social Change Review* 11(1978), 28–36.

31 N. Bourriaud, *Relational Aesthetics* (Dijon: Les presses du réel, 2002).

32 Increasingly, attempts to negotiate a materialist feminist art history became peripheral. Gen Doy's volume *Materialising Feminist Art History* (Oxford: Berg, 1998) is the only such (book-length) attempt that comes to mind.

33 On the critical import of intersectionality see A. Jones and J. Doyle, 'New Feminist Theories of Visual Culture', a special issue of *Signs: A Journal of Women in Culture and Society* 31/3 (Spring 2006), 607–15.

34 A. Jones, *Seeing Differently: A History and Theory of Identification and the Visual Arts* (London: Routledge, 2012).

35 M. Hardt and A. Negri, *Commonwealth* (Cambridge. Mass.: Harvard University Press, 2009).

36 Manuel Castells' concept of a 'space of flows', developed in the 1990s, has been essential to understanding the nature of production and communication in globalisation. See M. Castells, *The Rise of the Network Society, The Information Age: Economy, Society and Culture Vol. I* (Hoboken: Wiley-Blackwell, 2011 [1996]).

37 N. Bourriaud, 'Altermodern Manifesto – Postmodernism Is Dead', www.tate.org.uk/britain/exhibitions/altermodern/manifesto.shtm (accessed 1 November 2010).

38 N. Bourriaud, 'Altermodern', in N. Bourriaud (ed.), *Altermodern Tate Triennial* (London: Tate Publishing, 2009), unpaginated exhibition catalogue. A. Dimitrakaki, 'Beyond the Global Flâneuse: Travelling Women and the Politics

of Art as Labour' was presented in the session Dis-Locations: Movements and Migrations, organised by Rosemary Betterton and Dorothy Rowe as part of *Location: the Museum, the Academy and the Studio*, AAH Annual Conference, held at Tate Britain and Tate Modern, London, 2–4 April 2008.

39 See M. Hardt and A. Negri, *Empire* (Cambridge, Mass.: Harvard University Press, 2000). About Jameson's concept of 'cognitive mapping' see the relative entry in M. Foster Gage (ed.), *Aesthetic Theory: Essential Texts for Architecture and Design* (New York: W.W. Norton, 2011).

Feminist politics and art history: from 'postmodernism' to 'globalisation'

1

Rethinking 'feminist art history'

Feminist art history provides the broader and established theoretical framework for this study. The accumulated knowledge and diverse methodologies that have produced feminist art history as a field of critical enquiry have made it possible to raise questions concerning the impact of capital's global imperative on art as a gendered practice today. But it is for this very reason that feminist art history also constitutes a salient object of analysis within this study. Globalisation in the twenty-first century raises issues about the practice of feminist art history as such. This chapter is not, however, concerned with what it means to practise feminist art history in a general, absolute or prescriptive way – no matter how unambiguous the context, how obvious the injustice, how pressing the need to act. Such an aim would imply a lack of recognition of an important factor shaping this field: that despite its inherent radicalism, feminist art history is, and has been, the terrain of ideological struggle as much as any field of critical enquiry in the humanities and, especially, as feminism. To say this, however, is not to accept a pluralistic feminist art history where all positions hold the same *political* value in the historically specific context where feminist art history is practised. This chapter then is concerned with *how* to think about feminist art history in terms of its political value at present. If feminist art history is understood as a political intervention, how can this intervention be realised in the second decade of the twenty-first century? As explained in the Introduction, the visibility of capital as the framework of contemporary life at large has brought about a renewed interest in materialism and the left across the humanities. My aim here is then to consider, in more specific terms, what such a materialist turn might mean for feminist art history.

Let me begin by considering the designation 'feminist art history'. Its widespread use in academic environments conceals to an extent its complex evolution as a historical category of knowledge production as much as it permits the elision of its origins in a specific political discourse. In 2006 this led Francesca Berry and Amy Mechowski to publicly ask whether the time had come to imagine 'a future for feminist art history that is devoid of feminism as a political discourse'.[1] In their article from 1987 offering an overview of feminist art historical work, Thalia Gouma-Peterson and Patricia Mathews carefully traced the debates and ideological clashes that divided a feminist art historical community stretching mainly (though not exclusively) from the USA to Britain.[2] Their account captures the breadth of interlocking and diverging feminist projects in art history but, crucially, their article's title – 'The feminist critique of art history' – reveals the greatest and most radical contribution of feminism to the discipline, as perceived in the mid-1980s: feminist art history was as a critique *of* art history. In her important 1988 essay 'Feminism, Art History and Sexual Difference', Lisa Tickner contended that feminist art history could not 'stay art history', a position shared by Griselda Pollock occupying a central position in Gouma-Peterson and Mathews's exposition because of her deconstructive methodologies.[3] How could such a revolutionary prospect have led to imagining a feminist art history beyond politics, foregrounded by Berry and Mechowski? We are indeed confronted with the question whether feminist art history has ended up being just that: a 'specialism' within the discipline of art history, ultimately comfortable with its general disciplinary objectives. Commenting on her own position as a feminist scholar in a well-funded, liberal 'first-world' university, Amelia Jones has recently noted the paradox burdening the successful entry of feminism into the academy: 'the more one succeeds in infiltrating systems of power, the less radical one's work can be viewed as being'.[4] This perceived leakage of radicalism is closely connected with the threat of depoliticisation indicated by Berry and Mechowski, as a thin line divides 'infiltration' from 'incorporation'. One issue, then, for anyone identifying as an art historian working with feminism post-2000 is how to extend infiltration but fight incorporation. But, we may ask, should feminist art history be singled out in having been incorporated? Incorporated, after all, into what?

Significantly, feminism was not alone in its failure 'to end' art history. The challenges brought about by cultural studies and visual studies, as well as by radical, socially rooted discourses (including postcolonial critique and queer studies), did not lead to the dissolution of art history either. It is, however, unclear how the end of art history (as a traditional discipline) would have served the purposes of an emancipatory, political discourse – here, feminism. Presumably this 'how' can be answered as follows: the dissolution of art history would have made room for, and redirected energies towards, a new and less conservative field of knowledge. Yet this would imply that there could be 'progressive' fields of knowledge, inherently responsive to the political needs of a given era, somehow free from the ideological struggles and beyond the material conditions that permeate life outside the academy. Given the challenges faced by all disciplines in the humanities at the beginning of the twenty-first century, there is no ground for such a claim. Philosopher Martha

C. Nussbaum has observed in *Not for Profit* that the humanities are presently under attack precisely because of the ability of humanities disciplines to foster criticality, and especially forms of criticality that can threaten the smooth operation of capital in its structuring of all aspects of human life.[5] We begin then to suspect that in the current conjuncture, the struggle to undo art history cannot be a priority for a political discourse (including feminism), as such a struggle would be largely socially irrelevant. More importantly, such a move might well assist capital at its operation of curtailing the voices of dissent still contributing to sustaining an agonistic democratic space.

Since the mid-1980s art history has been reformed in significant ways and its boundaries have become permeable. Art history as a contested humanities discipline ('contested' because its alleged dependence upon a primary terrain, art, has been used to undermine its self-identity as a humanities discourse) was 'updated' and learned to exist and function on the principles of exchange, networking and flexibility, creating an environment of constant cross-fertilisation and intense self-reflexivity. This may sound like a positive development, and to a great extent it has been. Art history lived through the 'anything goes' demand of postmodern epistemologies, which means that it was reinvented as a democratic discourse, enjoying freedom of speech and intellectual movement. Yet such a perception of the 'democratic' was the spitting image of contemporary capitalist democracy where freedom of speech and movement, for those privileged enough to enjoy them, permitted *and* imposed interactions with a broad spectrum of agents – from social movements and intellectual discourses to the gigantic market space. The principles of exchange, networking and flexibility thus found very general applications, as art history was learning to converse, for example, both with feminism and postcolonial critique and with the corporate museum and funding bodies promoting a competitive research culture of transitory and token inclusivity. Art history, then, learned to operate within a knowledge economy; its survival, like that of other 'old school' disciplines, depended on that. The formulation 'feminist art history' is useful in so far as it reminds us that the space this phrase designates is entrenched within the same knowledge economy in which art history also operates. In this knowledge economy where universities (with Britain as a leading example) are expected and forced to perform as profitable corporations serving customers (students), both feminist and conservative art history can only be threatened by the same dismal possibility: the lack of sufficient demand for the 'product' in what is now a global higher education market.

Such an acknowledgement helps us see why in the twenty-first century we must seek a new differentiation between 'art history' and 'feminism' and apprehend them as two distinct but possibly (and hopefully) overlapping and conversant spaces. Simply put, in the material conditions subtending academic knowledge production today, the formulation 'feminist art history' implies the formation of a sub-category within an institutionalised humanities discipline as a process of taming and naturalisation. In due course, feminist art history was lured to behave not quite in terms of a disruptive, unsettling supplement, along the lines of a Derridean paradigm, since its survival and thriving required adherence to a competitive-funding higher education ethos. Contrary to that, the juxtaposition of 'art history' and 'feminism' reintroduces a differential space where an academic discipline, currently entrenched within the capitalist knowledge economy (art history), is confronted with a political, emancipatory discourse and social praxis, not necessarily institutionally bounded and setting as its primary goal the dismantling of structures, processes and subjectivities that produce women's oppression (feminism) always in concrete historical conditions. Even if in this instance I am misrepresenting 'feminism' as a unified space for analytical purposes (for feminism is subject to intense ideological battles and material divides that challenge its coherence at any point), this differential space may offer opportunities for thinking about these two entities' diverse histories and current positioning within the field of human action while also keeping alive a critical tension between them.

To emphasise this critical tension, we must take a further step in speaking not about 'feminism' but about 'feminist politics'. This move serves a triple purpose: first, it explicitly points to feminism as a form of social struggle that claims its visibility in the public sphere and seeks to place women in the *polis*: the community of citizens (the right to what kind of citizenship is an issue of both material and symbolic significance in the age of global capital). Speaking about feminist politics suggests that women's oppression, always contextual and non-uniform, must be addressed within the political rather than, say, ethical field, even if ethics and demands for social justice can greatly aid feminism's political battles. Two younger American feminists in the arts, Jen Kennedy and Liz Linden, argued in 2009: 'No longer connected to a living politics, feminism now represents a vague notion of "the good" that is associated with combating gender inequality.'[6] To place feminism within politics implies an understanding that feminism addresses actually existing social relations of power that no 'moralization of politics' – to quote political theorist Chantal Mouffe – can threaten to render invisible.[7] Even as I find problematic Mouffe's tendency to essentialise democracy by seeing it necessarily resting on conflict, it is far from accidental that she defended an agonistic political sphere that acknowledges a diversity of interests just when capital's globalisation appeared complete. Second, the phrase 'feminist politics' retains a strategic unclarity: is feminism *a* politics or can and should there be many forms of feminist politics? Third, 'feminist politics' situates feminism *within* and amidst all platforms of engagement negotiating relations of power. It thus becomes explicit that feminism is not an isolated, let alone separatist, discourse and praxis, pursuing its objectives irrespective of particular configurations of social forces, but exists in interaction with other struggles of a political character in a given historical conjuncture. This, arguably, weighs heavily on the articulation of a political sphere in the present, as anti-capitalist critique stresses the significance of building alliances and joining forces – a point to which I shall keep returning throughout this study.

Bearing in mind the above, we see that there is a need, at present, to negotiate the tactical convergence of art history *and* feminist politics. In other words, one cannot just assume that 'feminist art history' should continue to exist by force of habit, as a purely academic version of a once political discourse. Rather, the exchange between feminist politics and art history can begin by posing specific questions: What constitutes feminist politics in a world dominated by global capital and how can art history contribute to the realisation of feminist politics? In what sense does art history remain a relevant terrain for the realisation of feminist politics, so that we can speak about feminist politics in art history?

Gender, capital and contemporary art's history: rethinking the priorities of feminist analysis

The importance of art history for the struggles of feminism today has partly to do with the vitality and complex function of post-1990 art where a new 'social turn', to use Claire Bishop's phrase, exists in tension with art's integration into the dominant economic paradigm and its further capitulation to the culture industry, as an important branch of the economic sector relying on services and the provision of 'experience'.[8] This immediately suggests that 'experience' is a complex and multi-functional term in the contemporary art world, which complicates any straightforward appeal to the representation of gendered experience as the focus of the feminist art historical text. To introduce and exploit a tension between feminist politics and art history means also to raise the issue: what *kind* of relations does feminist analysis prioritise? What we might call the first wave of feminist art history retained to a great extent a focus on a *vertical* axis prioritising relations in time. But this approach, implicating continuity and the transformative capacities of women's work, can produce an inward-looking art historical discourse, of little value in addressing existing social relations where gender must be seen to matter politically. In a panel discussion on feminism and art published in 2003 in *Artforum*, Linda Nochlin is quoted as saying:

> Pipilotti Rist's *Ever Is Over All*, 1997, a wonderful video of an energetic woman marching down a city street smashing car window[s] with a kind of iron flower, is vitalized by the 'afterlife' of the antique maenad and her thyrsus – the female

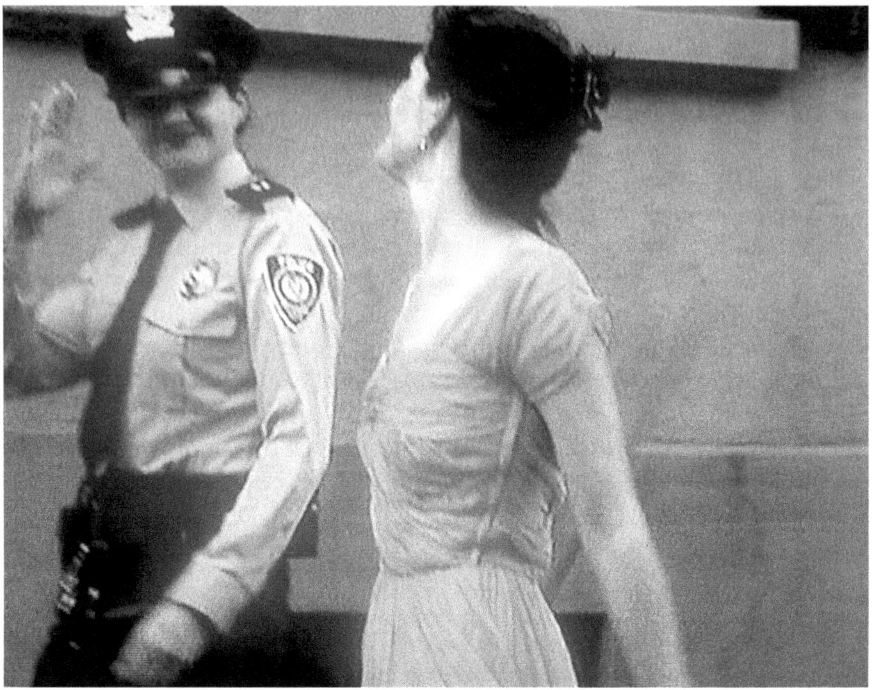

1.1 Pipilotti Rist, *Ever Is Over All* (1997). Audio video installation (video still).

activist is even dressed in drapery of a sort! Or take Sam Taylor-Wood's poignant large-scale self-portrait Fuck, Suck, Spank, Wank, 1993, which brings up antique and Renaissance memories in the contrapposto pose, the escaping strands of hair, the trousers falling about the sitter's feet (displaced classical drapery) – it's Venus, transposed by Botticelli and made utterly new in the artist's studio, with a cabbage instead of a scallop shell. This photograph is as harmoniously composed as any Greek frieze, and much the richer for its references, however unusual, to the past. I am not talking about anything as academic as influence here nor anything as trendy as appropriation. I am speaking, quite literally, of the afterlife of elements of the Western tradition achieving new meaning in the work of women artists who use them as both continuity and critique in the representation of women.[9]

However academically interesting this association may be between a contemporary woman artist's self-portrait with the art of other times, or of contemporary women's violent outbursts with the mythical maenad, it hardly helps us position such works, or the articulations of femininity they work with, within current political discourse and practice. The geopolitical order where feminist politics meets art history today suggests an urgent need to look at history in terms of relations *in, and of, the present* at least as much as with the past. But what does this mean when we think not just about gender but about gender in relation to the historical specificity of globalisation?

Let us first consider the relationship between femininity and activism. Indeed, the very mention of activism and its association with violence by Nochlin points to an inscription of the contemporary as an ideological 'moment' in the text, since in the period around 2000 the ubiquity of public protest against globalisation had already generated a historically specific resurgence of activism, highly visible in both mainstream and alternative media, and transforming in complex ways both art practice and theory. Nochlin's nomination of a young woman perpetrating a purposeless violent act in a public space as a 'female activist' suggests a reduction of activism to a form of blind public violence where gender becomes neutralised precisely through the ideological overdetermination of the activist moment by, and through, the invocation of violence. The attempt to connect 'femaleness' to the identity of the contemporary activist appears to rely on a heavily mediatised image of the latter as primarily and fundamentally destructive. In Nochlin's reading of Rist's video, the woman is constructed as claiming access to a certain social role, that of the activist, by reconstructing at a level of visual signification a powerful, widespread stereotype endemic in neoliberalism. Moreover, this is done in a manner reminiscent of women painters who have claimed access to the identity of the painter by reproducing stereotypical depictions of themselves as artists in the studio, with model or without. Yet as Griselda Pollock perceptively wrote in the early 1990s, from a certain point on, the efforts to connect femininity and painting were happening when 'everyone else had moved to another room'.[10] Something similar can be said in connection with this particular effort to secure a link between femininity and activist agency in the early twenty-first century. Contemporary art (by which I mean also its theorisations) has been of course very much invested in such efforts but to read such practices historically we must look elsewhere as much as differently.

To begin with, in its attendance to the articulation of gender and politics at present, feminist analysis may not need to maintain an exclusive focus on the work of women artists – unless there are specific reasons for doing so. Contemporary art's documentary turn of the past fifteen years permits and requires a much more complex negotiation about if – and how – the artist's gender can become a meaningful reference in situating works of art politically. Feminist politics in art history must today attend to the fact that male artists involved in anti-capitalist struggle may also engage and address gender and power. Swedish (male) artist Jesper Nordahl has, for example, used documentary techniques to make work that highlights the forms of resistance available to female sweatshop workers in Sri Lanka (*Katunayake Free Trade Zone, music by the Women's Centre,* 2006), that records the development of an

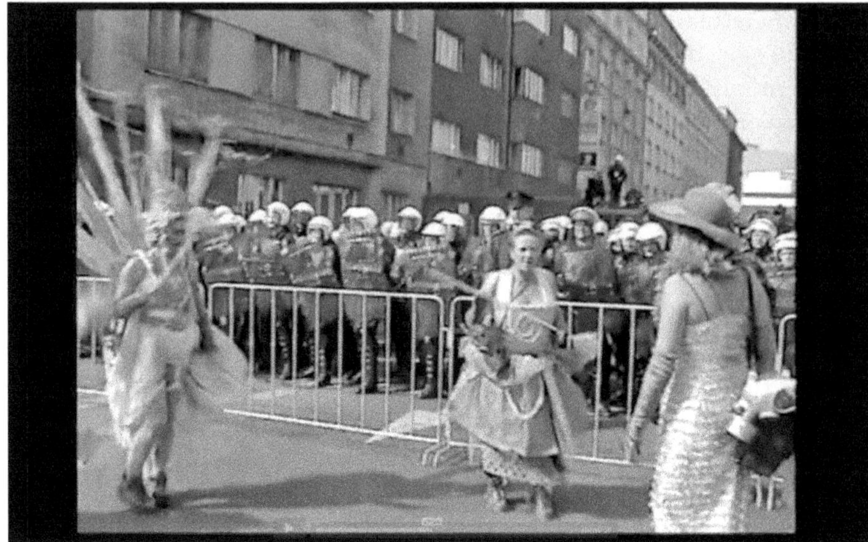

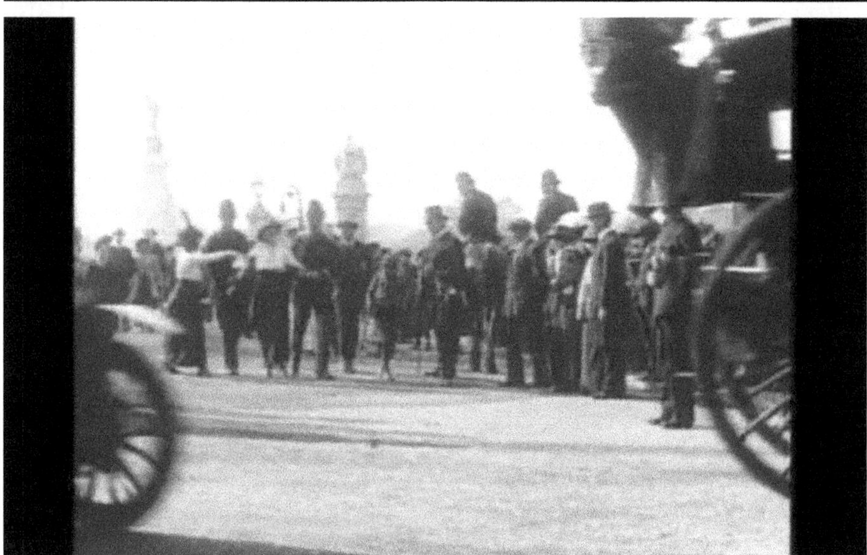

1.2–1.3   Marcelo Expósito and Nuria Vila, *Tactical Frivolity + Rhythms of Resistance* (2007). Video, 39′. Stills.

all-female Russian pop band in a media-inflected transformation of femininity in post-Soviet Russia (*The t.A.T.u. project*, 2009) and to construct a video-portrait of major feminist scholar and activist Chandra Talpade Mohanty (*Anticapitalist Feminist Struggle, and Transnational Solidarity*, 2007). Closer even to Nochlin's concern with the visual encoding of the encounter between femininity and activism we find Marcelo Expósito's work as a poetic mapping of the anti-capitalist movement. Expósito's video essay *Tactical Frivolity + Rhythms of Resistance* (2007), co-produced with female activist and video maker Nuria Vila, explores in particular the reconstruction of a carnivalesque femininity as a 'position' in the street rather than in language and instrumentalises it as an activist 'weapon', intending to disarm the police rather than perpetrate violence. With references to a well-known public protest event in Prague in 2000 that marked the meeting of World Bank and IMF strategists, following actions of an emergent anti-globalisation and anti-capitalist movement in Seattle and London, the video essay's most striking attempt at forging continuity is perhaps the weaving of footage from suffragist demonstrations of the early twentieth century into its narrative construct exploring the mobilisation of the gendered body in early twenty-first century protest and civil disobedience culture.

I now turn to Nochlin's second reference, registering the sexualisation of women's bodies in contemporary art by asserting a vertical connection between a contemporary woman artist's self-portrait involving nudity and masculinist art history's Venus. On this occasion, there is indeed a good reason to consider the gender of the artist because typically such sexualisation of women's bodies in art involves the artist's body, often proven to be a female body. Although it may well be the case that Sam Taylor-Wood's self-portrait *Fuck, Suck, Spank, Wank* (1993) enacts a subversive instance of a past formal convention (the contrapposto), the work's title also betrays its connection to its more immediate temporal context, and specifically pornography where images of women sucking, being fucked and spanked are intended to facilitate men's wanking. Julian Stallabrass furtively mentions that the message-shirt worn by this woman artist was 'made for gay activists'.[11] No doubt this portrait would read differently had this bit of information been included in the picture instead of a cabbage. The dilution of the hidden 'activist' message in this case may be intentional or not but stands: it is overwritten by the dominant association of a semi-undressed young woman-cum-dirty speak with heterosexual porn. The self-display of the woman artist with her trousers dropped to her ankles, revealing her naked legs, has a complex art historical ancestry, not just drawing on Venus imagery but also on the particular modes that produce the spectacularisation of women as sexual objects in popular culture, interwoven, as argued by Abigail Solomon-Godeau, into capitalism's visual cultures.[12] The gallery visitor would have no choice but to 'read' and decode the T-shirt message displayed on the woman's body, as in a chance street encounter, even if opting to ignore the work's accompanying caption (so as to appreciate this photographic self-portrait as a purely aesthetic object). The irony of the image emerges through the juxtaposition of a series of dry imperatives describing sexual activity and crafting a mechanical and repetitious form of interaction between the image's consumer (who must wank) and the female body's titillating half-nudity that is put to work. But in addition to the female sign at work, Nochlin's analysis forgets, it is also the (woman) artist whom we witness here *at work* – an effect attenuated by the mise-en-scene of the studio framing Taylor-Wood's body and later by the appearance of the image on, say, the Christie's site as 'Sale 6103'.[13] What are we to make of this imbrication of references to the mandates of a pornography industry and contemporary artistic labour that bears such a clear gender dimension?

Taylor-Wood's 1990s portrait of the artist at work has hardly existed as an isolated case of interwoven discourses and material practices. We can, indeed, turn to another prominent contemporary artist whose oeuvre has been seen to address gender in the post-feminist West. This is Tracey Emin, arguably one of the most successful women artists of the past twenty years, when capital realised its global imperative not as a matter of mere geographical domination but also as a form of biopower organising specific forms of life and work, or more appropriately, of life *as* work. To establish the relevance of art history for feminist politics today may then involve an effort to expose how art as a contemporary form of productivity partakes of this more general regime and help explain how gender is central to this process.

Emin's retrospective in Edinburgh in 2009, touring also to Bern, was advertised by a poster featuring the artist's body.[14] Photographed in profile, what we see of the artist is the part of her body from the waist to the ankles and her hand holding a paintbrush, a symbolic reference to her professional identity, the same as the paint-stained white apron she wears. It is harder to connect the black briefs worn under the apron, leaving exposed part of her buttocks and her legs, with her professional identity, as nudity has been typically associated with the model (a professional identity manipulated in modern art to gender the artist's profession and mythify it as the most privileged and creative one). Feminist art history has of course paid particular attention to how modern women artists negotiated in their art the dilemma of portraying themselves as women (involving nudity) or as artists (normally not involving nudity).[15] In this case, as the photograph is taken by Scott Douglas, Emin seems to have negotiated her identity through the marketing of the show by choosing this image to represent the latter. But to pursue such an analysis would merely produce Emin as yet another female artist having negotiated the same 'either-or' dilemma in pretty much the same way. But Emin is not just another woman artist, in the sense that her immense popularity in the

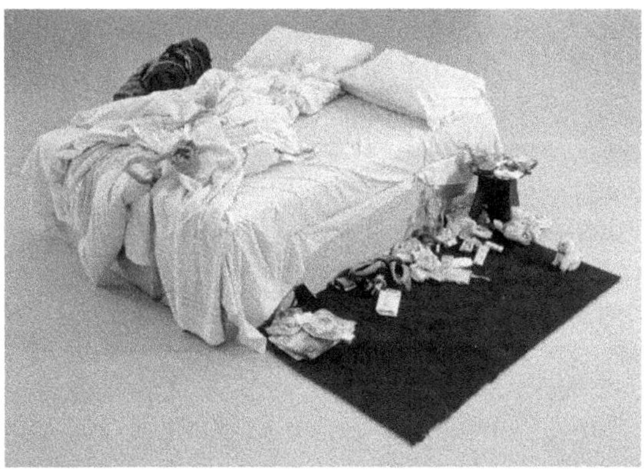

1.4   Tracey Emin, *My Bed* (1998). Installation.

past twenty years, and following the breakthroughs of feminist artists and historians in the 1970s and 1980s, prompts us to look at her methodologies as striking the chords of a contemporary gendered social imaginary. The best way to apprehend this is to turn to the discourse of the art market, a site that competes with feminist discourse in investing women artists' production with meaning. The Saatchi Gallery website offers the following description of Emin's work under an image of her famous installation *My Bed* (1998):

> A consummate storyteller, Tracey Emin engages the viewer with her candid exploration of universal emotions. Well-known for her confessional art, Tracey Emin reveals intimate details from her life to engage the viewer with her expressions of universal emotions. Her ability to integrate her work and personal life enables Emin to establish an intimacy with the viewer. Tracey shows us her own bed, in all its embarrassing glory. Empty booze bottles, fag butts, stained sheets, worn panties: the bloody aftermath of a nervous breakdown. By presenting her bed as art, Tracey Emin shares her most personal space, revealing she's as insecure and imperfect as the rest of the world.[16]

This institutional description is surely not concerned with feminist critique. Disregarding feminist concerns about the specificity and diversity of women's (or men's for that matter) experience, it appeals twice to 'universal emotions' and sees 'confessional art' positively, unmoved by the distance that separates it from autobiography as a radical strategy for feminist artists in past decades. The White Cube gallery's site provides a more nuanced description of Emin's work, acknowledging the artist's 'sexually provocative attitude that firmly locates her oeuvre within the tradition of feminist discourse'.[17] However such an acknowledgement hardly illuminates how Emin's work may have something to contribute to an understanding of the exchange between art and gender at present. To understand this, we must return to the Saatchi Gallery description which highlights the 'artist's ability to *integrate* her work and personal life' (my emphasis). This integration of work and life, at which contemporary art excels, is now a distinct feature of the organisation of labour in contemporary capitalism. This is the political economy of Emin's work, irrespective of whether the artist intentionally sought to pursue this point in the 1990s, when her turn to an art of experience proved so rewarding.

This point was, however, intentionally pursued by American artist and writer Andrea Fraser in her work *Untitled* (2003). This is a piece that the viewer can encounter as a video in the gallery, although the video is *not* the artwork per se but rather the document of the outcome of a more complex process. A leading figure of an artistic current known as institutional critique, Fraser offered to have sex with a male art collector who was bound by contract to buy the video documenting the sexual encounter. In this case, the artist's body is not quite the site of the artwork, although it might be tempting to see *Untitled* as a parody of those practices that claim their radicalism in transposing the artwork from an external object (say, a painting) to the artist's body. In 1981 Mary Kelly had already raised this issue in connection with performance art, of such great appeal to women and feminist artists since the 1960s: how is it different when the artwork's assumed authenticity, essential for the artwork's status as commodity, is associated with the artist's body rather than with what that body can produce?[18] Fraser intended to avoid this mistake. Rather, *Untitled*, of which only a very limited number of visual documents (videotapes of the artist–collector sexual encounter) were made, would be articulated through, and across, the relationships and negotiations that occur in the exchanges – discursive and corporeal/material – among the artist, the gallery, the collector but also the entire social space where it is acceptable for sex, art and labour to be bought. Indeed, *Untitled* alluded to the production process as 'the artwork': a remit of socio-economic relations where anything from sexual pleasure to video art had achieved a certain equivalence. As far as production processes go, this one highlights the links between sex, gender, heteronormativity, art and labour in the service and experience economies of global capital – links which demand a framework of analysis defined by political rather than ethical concerns.[19]

What must be visible from the vantage point of a feminist politics in art history today is that Emin and Fraser (and, not least, Taylor-Wood) *are* women artists, and for that matter, women artists of the same generation situated in the First World, where the expansion of a service and experience economy can be most clearly observed. But what does this have to do with women? As Hester Eisenstein has demonstrated, women's entry into paid labour coincided with – and, for Eisenstein, was integral to – the reconfiguring of late twentieth-century capitalism as a service economy of flexible and often part-time

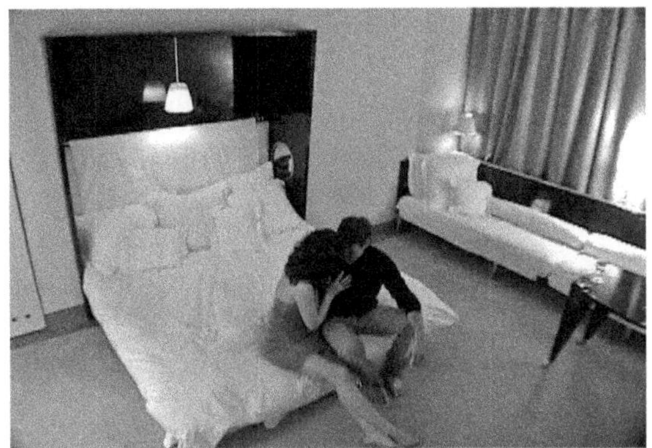

1.5   Andrea Fraser, *Untitled* (2003). Video, 60′. Still.

workers, especially visible in developed nations.[20] As an ideological position in a given historical context, 'being a woman' has been closely connected with service. What Eisenstein's study reports, however, is that this ideological position engendered both the material conditions of many working women and played a central role in producing contemporary capitalism. The conflation of sex work and service work as part of women artists' labour today can therefore be of great interest far beyond the confines of the art world. It points to several things at once: that making art continues to be gendered even in the West; that contemporary art making is fully incorporated in a more general labour regime; that precisely because of the myth of art as creative, non-alienated labour (a mythic legacy of hegemonic masculinist modernism), art provides ample opportunities for the glamorisation and valorisation of sexualised women's work in a way that pornography, prostitution and mass culture can never do, lending art's gendered production a unique ideological function.

Already in 1975 Marina Abramovic did *Role Exchange* in Amsterdam: for several hours on 2 July she replaced a prostitute, known as Suze or S.J., in her work environment, that is a shop window in Amsterdam's red light district, while Suze attended the opening of the artist's show at De Appel.[21] Abramovic felt like a seasoned artist: already ten years in the profession (as various sources inform us), she chose a woman who had been a prostitute for a decade. From an ethical perspective, *Role Exchange* can appear perhaps problematic, even cruel, given the *temporary* extrication of a human being from a context where her body and its capacity to offer pleasure are explicitly commodified: Abramovic notes that Suze had told her to absolutely not drop the price while taking her place.[22] Yet from a political (feminist) perspective, *Role Exchange* was illuminating, as it orchestrated and tested the conditional and gender-based exchange of labour time. More of a temporary job swapping, this prototypical relational artwork's title, 'role exchange', highlighted sexualised

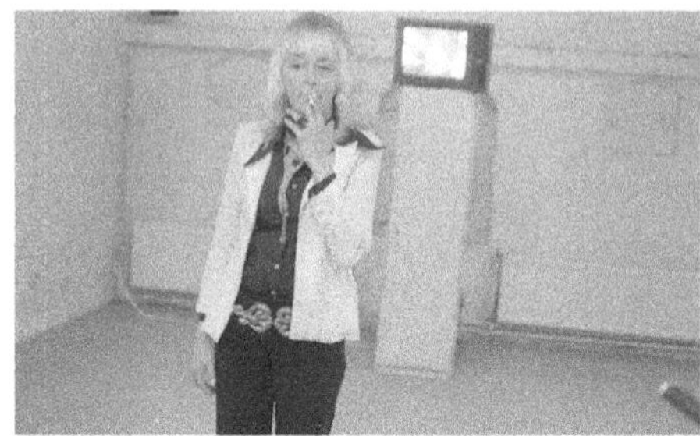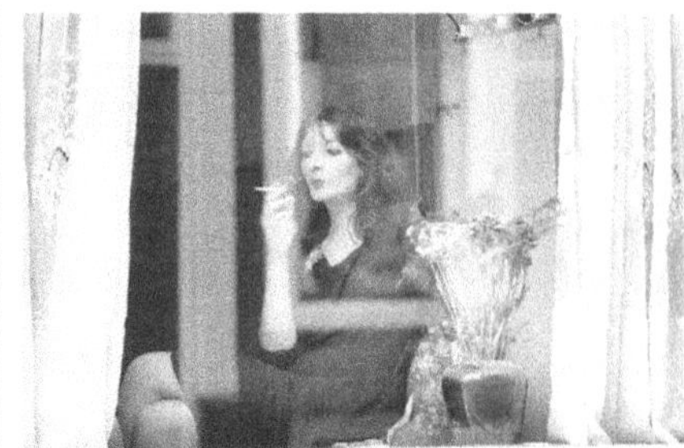

1.6   Marina Abramovic, *Role Exchange* (1975, Netherlands). Two Super 8 cameras. Installation, no sound, colour, 19′ 50″. Stills.

self-display as an aspect of women's work in a generic service economy: both Suze and Abramovic were primarily *seen* (in the window of a brothel and in a gallery). Yet the two jobs are not equivalent: Abramovic's authorship of this exchange script invests her sexualised self-display with a semblance of power (because those who consumed her image as a prostitute did not know she was an artist). Her authorship becomes more pronounced as a result of the contrast between the hyper-visibility of Abramovic's name and the requested anonymity of 'Suze'. *Role Exchange*, therefore, sets an important precedent for the need to carefully differentiate between artistic and other forms of labour in cases where both involve sex-related work.

But whereas *Role Exchange* led to a visual document based on the sexualised *display* of two women, Fraser's *Untitled* led to a visual document of a production process incorporating a heterosexual sex *act*.[23] What does this move from allusion to sex work to sex work in plain view within the contemporary artwork suggest when the artwork *is* its very process of production? Arguably, the twenty-five years separating *Role Exchange* and *Untitled* have seen the consolidation of emerging, in the mid-1970s, trends in labour, including the hegemony of services. In 2000 Hardt and Negri were able to render popular the concept of immaterial labour precisely because the transformation of labour that had begun much earlier was by then becoming ubiquitous and apparent, a consequence of informatisation. As Marina Vishmidt argued in 2004, the critique that necessitated a concept such as that of immaterial labour

> posits the *real subsumption* (at least in Antonio Negri's writing) of all forms of sociality, subjectivity, into capitalist production, and immaterial labour is described as a kind of production that trades precisely in affect, knowledge, arguing a very notable extension of the individual's productive capacity-life itself, in fact, with no more room even for alienation to occur. If the ideal worker is an information worker, then the ideal worker is an *artist*.[24] [my emphasis]

The shift from an exploration of women's 'roles' performed for a variety of public spectators (Abramovic) to the gendering of the sociality and labour sustaining the art market in the course of the twenty-five years separating Abramovic and Fraser is the loss of that space where alienation could have occurred. Fraser is able to go 'all the way', offering the actual sex to an art buyer because 'the artist' has by 2003 evolved into a biopolitical producer whose life and work are fully enmeshed and regulated by capitalist relations of production. Opposed to this, Yugoslavia-born Abramovic's *Role Exchange* inaugurated the Eastern European artist's encounter with a Western/capitalist urban space (Amsterdam) where female prostitutes on display stood for conspicuous consumption.[25] In *Untitled* the buyer-collector shows the same awareness as the seller-artist, and so a perverted form of market-based equality is achieved here: the artist's claim to authorship does not make her superior to her collaborator because he, the collector (unlike Suze, the prostitute), will own what this authorship produces. Making the viewer witness in the video record what authorship produces is important for the critical aspirations of *Untitled*: the indexicality of the moving image reveals a material ground (the body) right at the core of the artist's immaterial labour – a subject tackled by Fraser (albeit not considering the gender dimension of this subjectivisation) in her important essay 'The Artist as a Service Provider'.[26] If by 'looking at Marina Abramovic's work, one can see how the contemporary public artist evolved from the 19th-century passive observer to the 21st-century urban, sexually savvy nomad', Fraser eschews both roles to reveal the contemporary artist as a gendered economic subject.[27] And so we could rethink Vishmidt's connection between the information worker and the artist, and reformulate it so as to encompass an awareness of gendered labour: if in the immaterial, affective labour regimes of contemporary capital, the ideal worker is a prostitute, then the ideal worker is a woman artist.

Post-2000 feminist readings of contemporary pornography also place emphasis on work, and so Nina Power concludes her analysis by stating: 'contemporary pornography informs of one thing above all else: sex is a type of work, like any other'.[28] In *Lovely Andrea* (2007), a video essay of artist and theorist Hito Steyerl, the latter embarks on a search for a photograph of herself taken in Tokyo in the late 1980s. The narrative suggests that Steyerl had her photograph taken in the context of the bondage industry, a sub-genre of the pornography industry, under the name of 'Andrea'. The film presents Steyerl talking to various agents in Japan's bondage industry, accompanied by Asagi Ageha, a well-known bondage performer and also the interpreter in the film – the artist-and-bondage-girl temporary alliance replicating unwittingly the one of Abramovic and 'Suze'. Once more, the artWork establishes a complex interface between artistic labour and sex work – an interface that becomes possible because of the gender of the artist. The Documenta 12 website (*Lovely*

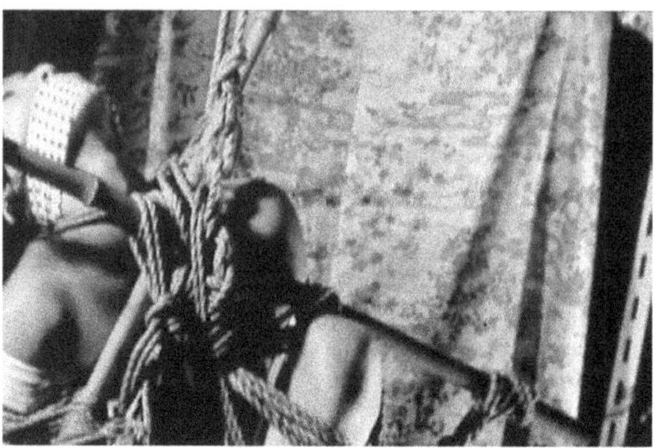

1.7   Hito Steyerl, *Lovely Andrea* (2007). Video, 30′. Still.

Andrea was included in the show) notes that the piece constitutes 'an examination of the precarious affective work of such women', but it is worth raising the question:[29] what happens to this kind of work when it enters the domain of immaterial labour identified with art?

On the one hand, and despite its sophisticated narrative where images of sexual bondage are seen to exemplify a global fascination with 'images of hanging and bondage' extending from popular culture to prisoners of Guantanamo Bay, *Lovely Andrea* deploys the confessional mode (the artist revealing something about her past) to both critique *and* expand the spectacularised consumption of the sexualised body of the artist.[30] *Lovely Andrea* is yet another output of gendered artistic labour (the facility of confessing associated with femininity in contemporary mass culture, as in reality TV). about an emblematic form of globally dominant gendered labour: sex as work.

On the other hand, the name 'Andrea' of the work's title is heavily coded, as this was also the name of the artist's childhood friend, Andrea Wolf, who started as a Western feminist in amateur films, joined the Women's Army of the outlawed in Turkey PKK (Kurdistan Workers' Party) and was murdered in Turkey in 1998. Her body was never found. Steyerl made the film essay *November* (2004), to 'observe the multiple transformations of 'her' [Andrea's] image: from Super-8 film heroine, to Kurdish martyr, to being appropriated as an alias for a Japanese rope-bondage model'. Alluding to the personal histories that feed into *Lovely Andrea*, Steyerl has said: 'Godard decided that he would insert some references to the war in Vietnam into all of his films . . . I suppose this is what I am unconsciously doing now. Bringing up the issue over and over again, especially in contexts where you would never suspect it, and where it even seems completely displaced.'[31] Steyerl stresses her interest in 'the material nature' of images associated with 'this event' – the event called

Andrea Wolf – noting their ability 'to travel', for example, from a PKK banner to a web page featuring a still from *November*.[32] As discussed in a later chapter, travel is a powerful figure in narratives of globalisation, outlining spatial rather than temporal relations, but in Steyerl's work we begin to grasp its complex bearing on art's engagement with articulations of contemporary figurations of femininity. There is no doubt, however, that globalisation encompasses an incredible array of ports of call where travelling images can reveal their material nature. *Lovely Andrea* is a profoundly melancholy and astutely political work. In addressing both gendered labour in contemporary capitalism and Andrea Wolf's attempt at an exodus from Western femininity, it simultaneously reveals art as the site where this critical question is posed: how is rebelling against gendered labour in twenty-first-century capitalism connected with abandoning Western models of femininity? The question far exceeds the scope of a singular discipline such as art history. Yet it is important to acknowledge that the woman artist's labour permits the question to be posed and explored.

The above discussion was intended as one possible response to the question: how to think about gender and art in the specificity of social and economic relations engendered by contemporary capital. Beginning with a response to Nochlin's comments involving the work of contemporary women artists, I argued that the exclusive emphasis on vertical relations (the relations of contemporary art to the past and maybe even its future) may not necessarily lead to a politically useful articulation of feminism in art history in the early twenty-first century. One outcome of capital's global imperative has been a spatialisation of the historical process, pointing to a need to consider cause and effect within the current synchronicity. Nothing in the etymology of the word 'history', deriving from the ancient Greek verb 'οιδα' (to know through research), suggests that the past should be the exclusive focus of what constitutes, in essence, an enquiry-driven record and truth-oriented narrativisation of events, relations and processes in human society. To maintain the political value of feminism in art history, it is important that feminist analysis today is, as in the 1970s, able to rethink any naturalised notions of what constitutes its field of enquiry. Overcoming a commitment to vertical relations, the analysis carried out above stresses both the need to disidentify feminist discourse from an exclusive focus on women's work and the complex context where the category of labour gains explanatory power in situating women artists within specific social relations. Prevalent here is the transcription of femininity as a set of internalised values (the same ones that enabled the rise of a woman-powered service economy) into the domain of material relations (the actual consumption of women's bodies in sexualised forms of labour) as well as relations of signification (the symbolic consumption or, conversely, political instrumentalisation of femininity) in the immaterial production of art.

We see then how the importance of art history for the contemporary struggles of feminism is also an outcome of the feminist battles of the past: for all their diversity, the insights gained in the 1970s and 1980s demonstrated the importance of keeping political energies focused on social process rather than on established objects of critique (such as the artist and the artwork). Introducing, for example, the 'writing of art's histories' as an object of critique in its own right has had everything to do with feminism's attention to social process in the 1970s and 1980s.[33] The question of 'writing' became a defining one partly because of feminism's attendance to the rise of a culturally hegemonic system of values, also a system of cultural hegemony: the one known as postmodernism. But at the same time, this attendance emanated from a necessary relation, as 'the condition of postmodernity', in David Harvey's words, provided the broader material setting for the articulation (or, in some cases, disarticulation) of politics.[34]

Feminism and postmodernism

Postmodernism followed the (alleged) defeat of the 1968 spirit of total revolt and the rise of identity and issue-based politics. For example, as an intellectual venture, postmodernism's radical challenge to dominant Western models of thinking was closely connected with a postcolonial condition and a presumed postcolonial subject.[35] Involving a massive technology-powered expansion of visual culture, postmodernism also entailed a privileging of the 'signifier' over the 'signified', or a culture of talking rather than doing, of the intangible over the material – shifts compatible with the exponential growth of a service economy in the 'developed' world. Post-structuralism became the signature intellectual venture of postmodernism precisely because it promised to focus exclusively on the text and claim 'destabilisation' as something that occurs in systems of language (as opposed to the materiality of street protest). The above may come across as a somehow reductive, binary schema but postmodernism's emphasis on language, textuality and the fluidity of meaning are hard to refute. Yet this emphasis on language introduced an opportunity to think through, and about, the significance of discursive and more broadly representational space for the circulation of ideology and the entrenchment of gender roles and hierarchies. Craig Owen's well-known claim about an affinity between feminism and postmodernism was one way of saying that postmodernism was the historically determined cultural habitus for post-1968 Western feminism, also known as the second wave.[36] And this despite the fact that strands of second-wave feminism sought to distance themselves from postmodernism as a dominant set of values and evaluations (in a world were women continued to be raised as second-rate citizens).

That feminist art history first emerged in postmodern times is then far from a historical coincidence, as an enlarged visual culture meant that identity politics would be tied to struggles for visibility – literal or metaphorical – and representation. Art historians brought important tools to the feminist cause in a postmodern context, where the heightened visibility of women's bodies in a mass visual culture served as a consumer good had to be challenged by other forms of visibility constituted in feminist terms. Griselda Pollock's important essay of 1977, 'What's wrong with "images of women"?', established a connection between gender-based oppression and images in art and mass culture, underpinned by the erosion of the high/low distinction in postmodernism.[37] But alternative forms of visibility were also claimed discursively. Offering visibility to 'other' subjects in signifying practices meant also the confinement of such subjects to textuality, their existence as instances of signification. 'Signifying practices', a term often encountered in the feminist art history of the period, became particularly important, and dominant feminist theories about the constitution of the gendered subject gradually paid excessive attention to spaces sustaining such signifying practices, identifying them with representational spaces.

In her 1989 discussion of aestheticisation and culturalism as the common elements of certain strands of Marxism and feminism in postmodernism, American cultural theorist and artist Laura Kipnis made an acute observation linking postcoloniality and the hermeticism of Western European (that is, French) feminist theory in particular. Given the impact of French feminist theory on feminist art history in general, it is worth quoting her at length:

much of European postwar decolonization took place out of practical and economic necessity more so than out of ideological conviction: the colonial mind persists long after its political and economic structures have been dismantled. Continental feminism offers a radical structural analysis of operations it prefers to call phallogocentrism, but then retreats from the implications of its own analysis into the autonomy of the text, seizing on a modernist refusal of reference to enact its ambivalence. Continental feminism would seem to be the most potentially radical current in contemporary political theory, freeing itself from the essentialism and the liberal tradition of American feminism. Yet, it also seems beset by the same conjunctural elements associated with the depoliticization of Western Marxism, prone to aestheticization, theoretical autonomy, and a deliberate distance from political praxis. It identifies the structural position of a new political subject, inscribing itself into that moment, and is then paralyzed by this knowledge and by its own first-world status, hysterically blind to the geopolitical implications of its own program. And legitimately so, because the knowledge offered here is not benign. It is that real shifts in world power and economic distribution have little to do with *jouissance*, the pre-Oedipal, or fluids, and that the luxury of first-world feminism to dwell on such issues depends on the preservation of first-world abundance guaranteed by systematic underdevelopment elsewhere and by the postponement, by whatever means, of the political decentering that will mean the close of that historical epoch.[38]

Although we know that such a political decentring is yet to come and although we are not in a position to foresee what shape it will take if and when it comes, Kipnis's attempt to situate the hegemony of what I shall call *post-imperialist feminist theory* against a background of global geopolitics is particularly relevant in 2013. Crucially, Kipnis's specific point is not about the inflation of theory (feminist or Marxist) in stark contrast to these discourses' diminished popular appeal at the end of the 1980s (though such a criticism appears earlier in her paper). Rather, her point is that post-imperialist feminist theory performed, through its hegemony, a hideous ideological and material function by ensuring the depoliticisation of feminism and placing the latter in the service of global capital's imperative to maintain economic misery for most of the world's population. Her scathing critique thus both accords great value to feminist politics in the struggle against capitalism and helps explain, more than twenty years later, the relative marginalisation of feminism in popular critiques of global capitalism – a point to which I shall be returning in parts of this study.

Yet for all the negative inflection of 'postmodernism' in her article's title ('Feminism: The Political Conscience of Postmodernism?'), Kipnis does not distance herself from the postmodern, arguing: 'If the popular is seen as an access to hegemony rather than an instrument of domination, what follows is a postmodern strategy of struggle over the terrain of popular interpellation, an acknowledgment that hegemony is won rather than imposed.'[39] It is this kind of postmodern struggle that she wishes feminism (and Marxism) to embark on in the hope that feminist politics would see its options expand beyond 'either "out of the mainstream and into the revolution", or out of the revolution and into the text'.[40] Yet one question is: would overcoming this binary require an understanding of social relations that postmodernism cannot offer? The second part of this chapter's title refers to a process of transition – 'from postmodernism to global capitalism' – that conceptualises, however schematically, a necessary shift of attention in feminist analysis. This does not mean that postmodernism and global capitalism are neatly differentiated: the formation of a global capitalism has lasted, and has been resisted, for centuries and the postmodern era can, with hindsight, be seen as the intense last few metres in the race – the last few metres before, that is, hitting the wall. But hitting the wall, or globalisation as terminus *and* crisis, is of course even more intense. This is what makes this shift of attention necessary. But then we need to ask: what does it entail?

From postmodernism to globalisation, or from the cultural to the economic subject

What I sought to establish in the previous section is that postmodernism as a social process and intellectual endeavour inevitably impacted on feminism's internal ideological divisions and marked the emergence of feminist art history. But by the mid-1990s postmodernism's hegemony felt fragile. Hal Foster concluded his study of contemporary art *The Return of the Real* with a chapter title phrased as a question: 'Whatever happened to postmodernism?'[41] The question continues to resonate today as much as it remains unanswered. Foster summarised postmodernism's difference from modernism in terms of postmodernism's articulation of a cultural subject as opposed to modernism's economic subject.[42] A few years back, Fredric Jameson had described post-modernism's 'logic' as fundamentally 'cultural'. His famous book title, *Post-modernism, or the Cultural Logic of Late Capitalism*, held a double meaning: firstly, postmodernism was posited as the cultural logic of late capitalism; but, secondly and more importantly, postmodernism was seen to arise when late capitalism managed to institute and mobilise the hegemony of a cultural logic (as opposed, for example, to an economic one).[43] We can indeed imagine that the demise of postmodernism begins when things stop being perceived as merely or predominantly cultural, when the *culturalisation* of social life under capitalism is no longer ideologically sustainable.

Making the above argument after the first decade of the twenty-first century is not hard: the global economic crisis of 2008 and the demonstration of the overdetermining role of the capitalist market in global, regional and state politics (for instance, the instability of the Eurozone since 2010) have now made apparent globalisation's economic rather than cultural matrix. However, a historical period does not conveniently end in an abrupt manner but lives on, even as a residue in what follows it. If in 2009 French curator Nicolas Bourriaud exclaimed 'postmodernism is dead!', we can always refer him to Karl Marx who argued long ago that the dead constitute a particular kind of weight on the minds of the living.[44] Precisely because feminist art history has been so strongly associated with postmodernism, its process of disassociation from it must remain conscious of postmodernism's primarily ideological after-life. Postmodernism informs in important, and perhaps in not entirely clear ways, the contemporary moment and its political articulations.

Yet it is also sensible to acknowledge that the ground of politics has shifted, and this shift has already been registered in emerging narratives of con-temporary art. If Foster publicly asked what happened to postmodernism in the mid-1990s, in 2002 curator Okwui Enwezor argued that, in the era of globalisation, oppositional subjects must openly distinguish their politics from postmodernism. In curating 'Documenta 11', the first grand-scale exhibition about art and globalisation, Enwezor sought to disentangle a specific oppositional subject, the one produced through postcolonial critique, from postmodernism both as ideology and analytical framework.[45] Enwezor saw a unique opportunity in Hardt and Negri's *Empire* for breathing new life into a postcolonial subject mired in the institutional trivialisation of identity politics of the 1990s, claiming for this rearticulated (one is tempted to say 'cleansed') postcolonial subject a central position in an emerging counter-hegemonic sphere that targeted global capitalism as the perpetrator of global social divisions, conflict and misery. In 2009 Nicolas Bourriaud curated the fourth Tate Triennial in London under the catchy, and rather optimistic, title 'Altermodern'. Opposition to postmodernism hardly mattered in Bourriaud's vision of a global paradigm of contemporary art, identified as altermodern, because postmodernism as such had been (supposedly) eclipsed. As already noted, Bourriaud's approach to the 'problem' of postmodernism lacked a dialectical, and indeed materialist, understanding of historical process. The critical lexicon deployed in 'Altermodern' provides a typical example of postmodernism (as ideology) informing readings of globalisation. To begin with, Bourriaud declared postmodernism's end in a manner that extended, rather than challenged, the fascination with 'endings' prevalent in postmodern discourse. It was postmodernism that announced with aplomb a series of 'ends', ranging from the end of history (Francis Fukuyama), the end of metanarratives (Jean-Francois Lyotard), the end of art (Arthur Danto) and even the end of (a certain kind of) art theory (Victor Burgin). But more importantly, Bourriaud based his curatorial gesture on the use of well-trodden postmodern concepts, such as that of 'cultural translation', referring us back to the primacy of the cultural. The description of a contemporary (alter)modernity as one premised on, or for that matter, permitting the comfort of cultural translation on a global scale is challenged as soon as we look for that altermodernity's historical ground, none else than global capitalism. And capitalism's global imperative is economic, not cultural. Indeed, the ubiquitous invocation of 'capital' in contemporary art discourse points to, as much as it implies, a supersession of postmodernism's cultural subject by a new and perplexing economic subject. Its perplexity is an outcome of capital's intensified biopolitical rule, its articulation as the overarching social relation and an embodied reality that, globally speaking, thrives on gender and racial difference. One issue here is whether the representation of globalisation's 'economic others', inevitably offered for consumption to privileged constituencies across art's many institutional sites, is replacing, and replicating, postmodernism's ethnographic commitment to the representation of 'cultural others'.[46]

But, we might ask, what was the position reserved for feminist politics in these two landmark shows mounted against postmodernism? As regards 'Documenta 11' specifically, it led feminists to wonder: 'where has the legacy of feminist intervention and participation gone? Has it been integrated into a project that no longer needs to advertise that specific dimension because it forms an integral strand of the plait or braid of contemporary concerns?'[47] By 2009 and 'Altermodern', it had become clear that such a project of integration had not occurred in the art world: not resting on the grand curatorial gestures of the above shows, the exhibition 'Uneven Geographies: Art and Globalisation' in 2010, promising to 'bring together the work of artists from five continents who find experimental ways of capturing the processes of globalisation, and its human consequences in various regions of the world' also failed to engage feminism.[48] Opening and closing the first decade of the twenty-first century, 'Documenta 11' and 'Altermodern' were not just global in scope but also explicitly sought to locate contemporary art vis-à-vis globalisation, prioritising a politics of geography that ignored, rather than openly attacked, feminist politics. Their silence over feminism's possible contribution to shifting the ground of politics from the staples of postmodernism to the actuality of capitalism's globalisation was an implicit dismissal of feminism's relevance to the production of a public sphere – an effective dismissal in that it did not have to reproduce the formula of excluding women artists. Because of the worldwide visibility and appeal of Enwezor's and Bourriaud's institutionally rewarded gestures, their rejection of postmodernism in a way that marginalised feminism, realised in projects that sought to refocus the political terrain in art on globalisation, raises a number of questions. The first and obvious such question is whether feminist politics is being relegated to a parenthetical position in relation to globalisation as contemporary art's new, historically dictated object of critique. The praise that 'Documenta 11' received from the mainstream press for allowing 'no body, no sex, no bodily fluids' to interfere with the show's tackling of 'serious matters' posed this threat already in 2002.[49] Ten years later this position is echoed in statements such as: '*Real topics* and *real questions* are on the agenda again' [emphasis in the original], as put by Karel Vanhaesebrouck in an essay that celebrates the death of postmodernism as apparently devoid of substance and oppositionality.[50] Beyond a facile dismissal of such comments as displaying a profound ignorance of feminist positions, it is worth considering whether they pointed at the time to the hegemony of a particular strand of feminist thinking, the priorities and methodologies of which were deemed incompatible with the demands introduced by globalisation as an object of critique.

Since 2002 other positions have emerged, and to an extent the short answer to the question concerning the possible integration of feminism into a broader oppositional project is 'yes'. This is realised both in curatorial practice (to be examined in Chapter 6) and in theoretical discourse. One, adequately complicated example, is Marion von Osten's editorial for an issue of the influential web art journal *e-flux* in 2010. This particular issue intended to launch 'the beginning of a debate that asks whether the (cultural) Left is still capable of thinking and acting beyond the analysis of overwhelming power structures or working within the neoliberal consensus model'.[51] Far from eclipsing the relevance of feminism to these debates, von Osten cites her 'own interest in contemporary feminist economists' engagement with new political imaginaries' as prompting her to pose the journal issue's key question. The turn to feminist economists, rather than feminist art theorists and historians, in an art journal, implies a scepticism towards the methodologies and concerns of dominant narratives of feminist art history and theory (that apparently tend to render other positions invisible). The invocation of economists, feminist or other, attests however to the reversal of the postmodern trend to translate the economy into culture.

But complications arise in von Osten's text precisely because 'feminist economists' are presented as a uniform group found to oppose the views of 'mainstream economists'. The production of feminist economists as a uniform group produces in its turn a singular feminist perspective that serves to sustain the 'search for the post-capitalist self' (the editorial's title). But this is not necessarily a future-oriented search (as one might expect), concentrating instead on readings of existing social and cultural practices through 'a post-capitalist lens', assumed to be available here and now! Von Osten attributes to feminist economists this particular view: 'Feminist economists warned that describing capitalism as a self-perpetuating structure – with its ongoing need for crisis, renovation, and so forth – ignores on the one hand the heterogeneity of multiple economies, including household activities and pre- or postcapitalist economies, already existing inside Western and non-Western contexts alike.' Despite the editorial's frequent references specifically to capitalism and the economy, the construction of a singular feminist perspective is used to prioritise an ultimately geographical reading of world divisions (Western vs Non-Western) while implicitly displacing global capitalism as globalisation's master narrative. The phrase 'decentering the economy', heading a section in the text, does not point to the fact that global capitalism is centreless (as Hardt and Negri have argued), implying instead that capitalism is not the only economy we inhabit. Finally, attention to difference (heterogeneity) is once more proposed as the solution to the problem – although it is no longer certain what constitutes the problem if post-capitalist practices already exist. In fact, von Osten concludes that 'although *the present is constituted by postcapitalist practices* (and politics as well), we still have to engage in the discourse and establish a new language, whether textual or visual, in order to make these practices apparent, articulated, and applicable' (my emphasis). This is an exemplary moment of postmodernism's survival as ideology – as the unconscious internalisation of values that appear obvious – since the 'problem' that remains, after asserting the heterogeneity of the economy and a post-capitalist present, is one of language and discourse. Moreover, postmodernism as ideology appears on this occasion to suppress post-structuralism's insight that 'practices', that is materially embedded processes, do not constitute a separate and primary field of relations that must then be reflected (made 'apparent'), rendered contextually meaningful (be 'articulated'), and valorised (made 'applicable') in some secondary space of discourse. Indeed, feminist art history, to which post-structuralism provided a vital methodological tool, would have a lot to say about reintroducing a polarisation between 'practices' and 'discourse' – a distinction also challenged today in the very terrain of so-called immaterial labour.[52]

The above discussion foregrounds the need to depart from postmodernism while also considering some of the ways that postmodernism can still be seen to inform radical thinking in the arts. In this context, negotiating the terrain of feminist politics in art history establishes a double goal: to assert the legacy of feminist art history and rethink the premises of a materialist feminist politics capable of addressing globalisation. This is important not least because feminism has not evacuated the scene of contemporary art. Exhibitions with a feminist agenda existed in the past decade but appeared to constitute a separate field of curatorial enquiry while an emerging generation of feminist art historians has noted, also in relation to such projects: 'the predominant understanding of "feminism" is coded by a body of works, actions, and texts produced in the 1960s and '70s, such that it has become nearly impossible to talk about contemporary feminism in a way that doesn't tie it to a historical moment'.[53] The vertical historicisation of feminism from within may have something to do with the peripheralisation of feminism in the arts today. To understand what this means, let me ask in the tradition of critical counterfactualism: what if the first major show on art and globalisation, 'Documenta 11', had claimed that the feminist rather than the postcolonial subject is where critical art practice must focus its energies in addressing globalisation? My intention is not to answer this 'what if' but rather to introduce the issues that this 'what if' brings to light, and which have everything to do with the transition from postmodernism to globalisation as the two discreet, and yet interconnected, phases of contemporary art.

To proceed with this discussion, a subtle difference between the terms 'postcolonial' and 'feminist' must be addressed, however briefly. As the site of critique, the postcolonial describes an explicitly historical condition of being, which may or may not be invested with political meaning: in its simplest and most literal formulation, a postcolonial subject is the one that emerged at the aftermath of colonial rule. Given that this aftermath was the outcome of extremely complex processes, including the struggle to end colonialism, there are good reasons to believe in the revolutionary potential of postcolonial subjects. The feminist subject did *not* however emerge at the aftermath of women's oppression. Rather, it is one that continues to 'irrupt', or gather force much like a wave, *within* conditions of oppression. It does not emanate as the outcome of struggle but it could best be grasped as the 'point' where the struggle becomes intensified and is situated as such. The postcolonial subject belongs to the twentieth century whereas the feminist subject, in its historically rooted variability (by which I mean both in space and time), crosses through centuries and continents to define and work towards the undoing of women's subordinate position as shaped in given social realities. It becomes then obvious that both subjects have a stake in the contemporary moment but that they are connected to this moment in different ways. One salient difference is that the feminist subject must always establish and communicate its relevance to each and every moment of its articulation whereas such connection is obvious in the case of the postcolonial subject. Neither can afford to ignore the moment's political specificity, and it is to this I now turn.

Thoughts on a possible art history: four entry points for feminism

Meanings of feminisation

Arguing for a feminist subject as a leading figure in the struggle against capital's global empire should not have been inconceivable. If a reviewer of 'Documenta 11' commended its chief curator for tackling subjects that really matter, such as poverty and conflict, in ways that disregard gender and sex, the data about globalisation directly contradict him. According to editor of *Signs*, political scientist Mary E. Hawkesworth, globalisation is not merely gender divided. Rather, there exist key 'dimensions of globalisation' that compel an engagement with women's position in this context.[54] Hawkesworth outlines the following such dimensions: (a) 'the feminisation of the labour force', (b) 'the feminisation of migration', (c) 'privatisation' as an 'aspect of the neoliberal agenda for globalisation' involving the 'shrinking' or even disappearance of the welfare state, and (e) (although Hawkesworth does not devote a special section to it but nevertheless discusses it) the 'feminisation of citizenship' with the 'emergence of a mode of partial citizenship that requires payment of taxes, yet affords no voting rights and tolerates diminished liberties pertaining to movement, conditions of labour, marriage, and reproduction'.[55] And most women became even more vulnerable after the global financial crisis of 2008.

Hawkesworth's use of 'feminisation' engages a range of meanings – from an increase in numbers (women economic migrants) to a demotion or subversion of rights and a decrease in quality (citizenship). In the world of global capital, 'feminisation' refers then to qualitative and quantitative data but in all cases it retains its strongly negative connotations. The negativity of 'feminisation' – by the 2010s a conceptual *sine qua non* in globalisation studies and political theory – is hardly ever considered problematic and a feminist project of reclamation of feminisation in positive terms is hardly underway. At the same time, 'feminisation' is rarely if ever used in art history, which to an extent betrays the distance between the concerns of feminist art history as shaped in the last quarter of the twentieth century and critiques of globalisation from the mid-1990s onwards.

The reasons why feminisation has not so far been deployed by feminist art historians are not obvious, since it could be usefully applied to address the precarisation of entry-point arts professionals and the 'dark matter' of (invisible) artists necessary for sustaining an arts economy divided in cases of exceptional 'success' and typical 'failure':[56] nearly half a century after the struggles of the 1960s and 1970s, art schools and art history classes are dominated by female students.[57] The relationship between the gender of most art students and the predicament of most artists requires broader acknowledgement within art history. The material-ideological make-up of 'female creatives', where feminist art history's politically invested category of 'woman artist' now falls, has not been subject to scrutiny in recent art history.[58] Occasionally, however, one can come across data about how much less than their male colleagues contemporary women artists fetch at auctions – a phenomenon that would absurdly allow us to speak about the feminisation of women artists' own production.[59] My point, however, is not to suggest useful applications in art history of a popular concept in recent globalisation theory. What is more relevant is what this concept – feminisation – suggests about the gendered socio-economic spaces where contemporary art-making becomes a job and whether this raises methodological issues that should be considered in formulating a feminist politics in art history.

A first observation to this end is the quantitative aspect of the term, which implies a turn from woman to women. In subsequent chapters, we shall see that post-1990 art embracing feminist critique already incorporates a problematic that shifts attention from the abstraction of woman (as sign, for instance) to the materiality of women's lives (to the trafficking of large numbers of women, to offer one example). In Hawkesworth's analysis across feminisation's spectrum of meanings, a common element stands out: the centrality of a general women's experience in globalisation, understood here in terms of a global organisation of labour, impacting also on citizenship. The glimpse of a general women's experience based on explicitly social grounds (labour and economy) may be seen to run counter to the psychoanalytic approach to femininity based on sexual difference. In the planetary enclosure that global capital demands, the 'shock value' of Jacques Lacan's famous dictum – 'woman does not exist' – becomes empirically affirmed as '*women* do exist':[60] their experiences may vary but it is possible to speak of women's general position in the global economy. And this aids the move from universality (woman) to generality (women).

That said, the qualitative interpretation of feminisation suggests that the feminine continues to be imbued with negativity in the social imaginary and explanatory discourses, including those that are embraced by feminists. If and how the feminist analysis of art can contribute to the reclamation and positive rescripting of 'feminisation' is a moot point at present. In this study, it is articulated as a desire rather than a goal within reach – and yet it is a desire that must motivate the quest for method that the conditions of globalisation impose on a feminism tackling the present.

Identity, agency, representation

The generality of women's condition in globalisation poses anew the problem of identity: do 'women' share an identity or is a politics of identity an impediment – either untenable or undesirable – at present? As the slogan 'the personal is political' (the personal being formed through internalisations of identity) found numerous applications in artistic practice and even in the writing of history, second-wave feminism in art history engaged with the question of identity from early on. Second-wave feminism became associated with a broader conception of identity politics, according to which the constitution of the subject (along the lines of gender, sexuality, race, ethnicity, age and to an extent, class) provided the grounds for the subject's politics. Especially in art, individual (or perhaps individualised) histories led to a radical deployment of autobiography that negotiated how what was hitherto intimate and private was the outcome of systematic exclusion, subjugation and mystification that had to be publicly contested. There was great emphasis on embodied experience and its discursive articulation, and there is little doubt that identity politics revolutionised the terrain of politics at large. This was a broader outcome of the demands expressed in the social turmoil of the late 1960s, supported also through theory not necessarily concerned with feminism: a number of French male thinkers, including Louis Althusser, Michel Foucault, Gilles Deleuze and Felix Guattari, focused on the articulation of power in, and through, the individual, embodied subject, which consequently became (also) the site of struggle.

Presenting the fractured image of a woman whose reflection is splintered on a shattered mirror, Barbara Kruger's *Untitled* (1989) remains, however, an emblematic reminder about the risks of this quest for radical identity. Superimposed on the image, the phrase 'your body is a battleground' can receive today an even more unsettling meaning than the one originally intended. If this piece existed within the context of the abortion debates in the USA in the 1980s, today we are aware that the body of woman was also the battleground of feminism. Identity politics became enmeshed in the relentless fragmentation of the social field and feminist politics were particularly affected. Questions of solidarity became less and less relevant, as the widely diverse experiences of women cast serious doubts on the possibility of a shared identity as the ground for political action. Amelia Jones' 1996 exhibition 'Sexual Politics' centred on Judy Chicago's *The Dinner Party* (1974–79), a landmark piece intended to celebrate women's contribution to human civilisation, produced instructive results.[61] The history of *The Dinner Party* proved to be not only a cause of celebration but also a symbolic object of injury, which made apparent the difficulty of creating a feminist community beyond, or at least across, racial difference – and, as the reception of the show demonstrated, ideological and material divisions. In feminism beyond the art world this was perhaps more pronounced. As Kathi Weeks has argued, citing black radical Angela Davies, the 'Wages for Housework' campaign failed to impress black women as most of them had already been doing paid housework for other people.[62] This had not made their work more visible nor given them greater agency.

At the same time, the extensive use of post-structuralist and psychoanalytic criticism, especially of Lacanian origin, in feminist art theory negotiated the inherent instability of identity, positing a subject always on the brink of collapse. This was seen as potentially liberating, since female identity could be recast as a mutable socio-cultural effect. But things were not so simple. Besides Kipnis's critique, already discussed, Judith Butler's performativity theory stressed the compulsive, daily reenactment of gender and sexual identity.[63] The effort to posit empowered female subjects and the belief that the subject as such is necessarily fractured, incomplete and unstable constituted an antinomy seen to hinder an understanding of how agency becomes possible in conditions of oppression.[64] In their 2005 volume *Reclaiming Female Agency: Feminist Art History after Postmodernism*, Norma Broude and Mary D. Garrard centred their arguments in an outright rejection of post-structuralism and psychoanalysis identified with 'an increasingly theoretical and largely masculinist postmodernism', though the agency they had in mind was that of women artists and their female promoters across the ages, and the volume overall marks the distance of its scholarship from contemporary articulations of the political.[65]

Contemporary theory addressing the discontents of globalisation is explicitly opposed to identity as the ground for politics but not because it accepts a subject forever incomplete and unstable. John Holloway, whose work has been massively influential in anti-capitalist circles, has argued about an opposition to global capitalism that begins from a position of negation.[66] The political project he advocates attempts to bypass the thorny issue of identity in that it leaves unacknowledged the widespread social desire for identity, especially as witnessed after the disaster of the American 9/11, when identity migrated from the 'soft' realm of culture to the 'hard' realm of politics proper, and when various permutations of 'us' and 'them' provided post-Cold War battle positions. In essence, Holloway suggests that in the current historical conjuncture identity cannot be an outcome of a freely executed act of self-definition. His starting point for anti-capitalist politics is 'the scream', that is the voiced despair that gives rise to protest and which indicates the need to build a coalitional culture of opposition that is as inclusive as possible. His thesis is not, in part at least, too far removed from the belief that if identity is provided from the site of power (if, say, women can only be defined as women in terms of not being men), then it is politically important to reject this imposed identity (to say 'we are not women'). In this act of not fulfilling the expectations of power, opposition and struggle emerge as constitutive of agency in the very process of becoming something or someone as yet unimaginable.

In favouring a politics of exodus, of subjectivity as 'departure', contemporary political theory working against global capitalism has attempted to address in more specific terms what the problem of a positivisation of identity is, in its articulation through a politics of difference. Vassilis Tsianos and Dimitris Papadopoulos have a lot of good things to say about the realm of micro-politics, which they associate with all those movements (including feminism) that paid particular attention to the constitution of subjectivity through the everyday. The struggles located in the micro-political realm provide a springboard for thinking about the next move in charting the path of exodus from capitalist relations, but are not at the same time adequate. For these authors, the limitations of a political discourse based on identity is that representation cannot be about leaving capitalism but about finding 'your' place in the ever expanding representational menu it offers:

> Feminism, civil rights movements, identity politics, urban activism, antiracism, all start from the embodied experience of exclusion on the level of the everyday and, by doing that, they intend to rearticulate it and to insert difference as a constitutive moment of the everyday. [. . .] In other words, the micropolitical form attempted to incorporate new social subjectivities into the established social compromise of the nation state – which was organised along whiteness, heteronormativity, waged labour, and property – by engaging in changing the dominant conditions of representation [. . .]. The micropolitics of difference is the fight for representation. [. . .] In this sense, the subjectivity connected to the event of representation is neither a departure, nor a facticity, it is an *arrival*.[67] [my emphasis]

The links of identity to representation remain then an acute problem in thinking about the political struggles of today. It is not so much that representation (especially of the subaltern) can only be illusory, leading to partial acceptance and token visibility, but that it constitutes an 'arrival' precisely into what ought to be rejected as the source of exploitation, injustice and inequality.

A critique of an oppositional politics based on identity and representation has been taken up by many other thinkers, including Hardt and Negri, feminist philosopher Rosi Braidotti and art historian Amelia Jones. Hardt and Negri are explicitly interested in the possibilities of networked resistance afforded by the concept of the multitude, the power of which, unlike that of 'the people', does not rest on the projection of a shared, collective identity. The multitude can thus be seen as the dispersed productive forces of contemporary capitalism, and that is why Enwezor's prioritisation of one subject (the postcolonial) as exemplifying the multitude misconstrues the historical specificity of this emergent subject. It is capital's global imperative that produces the multitude, just as the multitude's activity produces the interconnected spaces of 'empire'. Further than this, the multitude poses a challenge to the project of a politics of representation articulated in postmodern times. Undeniably, the politicisation of representation, in which feminism played a great role, was one of the most radical propositions of critical postmodernism in the arts. But it is at least questionable whether the multitude can be represented at all. The problem of the multitude is not how to make itself appear but how to act so as to claim back what the authors define, in their 2009 co-authored volume, as common wealth (the volume notably closes with a discussion of identity). This, in turn, raises two issues for a contemporary feminist politics in art history. First, that representation may no longer be a historically privileged site of politics. If contemporary art continues to be read as a site of representation, a crucial dimension of the formation of political subjects today may be lost. Second, it suggests that women should not have appeared (instead of the postcolonial subject) as the privileged subject of globalisation in an alternative 'Documenta 11', for that would have been an equally problematic misrecognition of where contemporary politics lie. Women, and feminists, are necessarily a constitutive element of the multitude and given the role of women in globalisation as outlined above, a question is whether Hardt and Negri have not paid due attention to the gendered condition of the multitude. Even if they highlight the role of immaterial labour (a term that this study will keep revisiting from various angles) and the importance, more specifically, of affective labour, connecting it (how could they not?) to women's work, a lot remains to be said or, better, understood.

Braidotti explicitly criticises 'the excesses of identity politics' and 'the sacralization of experiential knowledge'.[68] One problem she sees is that 'becoming minoritarian (becoming woman/animal/molecular) marks a shift from the dominant subject position, but nevertheless remains tied to it. These becomings-minoritarian unfold from the minorities and aim at a shift of consciousness, but they are like Benjamin's angel of history: always looking backward slightly, even as they advance toward the future.' Braidoti understands the rule of contemporary capital as not merely biopolitical but as covering both 'bios' (life in human society) and 'zoe' (the fact of life) arguing: 'in the age of bios/zoe-power, transversal interconnections make it impossible on the cognitive plane and irresponsible on the ethical level actually to uphold categorical distinctions between human and other-than-human subject positions'.[69] In this case, a politics of representation would be indeed unethical, as humans can represent but animals (and nature) must be represented. But the problem of humans exploiting both other humans and nature for profit cannot be resolved by claiming a lack of distinction between humans and non-humans on a discursive level, which is, after all, exclusively available to humans.

Braidotti's account is, however, useful to a feminist politics in art history in that it reminds us that intersectionality, currently used to extend the lifespan of identity politics, was according to Kimberlé Crenshaw who coined it in the landmark year 1989, 'a provisional concept linking contemporary politics with postmodern theory'.[70] Intersectionality can be seen as a concept marking precisely the process of transition from postmodernism to the realisation of global capital's enclosure project as globalisation. And interestingly enough, although Braidotti accuses Hardt and Negri of providing in their theory 'a meta-narrative of labour' (and so she shoots the messenger for the message), Crenshaw, a prominent American legal theorist, conceived of intersectionality by looking at the discrimination suffered by black women in their work environments.[71] Arguably, the term intersectionality gained momentum around 2000 when references to the economy – for example, in black feminism – began to achieve prominence against references to culture.[72]

Jones' extensive study of the trajectories of identity discourses in contemporary visual arts opens by offering a view to the other side of radical Left politics. She opens her analysis with the observation that the post-1990 repudiation of identity emerges primarily in the mainstream media, arguing that 'post-identity rhetoric functions to obscure 50 years of intense struggle on the part of civil rights, feminist, and other activists operating under the premises of twentieth-century identity politics to claim and act on coalitional identifications in order to produce social change'.[73] The move from identity to identification lies at the core of Jones' argument in ways that complement rather than undermine Hardt and Negri's emphasis on the function of singularity within the multitude. Singularity (a social being at a moment of action with others, an event-nodal point of convergences) can indeed be an expression of identification, and as Jones seems to suggest a form of 'queering' and subverting the compulsion of holding on to the illusion of an inalienable, immutable core. Jones' argument about the operation of a 'queer feminist durationality' is however concerned with the encounter of artworks that demand to be seen (or at least touched). It is an argument that invokes Jacques Rancière's positive investment in spectatorship; it is indeed about an active spectatorship where the memory of conventions (for example, what a mother has looked like as a cumulative effect of ubiquitous cultural signifiers) is constantly challenged, disrupted and reconstructed by what the work of art exhibits (for example, a butch lesbian mother in a Catherine Opie photograph).[74] The work, in other words, must have *it*, must be fully present and fully aware of the fact that it is called to perform for the spectator. The queer feminist durationality is, therefore, enacted in cases where the representational power of the artwork pulls the spectator into a temporary identification. This is then a theory about the challenges to identity in cases where the artist's work has led to the completion of an artwork, be it a sculpture or a photograph, which becomes an articulation of the artist's agency. What happens in cases where the artist's labour remains 'absent and hidden', to quote Boris Groys writing on art in the age of biopolitics (or globalisation) may be less rewarding, as we shall see in later chapters.[75]

Labour

The feminisation of citizenship is interwoven with the transformation of the labour market overall, seen to rely on mobile, precarious, service-oriented or, more generally, immaterial labour. Despite contentious aspects of this concept, immaterial labour's relevance to the project of feminist politics in art history is threefold: first, in capturing the specificity of 'art after deskilling', as John Roberts has referred to a process beginning with modern art and intensifying with the neo-avant-garde, it helps locate women artists within a broader framework of artistic production.[76] Second, materialist feminists have noted the centrality of women's devalued forms of productivity (especially in the home) in what immaterial labour encompasses. And third, the concept of immaterial labour can be helpful in tracing *how* the articulation of art as a gendered field of production is connected with gendered labour beyond art.

The unstable, insecure, often seasonal, low-paid work characterised as precarious labour has been a frequent reference in anti-capitalist thinking, both within and beyond the art world. The question of precarity is of particular relevance to those involved in the art sector where voluntary, seasonal and 'flexible' work arrangements sustain the art world as a sector of the service economy. Von Osten has stressed the gender-specific dilemmas faced by women in the new labour regime where flexibilisation has also meant to work 'from home'.[77] In 2009 the journal *Open* produced an issue entitled 'A Precarious Existence: Vulnerability in the Public Domain' where Brett Neilson and Ned Rossiter stress that 'in its most ambitious formulation, it [the question of precarity] would encompass not only the condition of precarious workers but a more general existential state, understood at once as a source of "political subjection, of economic exploitation and of opportunities to be grasped" ', further noting that 'related to this was the question of the gendered nature of precarious work'.[78] Strongly linked with capital's biopower, the precarisation of labour became thus associated with a historically dictated condition of being and was theorised by Tsianos and Papadopoulos in terms of 'embodied capitalism'.[79] This concept enables a departure from understandings of capital's global imperative in solely geographical terms, enacting in its place a dialectic between the diverse sites of capital's articulation, one of which is the body as the material ground of subjectivity.[80]

In developing the concept of embodied capitalism, Tsianos and Papadopoulos argue that 'immaterial labour cannot be conceived as a possibility for delineating a line of flight out of this system of domination', stressing: 'The question then is how to think of deterritorialisation and exodus beyond the concept of immaterial labour.'[81] To do this, the authors see as imperative a return to the presence of the body in current regimes of productivity, highlighting the importance of three strands of research in this endeavour: research in feminism, science and technology studies and border and migration studies. The crucial point made by these authors is that bodies at present produce an excess (primarily, of sociality) not captured by production. This leads them to raise the need for 'a new model of subjectivity . . . which is neither effect of production nor is it identical with the conditions of its exploitation, a concept which drifts constantly away from its social determinants'. But despite this insight, in their attempt to think of 'social transformation after representation', their thesis becomes too preoccupied with 'creating always new singular social actors' to prove of value to a redefinition of feminist politics. Indeed, their emphasis on the singular is reminiscent of Julia Kristeva's position in her 1979 essay 'Women's Time' – although Kristeva writing at the height of postmodernism predictably targeted 'the [imaginary] community of language as a universal and unifying tool' rather than connected the need to 'bring out the singularity of each person [. . .] and the *relativity of his/her symbolic as well as biological existence*' to material conditions.[82] Ironically, Kristeva's envisioning of a third generation of singular actors as the next stage in feminist politics did not stand the test of time.[83] The 'demassification of the problematic of difference', as she put it, was largely realised as a depoliticised post-feminism, startlingly blind to the grim reality of *most* women's lives in capital's articulated power.

Contemporary materialist feminism, largely visible outside art history, is both stressing the centrality of work in feminist politics today and guarding against the blindspots and amnesia of anti-capitalist theorisations of immaterial labour. In 2006 social scientist and activist Silvia Federici, strongly connected with the legacy of Autonomist Marxism, was already particularly mindful of the optimistic view that through immaterial labour 'capitalism is not only leading us beyond labor, but it is creating the conditions for the "commonization" of our work experience, where the divisions are beginning to crumble'. Arguing that this essentially optimistic view of precarious labour represents the interests of a privileged group of workers, Federici explains that 'the concept of "affective" [central to immaterial labour] . . . brings reproductive work back into the world of mystification, suggesting that reproducing people is just a matter of producing "emotions," "feelings" ' when in reality it produces 'not just "life," but "labor-power" ', that is 'the worker's "capacity to work," the worker's capacity to be exploited.' Women's struggle 'over/against reproductive work' created, on the one hand, the possibility of thinking about 'the ways in which capitalism has exploited [. . .] sexuality, and made it "productive" '.[84]

On the other hand, and more importantly, Federici reminds us of a key outcome of materialist feminist analysis already carried out in the past: that women's multi-faceted labour at home, incorporating motherhood, plays a crucial role in the very reproduction of systemic relations of power. At the same time, 'feminist scholarship has illustrated how global indebtedness, structural adjustment policies, and the hegemony of neoliberal development strategies have directly intensified women's *triple* roles in production, reproduction, and community management'[85] (my emphasis). It is not just that 'exclusion of the economic, cultural, and political spheres (often casual or informal) that operate in households and communities' is instrumental in distorting the true parameters of global capital's rule, when 'as profitability crises encourage restructuring, a series of spatial shifts (from factory to sweatshop to home) and ideological shifts (from family-wage work to poorly paid feminized work) cheapen production costs for global investors and producers.'[86] Such a distortion also renders invisible the practices of refusal that women enact vis-à-vis reproductive work and their flight from domestic space. This would be something different to the Autonomist tradition examined by Weeks and where women's liberation was not real so long as it meant 'slavery to an assembly line'.[87]

But what if practices of refusal did not mean slavery to the assembly line or the reception desk? When it comes to art, and despite feminist art history's close attention to the private and public dimensions of women's lives, we note that no feminist study of contemporary women artists (by which I mean artists coming of age after 1989) has systematically considered how their labour may in fact constitute such practices of refusal, irrespective of these artists' self-identification as feminist. As Teresa Ebert argued in the early 1990s, the problem has been 'the erasure of body/sexuality/gender as all *effects of labor*' within hegemonic strands of feminist theory that dominated also art discourse.[88] But such a distortion also hides from view how women's exodus from home, also occurring in the art world, is nevertheless imbricated in relations instituted through capital, as well as how it might be seen to undermine or sustain such relations.

Overall, what the above suggest is that for a feminist politics in art history in the early twenty-first century, the 'gendering of work', a major concern in feminist analyses of globalisation in the past ten years, must be as important as the gendering of signifying practices was in the feminist art history of the late twentieth century.[89] In the emergence of concepts such as 'embodied capitalism', we can recognise labour as a powerful mediator in the articulation of external and internal sites of reproduction of capital's global imperative (precisely as a master-narrative) and external and internal sites of resistance.

Transnationalism, or the return to feminist politics in capital's empire

One of the most frequently invoked concepts in today's feminist discourse, not least in relation to art, is that of the transnational. The unorthodox use of this word as a noun here helps bring to view, in parallel to Mouffe's iteration of the political as a space of antagonism/social relations, the significance currently attributed to a space where communication becomes possible beyond, or despite, the exclusionary logic of operative national spaces. Needless to say, much like the political, the transnational is also steeped in antagonism, especially in the era of deeply interconnected economies where, as many feminists have shown, what proponents of global capital see as 'development' in one part of the world guarantees or presupposes underdevelopment in another.[90] Feminist art historian Katy Deepwell also notes that ' "transnational" can refer simply to new flows of people, ideas, markets [. . .] but it can also imply, rather negatively, a racial, ethnic, linguistic, and national border, which is highly difficult to cross'.[91] For this very reason, transnational space is of interest to those who benefit from globalisation and to those who resist it. But it has been hard for feminists to inhabit transnational space politically in the arts.

In 1984, five years before Kipnis's harsh critique of continental feminist theory, Chandra Talpade Mohanty, a major proponent of transnational feminist solidarity today, published 'Under Western Eyes: Feminist Scholarship and Colonial Discourses'.[92] She identified specific analytic principles, apparently endemic in feminist scholarship dealing with Third World women, which prevented, rather than encouraged, alliances between First and Third World feminisms, arguing instead for a discourse that respected and described the heterogeneity of women's experience. The paper was to be extremely influential in its critique of Western feminism, but it is interesting to see how Mohanty revised her position twenty years after the essay's publication, following the consolidation of global capital from the 1990s onwards.

In her 2003 essay 'Under Western Eyes Revisited: Feminist Solidarity through Anticapitalist Struggles', Mohanty calls attention to her espousal of 'historical materialism as a basic framework, and a definition of material reality in both its local and micro-, as well as global, systemic dimensions', condemning the 'postmodernist appropriation' of her original position, consisting in interpretations of her argument as one that stressed 'difference over commonalities'.[93] In her revision's concluding remarks, Mohanty repeats that: 'A transnational feminist practice depends on building feminist solidarities across the divisions of place, identity, class, work, belief and so on.'[94] But to understand how difficult this is to achieve, two further points need to be noted. First, that Mohanty openly acknowledges the different context of writing as a critical feminist in the 1980s and after 2000. Whereas her earlier writing focused on a 'critique of Western humanism and Eurocentrism and of white, Western feminism, a similar essay written now would need to be located in the critique of global capitalism (or anti-globalisation), the naturalisation of the values of capital, and the unacknowledged power of cultural relativism in cross-cultural feminist scholarship and pedagogies', seeing 'the politics and economics of capitalism as a far more urgent locus of struggle'.[95] This is important not only because the concept of patriarchy is overshadowed by that of capitalism, but also because of the subtle disposal of a politics of geography. This politics of geography has been commensurate with an anthology-type of femo-multiculturalism, which is how transnationalism is understood in much feminist curating and writing of art history today striving to redress the balance by showcasing women artists from around the world. In accepting the systemic, totalising work of capital and in protesting the inadequacy of concepts such as Third World and First World women, the impulse Mohanty wants to cultivate is one of building bridges rather than condoning cultural relativism as a necessary evil in articulating women's position. Second, Mohanty acknowledges that 'although the context for writing "Under Western Eyes" in the mid-1980s was a visible and activist women's movement, this radical movement no longer exists as such'. What exists today is 'a more distant, but significant, anti-globalization movement . . . Activists in these movements are often women, although the movement is not gender focused.'[96] It seems superfluous to add that the absence of a women's movement is of paramount importance also for a feminist politics in art history today, when feminist art history emerged in the late 1960s and early 1970s precisely in the context of such a movement.

Let us then try to work with Mohanty's highly influential position on the search for a transnational feminist politics (but not a feminist social movement). Surely, suggesting the benefits of a comparative methodology, returning us to the concreteness and inter-connectedness of women's experience and impacting on pedagogy, is of exemplary value, but this claim has been made also in the context of postmodern feminism. A more accurate language and conceptual apparatus remains an objective in that context, but what such a change will not do – because it cannot – is to lift feminism beyond ideological divides that find expression textually even as rooted in material asymmetries.[97] It is also the case, as also stressed by Jones in an art historical context, that a solitary feminist project 'is no longer viable', to which Jones has counterpoised a 'para-feminism' developing in parallel with, or even enacted within, other contemporary articulations of politics.[98] Mohanty's argument about a transnational agenda is, however, different in that it specifies anti-capitalist struggle as the historically designated pool of a coalitional feminist politics. It is the multiple foci of this struggle which help her grasp the significance of 'the naturalization of the values of capital'.

But this opens a point of critique of Mohanty's own position. The naturalisation of the values of capital implies that bridges must not be constructed over difference but also over exploitation. In the last instance, the landscape of commonalities is interrupted by the fault lines of class antagonisms among women. Capital does not produce abstract difference but *difference through systemically reproduced exploitation* – having created a global framework where women's exploitation of women is also actualised in multiple, blatant or less conspicuous ways. The naturalisation of the values of capital is the mechanism by which what Mohanty calls 'the ladder of privilege' is maintained, because many women don't know they are climbing it or even want to know.[99] The issue therefore is not just how a sweatshop female worker will resist but also how a professional single mother who has to hire cheap female labour (not necessarily from the Third World) in order to keep receiving wages will resist. How will these women resist in ways that actively produce (rather than render visible) commonalities despite the materially embedded conditions of exploitation that connect them? The absence of a global feminist movement, to which Mohanty points, makes this an enormous challenge.

Also, Mohanty's concern over the naturalisation of the values of capital (meaning the internalisation of such values as ideology and the inevitable order of things) implies that transnationalism may be an inadequate concept for capturing the nature of resistance that must be built. What transnationalism can do is lend credibility to a 'practice of feminism across national and cultural divisions' but not necessarily address the complexities of a gendered and racialised economic subject. This concerns feminist politics in art history in two ways: first, if transnationalism (as an -ism that is practised) is complemented by 'the transnational' (a space of antagonisms and hierarchies), it is a first step towards moving away from the questionable solution of women artists' equal 'representation' and towards an analysis of the dynamics connecting the societies where these artists come from and/or produce work. If and how this can happen in the exhibition format is questionable: the liminal exhibition site tends to elide differences, no matter how many panels can accompany the works, carefully contextualising them. Second, it makes apparent the continuing relevance of art history for a contemporary feminist politics at large, as art history can look closely at how the naturalisation of the values of capital occurs, as much as it is resisted: for naturalisation can take place in an artwork as much as in an exhibition or curatorial project, in the policies of a funding agency or in the formation of grass-roots initiatives. The contemporary art world is a microcosm of the richness and scope of practices where the contradictions of 'autonomous' production become apparent as they are inevitably located in sites dominated by a market logic (an eminently transnational one).

Feminist politics in art history: a double awareness

Kipnis's suspicion that there has been a collusion of hegemonic feminist theory with a postmodernism keen to conceal from view material divisions in the restructuring of the world in the terms dictated by the markets was echoed twenty years later in Fraser's article in *New Left Review*. Close to Eisenstein's position who argued that capitalism 'used' feminist ideas as well as feminine values to effect changes in the economy, Fraser writes of

> a more complex and disturbing possibility: that the diffusion of cultural attitudes born out of the second wave has been part and parcel of another social transformation, unanticipated and unintended by feminist activists – a transformation in the social organisation of postwar capitalism.[100]

Fraser begins by considering the position that feminism changed attitudes but not institutions, that it 'wrought an epochal cultural revolution, but the vast change in *mentalités* has not (yet) translated into structural, institutional change'.[101] This position describes with remarkable clarity how things *appear* in the art world and could offer one explanation as to why around 2007 there was suddenly 'this renewed interest in feminist art – both historical and contemporary', in Jones' words, 'after decades of studied neglect on the part of galleries, museums, and the art market in general'.[102] The art institution, comprising all the above, has no problem accommodating *mentalités* in ways that do not amount to its structural reconstitution.

The present chapter clarifies thus why in the second decade of the twenty-first century a feminist politics in art history cannot remain concerned with developments in the art world but must prioritise its connection with the bigger world: the four steps I outlined above as a response to the question how such an updating of feminist politics in art history can begin taking shape far exceed the latter's disciplinary boundaries. Von Osten who, in discussing art and capitalism, turns to feminist economists rather than feminist art historians offers a route worth exploring: feminism is *not* the objective but rather a tool in understanding social process and acting on it in ways that highlight the interests of women. Similarly, a feminist art historian today cannot be committed to preserving feminist art history but to contributing to feminist understandings – also, via art history.

Notably, other arguments have also been made in observing the recent re-engagement of feminism in the art world. Jones has called attention to the need, after America's 9/11 in 2001, *to learn* from the practices of a non-violent activism, such as that established through second-wave feminism (the object of Fraser's critique).[103] Jones' comment was published in 2008, just before economic events threw the world into turmoil. Non-violent activism has not always been an option (I am thinking here of the Arab Spring in 2011 and what happened to it by 2013). But overall, as a I write these lines, there are massive mobilisations of populations and protest movements, unprecedented since the 1960s, even in the formerly privileged West. There is indeed a need to learn about how radical, interventionist politics come into being, what their limitations and successes have been historically: feminism thus becomes important with regard to its potential contribution to a politics of knowledge of the social, to a radical pedagogy targeting internalised values. Such an observation formulates a double and possibly challenging mandate for feminist politics in art history today: to keep searching the repository of (a past) feminist art history *and* work towards situating feminist politics in a broadly conceived oppositional practice directed against global capital and its reliance on gender hierarchies.

What makes this mandate challenging is that a materialist feminist perspective must learn to work with master-narratives (globalisation) and their complications (the survival of postmodernism despite its alleged death) *as well as* with the ideological fragmentation that is immanent in contemporary feminism, given that women's 'uneven' material realities, North and South, are structured through relationships of exploitation that constantly undermine solidarity. Feminist politics in art history must not work undialectically, in reiterating positions that *un*script the gains and losses of feminist struggle so far from the visions of a coalitional politics – simply because such gains and losses inform the current moment of, and for, politics irrespective of whether a conscious feminist discursive practice names them or not. The rethinking of priorities put forward in this chapter should not therefore be misconstrued as a dismissal but rather apprehended as a critical relocation of what-has-been in light of a reconfigured political landscape.

Notes

1 Quotation from the session description of 'Whither Feminist Art History?', organised by Francesca Berry and Amy Mechowski in the context of the

Association of Art Historians 32nd Annual Conference 'Contents, Discontents, Malcontents', University of Leeds, 5–7 April 2006.

2 T. Gouma-Peterson and P. Mathews, 'The Feminist Critique of Art History', *The Art Bulletin* 69/3 (September 1987), 326–57.

3 L. Tickner, 'Feminism, Art History, and Sexual Difference', Genders 3 (Fall 1988), 92–128. Here 94. Also see R. Parker and G. Pollock, *Old Mistresses: Women, Art and Ideology* (New York: Pantheon Books, 1981).

4 Amelia Jones quoted in A. Dimitrakaki, 'The Lessons of Sexual Politics: From the 1970s to the Empire, an Interview with Amelia Jones', in A. Dimitrakaki and L. Perry (eds), *Politics in a Glass Case: Feminism, Exhibition Cultures and Curatorial Transgressions* (Liverpool: Liverpool University Press, 2013), 101-2.

5 M. C. Nussbaum, *Not for Profit: Why Democracy Needs the Humanities* (Princeton: Princeton University Press 2010).

6 J. Kennedy and L. Linden, 'Making Ourselves Visible', *Alphabet Prime* 1 (Fall 2009), 16–24. Here 23.

7 C. Mouffe, *On the Political* (New York and London: Routledge, 2005). Mouffe's best known formulation in this book is her distinction between 'the political' and 'politics', the former referring 'to the dimension of antagonism [. . .] constitutive of human society' and the latter referring to 'the set of practices and institutions through which an order is created, organizing human coexistence in the context of conflictuality provided by the political'; ibid., p. 9. This distinction is less important for my argument here, which stresses the need for a feminism that is not rendered post-political in art history. The threat of the rise of a post-political society in light of globalisation is what I want to retain from Mouffe's thesis.

8 C. Bishop, 'The Social Turn: Collaboration and Its Discontents', *Artforum* (February 2006), 179–85, available online http://artforum.com/inprint/issue=200602&id=10274. Quotes are from the online version.

9 L. Nochlin in 'Feminism & Art (9 views)', *ArtForum* (October 2003). http// findarticles.com (accessed 28 November 2007).

10 G. Pollock, 'Painting, Feminism, History', in M. Barrett and A. Phillips (eds), *Destabilizing Theory: Contemporary Feminist Debates* (Stanford: Stanford University Press, 1992).

11 J. Stallabrass, *High Art Lite: British Art in the 1990s* (London: Verso, 2001), 142.

12 A. Solomon-Godeau, 'The Legs of the Countess', *October* 39 (Winter 1986), 65–108.

13 To see this image in this context go to http://www.christies.com/lotFinder/lot_details.aspx?intObjectID=1478109 (accessed 10 September 2012).

14 For a reading of this show that discusses its relationship to a feminist legacy see A. Kokoli, 'The Woman Artist as Curatorial Effect', in Dimitrakaki and Perry, *Politics in a Glass Case*.

15 Most relevant here is Rosemary Betterton's reading of Paula Modersohn-Becker's self-portraits. See R. Betterton, *An Intimate Distance: Women, Artists and the Body* (London and New York: Routledge, 1996).

16 www.saatchi-gallery.co.uk/artists/tracey_emin.htm (accessed 23 August 2010).

17 www.whitecube.com/artists/emin/ (accessed 23 August 2010).

18 M. Kelly, 'Re-viewing Modernist Criticism', in B. Wallis (ed.), *Art after Modernism: Rethinking Representation* (New York: New Museum of Contemporary Art, 1984).

19 For a more detailed discussion see A. Dimitrakaki, 'Labour, Gender, Sex and Capital: On Biopolitical Production in Contemporary Art', *n.paradoxa: international feminist art journal* 28 (July 2011), 5–15.

20 Eisenstein, *Feminism Seduced*. See in particular her chapter 'Globalization and Women's Labour'.

21 M. Richards, *Marina Abramovic* (Abingdon and New York: Routledge, 2010), 14.

22 Recorded in the Audio about the performance featured at the MOMA website www.moma.org/explore/multimedia/audios/190/1970 (accessed 10 September 2012).

23 Abramovic used two super-8 cameras to record the double, collaborative performance. The work, under the title *Role Exchange* is in Collections: NIMk (Netherlands Media Art Institute), De Appel.

24 Marina Vishmidt quoted in 'de-, dis-, ex- on Immaterial Labour: An Interview with Marina Vishmidt Conducted by Marion von Osten' at http://republicart.net/disc/precariat/vishmidt-osten01_en.htm (accessed 25 August 2010).

25 Marina Abramovic quoted in A. Novakov, 'Role Exchange: Desire, Beauty and the Public', in her *Veiled Histories: The Body, Place and Public Art* (New York: Critical Press, 1997), 27.

26 A. Fraser, 'How to Provide an Artistic Service: An Introduction', in S. Leung and Z. Kocur (eds), *Theory in Contemporary Art since 1985* (Oxford: Blackwell, 2005).

27 A. Novakov, 'Point of Access: Marina Abramovic's 1975 Performance 'Role Exchange', *Woman's Art Journal* 24/2 (Autumn 2003), 31–5. Here 34.

28 N. Power, *One Dimensional Woman* (Winchester, UK and Washington USA: Zone Books, 2009), 55.

29 http://archiv.documenta.de/uebersichtsdetails.html?L=1&gk=A&level=&knr=38 (accessed 15 May 2012).

30 Ibid.

31 The first quotation comes from Steyerl's interview to F. Boenzi, 'Do you speak Spamsoc?', *Mousse* 23, at www.moussemagazine.it/articolo.mm?id=540. The second quotation comes from J. Lack, 'Artist of the Week 22: Hito Steyerl' (31 December 2008), *The Guardian*, www.guardian.co.uk/culture/2008/dec/30/contemporary-artist-hito-steyerl-new-wave (both accessed 10 September 2010).

32 Steyerl quoted in Boenzi, 'Do you speak Spamsoc?'

33 G. Pollock, *Differencing the Canon: Feminist Desire the Writing of Art's Histories* (London and New York: Routledge, 1999).

34 D. Harvey, *The Condition of Postmodernity: An Enquiry into the Origins of Cultural Change* (Oxford: Blackwell, 1989).

35 For the breadth of this venture, see indicatively B. Ashcroft, G. Griffiths and H. Tiffin (eds), *The Postcolonial Studies Reader* (London and New York: Routledge, 1995).

36 Owens, 'Feminists and Postmodernism', in Foster, *Postmodern Culture*; and A. Jones ' "Post-feminism": A Re-masculinisation of Culture?', in H. Robinson (ed.), *Feminism-Art-Theory: An Anthology 1968–2000* (Oxford: Blackwell, 2001).

37 G. Pollock, 'What's Wrong with "Images of Women"?', in Parker and Pollock, *Framing Feminism*.

38 L. Kipnis, 'Feminism: The Political Conscience of Postmodernism?', *Social Text* 21, Universal Abandon? The Politics of Postmodernism (1989), 149–66. Here 163.

39 Ibid., 164.

40 Ibid.

41 H. Foster, *The Return of the Real* (Cambridge, Mass.: The MIT Press, 1996).

42 Ibid. See in particular the chapter 'The Artist as Ethnographer'.

43 See Introduction in F. Jameson, *Postmodernism, or The Cultural Logic of Late Capitalism* (Durham NC: Duke University Press, 1991).

44 N. Bourriaud, 'Altermodern Manifesto. Postmodernism is Dead' at www.tate. org.uk/britain/exhibitions/altermodern/manifesto.shtm (accessed 10 June 2009).

45 O. Enwezor et al. (eds), *Documenta 11_Platform 5: Exhibition* (Ostfildern-Ruit: Hatje Kantz Publishers, 2002).

46 On this see A. Dimitrakaki, 'The Spectacle and Its Others: Labour, Conflict and Art in the Age of Global Capital', in J. Harris, *Globalization and Contemporary Art*.

47 Quoted in the transcript of panel discussion organised by Griselda Pollock and Alison Rowley, 'Now and Then: Feminism: Art and History: Open Dialogue', AAH conference, Nottingham, 3 April 2004. Panelists: Martha Rosler, Sarat Maharaj, Catherine de Zegher, Mark Nash. CentreCATH Occasional Paper No. 1 AHRB Centre for Cultural Analysis, Theory & History, www.leeds. ac.uk/cath/ahrc/publishing/documenta11/aah.html (accessed 10 June 2010).

48 www.nottinghamcontemporary.org/art/uneven-geographies (accessed 5 July 2010).

49 On this see A. Dimitrakaki, 'Art and Politics Continued', *HM: Research in Critical Marxist Theory* 13/1 (2003), 153–176.

50 K. Vanhaesebrouck, 'Dead as a Dodo? Commitment beyond Postmodernism', in L. De Cauter, R. De Roo and K. Vanhaesebrouck (eds), *Art and Activism in the Age of Globalization* (Rotterdam: NAi Publishers, 2011).

51 M. von Osten, 'In Search of the Post-Capitalist Self', *e-flux journal* 17 (June 2010), www.e-flux.com/journal/view/159 (accessed 7 September 2010).

52 Von Osten draws on J. K. Gibson-Graham (Julie Graham and Katherine Gibson), representing what is often referred to as 'postmodern Marxism', an

eclectic mixture of post-structuralism, community-oriented feminism and radical anti-capitalist critique. See their books J. K. Gibson-Graham, *The End of Capitalism (As We Knew It): A Feminist Critique of Political Economy* (Oxford: Blackwell Publishers, 1996) and J. K. Gibson-Graham, *A Postcapitalist Politics* (Minneapolis: University of Minnesota Press, 2006).

53 Kennedy and Linden, 'Making Ourselves Visible', 16.

54 M. E. Hawkesworth, *Globalization and Feminist Activism* (Maryland: Rowman & Littlefield Publishers, 2006), 9.

55 Hawkesworth, *Globalization and Feminist Activism*, 22–3.

56 See G. Sholette, *Dark Matter: Art and Politics in the Age of Enterprise* Culture (London: Pluto Press, 2011).

57 The issue of the 'feminisation' of art students was discussed in the first UK symposium on art, women and labour entitled 'Art, Gendered Labour and Resistance on 15 June 2012 at Nottingham Contemporary. Available to watch online at http://nottinghamcontemporary.org/event/art-gendered-labour-and-resistance.

58 See S. Taylor, 'Negotiating Oppositions and Uncertainties: Gendered Conflicts in Creative Identity Work', *Feminism & Psychology* (2010), 1–18 and Angela McRobbie's extensive research, including her 'Reflections on Feminism, Immaterial Labour and the Post-Fordist Regime', *New Formations* 70 (Autumn 2010), 60–76.

59 Anonymous, 'The Price of Being Female' (20 May 2012) www.economist.com/blogs/prospero/2012/05/post-war-artists-auction.

60 See J. Copjec, *Imagine There's No Woman: Ethics and Sublimation* (Cambridge Mass.: MIT Press, 2004).

61 See Dimitrakaki, 'The Lessons of Sexual Politics: From the 1970s to Empire, an Interview with Amelia Jones', in Dimitrakaki and Perry, *Politics in a Glass Case*.

62 K. Weeks, *The Problem with Work: Feminism, Marxism, Antiwork Politics and Postwork Imaginaries* (Durham, NC: Duke University, 2011).

63 Judith Butler discusses performativity in much of her writing, articulating different aspects of it in at least three of her books: *Gender Trouble: Feminism and the Subversion of Identity* (London: Routledge, 1990), *Bodies that Matter: On the Discursive Limits of Sex* (London: Routledge, 1993) and *Excitable Speech: A Politics of the Performative* (London: Routledge, 1997).

64 On this see S. Clegg, 'The Problem of Agency in Feminism: A Critical Realist Approach', *Gender and Education* 18/3 (May 2006), 309–24.

65 N. Broude and M. D. Garrard, 'Introduction: Reclaiming Female Agency', in N. Broude and M. D. Garrard (eds), *Reclaiming Female Agency: Feminist Art History after Postmodernism* (Berkeley: University of California Press, 2005), 2.

66 J. Holloway, *How to Change the World without Taking Power* (London: Pluto Press, 2002).

67 V. Tsianos and D. Papadopoulos, 'Who's Afraid of Immaterial Workers? Embodied Capitalism, Precarity, Imperceptibility' (2006), http://preclab.net/text/06–TsianosPapadopoulos.pdf.

68 R. Bradotti, *Transpositions: On Nomadic Ethics* (Cambridge: Polity Press, 2006), 133–9.

69 Ibid., 131.

70 Kimberle Crenshaw, quoted in ibid., 62.

71 Ibid., 82; K. Crenshaw, 'Demarginalising the Intersection of Sex and Race: A Black Feminist Critique of Anti-discrimination Doctrine, Feminist Theory and Anti-Racist Politics', *University of Chicago Legal Forum* (1989), 138–67.

72 See P. Hill Collins, 'Gender, Black Feminism, and Black Political Economy', *Annals of the American Academy of Political and Social Science*, 568 (2000), 41–53.

73 Jones, *Seeing Differently*, xx. See J. Rancière, *The Emancipated Spectator*, trans G. Elliott (London: Verso, 2009).

74 Jones, *Seeing Differently*, 205–10.

75 B. Groys Enwezor et al., 'Art in the Age of Biopolitics: From Artwork to Art Documentation', in *Documenta 11_Platform 5: Exhibition* (Hatje Cantz Publishers, 2002).

76 J. Roberts, *The Intangibilities of Form: Art after Deskilling* (London: Verso, 2008).

77 M. von Osten et al., '"She Now Works Flexible. . ."', in J. Billing, M. Lind and L. Nilsson (eds), *Taking the Matter into Common Hands* (London: Black Dog, 2007), 68.

78 B. Nielson and N. Rossiter, 'Precarity as a Political Concept: New Forms of Connection, Subjectivation and Organization', *Open* 17 (2009), 49–50.

79 Tsianos and Papadopoulos, 'Who's Afraid of Immaterial Workers? Embodied Capitalism, Precarity, Imperceptibility' (2006), at: http://preclab.net/text/06–TsianosPapadopoulos.pdf (accessed 9 June 2012).

80 In 2007 Malcolm Bull noted already the need to differentiate but also preserve the tension between the concepts 'globalisation' and 'biopolitics'. See M. Bull, 'Globalization and Biopolitics: Introduction to New Left Review 45', *New Left Review* 45 (May–June 2007), 1–2.

81 Ibid.

82 J. Kristeva, 'Women's Time', *Signs* 7/1 (Autumn, 1981), 13–35. Here 35.

83 Ibid., 34.

84 S. Federici, 'Precarious Labour: A Feminist Viewpoint', lecture, 28 October 2006 at Bluestockings Radical Bookstore in New York City, as part of the 'This is Forever: From Inquiry to Refusal Discussion Series'. http://inthemiddleofthewhirlwind.wordpress.com/precarious-labor-a-feminist-viewpoint/ (accessed 10 May 2010).

85 R. Nagar, V. Lawson, L. McDowell, S. Hanson, 'Locating Globalization: Feminist (Re)readings of the Subjects and Spaces of Globalization', *Economic Geography* 78/3 (July 2002), 257–84. Here 262.

86 Nagar, Lawson, McDowell, Hanson, 'Locating Globalization', 60–1.

87 Weeks, *The Problem with Work*, 124.

88 T. L. Ebert, 'Ludic Feminism, the Body, Performance, and Labor: Bringing 'Materialism' Back into Feminist Cultural Studies', *Cultural Critique* 23 (Winter, 1992–93), 5–50. Here 39. Emphasis in the text. Ebert argues that 'the ludic notions of discursive subversion, semiotic activism, disruptive pleasures, and flexible notions of gender have a strong appeal to (upper) middle-class women. They play to the (upper) middle-class desire for

individual freedom from economic constraints and the obsession to escape the demands of labor, through gestures of self-expression, pleasure, excess', pp. 39–40.

89 Nagar, Lawson, McDowell, Hanson, 'Locating Globalization', 271.

90 See for example M. Mies, *Patriarchy and Accumulation on a World Scale* (London and New York: Zed Books 1986).

91 Deepwell quoted in M. Connor and K. Deepwell, 'Working Notes: Conversation with Katy Deepwell', *Art Journal* 61/2 (Summer 2002), 32–43. Here 36.

92 C. T. Mohanty, 'Under Western Eyes: Feminist Scholarship and Colonial Discourses', *Boundary* 2, vol. 12/13 (nos 1 to 3) (Spring–Autumn 1984), 333–58.

93 C. T. Mohanty, *Feminism without Borders: Decolonizing Theory, Practicing Solidarity* (Durham, NC: Duke University Press, 2003), 223 and 225. See also C. T. Mohanty, ' "Under Western Eyes Revisited": Feminist Solidarity through Anticapitalist Struggles', *Signs: Journal of Women in Culture and Society* vol. 28, no. 2 (Winter 2003), 499–535.

94 Mohanty, *Feminism without Borders*, 250.

95 Ibid, 230.

96 Ibid, 236.

97 See A. Dimitrakaki, 'Researching Cultures and the Omitted Footnote: Questions on the Practice of Feminist Art History', in A. Jones (ed.), *The Feminism and Visual Culture Reader, 2nd edition* (London: Routledge, 2009). First published in B. Biggs, A. Dimitrakaki and J. Lamba (eds), *Independent Practices: Representation, Location and History in Contemporary Visual Art*, (Liverpool: Bluecoat Arts Centre, Liverpool School of Art and Design and Saffron Books, 2000).

98 A. Jones, 'The Return of Feminism(s) and the Visual Arts, 1970/2009', in M. Hedlin Hayden and J. Sjöholm Skrubbe (eds), *Feminisms Is still Our Name: Seven Essays on Historiography and Curatorial Practices* (Newcastle: Cambridge Scholars, 2010).

99 Mohanty, *Feminism without Borders*, 231.

100 Fraser, 'Feminism, Capitalism and the Cunning of History', 99.

101 Ibid., 99.

102 Jones, 'The Return of Feminism(s) and the Visual Arts, 1970/2009'.

103 A. Jones, '1970/2007: The Return of Feminist Art', www.xtraonline.org/past_articles.php?articleID=184 (accessed 5 July 2012)

'The gender issue': lessons from post-socialist Europe

What and where is post-socialism?

Capital's global imperative was in many respects realised – not least, symbolically – in the accelerated, spectacular and violent dissolution of Europe's 'Eastern Bloc' between 1989 and the mid-1990s.[1] For this reason, questions framing the dialectic of 'presence' and 'representation' in relation to gender in the art of the region post-1989 are integral to this study. Eastern Europe's transition to capitalism involved a process of regendering women's lives at the same time that it enabled the spread, but also contestation, of feminist politics. As Western feminists have been repeatedly told, Eastern Europe has not been a unified cultural and social space. It is not treated as such in this study, which remains, however, aware of the manufacturing of 'Eastern Europe' as an ideological tale of otherness in ongoing, hegemonic global political narratives (precisely what capitalism's victory in 1989 meant). This is what has dictated the need for a whole chapter dedicated to Eastern Europe – one that would probe the meaning of the departure from 'actually existing socialism'.[2] And although recent studies have claimed a long-standing feminist presence in parts of Eastern Europe before 1989, this claim gained visibility in the past twenty years, when the relationship between East and West was generally transformed as follows:[3] the border separating East and West opened for ideas and remained, until the recent eastwards expansion of a capitalist European Union, closed to people. Economic unevenness, massively disadvantaging the former East and expanding the contexts of precarious labour East and West, provided the ground for the negotiation of feminism in Eastern European art scenes.

The formation of post-socialist Europe was not a process of eliminating but of regenerating and recalibrating borders, of regulating the movement of whole populations, and of creating within what is somehow ironically called 'Former West' new armies of second-class citizens.[4] Gender, and sex, became important. An examination of the inter-European border in connection with the sexualisation of migration – the sexing, that is, of the act of crossing – and how art dealt with it is one aim of this chapter. Realising this aim is commensurate with understanding how gender relates to the objects of desire produced by capital's restructuring of *inter*national space. Arguably, feminism can also be understood as such an object of desire – the desire to belong to a collective, transnational, transformative subject – a topic I discuss in more detail in the last section of this chapter.

For the time being, it is worth asking whether this desire to belong can challenge the constant historicising of Eastern Europe as exceptional, particular and intensely local, having always its own story to tell – and tell in 'its own' words in the process of fashioning an allegedly authentic identity. Such authentic identities of the local, the exceptional, the particular have been at the heart of the postmodernist ideology underpinning neoliberalism. When operating in the realm of culture, neoliberalism has translated into a logic of competition among national or regional art scenes struggling for visibility and market value. 'The case of' Eastern Europe has been subject to much theorising in recent attempts to grasp what connects the ubiquitous ideology of 'transition' with the reality of global capitalism. In 2007 Marina Gržinić argued that the 'neoliberal global system…should be read as the dark side of Communism, and not vice versa! What we face in this time of neoliberal global capitalism is something that we "Eastern Europeans" have already tested on our bodies in the time of Communism.'[5] Curiously, this statement both acknowledges the biopolitical rule of contemporary capital and succumbs to the competitive logic of neoliberalism by implicitly declaring: 'We experienced *this* first! We are not really different because we have been what you are now becoming.' What I am trying to articulate here, however, is not a refutation of difference; rather, as instructed by Chandra Mohanty, I am interested in feminist scholarship that can see through and act across (or despite) differences.

Generally, feminist discourse has not been immune to capital's competitive logic, never quite managing to overcome narratives of origins – that is, who did first what and, crucially, where. Of course, the narratives responsible for the exclusions and inclusions of art history engage an incredibly dense nexus of causes and effects: feminist art historians in Eastern Europe have detected a hegemonic attitude on the part of Western feminism, often conflated with a universal(ising) narrative of feminist rebellion launched in the late 1960s and 1970s. Inevitably, thorough art historical projects disprove a shared trajectory of feminist politics whereas a project attempting to connect the dots giving us the full landscape of localised feminist revolutions is missing. Simply put, *we do not know how feminism in Eastern European art scenes is connected with feminism in the West or with feminism in Latin America*, though we may suspect that such connections may have something to do with the history of capitalism in the late twentieth century. Producing a map of feminism's mobility in this complex terrain exceeds the scope of this study but the absence of such a map informs my choice to read the story of Eastern Europe not as one of exception but as indicative of broader changes delineating the greater social truth of globalisation.

Let us consider the following example: Estonian artist Kai Kaljo made *Loser* in 1997, during the first decade of a de-Sovietised Estonia. *Loser* is a short video (1 min. 24 sec.) where the protagonist (the artist herself) recites the figures (her monthly income, her weight and so on) that position her as a social failure. She weighs too much and earns too little. Despite the fact that she is employed teaching at an art academy, earning as little as what would, say, be €150 per month means that she can only afford to live with her parents. It is unclear whether such a self-description on some level implies that she has also failed to find a man to support her or that models of communal living with peers did not constitute an option for Estonian women at the time. Although this work is produced in post-Soviet Estonia, the reference to the precarious position of the cultural worker that structures the work is certainly not limited to post-socialist states.[6] This becomes obvious as the specific position is underwritten by the protagonist's failure 'as a woman' or her 'social failure', or the new system's failure to support independent citizens. On the contrary, they suggest that the (woman) artist in contemporary Estonia shares her state of uncertainty and despair with artists and workers in the countries of advanced capitalism. If anything, the position of the woman artist, as described by Kaljo in 1997, prefigured developments in Europe, which around 2003 witnessed the rise of the 'precarity movement', complete with its own (male) patron saint, San Precario. There is no good reason then why *Loser* should be seen to refer to a localised 'transition' rather than to a global condition of contemporary labour, which of course it is easier to assert from the vantage point of the first deep financial crisis of global capital from 2008 to date (that extended a state of precarity to many formerly secure Western citizens).

If the logic of exception, espoused East or West, serves to return Eastern Europe to its point of origin, as either a heroic or denigrated otherness (an exotic yet tamed and, in the right circumstances, marketable 'identity'),[7] repositioning Eastern Europe as merely another site that demonstrates the failure of capitalism to organise sustainable forms of social existence may hold some benefits for feminism. As Anna Dezeuze has argued, popular culture in the 1990s, at least in the West, had glamorised the figure of 'loser', often associated with the 'slacker', and nearly always coded male.[8] It is therefore far from accidental that after 2000 and in the first signs of a crisis in labour relations affecting scores of young Western men, the patron saint was male. Kaljo's appropriation of the term 'loser' amounted to an early and effective gendering of precarity as much as to a warning about the entanglement of precarity and labour in the sector of economy known as 'culture'. What *Loser* suggests is that post-Soviet social contexts were the shape of things to come, foreshadowing astute examinations of the artist as a labouring subject today beyond these contexts.[9] *Loser* thus signals a different moment of origin for contemporary feminist critique, not so much as regards the artist's intentions but the gendered narrative that this work puts into circulation, establishing connections (between the 'failing' female subject, post-socialist societies and cultural labour) that still remain to be unpacked. Fifteen years after its release, *Loser* invites us to reflect on post-socialism as the shared condition of Eastern and Western Europe, far exceeding the geographies of 'transition'. It is one of the lessons to be learned when attending to gender and power as a prevalent concern in much of the art of Eastern Europe since 1990.

If among the features that historically unite, rather than divide, the art world East and West is that women carry the burden of gender as well as of 'gendering' the artwork, it makes sense to turn to women's practice in order to examine the parameters of an artistic critique that assumes both a local and global face. I shall discuss this gendering process through art from two different parts of the former East, the Baltic republics and the Balkans. Specifically, I look at the work of Mare Tralla from Estonia and Tanja Ostojić from former Yugoslavia. One reason for this is that Estonia has been identified with a positive process of *appearing* whereas Yugoslavia is associated with a negative process of *disappearing* – and yet both appearing and disappearing are connected with the advance of global capital. In the last part of the chapter, I turn to an examination of projects involving curatorial and art historical thinking in order to consider the development of broader frameworks organising the encounter of cultural practices and feminist politics in the region.

The spaces comprising the former East are, of course, diverse and, as it has been pointed out, the more culturally liberal Yugoslavia generated a feminist consciousness (evident, for instance, in the art of Sanja Iveković) not experienced in most Eastern European countries in the 1970s. But overall, art in Yugoslavia has been seen to have 'evolved under very exceptional social and political conditions' (the destablisation of which contributed to the sense that something more was lost along with Yugoslavia's fragmentation in the 1990s), beginning with President Tito distancing his rule from Stalinist totalitarianism during the Cold War.[10] On the other hand, Tralla's piece entitled *So we gave birth to Estonian Feminism* (1994), expressing an ironic but ultimately positive response to Estonia's own rebirth, is representative of the broader regional tendency: the rise of gender critique, nationally framed, in the redrafted map of the region in the 1990s. The work's title locates the birth of Estonian feminism at the time when Estonian visual culture, and especially TV, was flooded by West European pornography and so this video piece was based on the accidental recording of German porn by the artist (when she had programmed her video to record a late-night Finnish TV news broadcast). This transformation of the Estonian airwaves, so suggestive of women's role in capitalist industries and heavily promoting this role to post-Soviet women, played a crucial role in the emergence of feminism in the Estonian art scene. As opposed to this, Serbian curator Bojana Pejić participated in the first feminist conference known to have taken place in the Eastern Bloc, in Belgrade in 1978. Yet as she admits, the conference, even if interdisciplinary, did not impact the art world: feminist art criticism did not develop.[11] However, Yugoslavia's liberal policies and greater contact with the West can help explain the 'mystery' of a woman artist active behind the iron curtain (Iveković) making feminist art.

As is well known, Iveković transformed the long-standing tradition of dissident art in state socialism by addressing women's fetishisation in advertising, in parallel with a similar critique in the West. But Iveković (and any similar 'case') is a mystery only if feminism is perceived as a strongly localised discourse, expected to address strictly its immediate surroundings. Such an expectation has indeed burdened second-wave feminism. And such an expectation intersected with a demand imposed on artists of 'the periphery': to circulate in the global art market images of 'their' exotic and often quixotic identity. The pragmatic need in the 1990s to address the 'transition' of a local/regional social reality made the situation all the more complex: this transition was imbued with the spirit of catching up – which in turn involved the alignment of Eastern European art scenes with Western cultural narratives such as postmodernism. Postmodernism's geographic, anti-universalist and anti-humanist rhetoric of always localising discourse, cancelling out the prospect of transnational feminist solidarity, generated expectations about what each 'local' feminism could, or should, be about.

This background has been important in shaping this chapter in terms of its theoretical reflections. The issue raised here is whether global capital has since the 1990s actualised a different horizon for thinking about feminism across borders, or at least *in spite of* borders. (As put in this volume's introductory essay, has there been a feminist global imperative?) One key element in this mobilisation of the border was the *internalisation* of geography as a habitual behavioural mode, an (unconscious) ideology, in its own right productive of contemporary subjects. In the gendered world that the practices I now turn to take as their reference and object of critique, this has meant the proliferation of primarily inter-spatial positions as the test ground for contemporary articulations of gendered subjectivity. These are positions constructed in the course of establishing or, in some instances, unveiling connections across spaces ranging from the stereotypically private to the stereotypically public. Where art is concerned, my analysis situates labour as the matrix of their manifestation.

What does the Eastern European woman artist do for a living? And where does she do it?

Mare Tralla's and Tanja Ostojić's approaches to gender relations are indicative (though by no means representative) of the diversity and complexity of critical positions in the field of contemporary Eastern European art. The prevalent differentiating factor in their work is that whereas Tralla, as a first-generation Estonian feminist artist, focused on developing a feminist politics of representation, Ostojić questions the representational capacity of the gendered sign. In effecting a move from the artist's body (performance) to the artist's life (biopolitical art), Ostojić is preoccupied instead with the terms in which the Eastern European female subject can be understood as pure presence: always already caught within the turmoil of actual socio-economic relations. But although her work can be (and has been) seen to test the gendered specificity of Giorgio Agamben's 'bare life', it also reveals how 'pure presence' can find its most adequate form in the commodity.[12]

If Tralla discovered in the 1990s that her persona as the voluptuous, loud, post-punk 'disgusting girl' could be a supporting, media-sustained mechanism for the feminist 'provocation' she intended to achieve through her technologically-oriented art, petite Ostojić displaced altogether the distance between her embodied self and the site of social critique: reducing herself to the corporeal basics, she placed a photograph of her naked, skinny, shaved body on the web, prepared to enter a widely accepted form of contemporary arranged marriage: the one where one party gets the right (Western) passport.[13] The image used in the personal ad as part of Ostojić's five-year project *Looking for a Husband with EU Passport* (2000–5) is designed to let any prospective buyer inspect the 'product' in full detail. To speak about offering *this* body to a male gaze globalised through the World Wide Web would sound ridiculous: the hair removed from the head to the pubis was the last 'protective' veil to drop in a public show of extreme self-inflicted nakedness. The eyes facing straight ahead, the closed mouth, the arms hanging on the side, attenuate the body's docile, unthreatening pose – fitting perfectly the quiet stillness of the photographic image. At first sight, Ostojić's portrait, a voiceless register, appears to record the *absence* – or possibly, suppression – of what John Holloway detected at the core of contemporary oppositional politics: the 'scream' that negates the rule of capital.[14]

However, before I move on to look more closely at the two artists' work, I must explain the purpose of including in the above descriptions references to the artists' physical appearance. Why mention Tralla's public image of corporeal excess and post-punk aesthetic and Ostojić's quasi-deliberate smallness? Because in both cases a certain corporeal reality is instrumental to the labour of the sign – the sign, that is, of the female artist's body. The ample (excessive),

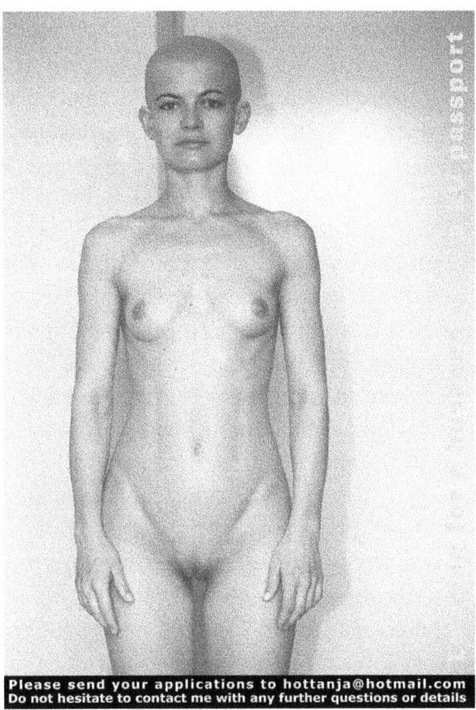

2.1 Tanja Ostojić, *Looking for a Husband with EU Passport* (2000–5). Participatory web project/combined media installation. Detail: The ad.

and the meagre (child-like), are far from unknown categories in the regimes of an over-corporealised feminine, bearing complex genealogies in the history of art. But what is interesting here is how these categories are undercut by the historically specific demands of the social realities where they are located. The refusal to contain (the flesh) in Tralla's projected media image must then be 'tested' against both the over-sexualisation of the female body experienced in Estonia in the 1990s and the disciplined female body of Soviet culture. Similarly, the available readings of Ostojić's *Looking for a Husband with EU Passport* have rightly included comments on her famous web portrait, where the pornographic image of the shaved pubis is disciplined by the shaved head's allusion to the dehumanisation and annihilation of the body in Nazi camps. The clash between the promise of possibly illicit pleasure (shaved pubis) and authorised terror (shaved head) is already a gendered narrative – intensely so for those who recall that in the war-torn mid-twentieth-century Europe the shaved head was also the humiliating punishment for women who had slept with the enemy. Positioned between being slim and emaciated, Ostojić's body-as-sign can be identified as both fragile (desirable/gendered) and tortured (moralising, pointing-the-finger/merely human). Yet either way this body-assign succumbs to the logic of the market. The point is precisely this: the ambiguity of the image-sign becomes *irrelevant* in the context of the attempted transaction facilitated by and, as we shall see, materialised through capital's global imperative.

Looking for a Husband with EU Passport has been an enquiry into the gendered terms of participation to global capitalism. Described by the artist as a 'project' always under her 'control', it was initiated when Ostojić placed a web ad combining both text and image.[15] In the ad Ostojić also provided her email address under the name 'hottanja', tipping perhaps the balance towards the sexy/desirable/pornographic reading of the image by the potential cybersurfer. In the span of several months Ostojić received about 500 responses, mostly by men, that varied in their intentions, yet many of them responding seriously. In 2002 Ostojić had her first meeting with the man who would shortly after become her husband. This was German artist C., one of the men who responded to the ad and possessed an EU passport. Their first meeting was held (as if following the safe date instructions of an online dating agency) in a public space and, under the directorship of Ostojić, it assumed the form of a performance. The encounter was indeed performed in front of an audience in the garden surrounding Belgrade's Museum of Contemporary Art. It was recorded on video and now habitually joins the series of documents that remains of this project. The full realisation of this artwork continued through a series of acts: signing a pre-nuptial agreement, the actual marriage, the acquisition of a visa that permitted Ostojić to live in Germany for three years, her German language lessons as a demand of the German state when resident in Düsseldorf, the eventual divorce and divorce party that concluded the artwork.

In the span of this artwork, Ostojić realised a series of other artworks under the general title *Crossing Borders Series*, described by the artist as 'engaged with the issues of diverse border crossing strategies'.[16] The mention of 'strategies' as opposed to 'tactics' suggests that such practices were initiated and executed from a specific site that afforded a directionality of action. The series comprised: *Illegal Border Crossing* (2000), a three-day art action during which Ostojić illegally crossed the Slovenian-Austrian border, assisted by friends on both sides, in order to attend an international artists' workshop in Austria (an art action prompted by the fact that she could not obtain a visa); *Waiting for a Visa* (2000), a six-hour 'situationist performance', as described by the artist, during which she joined the visa queue of the Austrian Consulate in Belgrade to apply for a visa (the action concluded frustratingly enough when the visa office closed at noon and the artist shared 'the fate of failure with more than a hundred of other people who were 'too late')';[17] *Wait behind the Line* (2004), a collective performance/action at the opening of the

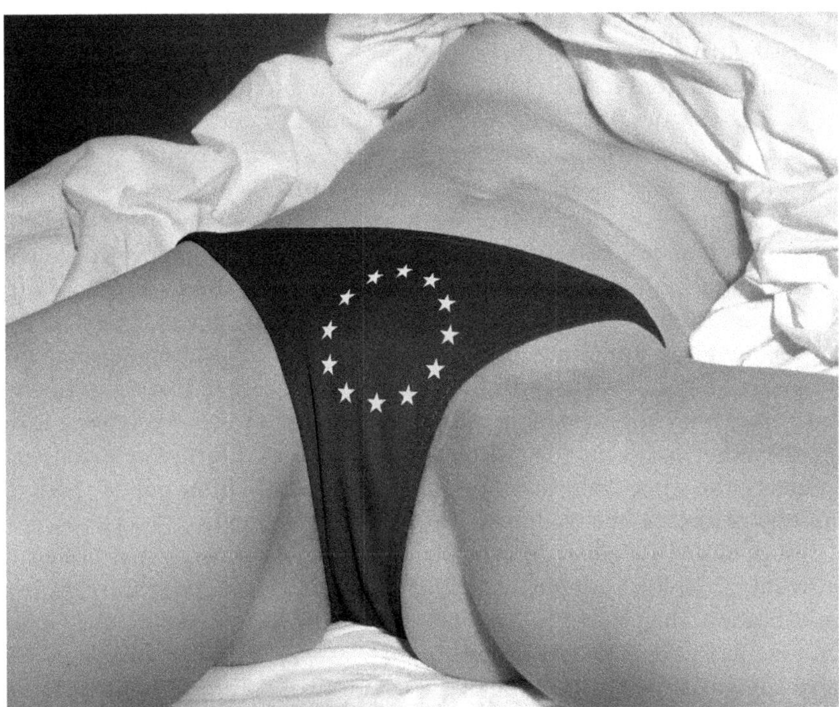

2.2   Tanja Ostojić, *Untitled/After Courbet (L' origine du monde 1866, 46 × 55 cm)* (2004).
Colour photo, 46 × 55 cm.

exhibition 'The Post-Communist Condition: Privatizations, Contemporary Art from Eastern Europe' in KW in Berlin during which visitors were subjected to a process of identification that involved their bodies and their fingerprints; and crucially, also in 2004, *Untitled/After Courbet ('L' origine du monde', 1866, 46 × 55 cm)*, a photographic rendition of Courbet's famous painting presenting a naked female torso on a bed in an angle that directs the viewer's gaze to the exposed genitals. In *Untitled/After Courbet* the artist's body is presented in the same awkward position with her genitals covered by panties bearing the European Union flag motif of 12 yellow stars against a blue background. *Untitled/After Courbet* differs from other works in the series in that it returns to a representational mode. That this work concluded, as its life was extended through an exhibition circuit in 2004–5, a cycle of non-representational works becomes therefore important.[18]

Having started its life as a double spread in the Canadian art magazine *ESSE* and after featuring in a couple of institutionally hosted shows, *Untitled/ After Courbet* acquired its notoriety in 2005 when it was exhibited in public space, on a rotating billboard in Austria, as part of the show 'Europart' intended to mark and celebrate Austria's Presidency of the EU the following year. Realised during the period of Ostojić's marriage, this portrait of the artist was eventually removed from public display after the curators received complaints 'from various sides' that were allegedly offended by such a 'sexist' display of the female body.[19] Noting that *Untitled/After Courbet* 'shifted the political instrumentalisation of art into an aesthetic instrumentalisation of politics', Marina Gržinić associated this artwork with a strategy of over-identification. 'A strategy that can be recognized in many works by contemporary artists coming from Eastern Europe', over-identification is in this case, according to Gržinić, a purposefully assumed position in gender relations.[20] Gržinić does not see anything humorous in *Untitled/After Courbet*, stating: 'Ostojić does not present a kind of partial identification as is the case in parody: a mockery that begins with appropriation and identification, but then becomes a joke.'[21] On the other hand, in their letter explaining the unfortunate situation of removing the work from the show and consequently from public space, the curators regret the 'misreading' of the work by the public.

Yet does not a strategy of over-identification *intentionally* provoke such a misreading? If, for example, an artist is to critique a dictator through over-identification, then the artist must *become like* the dictator so that the dictatorial practices come into plain view. In that case, the artist enables precisely a misreading of what she is doing in order to provoke a greater understanding. In other words, in over-identification as an aesthetic strategy a misreading is *expected* to be the artwork's outcome: the misreading forms an integral part in the process of exposure that constitutes the artwork's political work. The misreading, rather than the truthful representation of an individual or collective as such, is at the core of the artwork's dialogical constitution, in the sense that the misreading is also proof that a response to the visual statement of the artwork has been triggered. That the outcome of this dialogue was the removal of *Untitled/After Courbet* from public view completed the artWork by demonstrating, as second-wave feminists had been insisting all along, that power relations overdetermine the reading of visual signs. The efficacy of any signifying configuration is intensely contextual but the context is materially grounded: not necessarily in relation to the specific body represented but in relation to the real socio-economic circumstances of bodies symbolically rather than indexically linked to a given image. This last point is important. Ostojić made a piece about what entry to so called Fortress Europe means to many women from elsewhere: the sexualisation and reification of their bodies and lives. This was the social context addressed through the work. Complaints sent to the curators about how *Untitled/After Courbet* dehumanised women were, interestingly enough, recognising the dehumanisation of a collective subject merely alluded to in the billboard image. So here over-identification was successful. The image was convincing. And yet something went wrong.

Gržinić's remarks about *Untitled/After Courbet* deploying a strategy of over-identification can help clarify something about public reactions to this piece which can be captured in this imaginary statement of its censors: 'we know that women are already objectified and we believe that this image is yet another instance of such objectification, and we don't need to add more such instances to those that already exist'. And yet in this imaginary statement a crucial point is missed. *Untitled/After Courbet* on a billboard was in the end merely a signifying space, whereas women's human rights are undermined through the actual subjugation of women's material existence. This takes place not just through prostitution and trafficking but also through the institution of marriage, as *Looking for a Husband with EU Passport* demonstrated so aptly. Unlike *Untitled/After Courbet*, *Looking for a husband with EU Passport* could not have been, and was not, censored. It could not have been censored because its political work, exposure and critique was *not* condensed to a (visual) moment but was enacted through a refusal to retort to the image. Rather, this artWork was spread in time, utterly embedded in the materiality of the artist's life and that of others. This is a crucial parameter articulating the distance that separates visually oriented art (*Untitled/After Courbet*) and biopolitical art (*Looking for A Husband with EU Passport*).[22] This distance marks and renders incredibly complex the choices that feminist critique in art has to make today. Ostojić's return to a representational mode in *Untitled/After Courbet,* when the resolution of the extraordinary *Looking for a Husband*…was perhaps in sight, demonstrated the limits that the exhibition form, as the conventional and prevalent site of the public's encounter with art, holds for radical feminist art practice today.[23] And notably, it mattered little that 'Europart' was an exhibition that engaged public space.

Looking for a Husband with EU Passport renewed the relevance of the former West's feminist slogan 'the personal is political'. But as Ostojić's work suggests, the terrain of the political today emerges as biopolitical in a complex sense. Overall, in the *Crossing Borders Series* the artist opted to call 'art' actions and processes that occurred in her real life and that defined and regulated her remit of possibilities as a socialised, gendered human being. Her investigation addressed primarily the gendered condition of free move-ment, and not the negotiation of a culturally situated femininity. Arguably, her gender was deployed tactically within this broader investigation. Femi-ninity is thus instrumentalised in *Looking for a Husband with EU Passport,* but this is only possible because of the historically specific power relations in which Eastern European femininity became caught in the shaping of post-socialist states. The phrase 'Eastern European femininity' does not of course indicate the existence of a cross-cultural experience but designates the pos-sibility of a prevalent articulation in the constitution of femininity within a regional socio-economic reality. This is what establishes a connection between the construction of femininity in women's art from the Balkans and from the Baltic region. The connection comes from the present, not from the past.

Mare Tralla has remarked that the transition to capitalism in Estonia involved the overt 'sexualisation of society; this sexualisation did not just enter Estonian society through consumerism but was evident, for example, also in the job market. Looks became important in that area too.'[24] An awareness of this intertwining of sex and work holds important implications for the construction of femininity in post-socialist Eastern Europe in particular, because there women were supposed to be fully integrated in the 'proper' structures of production, that is, in remunerated work outside the home. Moreover, the grim reality of Soviet women carrying also the double burden (of work outside the home and domestic labour) was ameliorated, and mediated to women, through the concept of the 'heroine'.

The speedy evacuation of this mythical identity, the heroine, is a theme that runs across Tralla's art. It is encountered both in *her.space* (1996–97) and in *Heroine of Post-Socialist Labour* (2004). The interactive CD-Rom and installation *her.space* considers, as the title suggests, the spaces of femininity in Estonia. Here, the computer (one of the artist's main sites and tools of labour) is enfolded in layers of flowery fabric that attempt to domesticate technology. Estonian viewers would have been able to identify the fabrics used as those widely available during Soviet times. The touch-screen offers an opportunity to navigate the two 'groups' of spaces where femininity concretised into gendered social roles in late twentieth-century Estonia, in the transitional 1990s but also before. The first group identifies its feminine spaces through a series of objects, from the teacup to the dildo – a crucial addition to the sexualisation of the domestic in Estonia made available through capitalism. The second group turns to the woman as labourer in the public domain, and it is here that we find references to a heroic femininity – predictably not in connection with women's domestic work and reproductive labour, which remained just as undervalued in state socialism as in capitalism. But in this grouping of spaces the implicit 'equality' achieved as women were taught how to build a Kalashnikov and shoot, or, in some cases, work in the mines, is challenged by two things. First, references to the drudgery of work in a production regime where labour stood as an obstacle to life, as the text that appears on the screen suggests: 'After years in the mines Natasha and Tatjana only saw life like this: "in circles". They only could hear drilling noise. Their lungs were filled with dust, and consequently their dream romance was lost in the process of "equalisation"'. Second, there is the particular framing of the female cosmonaut. The text that appears on the screen makes a reference to Soviet cosmonaut Svetlana Savitskaja. The artist claims an immediate connection between Savitskaja's life and public images of femininity, shattered by the advent of capitalism: 'Svetlana: one of my childhood heroines, a soviet cosmonaut. She was sent to

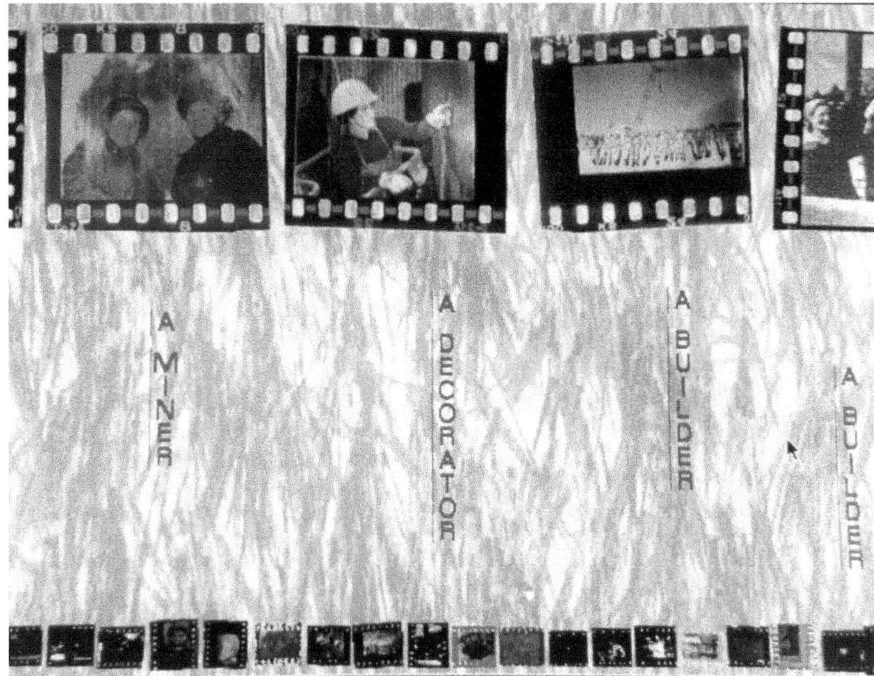

2.3   Mare Tralla, *her.space* (1996–97). CD-ROM installation. Detail.

space to see if /however this is a bad joke: to see, can a woman get pregnant in a space. Truly, I did not know that this was her mission. She was my heroine, because she did something I cannot do, ever. I do remember myself looking at the space and thinking: how could it be to be Svetlana? In a space.' Tralla made this work after she migrated to London and considers it strongly auto-biographical: the disidentification with the heroic female labourer in the stars marked a beginning where an artistic career based on earthly mobility would become interwoven with the life of an economic migrant. Here the appropriation of autobiography as a feminist strategy leads to a narrative of female labour that ultimately subverts the promise of identity.

Eight years later, the single-channel video *Heroine of Post-socialist Labour* (4 mins) offers an ironic meditation on the past and present of female labour in Estonia. Drawing on material from the Estonian TV archives, the video uses footage of female factory workers during Soviet times performing their manual tasks. The artist appears as a sign language interpreter in a small square at the bottom of the screen. As an interpreter, she translates the bygone Soviet work regime into the 'work language' of today, and so it is little surprising that the female workers' movements are translated into actions that attend

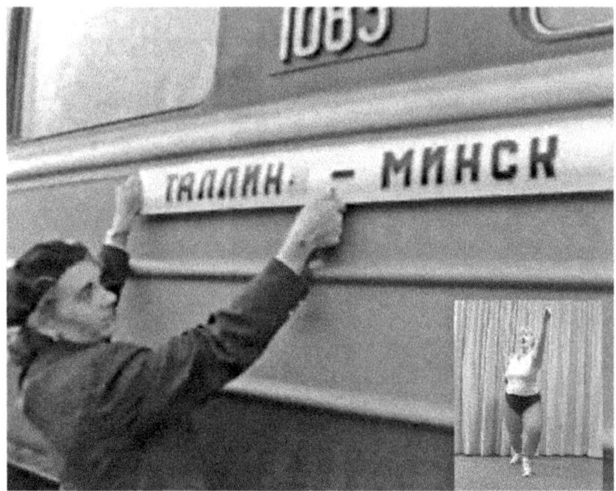

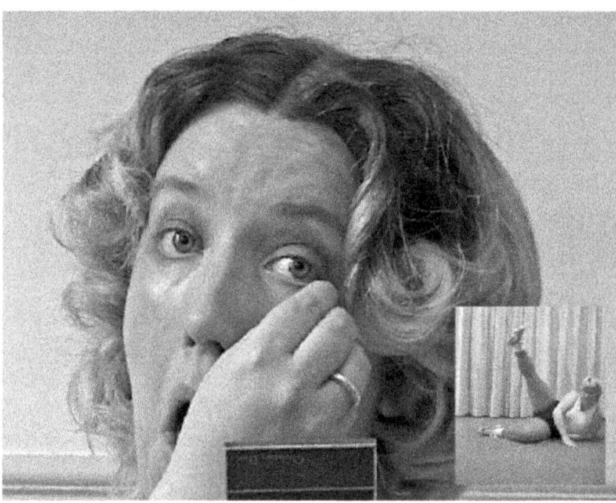

2.4–2.5   Mare Tralla, *Heroine of Post-Socialist Labour* (2004). Video, 3′55″. Video stills.

to the body's appearance (exercise, application of make-up and so on). Women's post-socialist labour centred on the production of the body – a production inscribed as a new type of mechanical, exhausting form of manual labour. At the same time, the footage does not document the mere act of female labour but also, inadvertently, the response of the female workers to the camera as a documentation tool. In the knowledge that they were being filmed, the female workers would take care to appear 'more feminine'. This piece was also part of Tralla's investigation into the regional histories of female subjectivity orchestrated around labour. But Tralla detects here a hidden connection between the socialist past and the capitalist present, one effected through women's self-identification with an always already sexualised gender position. As regards, then, women and work, the difference between the two systems of production (state socialism and capitalism) emerges as one of degree. Women as working subjects became *more* associated with sex during capitalism, and it is this essentially quantitative relationship between past and present that permits the very act of 'translation'.

What comes between these two works is Tralla's take on prostitution as work. Unlike the two works discussed so far, *Estonian Girl* (1999/2000) and *Estonian Beauty* (2000) implicate national identity in their titles. For *Estonian Girl*, Tralla rented a shop in Turku, Finland from where she distributed pink calling cards, occasionally hiring a pimp to distribute the cards around town. *Estonian Beauty* is an installation where the viewer discovers images (photographs) of the same woman posing in various sites in London. The photographs, concealed under flaps in the centre of soft pink cushions, mark the artist's own itinerary in London when in search of 'calling-cards' left in public places (such as telephone booths) advertising Estonian prostitutes to a prospective clientele. Intended to explore the widespread acceptance of prostitution as work among the female Estonian population, *Estonian Beauty* and *Estonian Girl* highlight also geographical relations as economic relations, in which women find their (new) place but also where a new stereotype takes hold. These two artwork titles reference nationality and gender but not class, as this would have been superfluous: the specific female national subject *is* a classed subject in the global context of power relations where it is positioned, and where film titles such as *American Beauty* (1999) and *American Girl* (2002) bear quite different connotations in their sexualisation of femininity. In stark contrast to the two contemporaneous American films that constitute a critical meditation of, and within, a strictly American society, the hierarchical gender relations negotiated in *Estonian Beauty* and *Estonian Girl* involve post-Soviet Estonian women and foreign, Western men. Whereas the American films merely add to conventional popular culture's manipulation of young women's bodies by featuring them in the global market of signs, the artWork examined in this chapter resolutely places gender relations in a geopolitical reality defined by the necessary mobility of labour (labour that must travel to reach the labour market). The economic asymmetries sustaining global capital are expressed in the literal, material consumption of women's bodies from poor countries by men from wealthy nations. It is this emphasis on the relocation of consumption from the level of the sign to the properly material level that both Tralla's and Ostojić's work points to.

As we shall see in following chapters, this move from significatory to material consumption is a more general thread in women's work of the past fifteen years. Yet in work from Eastern Europe we encounter an acute awareness of how this consumption is both a symptom and an actually existing condition of capital's global economic relations. One question here concerns the relationship between the significatory and the material register, as negotiated in situated paradigms of contemporary art. Readings of Ostojić's *Looking for a*

Husband with EU Passport throw the complexity of this position into sharp relief. In discussing the work's reception in the USA, Pamela Allara notes that 'because the performance [Ostojić's videotaped first meeting with her prospective German husband] burst the bubble of romantic love that has successfully fuelled the backlash against second-wave feminism in the United States, Brandeis students were generally outraged by her actions, arguing that Ostojić had "used" that nice Herr Golf'.[25] This was hardly an isolated incident as the artist came across similar reactions in Sweden where she was seen as 'intimidating' the men who had, kindly, 'tried to help' her.[26] Judith Surkis notes how Ostojić's artwork 'depicted migrant life…as literally "bare life"' and 'further highlights how, even and especially when stripped to its essentials, the migrant body is positioned in sexualised, racialised and national hierarchies'.[27] Rune Gade detects a strategy of 'queering' in this artwork that 'make[s] real circumstances and facts that exist but are usually reduced to non-existence and invisibility, rather than being culturally acknowledged'. Arguably, this queering, this making strange and therefore specific and real, takes place through transgressing 'the distinction between performance and performativity' expounded by philosopher Judith Butler.[28]

Gade further makes an illuminating comparison between the intermingling of representation and reality encountered in Western second-wave feminism and that practised in the early twenty-first century by Ostojić. In discussing the real-life performing of Lynn Hershman as her alter ego Roberta Breitmore between 1974 and 1978, when American feminism was flourishing, Gade comments that in doing away with the alter ego, Ostojić also does away with masquerade:

> For Ostojić, it is not a question of playing different roles, playing with the possibility of momentarily being or becoming someone else. It is a question of actually transforming the conditions of her existence, producing possibilities for changing her life, rather than changing her identity…The analytical distinction between the manipulation of psychic structures found in the work of Hershmann and the manipulation of social structures found in that of Ostojić may prove fruitful.[29]

Indeed, the implicit contrast between 'life' and 'identity' by Gade raises several issues: is not identity part of this larger category, life? From which vantage point can they appear distinct? Is such distinction a cultural and economic privilege, available to culturally and economically specific subjects? Or is such distinction instead a possibility determined by, and within, discrete moments in a historical process? For instance, was postmodernity the right ground for effecting strategies of role-playing in the context of American feminism and is the totalising horizon of globalisation the right ground for effecting the absorption of art within geo-politically determined gender relations?

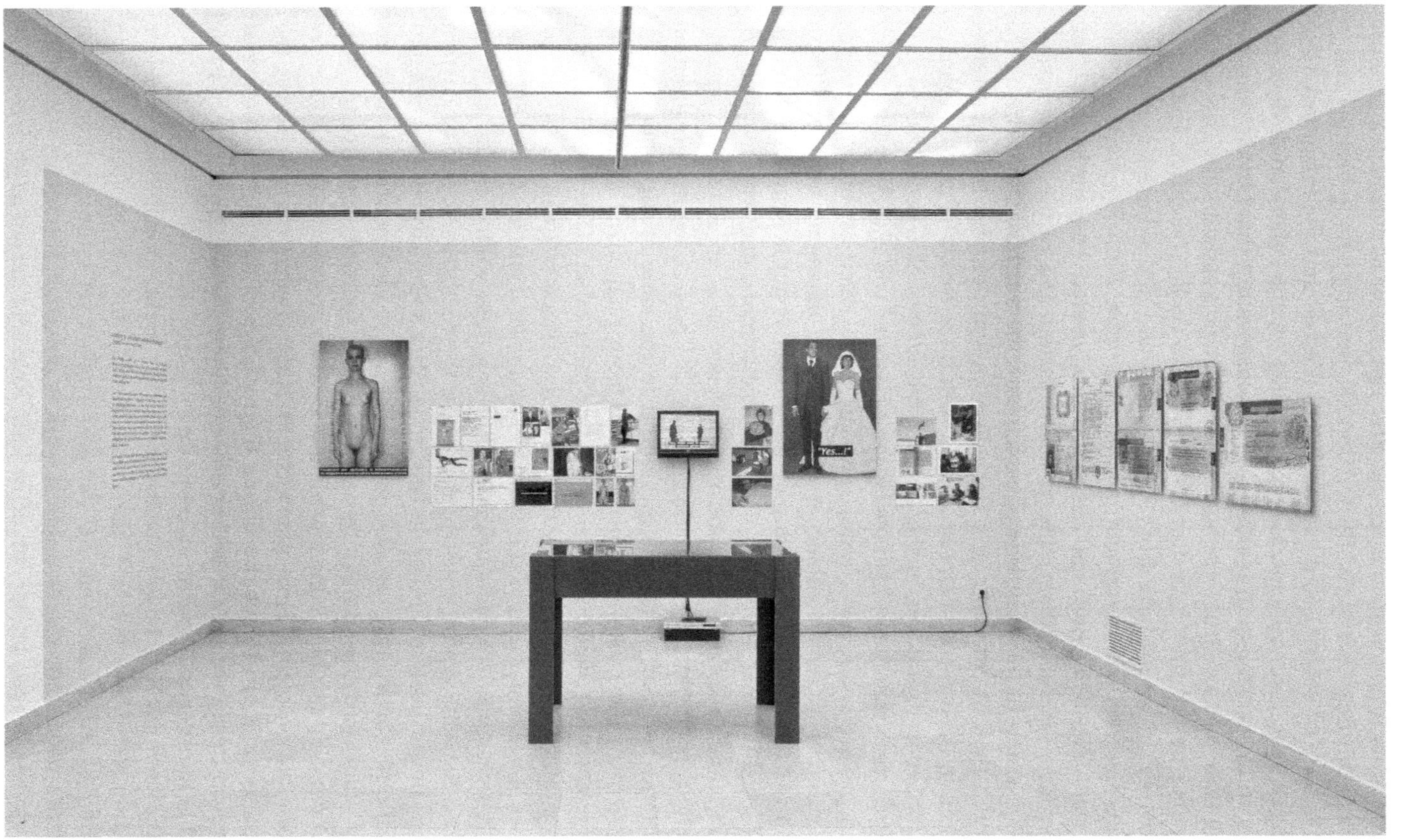

2.6 Tanja Ostojić, *Looking for a Husband with EU Passport* (2000–5). Participatory web project/combined media installation. Installation view 'Integration Impossible?'.

Hershmann's investment in a female alter ego did in fact display a pleasure not in becoming other but in the freedom of choosing who to become and in the freedom of entering and exiting at will the real and the imaginary (also rendered real in an ephemeral way). Ostojić, on the other hand, does not invest in the possibility of pleasure. Gade's observation that Ostojić does not manipulate psychic structures but social ones makes apparent the core of the problem: the full subjugation of Ostojić's life in social structures. Her life is impossible to disentangle from the bureaucratic and administrative constraints that regulate movement in capital's empire. Both her starting point (the fact of her being born and raised in a 'disappeared' Yugoslavia, that is, on the wrong side of capitalism), the conceptualisation of a journey (the possibility of crossing to the right side of capitalism), the finishing point (being the wife and then the divorcee of a German man and even her being currently resident in Berlin) are all circumscribed within the reality of global capital as social relation producing, in this scripted life, *all* available positions.

The artist's statement that *Looking for a Husband with EU Passport* was, for her, a project under her control can thus be revisited as follows: Ostojić's authorship as a creative subject is constituted in managing her own life on behalf of capital. Her directorship of 'the project' is not fictitious, far from it. But as the five-year art project was completely imbricated with five years of her life (and probably more) and was designed so as to actualise a specific direction in this life, the managerial work this project required realised an important circle of transferences. Central to the latter is the ethos of self-management that sustains contemporary labour relations. The impossibility of differentiating life from work in this case means that life as such is subject to an administrative logic – one that certainly permeates life in the 'advanced' former West. We do indeed see, then, in *Looking for a Husband with EU Passport* a strategy of over-identification. But if we are willing to test this not against the stereotypical construction of the over-sexualised, female Eastern European prospective immigrant (tied to locative specificity) but against globalisation's labour logic, we also see that the over-identification is *with the 'ideal' subjectivity* promoted by capital today: focused, resourceful, self-managed. More or better management is capital's proposed solution to every conceivable problem. 'Time management' skills is what students across the board are expected to acquire during their studies in developed nations and what immaterial workers, whether office or home-bound, are expected to be good at in order to perform successfully.

The commitment to self-management that makes possible the 'mastery of…humiliation', as put by Gade – conceivably, the real project sustaining *Looking for a Husband with EU Passport* – raises yet more questions about how and where this piece's political work is done.[30] It is perhaps important that already in 1980 Hungarian artist Judit Kele sold herself as an artwork in

Paris, thus explicitly using the commodity form as a means of accessing the West.[31] But Ostojić's project was different in that it invested in duration. Duration, or time, permitted both the realisation *and* the gradual unmasking of administration as the key element in the production/transformation of 'a life'. Administration is also what constructs a relationship between the symbolic articulation of *bare life* in the artist's portrait and *bios* as the planned life that the EU passport will permit her to have. As Šefik Tatlić notes:

> This is what happens to bare life: the more it suffers, the more it wants to become integrated into the work processes of neo-liberal capitalism; the more it wants to become bios, life with style. It has the tendency not to resist the oppression, but to become the oppressor…Thus, bare life is not the only form produced by the sovereign [capital], but the sovereign produces the relationship between two forms of life, in which one, bios, wants to stay included, while the other, bare life, *struggles* to be included. This obscene relationship marks the situation in which politics are slowly killed by capitalism, where the tortured body of politics is not hidden, but presented as culture.[32] [my emphasis]

Significantly, Tatlić's essay, from where the above remarks come, concludes the volume of documents and essays on Ostojić's work from 2000 to 2007. Overall, the essay discusses the social relationship between those who belong and those who aspire to belonging within the ever-totalising world of capital, implicitly asserting that these are the only two available positions as an outcome of capital's global imperative. To revisit Tsianos and Papadopoulos' concept discussed in Chapter 1, 'embodied capitalism' is a generalised condition constantly pulling towards representation, towards an arrival, towards gaining or sustaining a 'being in'. The terms used by Tatlić are telling, cutting short the dream of an exodus that today animates so much theory on the left:

> After the era of colonisation, the purpose of bare life (as a result of the imposition of the truth of capital) shifted from 'being a slave' to 'wanting to be a slave'; which reflects today's bare life position that (mostly) tends to [want to] succeed in the First World, to become a lifestyle. It is not about achieving a decent life, but about embracing the perverted notion of a decent life as mindless consumerism.[33]

What is the significance of this essay, concluding the commentary on Ostojić's artistic exercises on the possibility (or not) of integration? In a volume entitled *Integration Impossible?*, Tatlić's essay implicitly at least suggests that integration is not only possible but already perhaps effected in, and through, the atomisation of migration – to which 'gendering' contributes. 'Integration', as such, is part of a relatively new management-of-immigration parlance. Curiously, the self-management principle as the structuring feature of the artist's labour

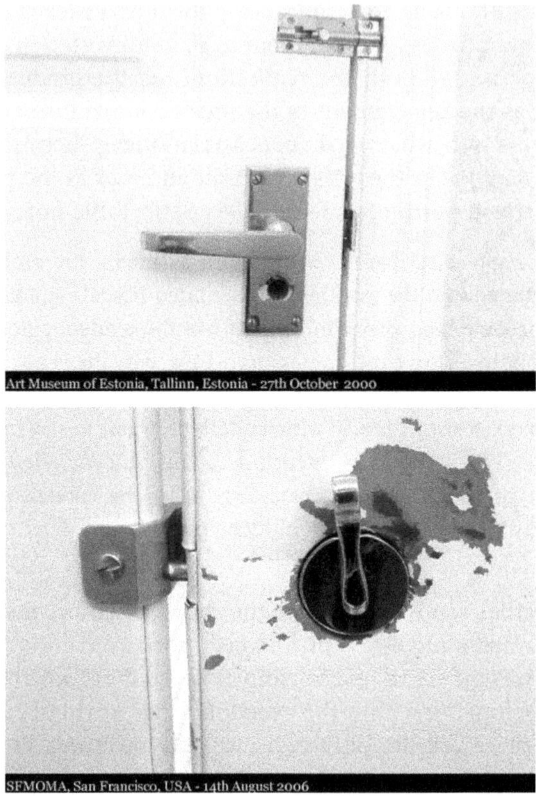

2.7–2.8   Mare Tralla, *WeeViews* (1997 to date). Looped video, 7′. Stills.

helped subsume all other aspects of this labour (including networking, communication and the journey) into the production of an individual's success, both in terms of the accomplished artwork and of 'her' life. The final unmasking that this work performs is to reveal capital's power to regulate, through the very atomisation of work, evident in the continuing value of authorship in contemporary art, the reproduction of social divisions even where, one imagines, collective resistance would be possible. Women's work, we learn through Ostojić, is not exempted from the melancholy of this position – that, at the same time, the context of art permits it to be elevated (within the protected space of art-world politics) to the plane of critique.

This critical melancholy and melancholy of critique is also encountered in Mare Tralla's *WeeViews*, initiated in 1997, a year after the artist had moved to the West. Currently a seven-minute long, looped video, so that it could be collected (it has), *WeeViews* comes as an afterthought on the meaning of integration and success for the post-Soviet artist.[34] *WeeViews* is in essence a work about travelling as work, and although I consider this prevalent concern (travel) in more detail in Chapter 3, placing this piece here facilitates the dialogue between Ostojić's purposeful instrumentalisation of the migrant subject as well as Eastern European femininity and the 'follow-up' moment of this femininity's proper incorporation into the global network known as the art world.

WeeViews could not have been realised without the 'freedom to travel', a desire successfully exported from the 'liberal' West to the 'totalitarian' East during the Cold War and to which Tralla's favourite Soviet heroine, the female cosmonaut travelling to the stars, provided a radical but unconvincing counter-narrative. *WeeViews* is very much about the reality for the sake of which the mythic female cosmonaut was rejected by post-Soviet women. Constructed as an image and text archive, the video is an idiosyncratic, ironic documentation of Tralla's travels around the world – or, more accurately, the art world. The image archive shows close-ups of doors photographed hastily with a mobile phone camera, revealed to be the toilet doors in the art venues visited by the artist. Each image is accompanied by an excerpt from the artist's private travel journal. These range from personal thoughts to social commentary but, as one would expect, images and excerpts defy any formal attachment to one another: the visual part of the work records the sameness of experience from London to Moscow and Tokyo. The banality of the exercise as much as the prospect of endlessly repeating it is what remains. Tralla does not disclose whether a trip involved her installing work, seeing others' work, meeting artists or curators or giving a paper at a conference. All trips are art-related and appear to be devoid of pleasure, with the journal excerpts recording emotions ranging from calm indifference to cynicism about the fact that this (the journey) is what *must* be done, much like as if Tralla were a travelling saleswoman.

Tralla started *WeeViews* when she learned that the Estonian Art Museum in Tallinn had been advised to urgently seek funding to upgrade its toilet facilities which were deemed to not meet (Western) European standards (under threat that it would not feature in European tourist guides). This prompted the artist to start taking pictures of toilet doors wherever she went as if patriotically committed to discovering a globally acceptable 'standard'. But what started as a reaction against a pervasive cultural stereotype (Eastern Europe's association with poor standards, the failure of modernisation and modernity exemplified in Gržinić's psychoanalytic reading of Eastern Europe as 'a piece of shit')[35] soon transformed into a visual and textual meditation on the artist's experience of permanent displacement and residual distance from her 'global' art-world surroundings.

With just occasional references to instances of 'local' gender politics, *Wee-Views* differs from Tralla's main body of work. And yet it remains connected to post-Soviet feminism. If the dialogue with Western feminism in Estonia in the 1990s enabled a reflective outlook towards the interwoven histories of gender and power (even within discourses of social equality such as socialism), the language of post-Soviet feminist artists had, nevertheless, to communicate the 'particular' experience of women's marginalisation – or perhaps better, re-feminisation – that few were keen to identify with. Identifying with a nation (Estonia) emerging out of the rubble of Soviet times seemed like a more optimistic choice, for instance. When adopted by the post-Soviet woman – and in Tralla's case, openly feminist – artist, a strong narrative 'I' of the kind that animates *WeeViews* was not an instrument of self-definition in any straightforward way. Rather than register a positively invested, autobiographical feminine in the making, post-Soviet Estonian feminism appropriated the 'I' within a question: do I belong *here*? What *WeeViews* achieves is relocating the question from Estonia to the promised land (promised, that is, by capitalism) of an accessible global space. Perceived largely as *of* the West, this global space was formerly identified with the very possibility of 'self-definition': first, by way of breaking free from the oppressive 'we are Borg' identity of Soviet times and second, as the rallying cry specifically of Western feminism – an issue to which I return in the last section of this chapter.

Alongside its probing of gender norms through the work of feminist artists, the Estonian art scene was beginning to grasp that the freedom to travel was to be more of an obligation for arts professionals. The merger with the West meant that a 'local' art scene had to pursue every networking opportunity, abiding to the general rules of capitalist development. Investing heavily in video and media art (a tendency that closely followed developments in neighbouring Finland and was promoted by the Soros Contemporary Arts Centres throughout 'transitional' Eastern Europe),[36] the Estonian art world developed as instructed: its artists began producing the surplus cultural value of the transition period, ensuring their own circulation in the spaces that really mattered and which turned to be everywhere – including, for example, Moscow as the city most identified with the despised Soviet imperium. In short, Estonian artists began travelling just as much as artists from anywhere are expected to travel today: to instal work, to see work, to give talks, and so on. And despite the absence of the human figure in *WeeViews*, the video enacts an enquiry into the passage of the embodied traveller through the material and yet abstracted (in their predictability) sites where cultural exchanges take place. Is the 'successful' feminist artist successfully integrated in this new context? And if so, is this good or bad news for feminism?

Frameworks and their discontents: from 'Capital & Gender' to 'Gender Check'

The entanglement of feminist politics and Eastern European art did not occur exclusively in the artwork but also in the frameworks that sustained the dissemination of art. The account that follows focuses on the shaping of such frameworks. It is a highly selective account and also concentrates on developments since 2000, though, as I have argued elsewhere, the rise of feminism in the art scenes of Eastern Europe had already raised important issues for feminist critique overall in the 1990s.[37] The prevalent such issue was that any points of contact between Eastern European and Western feminism appeared already multiply, yet often negatively, determined by the division East/West and the materially grounded hierarchies that informed it. In a recent review of the rise of feminist critique in Baltic art scenes, Lithuanian curator Lolita Jabloskiene corroborated this view in noting that in certain cases and places introducing a feminist discourse seemed as a requirement for meeting the objective of a successful alignment with Western art scenes.[38] If, however, in the 1990s this had (partly, at least) led to an intense search for the contemporary in ways that privileged the West and its art historical narratives, the decade that followed provided ample reasons for a serious rethinking of priorities and the intentional development of frameworks. The latter often involved curatorial practices that attempted to elucidate the relevance of feminist politics to shaping a contemporary moment *from within* in Eastern Europe.

In January 2001, curator Suzana Milevska presented in Skopje the project 'Capital & Gender', which included a conference, workshops and an exhibition featuring both male and female artists. Over ten years later this remains a rather unusual curatorial project. Not many feminist curators East or West have sought to explicitly investigate the connections between capital and gender – with feminist curatorial projects bridging the gap between East and West in relation to capitalism being conspicuously absent. Milevska invited primarily Eastern European theorists and artists to take part in conference sessions and roundtables such as 'Capital, Information and Difference', 'Who Is Afraid of the Big Bad Capital?' and 'Gender and Management'. The exhibition was conceived and presented in the relevant literature as a 'public art project'. Entitled 'Perfect Match', this public art project lasted just three days and was installed in a shopping mall – a curatorial choice both ironic and affirmative in many respects. Built in the 1970s, Skopje's City Shopping Mall, formerly known as the City Trading Centre, was managed by the state until the change of regime, which led both to the formation of the Former Yugoslav Republic of Macedonia (FYROM) and the advent of a new and aggressive shopping culture based on excessive advertising about everything. Many of the artworks in this public project took as their focus the explicit incorporation of human relations, commonly perceived as interpersonal, into frameworks of consumption. For example, Zdenko Buzek's *Personal Contacts* (2001) consisted in the artist advertising in the local free press (devoted exclusively to ad placements) his eagerness to meet middle-aged intellectual women for a mutually pleasant chat and then actually meeting respondents in a café.

Ostojić did not so much 'show' work but rather engaged the exhibition site as such in the production of *Looking for a Husband with EU Passport*, initiated the previous year and of unpredictable outcome in 2001 (she used the commercial site of the mall as an opportunity to advertise her call).

The curator's choices of artworks thus made the conference session/workshop titled 'Gender and Management' sound much less surprising and perhaps urgent. Eastern European artists were indeed in a process of reinventing themselves and learning to manage their gender attributes to build both new lives and careers. This necessarily entailed an acknowledgement that capitalism, arriving in Eastern Europe both as an economy and a way of life, had assimilated gender difference into entrepreneurialism and that entrepreneurialism was reconfiguring the social role of the Eastern European artist. In the edited volume published as part of the project, Milevska notes: 'When the individuals of the countries of the East understood that they can completely take responsibility for the management over their own bodies and lives...many suppressed issues appeared that were not answered by the state in the preceding phase of development of these societies.'[39] Around 2000, a thin line seemed to separate the traditional distrust of the state in Eastern Europe (that had led to local and regional cultures of dissidence evident in art) and the new demand for reinventing oneself in a nascent entrepreneurial capitalism.

Overall, 'Capital & Gender' suggested that Eastern Europe after the fall of the Berlin Wall had provided the ground for an accelerated model of capitalism –which was why the significance of gender in redesigning a socioeconomic context could be readily observed. 'Capital & Gender' indicated that even if Eastern European feminists turned to the West for methodologies and concepts, the reasons why feminism had emerged as an oppositional discourse in the region were far from imported, to be found instead in the very process of social refashioning. For instance, Serbian curator Bojana Pejić has rejected arguments that present Eastern European women's peaceful withdrawal from waged labour as a reaction to state socialism, contending instead: 'we know that in the period of "transition" it was primarily women who lost their jobs and remained unemployed', which was also when emergent nationalist narratives, not so coincidentally, required of women a return to full-time motherhood and economic dependency at best.[40] In Eastern Europe, capital became a force for undoing gender relations in the public sphere as the sphere of productive labour (since reproductive labour, normally confined to domestic space, remained to a great extent hidden in Soviet times as well). As a curatorial project, 'Capital & Gender' testifies to this, providing itself a site for experimenting with gendered artistic labour and for investigating practices of management of the gendered self.

But, in addition, 'Capital & Gender' was conceived when, as Maja and Reuben Fowkes note, the cumulative disappointments of the first transition decade, the 1990s, were leading to a decade of 'post-transition' where 'belief in the utopian promise of that transition has given way to a more cynical assessment of economic and social reality in a globalized Eastern Europe'.[41] The realisation that a certain political process was over (that political change was 'accomplished', as put by the Fowkes), and that things were therefore settling, was cause for concern rather than relief. Maja and Reuben Fowkes detect 'a distinct shift in artistic interests at that point', which they associate with a diminished emphasis on the nation within the art community. This was perhaps easier to observe in Hungary than in FYROM, where 'Capital & Gender' presented a rather disruptive position on privileged state narratives strongly dependent on nationalist sentiment (fuelled by the naming dispute of this post-Yugoslav state). But also, feminist criticism after 2000 felt compelled to not give up on the politics of (European) space. In this discourse, the terms in which national space is discussed change and national space becomes meaningful in so far as it fills larger, transnational maps of discontent.

Curated by Slovenian Zdenka Badovinac, the exhibition 'Schengen Women' took place in Ljubljana in 2008 and included just ten artists (nine women and one man) from Eastern Europe, in particular from countries that emerged out of the violent dissection of Yugoslavia.[42] Yet the exhibition was important precisely in articulating the impossibility of achieving Jurgen Habermas's 'cosmopolitan solidarity' cited by the Fowkes.[43] 'Schengen Women' placed emphasis on the extended centrality of the border as defining a transnational gendered zone of exclusion so entrenched in formal structures as to undermine the prospect of transnational feminist solidarity even among all women actually excluded from the Schengen Treaty. This assessment was implicit in the curatorial decision to disregard the fact that not all European Union countries are part of the Schengen area (for example, the UK), even if 'cooperating in Schengen'.[44] Schengen therefore provided a case study where the border ultimately proved to be a *symbolic* rather than actual figure of division. The internalised otherness experienced by Eastern European women was not an effect of the border per se but rather an outcome of a combination of factors that ultimately placed women as economic subjects in a geo-political nexus: Britain could opt out of being in the Schengen area whereas other countries did not fulfil the criteria for inclusion. On the other hand, 'Schengen Women' was particularly important in, precisely, appropriating the meaning of 'Schengen women' for a majority of female subjects on the wrong side of the Schengen border. The strategic appropriation defining the curatorial narrative of excluded and included was less concerned with the accuracy of its politics of geography and more with investigating the possibility of agency, working against 'stereotypical images of Eastern European women, from the androgynous partisan and communist to the poor woman who does not match up to the western media images, and in the time of the transition, to the refugee and prostitute…formerly a victim of the regime, currently a victim of unbridled capitalism'. To these stereotypes of passive otherness, the exhibition sought to counterpose 'active otherness', providing thus a positive framework of reception for biopolitical works such as Ostojić's *Looking for a Husband with EU Passport*, already completed and exhibited through its documentation by 2008 and highlighting how ultimately capital defined all available positions (to be included, to be excluded, to reject inclusion). To present the possibility of active otherness, the curatorial narrative in 'Schengen Women' revived and reconfigured the Western feminist discourse of self-definition, promising to 'stress the significance of the Eastern European women artists' self-defining' against 'views from the outside'. [45]

This emphatic assertion of the need to mobilise a shared, regional consciousness relying on agency and working towards self-definition found an even more concrete and complex expression in the momentous curatorial project 'Gender Check: Femininity and Masculinity in the Art of Eastern Europe'. Directed by Pejić, the exhibition, which featured about 400 works by 200 male and female artists from 24 countries, was shown in Vienna's MUMOK in 2009 and then in Warsaw's Zacheta Gallery in 2010. Here, the curatorial strategy consisted in articulating a comparative approach with research conducted locally –that is, nationally – by art historians who had first-hand experience of the socio-cultural contexts they were researching. In doing so, 'Gender Check' implicitly at least extended the remit of self-definition from the artwork to art historical research, with a collectively produced curatorial narrative being ultimately responsible for asserting agency. The immense effort that went into producing such a transnational narrative merits a context. And this, unsurprisingly, returns us to the relationship between East and West.

Twenty years after the end of European state socialism, scholarly projects demonstrate the level of division, as charges of 'mis-representation' brought against Western feminism abound. The issue I want to raise is the extent to which 'mis-representation' does not so much occur at the interface of regional feminist politics but is a structural feature of global hierarchies and privileged sites of communication defining the dissemination of research. Consider the following: In her introduction to *The Feminism and Visual Culture Reader* (2009), Amelia Jones explained her conscious decision as an editor to 'limit the second edition to texts written and/or published originally in English' adding: 'no matter how good the advice I am getting from colleagues around the world…I cannot begin to pretend to cover in any remotely comprehensive way material written or published outside the Anglophone context'.[46] The volume thus includes an essay on Eastern European women's art that first appeared in the exhibition catalogue of 'Global Feminisms' – an exhibition organised in 2007 in the USA. Coincidentally, the included text, written by an

Eastern European scholar based in America for many years, is the one that Pejić berates as misrepresenting Eastern European women in the context of the American show, commenting further: 'After this exhibition catalogue, I thought: if we don't start to deal ourselves with our art history, nobody will do it'.[47] Jones' sensitivity to the intellectual and political context of feminist scholarship did not provide a resolution, highlighting instead inadvertently how practical matters (access to language) impede feminist scholarship as a transformative global project.

But to Eastern European artists, scholars and curators access to language has not been a mere practical matter. Croatian Mladen Stilinović made in 1992 the now landmark installation featuring this phrase: 'An artist who cannot speak English is no artist'. In her introductory essay to the *Gender Check* catalogue, Pejić explains her own choices as follows: 'my analysis does not take into consideration studies in national art histories, but only publications that deal with a broader Eastern European framework that have appeared in the English language and been written by "embedded" art historians, that is, by Eastern European authors'.[48] Although strategic and also having to do with the practicalities that arose in the context of their respective publishing and research projects, Jones' and Pejić's choices testify to the immense difficulties of operating beyond dominant frameworks of global purchase – difficulties that generate considerable bitterness to those who feel, and often are, excluded from them. These choices also suggest that transnational feminist research as an attempted act of communication is 'embedded' in its own right – entrenched, that is, within established geopolitical hierarchies that are systemic and compulsively reproduced. The cosmopolitan globalism of art-history writing constructs a space for feminist politics where the rules of global hegemony, grounded on economic divisions, are self-consciously performed by the situated author. As Pejić's necessary and pragmatic choices in particular teach (how can you conduct large-scale intercultural research across the multilingual social sites of European geographies?), the desire to acknowledge the diverse histories that comprise post-socialist geographies was compounded by the desire to construct a framework for their presentation that could afford them maximum, indeed global, legibility. This is what the choice of English offers at the same time as it acknowledges the hegemony of 'writing in English'.

The above compel, however, a rethinking of 'cultural translation', a concept popular in the postmodernist discourses of cultural difference that has also found some application in more recent endeavours: the deployment of this concept in Nicolas Bourriaud's 'Altermodern' discussed in Chapter 1 is indicative of its current usage *after* postmodernism. The premise of 'embedded' art historians, writing in English, places faith in embodied cultural identity and the first-hand, long-term, personal experience of a socio-cultural context. It exemplifies and extends the logic of identity politics, transferred now from the artist to the historian-curator who remains doubly burdened: she has to signify both the authenticity of the experience transmitted – in fact, the experience of being 'Eastern European' rather than belonging to a specific socio-cultural space – *and* the ability to converse with a transnational framework where experience can be communicated through a globally hegemonic language. Could it be that at present as long as the curator can speak English, it matters little if the artist cannot? In this sense, the framework provided by 'Gender Check' is symptomatic of the greater authority achieved by the curatorial role in negotiating cultural narratives within the ethos of administration promoted by global capital. And, notably, 'Gender Check' as the most systematic collectively undertaken regional investigation (by feminist curators) of gender and art anywhere in the world, became possible not through government or EU funding but through private sources – specifically by ERSTE Foundation as 'the main shareholder of Erste Group', which 'invests its dividends into those societies where this money was earned'.[49] 'Gender Check' was realised as a response to an ERSTE Foundation call for curatorial proposals that commemorated the fall of the Berlin Wall. Securing funding from one source permitted the curatorial team to focus on scholarship and research rather than engage in step-by-step fundraising, at a moment when state funding in the arts was disappearing. When then looking at Eastern Europe, it becomes clear that no singular narrative can uphold the complex encounter of feminism's and capital's global imperatives – if, that is, from the position of materialist feminism we wish to maintain them as distinct.

Marina Gržinić's polemic against 'Gender Check' (despite her participation in the project as both artist and theorist) may well suggest that such distinction is becoming impossible for some. Gržinić regarded 'Gender Check' as underpinned by 'the co-propriety of capital and power (Erste/MUMOK/the institution of the curator)', arguing that 'the control over representation is done through an enumerative logic [e.g. so many artists from so many countries] as a new juncture in-between neoliberal capitalist epistemology and neoliberal capitalist governmentality'. Her furious criticism rested on her assessment that the project –any such project, apparently – expressed 'a brutal colonial logic of forced subjugation of whole territories and art and social practices to a gender administrative logic of counting nameless bodies in order to be governed in the future properly'.[50] But although Gržinić is right in identifying new configurations of vectors of power (finance/museum/curation), her perspective is problematic in its refusal to address either contradictions in the operations of global capital or the struggle that takes place at the zones of contact between capital and transnational emancipatory politics. In the case of 'Gender Check', did capital serve to generate collectively produced feminist knowledge? Yes. Can we see a contradiction in capital generating feminist knowledge and in having brought about the conditions that such feminist knowledge seeks to change? Also yes. Can we foresee how such feminist knowledge *will* be used – that is, will it be used to engineer capital's further control or to advance feminism's subversion of capital? No, we cannot, because such use can only be determined in historically specific contexts where struggle acquires distinct forms.

The 'Gender Check' project becomes particularly important, intending to provide an authoritative summary of the social processes it unearths as the first step towards further action by making meaningful a 'we' addressing Eastern European feminists.[51] As the outcome of a collective yet centrally coordinated effort, the exhibition (as part of the broader project) did not invent new categorisations but worked with concepts already familiar through Western feminism. It did not displace Western feminism's emphasis on a politics of representation and although the theme of gender and work was strongly present throughout the show, the curatorial narrative did not, for example, provide a rethinking of the relationship between artist and model that prioritised conditions and relations of labour.[52] The project's underlying aim became clearer in the exhibition catalogue which documented the development of art historical thinking centred on gender across Eastern Europe as a process resting on an interplay between a nascent feminist consciousness and the various contexts of resistance to it. An edited reader that offered a necessarily selective but representative sample of interventions in art criticism added to this narrative. Much more than a survey show, 'Gender Check' was therefore posited as a document of larger processes framing the convulsive emergence of feminist politics in a part of the world very much defined by the moves of global capital. As such, it remains an invaluable document, the meaning of which is likely to change in time.

When considered for its documentary value, 'Gender Check' raises a number of issues for any future research in the histories of feminism. To begin with, Czech art historian Martina Pachmanova noted in an essay that Pejić chose to include both in the exhibition catalogue and the reader that 'in spite of this unwelcoming situation [the resistance to feminist analysis in Eastern European art scenes], there were remarkable women artists working behind the Iron Curtain whose works were *strikingly similar* to women's and feminist art in the West'[53] [my emphasis]. The claim that women artists in Eastern Europe produced work 'strikingly similar' to that of their Western colleagues during the Cold War period must be carefully considered. The Cold War was also a time when second-wave feminism appeared in the West, allegedly transforming women's art in terms of form and content. This transformation is the very meaning of 'feminist art', popularised to the extent that it has acquired its own Wikipedia entry: 'Feminist Art Movement'. So, if women artists in Eastern Europe, where a feminist art movement did not exist in the 1960s and 1970s, produced strikingly similar work to that of women artists in the West where such a movement did exist, what difference did feminism actually make? This question suggests that there is an urgent need for not just comparative methodologies in feminist research but for a relational feminist historiography in the arts. How and why did such affinity between East and West exist? To merely assume that a common patriarchal ground sustained liberal capitalist societies *and* state socialism in the second half of the twentieth century is unsatisfactory because it naively construes gender relations as autonomous, not fully integrated into historically specific webs of socio-economic relations.

Despite Pachmanova's claim, the exhibition and the investigation into the region's art criticism suggest that something did change during the 1990s and the first decade of the twenty-first century: since 1989 there has been an intensification in the engagement with gender and sexuality in most parts of the region – indeed, an engagement with feminism as a framework with a particular agenda about gender and sexuality. *The Gender Check Reader* provides reflections on the many exhibitions and public exchanges openly addressing gender in relation to a transformative politics – including 'Capital & Gender' and 'Schengen Women' as curatorial initiatives providing frameworks of analysis that precisely opposed an understanding of gender as an autonomous structure. Curatorial projects such as these displayed an awareness concerning the intersection of economy and geography as determinants of gender relations but hardly represent the full range of positions on feminism in the art scenes of Eastern Europe. The *Gender Check Reader* addressed this issue by including an essay by Latvian Inga Steimane called 'An Alternative to Cynicism'.

First published in a reputable Eastern European art journal in 1998 (nearly a decade after the first wave of feminist art criticism in some post-socialist countries), Steimane's essay asks whether alternative empowering discourses for women exist, since feminism is deemed to be infantile, nervous, vulgar and, as per the essay title, a form of cynicism. Steimane discusses the work of a Latvian group of women artists as attempting to provide such an alternative (that remains, however, unspecified in the essay). In her Introduction to the volume, Pejić characterises the group as 'feminist', further stating that their interventions stood in opposition specifically to Western feminism and connecting Steimane's essay (she was a member of the group) with the mixed feelings towards Western feminism in Eastern Europe overall. Yet Steimane does not address Western feminism as such in her text, rejecting instead feminism *tout court*. Pejić's reading rests on her awareness of a historically specific framework of reception: that of a 'transitional' Eastern Europe that saw Western feminism not just as a discourse of the other side but of a privileged social space (the West) in global geopolitics. There is a crucial slippage here in the perception of Western feminism, seen to have developed and operated *as*, rather than *in*, a space of privilege. The inclusion of Steimane's essay serves as more than the mere documentation of diverse perspectives on feminism encountered in the region. What is rather documented here is the geopolitical, rather than merely cultural, translation of feminism and the ideological impediments to establishing a transnational feminism in the arts.

Although in the late 1990s one might have rebutted this dismissal of feminism by arguing about its essential transnational vision, this sounds less convincing today. Feminism's vision in globalisation may indeed be transnational but, as seen in the Introduction, in the preceding decade materialist feminists such as Eisenstein and Fraser explored the deep connections between the rise of second-wave feminism in the 1960s and the transformation of capitalism. Fraser situated the genesis of second-wave feminism explicitly in state-organised capitalism, arguing that feminist demands were 'resignified' and ended up playing a key role in a transition that involved not merely a region but the whole planet. Feminism's 'utopian desires found a second life as feeling currents that legitimated the transition to a new form of capitalism: post-Fordist, transnational, neoliberal'.[54] She further notes:

> In general then, the fate of feminism in the neoliberal era presents a paradox. On the one hand, the relatively small countercultural movement of the previous period has expanded exponentially, successfully disseminating its ideas around the globe. On the other, feminist ideas have undergone a subtle shift in valence in the altered context. Unambiguously emancipatory in the era of state-organised capitalism, critiques of economism, androcentrism, etatism and Westphalianism now appear fraught with ambiguity, susceptible to serving the legitimation needs of a new form of capitalism. After all, this capitalism would much prefer to confront claims for recognition over claims for redistribution, as it builds a new regime of accumulation on the cornerstone of women's waged labour, and seeks to disembed markets from social regulation in order to operate all the more freely on global scale.[55]

Fraser's courageous analysis helps us also rethink the dilemmas faced in the reception of feminism in Eastern Europe, which impacted greatly on its art scenes as platforms for subverting gender hierarchies. The dismissal of feminism by some Eastern European women still keen to promote women's empowerment may well display an ignorance of the many currents of and ideological battles within Western feminism but may also be seen to express a resistance to the very process of transition. In some sense, to jettison feminism implied a misunderstanding of what the transition was about and where it could be observed. The transition of Eastern Europe was not one from a nominal communism – or better state socialism – to capitalism in general. Instead, it was realised in the 1990s as the cherry on the cake: as a crucial and concluding step in a global passage from one phase of capitalism to another, that is, from state capitalism to the interconnected economies of global capital and the generalisation of crisis. As Fraser remarks, the neoliberal policies that appropriated and made exemplary use of the demands of second-wave feminism were 'road-tested in Latin America' and 'served to guide much of the transition to capitalism in East/Central Europe'.[56] Understanding the encounter with Western feminism as taking place after the 're-signification', in keeping with Fraser's term, of feminist demands can help refocus the dialogue between Eastern European and Western feminisms in the arts on emergent commonalities rather than past differences. More generally, elaborating on this knowledge can aid a more constructive dialogue on the roots and direction of transnational feminism, as long as we bear in mind that transnational feminism is also fraught with materially grounded and ideologically expressed divisions.

The above discussion, concerning both women's art and debates around feminism in Eastern Europe, suggests a complex signification of gender in the given context. Arguably and paradoxically, it makes apparent both an (internalised) position of difference and the need to reconceptualise transition as a process of wider relevance. Perceiving transition as regional (that is, localised) misses its essential meaning in a global context, isolates Eastern Europe under the banner of exceptionalism and places its feminism in a dead-end generational relationship (or, better, conflict) with Western feminism. The reason why this chapter concludes with an exploration of 'Gender Check' is that the project is articulated as a moment of pause and reflection on what has been in order to facilitate a future-oriented feminism in the arts. This hardly means that 'Gender Check' can be seen as the last word on the subject. But it does mean that the new data that will undoubtedly keep coming can enter a dialogue with an already existing narrative that explicitly posits a 'we' based on the will to set in motion a feminist historical consciousness.[57] At the same time, it is becoming apparent that this 'we' cannot be summarised and transmitted through the discourse of cultural translation, being instead enmeshed, much like Western feminism, in historical processes that guarantee the constant reproduction of economic rather than cultural otherness.

Notes

1 Notably, even when globalisation stretches back in time to encompass European imperialisms, the collapse of the Soviet world retains its significance. Effectively locating the Soviet experience at the heart of Western modernity, Susan Buck-Morss writes: 'The spread of Western scientific and cultural hegemony was the intellectual reality of the first five hundred years of globalisation, lasting from the beginning of European colonial expansion to the end of the Soviet modernising project (1492–1992)'. See S. Buck-Morss, 'The Post-Soviet Condition' in IRWIN (eds), *East Art Map: Contemporary Art and Eastern Europe* (London: Afterall, 2006), 495.

2 R. Williams, 'Beyond Actually Existing Socialism', *New Left Review* I, 120 (March–April 1980), 3-19.

3 F. de Haan, K. Daskalova and A. Loutfi (eds), *Biographical Dictionary of Women's Movements and Feminisms in Central, Eastern, and South Eastern Europe: 19th and 20th Centuries* (Budapest: Central European University Press, 2006).

4 'FORMER WEST is a long-term international research, education, publishing, and exhibition project (2008–2014), which from within the field of contemporary art and theory: (1) reflects upon the changes introduced to the world (and thus to the so-called West) by the political, cultural, artistic, and economic events of 1989; (2) engages in rethinking the global histories of the last two decades in dialogue with post-communist and postcolonial thought; and (3) speculates about a "post-bloc" future that recognizes differences yet evolves through the political imperative of equality and the notion of "one world." Quoted from www.formerwest.org/ (accessed 5 April 2010).

5 M. Gržinić, 'From Transitional Postsocialist Spaces to Neoliberal Global Capitalism', *Third Text* 21/5 (2007), 563–75. Here 572.

6 I use the term 'post-socialist' to refer to the states that emerged at the aftermath of the Soviet world following Antonio Negri's distinction between 'socialism' and 'communism'. See A. Negri 'Communism: Some Thoughts on the Concept and Practice' in C. Douzinas and S. Žižek (eds), *The Idea of Communism: Some Thoughts on the Concept and Practice* (London: Verso, 2011).

7 See R. Močnik, 'East!' in IRWIN, *East Art Map: Contemporary Art and Eastern Europe*.

8 A. Dezeuze, 'The Poetics and Politics of Precariousness in the 1990s', lecture delivered at the Department of History of Art, University of Edinburgh, 5 October 2011.

9 G. Sholette, *Dark Matter: Art in the Age of Enterprise Culture* (London: Pluto Press, 2011).

10 L. Becker, 'Art for an Avant-Garde Society: Belgrade in the 1970s' in IRWIN, *East Art Map*, 391. See also D. Djuric and M. Suvakovic (eds), *Impossible Histories: Historical Avant-gardes, Neo-Avant-Gardes and Post-Avant-Gardes in Yugoslavia* (Cambridge, Mass.: MIT Press, 2003), also cited by Becker.

11 I. Kowalczyk, D. Łagodzka and E. Zierkiewic, 'Anger of Bojana Pejić: An Interview', Warsaw 23.2.2010, *Obieg*, www.obieg.pl/artmix/18402 (accessed 10 October 2011). The conference was organised by Pejić's friend, feminist sociologist Žarana Papić and Dunia Blažević, art historian.

12 See S. Milevska, 'Femina Sacra: Bio-Power and Paradoxes of Humanity in the Art of Tanja Ostojić', in M. Gržinić and T. Ostojić (eds), *Integration Impossible? The Politics of Migration in the Artwork of Tanja Ostojić* (Berlin: Argobooks, 2009).

13 Appropriating her stereotypical treatment in the Estonian press, young Tralla referred to herself as a 'disgusting girl' constantly engaged in 'provocation'. See Tralla's interview in A. Dimitrakaki, P. Skelton and M. Tralla (eds), *Private Views* (London: Women's Art Library, 1998). On the symbolic attack on the institution of marriage and women's work in Eastern Europe, see B. Hock, 'Agency

Gendered: Deconstructed Marriages and Migration Narratives in Contemporary Art', *ArtMargins* (8 July 2011), www.artmargins.com/index.php/2–articles/636—marriages-and-migration-in-art (accessed 19 October 2011).

14 J. Holloway, *How to Change the World without Taking Power* (London: Pluto Press, 2002). See Chapter 1.

15 Author's interview with the artist, Berlin, June 2010.

16 Unsigned introduction to project, Gržinić and Ostojić, *Integration Impossible?*, 33.

17 Artist's statement in ibid., 38.

18 The work was first exhibited in 'Double-Check: Re-Framing Space in Photography: The Other Space, Parallel Histories' in Slovenia and Austria in 2004–5 and 'Europart' in Austria in 2005–6.

19 The curators' letter is reproduced in Gržinić and Ostojić, *Integration Impossible?*, 74.

20 Gržinić, 'Decoloniality of Knowledge', 190.

21 Ibid.

22 See Dimitrakaki, 'Labour, Ethics, Sex and Capital: On Biopolitical Production in Contemporary Art'.

23 See A. Dimitrakaki, 'Art, Globalization and the Exhibition Form: What Is the Case, What Is the Challenge?', *Third Text* 26/3 (May 2012), 305–19.

24 Interview with the author, London, 2 July 2010.

25 P. Allara, 'Geo-Bodies: Feminist Activists Crossing Borders', in Gržinić and Ostojić, *Integration Impossible?*, 178

26 This was confirmed in electronic communication with the author, 13 September 2012.

27 J. Surkis, 'Tanja Ostojić's European Border Work', in Gržinić and Ostojić, *Integration Impossible?*, 197.

28 R. Gade, 'Making Real: Strategies of Performing Performativity in Tanja Ostojic's *Looking for a Husband with EU Passport*', in Gržinić and Ostojić, *Integration Impossible?*, 202–3.

29 Ibid., 207.

30 Ibid., 218.

31 B. Hock, 'Gendered Artistic Positions and Social Voices: Politics, Cinema, and the Visual Arts in State-Socialist and Post-Socialist Hungary' (unpublished PhD thesis, Central European University, Budapest 2009). Published in 2012 by Franz Steiner verlag, Stuttgart.

32 S. Tatlić, 'The Truth Machine: The Relationship between Life and Sovereign Power', in Gržinić and Ostojić, *Integration Impossible?*, 233.

33 Ibid., 237.

34 *WeeViews* belongs to the collection of Threshold Artspace in Perth, Scotland.

35 M. Gržinić, 'On the Re-politicisation of Art through Contamination', in IRWIN, *East Art Map*, 484.

36 On the impact of American billionaire George Soros' art centres in post-Soviet Europe, see N. Czegledy and A. Szekeres, 'Agents for Change: The Contemporary Art Centres of the Soros Foundation and C3', *Third Text* 23/3 (2009), 251–9.

37 See Dimitrakaki, 'Researching Culture/s and the Omitted Footnote: Questions on the Practice of Feminist Art History', in Jones, *The Feminism and Visual Culture Reader*, 2nd edn.

38 L. Jablonskiene, ' "Just an Artist?": An Imaginary Exhibition Project', in Hedlin Hayden and Sjöholm Skrubbe, *Feminisms Is still Our Name*, 145.

39 S. Milevska, 'Introduction', in S. Milevska (ed.), *Capital & Gender* (Skopje, 2001), p. 7.

40 Pejić quoted in Kowalczyk, Łagodzka and Zierkiewic, 'Pejić's Anger'.

41 M. and R. Fowkes, 'Contemporary East European Art in the Era of Globalization: From Identity Politics to Cosmopolitan Solidarity', *ARTMargins Online* (29 September 2010), www.artmargins.com/index.php/2–articles/ 598–contemporary-east-european-art-era-globalization-identity-politics-cosmopolitan-solidarity#ftn_artnotes1_1 (accessed 10 October 2011).

42 Artists were Maja Bajeviæ (Bosnia – Herzegovina), Danica Dakic & Sandra Sterle (Bosnia – Herzegovina, Croatia), Vlasta Delimar (Croatia), Sanja Ivekoviæ (Croatia), Šejla Kameric (Bosnia – Herzegovina), Zofia Kulik (Poland), Andreja Kulunèic (Croatia), Tanja Ostojić (Serbia), Tadej Pogaèar and the P.A.R.A.S.I.T.E. Museum of Contemporary Art (Slovenia), Marija Mojca Pungercar (Slovenia).

43 See P. Cheah, 'The Cosmopolitical', in M. Rovisco and M. Nowicka (eds), *The Ashgate Research Companion to Cosmopolitanism* (Farnham: Ashgate, 2011). See also J. Habermas, 'Why Europe Needs a Constitution', *New Left Review* 11 (Sept.–Oct. 2001), 5–26.

44 http://europa.eu/legislation_summaries/justice_freedom_security/free_ movement_of_persons_asylum_immigration/l33020_en.htm

45 The curatorial statement is available on www.re-title.com/exhibitions/archive_ GalerijaSkuc1448.asp (accessed 10 October 2011).

46 A. Jones, 'Introduction: Conceiving the Intersection of Feminism and Visual Culture, Again', in Jones, *The Feminism and Visual Culture Reader*, 5.

47 Pejić quoted in Kowalczyk, Łagodzka and Zierkiewic, 'Pejić's Anger'.

48 B. Pejić, 'Proletarians of All Countries, Who Washes Your Socks? Equality, Dominance and Difference in Eastern European Art', in B. Pejić (ed.), *Gender Check: Femininity and Masculinity in the Art of Eastern Europe* (Vienna: MUMOK Museum Moderner Kunst Stiftung Ludwig, 2009), 20.

49 The Erste Foundation website offers a detailed description of the foundation's policies and remit of activities based on the transformation of Europe after 1989. See http://www.erstestiftung.org/countries/ (accessed 14 October 2011).

50 M. Gržinić, *'Analysis of the Exhibition "Gender Check – Femininity and Masculinity in the Art of Eastern Europe", Museum of Modern Art (MUMOK), Vienna, November 2009/February 2010'* (December 2009), http://eipcp.net/ policies/grzinic/en (accessed 10 November 2010).

51 Pejić, 'Proletarians of All Countries, Who Washes Your Socks? Equality, Dominance and Difference in Eastern European Art' in *Gender Check*, 21.

52 No comment on the relationship between artist and model in terms of labour was made in the show captions and panels in the MUMOK exhibit in Vienna or in the exhibition catalogue.

53 M. Pachmanova, 'In? Out? In Between? Some Notes on the Invisibility of a Nascent Eastern European Feminist and Gender Discourse in Contemporary Art Theory' (2009), in B. Pejić (ed.), *Gender Check – A Reader: Art and Theory in Eastern Europe* (Cologne: W. König, 2010).
54 Fraser, 'Feminism and the Cunning of History', 99.
55 Ibid., 113.
56 Ibid., 107.
57 B. Pejić, 'Introduction' in Pejić, *Gender Check – A Reader*.

3

Travel as (gendered) work: global space, mobility and the 'woman artist'

Notes on a work accident

In the mid-1990s Martha Rosler published in book form her art project *In the Place of the Public: Observations of a Frequent Flyer*, initiated in 1981.[1] Comprising photographs of the transit sites marking the artist's air travels and textual commentary reflecting on travel as a social relation, the project was among the first to articulate a fundamental condition of contemporary art: the imperative to travel generated by global capital. Rosler, a leading figure of feminist art in the 1970s, did not in this instance provide a gendered reading of her experience as an artist compelled to travel – as a woman artist, that is, pulled outside the home–studio nexus and productive in an increasingly global setting. Yet in her iconic video-performance *Semiotics of the Kitchen* (1975), Rosler explicitly gendered the requirement of remaining still and homebound: the video showed the (woman) artist herself in a kitchen setting, with the TV screen as her interface with the world. Holding, naming and putting aside a variety of objects/tools used for cooking, the woman artist's rigid and minimal hand movements attenuated her stillness in the enclosed space – with the screen as the fourth wall, from the spectator's perspective.

Semiotics of the Kitchen has been highly visible in feminist art history and contemporary art histories, articulating a connection between women's subordination and the domestic as the primary site of female labour. *In the Place of the Public: Observations of a Frequent Flyer* has enjoyed more modest visibility. Excluded, for instance, from the exhibition site of 'Documenta 11', it appeared as a single photograph in its catalogue, its hesitant inclusion speaking rather about the difficulty of pursuing a link between feminism, women artists, work and capital as the force shaping global space – space, that is, away from home. It is the possibility of establishing such a link that I explore in this chapter. If, as Janet Wolff observed in 1993 (noting also the sudden proliferation of travel metaphors in cultural criticism), 'the practices and ideologies of *actual* travel work to exclude or pathologise women', travel can be a very complex form of political artWork for contemporary feminism.[2]

In 2008 Giuseppina Pasqualino di Marineo, also known as Pippa Bacca, began the project *Brides on Tour* in Italy, with fellow woman artist Silvia Moro.[3] The two artists intended to travel east, dressed in flowing, white wedding gowns: they would hitch-hike through northern Italy, part of the Balkans, Turkey, Lebanon, Jordan, arriving finally in Egypt to assert that a peaceful crossing of troubled regions is possible. The wedding gowns, provided by Byblos Art Gallery in Verona and designed by the artists, were to be a symbol of joy, celebration, womanhood (their journey started on 8 March or 'international woman's day') and the possibility of new beginnings. They also stood for a retreat from cultural exchange policies, as often put in the parlance of token government directives; instead, the artists intended to explore the 'marriage', the becoming one in a context of informality, of cultures in peoples' everyday realities.[4] To cover more of the region's cultural diversity, the artists separated before Istanbul and would reunite in Lebanon. In April 2008 this collaborative artwork, realisable through the participation of drivers, most of whom would be men (it is mostly men who drive trucks on highways), was cut short. Di Marineo was found raped and strangled in Turkey – not too far from cosmopolitan Istanbul and near town Gezbe, by a (male) driver who had picked her up, as reported by news agencies. News agencies kept reproducing the words of di Marineo's sister: 'Her travels were for an artistic performance and to give a message of peace and of trust, but not everyone deserves trust.'[5] Gendering this 'everyone' was not something that the media were prepared to do – such a reading of the tragic journey was attempted a couple of years later by Kurdish female documentary filmmaker Bingöl Elmas who, dressed in black, continued the journey from where the Italian artist had been brutally murdered to the Syrian border. Elmas filmed her journey with the explicit purpose of 'rais[ing] awareness about society's attitudes toward women'. This time such awareness was not to do with women's right to urban space – Leslie Labowitz and Suzanne Lacy's *In Mourning and in Rage* (1977) addressing women's rape and murder in Los Angeles did this – but with women's right of access to territorial movement. *My Letter to Pippa* (2010, 60 mins), funded by European organisations, was described by Elmas as very hard to make: knowing about the risks awaiting a woman on a journey had hardly prepared her for the reality check of the journey itself.[6]

In the two decades that witnessed the beginning of Rosler's air travel project and the terror-filled ending of di Marineo's ground travel project, critics and curators spoke increasingly about artists' exodus from the studio. First, Claire Doherty's observation that the protected space of the studio was no longer where art was born and Bourriaud's coining of the term 'journey-form', as the contemporary artwork's essential mode of being, defined the transformed conditions of contemporary art making in globalisation.[7] In assuming that these conditions do not constitute a curiously non-gendered terrain of action, the question if, and how, women artists exited the studio becomes an obvious one. Second, after 2000 a geographico-cultural understanding of globalisation generated interest in earlier instances of women artists' relationship to the 'other' of domestic space: the edited volumes *Intrepid Women: Victorian Women Artists Travel* and *Local/Global: Women Artists in the Nineteenth Century*, both appeared in 2006.[8] The first researched histories of women artists that did not remain homebound (as the volume's title indicates) at their own peril, while the second appropriated concepts associated with globalisation as a late twentieth-century phenomenon to propose an alternative reading of nineteenth-century female creativity defined by movement rather than boundaries. The book focused on women 'who crossed continents and cultures, artists relocated and displaced by the pressures of global and local change'.[9] Third, the critique of contemporary art's ethnographic turn, as put forward by Hal Foster in 1996 and Miwon Kwon in 2004, began being displaced by efforts to chart a critical cosmopolitanism as a major project in contemporary art.[10] Nikos Papastergiadis argued that post-2000 'the cosmopolitan imaginary is… not just a zone of pure fantasy and aloof speculation. It is part of the realm of representation that is constantly criss-crossing both the real conditions of existence and future-present forms of possibility'.[11] In a book devoted to the subject, Marsha Meskimmon explains that the cosmopolitanism she deploys is

> grounded, materially specific and relational; it is a committed address to cultural diversity, and movement beyond fixed geo-political borders. It is linked to the concept of home through processes of belonging (making yourself at home) and to ethics, through both the ideas of dwelling and hospitality [...] cosmopolitanism asks how we might connect, through dialogue rather than monologue, our response-ability to our responsibilities within a world community.[12]

Both Papastergiadis and Meskimmon reclaim a positively inflected cosmopolitanism, one of relevance to an art that is (mostly) realised rather than an art in/of utopian terms (as a future that art is imagining on our behalf). One of the main characteristics of the new and desired cosmopolitan subject that such analyses pose is its articulation, partly at least, 'in the real conditions of existence' (Papastergiadis), which makes this subject 'grounded, materially specific and relational' (Meskimmon). This is a cosmopolitanism that seeks to re-establish its connection with reality in terms of materiality, having provided, for this very reason, the principal framework for critical theorisations of journeys and travels. That this framework exists in 'a global world' where contemporary art is 'at home', as stressed by Meskimmon, suggests why it is important to connect the dots between the journey and women artists' production.[13] But so far, as di Marineo's and Elmas's gendered, performative (white-dressed bride/black-dressed mourner) journeys indicate, women artists' terrain of action outside the home remains apparently fraught with risk. What kind of risk? I do not wish to see di Marineo's rape and murder during her journey as a case of a temporarily defeated cosmopolitanism. I do not wish to see it as a freak accident and a momentary disruption of an otherwise smooth realisation of a global citizenship pursued through art mobility. Rather, I want to see it as a work accident that can alert us to art making *as historically*, rather than essentially, gendered labour. Di Marineo was killed on duty. She died during, and as a result of, her work, which could only be experienced on site (in the crossing), which in turn permitted an unknowing 'participant' to complete the work by becoming her murderer. The association with Marina Abramovic's *Rhythm 5* (1974), a performance where the viewers of her conditions of risk in the flaming star entered the field of participation by carrying the artist away and saving her life, is inevitable – this being one of the many examples one could conjure to highlight the significance of 'where' in any meaningful account of art that requires, or even pursues, an entanglement with risk. Di Marineo's rape and murder were ultimately part of what Bourriaud has called the 'journey form', persistently visible – and mostly as a work method – in the landscapes of contemporary art but naively construed (for the French curator who coined the term) as eclipsing the differences between the journeys of living subjects and the journeys of signs, codes and information. Bearing in mind this distinction, which compels me to speak about the biopolitical journey as a work method in contemporary art paradigmatically articulated under capital's global imperative, my question is whether, in what ways and to what effects this work method can be available to women artists.

As I have argued in previous chapters, the globalisation of capital is intricately articulated with notable transformations in the regime of labour and I see this as the main reason why we have been witnessing a critical 'labour turn' in the art world. An indicator of this trend has been the engagement with labour through exhibitions that involve feminism and that historicise feminism. 'Labor' was one of the 15 sections that provided *Wack!*'s conceptual typology of 1970s feminist art. Curator Cornelia Butler explicitly related 'labor', as part of this conceptual typology, to 'collaborative projects as a way to decentralize authorship, experience collaborative activity as a microcosm of the larger society, and generate new, non-hierarchical models of organization and production'.[14] In this context, labour operates as a dynamic, open and liberating category, a sphere of human action where an opposition to dominant social relations can be productively articulated by juxtaposing collaboration (progressive and emancipatory) with atomisation (regressive and, in Marxist terms, alienating). In other quarters, not necessarily engaging feminist perspectives, the recent introduction of collaboration into art and curatorial discourse appears to have an experimental character. Even when a link is not established between the visibility and possible increase of collaborative, participatory art practice and the cooperative productivity that the contemporary stage in the capitalist mode of production requires, the emphasis on collaboration in terms of an artistic method raises a number of questions that implicate labour. Can art as labour assume the guise of an experiment with greater social consequences? Can art as labour generate paradigms of labour relations that are not oppressive, or that at least engender the possibility of imagining a less oppressive regime of labour? And what happens when such paradigms and experiments are seen in gendered terms?

Theorists addressing the condition of global capital and imagining forms of resistance to its authority have highlighted the increasing relevance of affective labour in contemporary economy. The popularisation of affective labour (in the wake of Hardt and Negri's *Empire*) has generated a widespread use of 'affect' in art discourse since 2000, often detracting from how affect enters relations of production shaping the terrain of waged and unwaged gendered labour. But, as seen in Chapter 1, the labour turn in the humanities and social science has also raised the issue of a 'feminisation of labour', according to the qualitative interpretation of which men's work is now increasingly subject to the 'laws' of precarity, flexibilisation, home-based production, part-time work, low and uncertain wages and so on – conditions with which women have long been familiar. The relationship of femininity, women and labour takes place within a troubling context, orchestrated by capital's impetus to transform in order to maintain and increase the rate of profit. In the *Communist Manifesto's* famous words, 'all that is solid melts into air' and gendered labour, in art and elsewhere, is not an exception to this general rule. In essence, the study of contemporary art in this chapter takes capital's current (that is, historically specific) impetus to transform as its starting point and investigates the impact of this impetus on women artists' labour. Instead of attributing to women artists a subjectivity emanating from a desired cosmopolitanism, the analysis asks how travel as work defines women artists as productive subjects. More specifically, I am interested in how globalisation can be seen to transform the historical category of the 'woman artist' – a historical category that second-wave feminist art historians and artists invested with political meaning.

Labour, art and feminism: the interrupted materialism of the 1970s

As a practice of territorial and institutional subjugation to global capital, globalisation is not the sole operator in this recent transformation of the category of 'woman artist'. Political discourses and experiences, such as those provided by feminism, are integral to the process this chapter seeks to describe and approach critically. Labour was on the agenda of early feminist interventions in art. The two best-known cases are in Britain and the USA, the two countries where the feminist art movement thrived in the 1970s. Mierle Laderman Ukeles's series of performances under the title *Maintenance Work* in the USA exposed the art museum as a space where women's labour and working-class labour were actively exploited. Cleaning the museum space required the invisible 'performance' of working-class people, and Ukeles's action was a way of exposing the invisible. Arguably, her action made also visible the expanse of service work characterising late twentieth-century capitalism and, more importantly, repositioned the spectator as a user-consumer of museum space, apprehended through Ukeles's work as the site of a social experience. In this sense, *Maintenance Work* entailed elements of participation at the same time as it disinvested participation from its positive (collaborative) meaning, by demonstrating how users-consumers participate in institutionally ratified forms of the exploitation of women's (and men's) labour. Yet Ukeles's action was not strictly speaking a performance, requiring and generating a community of spectators passively registering the artist's action (even if such an audience was present), and this participatory aspect of her work became more prominent in other projects (especially in collaborative projects with the New York Department of Sanitation in the 1990s) that only recently began being considered by feminist art historians.

Andrea Liss traced the origins of Ukeles's public projects involving maintenance labour to the 'painful experience as a young female artist [in the late 1960s] who was soon to become a mother' and was told by her art school professor that she couldn't be an artist *and* a mother.[15] Liss is right to note that '"The Manifesto for Maintenance Art, 1969" is a feminist and humanist text that continues to resound in the twenty-first century.'[16] The turn to affective labour has, more accurately, made it acutely contemporary. And yet in Liss's argument that the four photographs of the artist accompanying the manifesto describe 'maternal activities', where Ukeles 'photographically named herself to be a housewife, a mother, and an artist, breaking the taboo of the mother-artist in the face of the established systems of the commercial art world', a crucial relation gets obscured.[17] The four photographs (reproduced in Liss's book) show Ukeles cleaning a shower curtain, rinsing a diaper, mopping the floor and cooking (cleaning a chicken leg). Taken by her husband, the photographs implicitly comment on the risks entailed in this division of labour between represented and representing subjects. The maternal 'activities' turn out to be unwaged domestic labour. What appears as a 'taboo' is an incompatibility between artistic and maternal labour as shaped in the late twentieth century in advanced economies. Both forms of labour demand, in reality, all of one's time, unless part of this labour time is delegated to someone else.

This is clearly demonstrated in Ukeles's *Some Kinds of Maintenance Cancel Out Others, Keep Your Head Together – 1,000 Times or Baby-Sitter Hangup – Incantation Ritual* (1974), which consisted in the artist leaving her children with a babysitter in New York so she could perform, literally and metaphorically, as an artist at the Institute of Contemporary Art in Boston. Liss's discussion focuses on the morals of the story – that maternal absence for the purpose of work outside the home should be socially acceptable – but does *not* comment on how the absence of the mother-worker from her designated site of labour is compensated for, since another (most often female) worker must be hired to do the maternal 'affective' work. Far from merely 'performing the pain and indecision…created for her, and for countless feminist mothers-artists then and now', Ukeles showed, possibly without intending to, that mobility, emerging as a feature of artistic labour already in the 1970s (as Rosler's *In the Place of the Public* makes clear), clashed with homebound maternal/domestic labour.[18] This parenthetical remark on maternal labour in the mid-1970s was in 2009 presented as the key problem facing the US workforce, of which women (working for wages outside the home) were to constitute over 50 per cent in 2010.[19] In a wealthy nation such as the USA a whole army of underpaid and often immigrant female labourers have replaced middle-class mothers as primary 'carers'. Obscuring this clash of two different labour times behind ethical dilemmas addressed exclusively to women ultimately helps keep hidden from view how the organisation of labour in contemporary capitalism relies and reproduces not only male/female hierarchies but also antagonisms and competition among women.

Although my analysis only parenthetically addresses women artists and the domestic, it is worth noting that the turn to collaborative production and Hardt and Negri's theoretical promotion of the 'commons' (as the outcome of cooperative production that must be reclaimed from capital) has boosted a new interest in domestic labour among feminist theorists, women artists and cultural practitioners at large. *User's Manual: The Grand Domestic Revolution* in the Netherlands (2009–11), an interdisciplinary art project led by the collective Casco, focused on how the feminist critique of domestic labour could lead to 'forms of living that subvert capitalist organization of society'. The project sought to resituate women's work at home in a broader investigation concerning 'the notions of the social, the public and, eventually, the commons'.[20] Beginning from the old feminist goal of breaking women's isolation at home, the research connected nineteenth-century feminist design of communal domestic labour spaces with the possibility of cooperative production set against the privatisation of both space and labour (the commons). Summarily, we witness here an attempt to relocate the private in the public (or, better, the desired commons) in ways that betray the rise of grass-roots activism in the domain of art and the diminished expectations of citizens from a centrally organised democratic state – a thread that is picked up more consistently in the last chapter of this study.

Yet women's labour outside the home was originally, in the early 1970s, on the feminist art agenda. There was a particular interest in working-class women. In Britain, artists Margaret Harrison, Kay Hunt and Mary Kelly put together in South London the exhibition *Women's Work: A Document of Women's Labour in Industry* (1975) while Kelly, a member of the Berwick Street Film Collective, produced the film *Nightcleaners* (1975, 90 mins). *Women's Work* became possible because of governmental funding 'for projects that would be of benefit to lower-paid sections of the Greater London Community' as a reminder of how the realisation of feminist interventionist practice has not been wholly autonomous but was facilitated, or conversely hindered, by state ideology.[21] Largely neglected by feminist and art historical scholarship, *Women's Work* can now be considered a precursor of art's current methodologies (documentation and intensive research) and concerns (the economic subject), recently adopted *en masse* by artists and curators keen to understand the social ramifications of globalisation.

One pioneering aspect of *Women's Work*, as an exhibit curated by artists and based on two years' collaborative research, was that the curatorial-artistic act was directed at the presentation of a social document rather than representational 'art'. The research carried out by the three artists-curators produced a record of women workers' specific conditions, one of the empirical findings being that 'the division of labour at the point of production' had everything to do with 'the division of labour in the home', as interviews with employees made clear.[22] *Nightcleaners* focused, as the title suggests, on the conditions of a particularly underprivileged feminised profession.[23] There was a direct link between choosing this particular profession as the film's focus and 'a key campaign for the WLM [Women's Liberation Movement]' where one witnessed 'the night cleaners' struggle for union recognition in an occupation that epitomized women's exploitation in low paid jobs at its most acute'.[24] It is therefore not entirely true that the current of recent art identified as 'aesthetic journalism' merely filled a gap produced by the withdrawal of funds for old-fashioned *in situ* investigative journalism brought about by the digitisation of information.[25] Materialist feminism in the 1970s had succeeded in transferring its struggles in the art world fringe. Yet the emphasis on the textual construction of female subjectivity favoured by a hegemonic postmodernism gradually but decidedly pushed aside feminism's materialist and class preoccupations. Articulating the connection between the *Manifesto for Maintenance Art, 1969* and *A Document for the Division of Labour in Industry* did not feature among feminist art history and theory's concerns in the 1980s and 1990s despite its revisionist tendencies.

One reason for this was the conspicuous lack of attention by feminist art historians on how artistic labour was formed by a more general transformation of labour. Partly, what the works discussed above suggest is that in the 1970s feminist artists in the West enacted a brief dialogue with the working-class women of their times. Women artists approached the labour of working-class women as an issue worthy of analysis and reclaimed the art exhibition as the site where such an analysis could be inscribed, reaching the public (importantly, the exhibition site for *A Document for the Division of Labour in Industry* was close to the factory were the research was conducted). Feminist art historians paid much more attention to the female model as the 'hidden' working-class subject that had shaped modern art – a choice partly justified by the gradual reluctance of Western feminist artists to focus on the female (or male) labouring subject of their times. A particular interpretation of 'the personal is political' meant that attempts to extend this dialogue on women and work were eventually marginalised, with the personal rarely being relocated within relations of production. Mary Kelly's *Post-partum Document* (1973–79) did *not* become known as a serious attempt to rethink the mother as a labouring subject, whose work is fundamental both to women's unacknowledged exploitation by capitalism and the reproduction of the child as tomorrow's labour power but was seen as an investigation into the complexities of maternal subjectivity or 'inter-subjectivity'.[26] Yet rethinking of *Post-partum Document* as an outcome of a complex form of productivity, requiring two intersecting forms of labour (artistic and maternal/domestic) previously thought of as mutually exclusive, may cast new light on the woman artist's association with domesticity. We see that in the feminist imaginary, domestic work was not utterly incompatible with artistic labour, *as long as artistic labour excluded mobility.*

In their efforts to render visible the terms in which women artists' exclusion from histories of art had been effected, feminist art historians highlighted women artists' restricted, or forbidden, access to the spaces that comprised modernity's intricate and evolving public sphere. In the 1970s women artists continued to be associated with domesticity and grass-roots projects were generated in order to break women artists' isolation and confinement to the home. Indeed, one question was how to recast domestic space into a 'productive' space for the woman artist. Roszika Parker and Griselda Pollock's *Framing Feminism*, a record of the activities of the women's art movement in Britain, offers ample evidence of efforts directed at answering this question imaginatively.[27] The emphasis on the dialectic between 'private' and 'public' in the constitution of gendered subjectivity, and in relation to issues pertaining to women's association with the private rather than the public, remained of paramount importance. Feminist theory and practice in the 1970s, 1980s and even part of the 1990s stressed the political usefulness of grasping space in terms of 'private' or 'public'. Women – artists included – were very much associated with the first term: the private, as in 'the garden', 'the kitchen', 'the bedroom' – words-spaces that were drawn into political speech. From Rosler's theatrical, rebellious housewife in *Semiotics of the Kitchen* to Kelly's nappies in *Post-partum Document* and even to Sanja Iveković's *Triangle* (1979), where the Eastern European woman artist establishes her concrete-walled balcony as a space of freedom (bodily and sexual freedom since Iveković opted to mastur-bate) from an oppressive state, the private was the privileged signifier of an earlier, foundational feminist moment in contemporary art. But as women artists and historians were working in this direction, global capital started prioritising mobile labour. When it came to art, mobile labour reconfigured global space, and not just urban space, as a new public sphere.

Mobility

In contemporary production, as understood by global capital, mobility and work are intertwined. Mobile labour normally describes an organisation of labour where people are expected to travel in order to find work. But mobility structures contemporary labour in other ways too. Mobility can be embedded in the labour process as such. As Hardt and Negri have argued, in capital's global empire 'jobs for the most part are highly mobile and involve flexible skills... They are characterized in general by the central role played by knowl-edge, information, affect and communication.'[28] This pretty much describes the work done by artists today, meaning that art comprises all the attributes of a presently hegemonic form of labour. What the artist shares with economic immigrants is that mobility structures their productivity. 'Movement' is the very condition of global capital and of the subjectivities it shapes through the organisation of labour. That labour plays a key role in the production of subjectivity can be adequately demonstrated by looking at women as a pro-ductive group, as defined especially after the Second World War: the combined burdens of unwaged domestic/maternal labour *and* waged labour has meant that most women's existence has been structured by work throughout the day. In contemporary articulations of capital as social relation, women's movement plays a structural role. As summarised by Sandro Mezzadra, the ' "feminiza-tion" of labor coexists with a more substantial (and hard to refute) feminiza-tion of global migration. Women are on the move as never before in history, this is a sentence that you can read as commonsense in many works on migra-tion.'[29] Yet Mezzadra has also contributed to developing the concept of the 'autonomy of migration':

> What we mean when talking about the autonomy of migration is precisely that it is impossible to understand migratory movements reducing them to the 'laws' of labor demand and supply which should govern the 'international division of

labor', that migratory movements are crisscrossed by a set of subjective behaviors, claims, desires, affects, imaginations structurally *exceeding* the 'objective' and structural causes which are of course very important in determining them. It is this moment of *excess* which is politically strategic, since in regulating and disciplining it new technologies of domination and new modalities of exploitation are forged, while only in valorizing it a politics of the multitude can reinvent the concepts of liberty and equality.[30] [emphasis in the text]

How interesting that the autonomy of migration is negotiated when the autonomy of art is yet again questioned (the concept of 'empire' implies the full assimilation of space into capitalist relations of production) – or at least redefined in terms, precisely, of an excess of sociality that eludes capture by the capitalist art establishment. And what is more, the 'autonomy of migration' has prompted a rethinking of the Deleuzean distinction between migration and nomadism. Tsianos and Papadopoulos have argued that it is no longer possible to sustain such a distinction between nomadic and migratory subjects, in essence reasserting mobility as that which 'generate[s] a persistent and insatiable surplus of sociality in motion'.[31] This is important because the nomad (as in the nomadic or 'itinerant' artist) has featured strongly in critiques of the contemporary art-world structures. To offer the glaring example, biennials and other institutional sites have been attacked on the grounds of issuing invitations to an artist from elsewhere to produce work about, and in, a social context about which he/she knows nothing. In this sense, the biennial and formal museum circuit, where such practices are endemic, have clearly engendered an appropriation of travel as work within a formal economy, that is, the art economy. They have also been incredibly active in ushering cultural producers within the regime of a traditional cosmopolitanism, in providing a subsidised, privileged art-world citizenship open to artists, curators, dealers and, not least, theorists. (This cosmopolitanism is not gender-free: female curators, for instance, do travel with their young children, when neither the children's travel nor childcare is subsidised by the institutions inviting their mothers, making the mother-cultural worker more 'expensive'.)[32] Such developments in the art world do not exist in isolation. Instead, they form part of a generalised organisation and co-articulation of work and life. Migration accounts for a great deal of travelling and border crossing, but what the art economy, alongside tourism, activism and even 'terrorism' suggests, is that today we are confronted with the autonomy of mobility rather than the autonomy of migration. Mobility and circulation may take the currently hegemonic form of migration or they may not.

Rather than attending to mobility, feminism in the arts has so far primarily approached movement in connection with (gendered) postcolonial subjects or through a broader investigation into the gendered diasporic experience.

The border has emerged as a powerful figure in these discourses, one associated with a politics of identity. Irit Rogoff's analysis of Ana Mendieta's earth sculptures in relation to their claims on earth–space reveals the long-standing presence of the 'border' in a mode of thinking and acting that connects the feminine to the world.[33] Yet Mendieta consistently presented herself as inhabiting the trauma of exile and a life permeated with loss (despite the favourable, by comparison, conditions of her relocation to the USA). Undeniably, globalisation, as the stage of permanent war and the scene of myriad of crimes against human rights, provides plenty of opportunities to reflect on woman as the exilic subject. It also provides opportunities for a reflection on the contextual meaning of intersectionality. Much like multiculturalism in the public sphere, intersectionality (as a concept that describes the co-articulation of multiple identifications in the production and transformative potential of a subject and an individual's position in interwoven practices of interpellation) does not reveal how such identifications may *not* coexist in equal terms. Let me speak through an example.

Emily Jacir is a woman artist, described either as 'American' (MOMA website) or 'a Palestinian' artist (Facebook and Wikipedia). She is one of the most prominent and institutionally rewarded artists of our times: born in 1970, she received the Golden Lion award of the Venice Biennale in 2007 and Guggenheim's Hugo Boss Prize in 2008. Jacir's work, often relying on travel, addresses systematically the tragic fate and continuous struggle of the Palestinian people and the condition of exile that structures the lives of the Palestinian diaspora. Her photographic and textual installation *Where We Come from* (2001–3) in the collection of SF MOMA is merely a document of an artwork that actually took place outside the institution of art over the span of two years. The artwork was realised through extensive travelling and its realisation depended on the artist's right to travel as a holder of a US passport. The artwork began when Jacir asked exiled Palestinians: 'If I could do anything for you in Palestine, what would it be?' She comprised a wish list that included: 'Bring me a photo of my family, especially my brother's kids', 'Go to Haifa and play soccer with the first Palestinian boy you see on the street' and so on. We can assume that these journeys, as an integral part of the project, carried some risk. In 2004, Jacir issued a statement explaining the termination of the project:

> It is now May 2004 and the situation has worsened. I can no longer move freely through the borders with my American passport. I cannot make the project 'Where We Come From' today. I am no longer allowed to enter Gaza, and certain Palestinian towns in the West Bank. Israel is relentlessly moving forward in the construction of the Apartheid Wall which began in the spring of 2002. Palestinians with foreign passports are increasingly being denied entry into the country by Israel at all border crossings and are being forced to

immigrate. Israel has decided that 'freedom of movement' is no longer a right for American passport holders and has created measures to ensure this.[34]

According to the above statement, the risks and, from a point on, impossibility of the journey had little to do with Jacir being a woman. They had everything to do with her self-identifying, and being identified by others, as Palestinian and the geopolitical dynamics currently limiting the movements of anyone carrying this identity, irrespective of formal documents (through which Jacir is identified as American). Jacir has at least implicitly prioritised her ethnic (Palestinian) over her gender identity in her intersectional constitution as a contemporary exilic subject. The narrative and material reality of oppression she chooses to identify with emanate from the historical constitution of her ethnicity in terms of a collective identity. The installation *Where We Come from* avoids references to gender either with respect to Palestinian society and diaspora or the journeys undertaken by the artist. If anything, carrying out the wish 'play soccer with the first Palestinian boy in the street' and the photograph that documents its realisation allude both to the street as a gendered public space in the Palestinian territories as well as to the right of the freely moving woman artist to temporarily transcend this gender boundary within the process of producing the work. It is not therefore that *Where We Come from* actively conceals gender relations in the society it takes as its focus but that global geopolitics have directed this woman artist's historically shaped consciousness away from narratives of intersectionality. They have significantly limited her remit of 'identifications' – a term that Amelia Jones uses to think a contemporary subject no longer comfortable in being described through the rigidity of identity.[35]

Global capital is connected with forms of gendered mobility in complex ways. What attendance to mobility, rather than migration, implies is that the primacy of the diasporic in the emergent subjectivities associated with movement across the empire of capital is challenged – since diaspora is connected with taking residence elsewhere, with planting the seed (of the nation, one assumes) in other lands. The permanent displacement of the subject that the term 'diaspora' promises is but one among the many realisations of movement in capital's empire, tied to the will to travel that globalisation has brought forth. The question posed here is if, and how, this will to travel finds also an expression in gendered artistic labour. Or, conversely, is it that women artists' appropriation of travel as work constitutes a contemporary form of refusal – what globalisation theory has called 'diritto di fuga', the same 'right to escape' that animates migration? This is hardly a rhetorical question, given that the political economy of travelling in the art world has been associated with global capital's expression as culture. To address these questions, I now turn to specific examples where women artists deploy travelling as their core work method. The artWork discussed in this chapter highlights the relational aspirations of the journey as much as it directs attention to the journey's gendered specificity.

Beyond the global flâneuse? En(gendering) the journey as collaborative production

The value of female teamwork when it comes to travel as a work method is also asserted in Lin+Lam's project *Departure* (2004–6). Lin+Lam is a moniker assumed by collaborating artists H. Lan Thao Lam and Lana Lin, both of Asian background but resident in New York City. Having worked together for well over a decade, they embarked on *Departure* as a labour-intensive project that involved them personally and politically. Politically, in the sense that *Departure* would be about the transformation of Asian urban space as postcolonial realities fade into the world of global capital; personally, because the artists are displaced subjects where Asian geographies are concerned. Both Lam and Lin found themselves in North America when their families migrated from Asia in the 1960s and 1980s – Lam's family escaped Vietnam when she was 12 years old while Lin is of Taiwanese descent.[36] *Departure* was the first collaboration between the two artists for which they had to travel extensively to Asia, where they had not been since their childhood (Lin was born in Canada and had not visited Asia until her teenage years.). This can perhaps help explain the evocative title given to the video essay: departure – alluding both

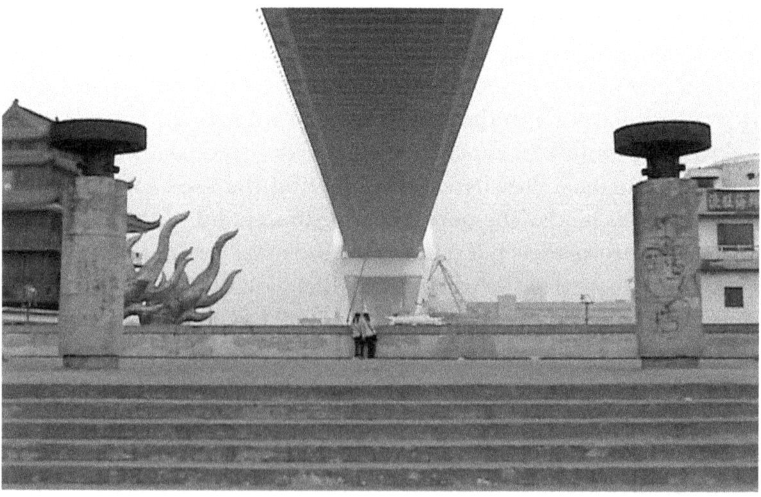

3.1   Lin+Lam, *Departure* (2004–6). 48′, single-channel video and three-channel video installation. Still.

to the language habitually framing contemporary travel (mostly air travel) where distance is typically compressed and the act of leaving behind (in this case, a land of assumed 'origin').

In the 48-minute video essay, five women narrate in their languages (Mandarin Chinese, Taiwanese, English, Shanghainese and Vietnamese) tales of the modernisation process of three Asian cities, Taipei, Shanghai and Hanoi. Once defined through their colonial relations to Europe, these cities are now recalibrating their positions in a global economy. Beyond the narrative voices (as detached as a voice-over), human presence is far from prominent. What is prominent is movement and 'activity' performed mostly by various types of machines – transportation machines, cranes, moveable bridges, even the camera. The contrast between the inclination to constant movement – horizontally because of means of transport, vertically because of construction – and the desire to stay still (permeating the narrative voices) is a defining feature of *Departure*: departure is in fact a slice of time where the inertia keeping one in place fails to stop one's body being propelled forward. And movement does not necessarily entail liberation for the women who offer bits and pieces of their (gendered) experience of modernisation as partly an effect of colonialism. The female narrators do not always, or necessarily, place modernisation in gendered terms – although they were chosen, by the two women artists, specifically because they are women. There was at least an implicit expectation that even without inhabiting a specifically female consciousness, the female narrators would provide a composite, 'stitched', yet situated and experiential account.

The video essay does in fact open with an image of two young women seen from afar. They are literally 'set' in an impressive urban landscape, much like they would appear as diminutive figures in an architectural maquette. The young women move across a space defined – or better, contained – by perspective, continually being observed (by the camera/the artists) from a distance. What must in reality be a horizontal bridge appears as a phallic vertical mass dominating and dwarfing everything else. Stretching to the sky, the bridge appears pathetically stiff and immobile, unlike the two young women's energetic movement on the ground. Later on we are told about a woman who never crossed the massive bridge having been built for years across from her house. She becomes the stuff of legend as her refusal to move blends into imagined opposition to capital's global imperative. And yet, as the artists admit, the Asian societies they visited were 'demystified' – to their disappointment – as paradigmatically patriarchal. The postcolonial Asian cities, vital economies in globalisation threatening to shift the development axis eastwards in the early twenty-first century, are condensed into images captured by a hand-held camera – always 'held' by someone using a means of transport: a moving car, a 'cyclo', trains. The journey itself is a survey mechanism of classed urbanscapes, the poor and the affluent ones. The five stories narrated never criss-cross each other, never connect, never become politically relevant in an explicit way. Shot well before 2008 and the global economic crisis, the video essay closes with yet another 'construction & development' scene, full of light and noise.

It is not hard to see how *Departure* may be seen to constitute an investigation into the economic, political and psychic contexts that, via a displacement, led to Lin's and Lam's unstable identification with the contemporary American 'woman artist'. The opening image of the two young women on the move, defiant of the phallic bridge (which, nevertheless, signifies engineering and progress in late nineteenth-century terms) points strongly to the artists' partnership as a necessary condition for realising the durational work, much of it consisting in learning to inhabit the very conditions visualised in, and by, the video essay. The two young women filmed symbolically articulate the two women artists' vital cooperation, emotional togetherness and the sharing of responsibility with regard to how they are positioned in territories defying a sense of the familiar and the unfamiliar alike – territories where they felt 'culturally disoriented' and occasionally limited by their knowledge of language. The experience of travelling *as women* unavoidably informs *Departure* – but as a more temporary, or even transient, identification rather than an inalienable right to an identity from which to organise experience securely.[37] Lin+Lam's intimation of the road movie formula is perhaps slightly ironic. Here, the woman artist's refusal to be contained to/by the domestic is scripted not as a return to lost homelands but as a visual fetishisation of the materiality of global 'development': bulldozers, construction sites and motorways populate the video, sure signs of finance capital's material remaking the world and, not least, of masculinity at work. The five female voices commenting on the modernisation of Asian urban space are counterpoised to the masculine principle organising this space, demonstrating its already gendered process of transformation. That Lam and Lin could 'pass' (for local/Asian women) because of their physical appearance put them in a difficult position: they were often told that they 'should know' how to behave as local, non-Western women and what to make of their surroundings. *Departure* thus ended up as the record of an unlearning: of letting go of the myth of belonging 'somewhere', of discovering places of irreducible difference (rather than cultural disorientation and the predictability of capitalist ventures). The visual marginalisation of the human figure in the video essay was a choice very much connected with such an unlearning and with the artists' ambivalence towards the possibility and need for an art paradigm tied to representation.

The mobility sustaining such projects is hardly reducible to vague 'flows' of disembodied subjects, so strongly associated with postmodernism. The exodus of women artists from the domestic does not (necessarily) begin in loss but connects them to a space of global friction, one of acute and conflicting materialities. At the same time, this dis-identification with the domestic does not occur within an art or social movement and neither is it protected by something akin to a collective consciousness, which suggests that it does not operate strategically within a feminist politics – unless of course we accept a perversion of 'the personal is political' as 'the political is personal'. Yet such journeys further challenge the centrality of a global flâneuse, a solitary creature celebrating a new-found freedom and loosely surveying a territory with her meaning-making gaze. Whereas the global flâneuse, often associated in the 1990s with a digital existence and cyberspace, believed in connectivity, the women artists for whom the ground of global space becomes a terrain of labour expect disconnectedness. Travelling here is performative, a form of bridging spaces that the empire of capital has every interest in keeping apart outside the tourist industry or economies of conflict (often organised around 'resources'). In some cases, such bridging requires concerted action, collaborative research and establishes models of shared learning.

Generating a number of projects, *Transcultural Geographies* (2003–4) was the umbrella title given to a collaborative research programme, initiated by Ursula Biemann, Angela Melitopoulos and Lisa Parks, three women whose complex forms of cultural production cross through, and engage art, while disrupting any notions of the latter as a singular, safely isolated apparatus of aesthetic concerns. Developed through 'work sessions' and studies realised and distributed across multiple sites, *Transcultural Geographies* constitutes an exemplary case study with regard to the new links between art and interdisciplinary knowledge production in the twenty-first century. *Transcultural Geographies* comprised three core projects, *The Black Sea Files* by Biemann, *Timescapes/Corridor X* by Melitopoulos and *Postwar Footprints* by Parks, and

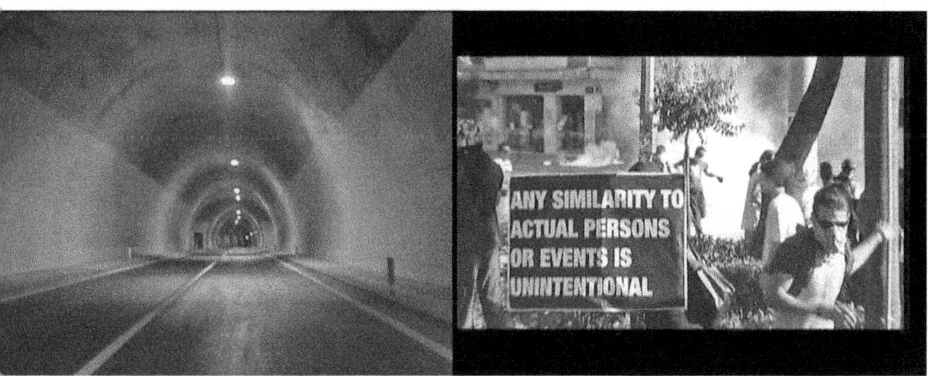

3.2 Angela Melitopoulos, *CORRIDOR X* (2006), DVD (still), double projection, colour, sound, ca. 130′.

three work sessions, in Amsterdam (2003), Istanbul (2003) and Ljubljana (2004). *Transcultural Geographies* is documented in detail on the project website, where one can read both analyses of each work session, study and artwork and observe visual material, while the general description of the project reads as follows:

> Transcultural Geographies is an art and visual research project focusing on the transitory geographies of the Balkans, Turkey and the Caucasus. Immersing ourselves in sites stringing along the Southern axes that join Europe and the East, we examine dynamics of their economic and social transformation through a number of large-scale infrastructures and transcultural campaigns. In three distinct but interrelated research projects, we explore topographies that are increasingly marked by the transitions occurring in the post-socialist/post-Cold War period and we individually and collectively work to generate new audiovisual representations, geographic mappings and critical imaginings of the region.[38]

In the documentary material of the work sessions it becomes clear that most participants were women. Indeed, the first work session at the University of Amsterdam is documented visually through snapshots that present an informal gathering of women in a classroom or having a meal. And yet *Transcultural Geographies* is not defined by its initiators, all of whom have produced work on gender and/or feminist politics, as a feminist project. Nor does the description of the project cited above claims any connections to feminism. This hardly means that the analyses, mappings and imaginings, as the intended project outcomes, did not critically engage gender relations. Given the project initiators' involvement with gender politics and the overwhelming presence of women collaborators (including, for instance, feminist philosopher Rosi Braidotti), the choice to not flag up feminism in this particular project may strike one as bizarre. I might as well add that none of the projects discussed further on seeks to achieve an unequivocally feminist intervention, although all address gender relations through specific social contexts and themes – social contexts and themes approached through the (woman) artist's journey. This suggests perhaps that the transition from the domestic to the global remains the untouched issue in feminist thinking involving the historical category of the 'woman artist' – not least the feminist thinking that the artists themselves might be expected to bring forth. On the other hand, and as concerns the specific project, there seems to be a deliberate and tactical suppression of a narrative that would highlight the gender of the researchers/artists/collaborators. What such a tactical suppression presumably achieves is placing the operation of women in the critical surveying of a global terrain as a *fait accompli*, an irreversible, accomplished claim, and *right*, to this space. A critical feminist view of this space must be embedded in any broad surveying of the latter since, according to Biemann, theorisations of globalisation that do not reflect on gender relations produce by default a distorting perspective of their object of analysis.[39]

Indeed, globalisation is the object of analysis in *Transcultural Geographies* and it is interesting to see how the journey is inscribed as a critical tool therein. The work sessions did not just provide opportunities for discussion among the group members and with invited guests. That was also where Biemann, Melitopoulos and Parks screened footage collected through their *in situ* research in between the workshops. The work sessions were therefore a dialogical space for the planning of activities (often further trips), a collective evaluation and cross-reference of a vast amount of data that would then be disseminated through the project outputs, ranging from art to publications to further sites of dialogical exchange. But the work sessions also provided the space for critique *and* encouragement, sustaining this labour-intensive project emotionally and intellectually. In constituting a mechanism of support and an environment of reflective affirmation, the work sessions had to be realised materially, depending on the artists/researchers' willingness and ability to realise further trips. These were not always risk-free, but risk was actively incorporated in the work process. And so, the Istanbul work session took place 'one week after the bombing of the British Consulate in Istanbul and additional bomb attacks on the British HSBC bank in Istanbul on November 20th 2003. Despite doubts and many mails sent the days after the attack and despite the travel warnings issued by European Embassies, the group decided to hold the meeting and to productively integrate the strained political situation into their discourse.'[40]

This brief presentation of some of the work sessions' elements makes it obvious that the mappings and imaginings of *Transcultural Geographies* were not intended to be from above (imposed by a superior external power); but neither could it have been from below (emanating from 'authentic' internally obtained experience). This was a particularly sensitive aspect of the project, given that the artists/researchers had no direct connection to the geographies they undertook to study: Biemann is Swiss, Parks is American and only in the case of Melitopoulos, a German citizen of Greek ancestry originating in Asia Minor (Turkey), a connection could be claimed in terms of (ethnic) identity. The instability of this identity has been very much an outcome of the historical co-articulation of labour, displacement and mid-twentieth century fascism, as Melitopoulos's father ended up in central Europe from northern Greece after serving as a forced labourer under the Nazis in Austria and Germany during the Second World War.[41] But if these mappings and imaginings were neither from above nor from below, where were they placed? In other words, did these women's critical practice create a dynamic that displaced, or at least worked through, the above/below binary? Even as no ready-made answer exists, I want to argue that the journey, as a work method of undiminished

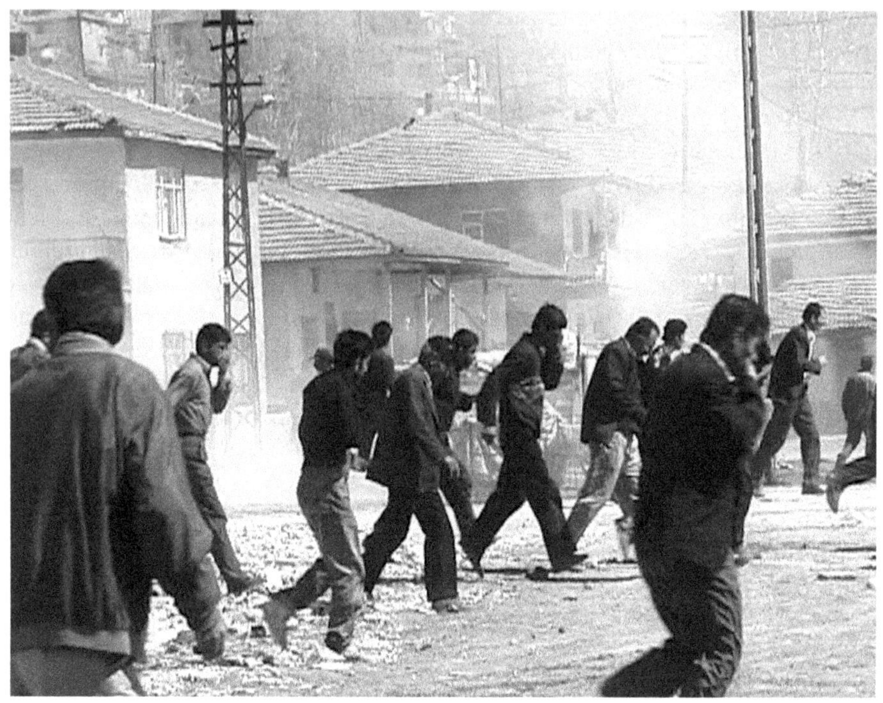

3.3   Ursula Biemann, *The Black Sea Files* (2005). Synchronised video essay. 43′. Still.

materiality played a crucial role in achieving such a dynamic. Although a detailed presentation of the numerous ways that the journey entered the project is not possible here, I would like to consider specific aspects of Biemann's *Black Sea Files* and Melitopoulos's *Timescapes/Corridor X* as the sub-projects of *Transcultural Geographies* that constituted the project's artistic output.

As described by Melitopoulos, *Timescapes/Corridor X* (2003–4) was conceptualised as intensely collaborative – indeed, it seems to introduce a new medium/practice: 'collective video editing'.[42] In this case, the artist did not traverse herself all the geographies that provided the project's focus but instead sought to mediate the multiple sites of the work's production. As explained on the project website:

'Timescapes/Corridor X' was to be 'a collective video-database built by five video artists/activists from Cologne (Angela Melitopoulos), Berlin (Hito Steyerl), Belgrade (Dragana Zarevac), Athens (Freddy Viannelis) and Ankara (Videa: media collective) who shaped different subject matters on the theme of mobility and migration in so-called 'B-Zone territories' in South-East

Europe and Turkey after 1991. The authors apply the term 'B-Zone' for a still fictitious yet emerging state of the EC. This particular transnational post-war territory is perceived as a field of political experimentation. New structures of political domination arise through the building of infrastructure. Natural resources are exploited against local economic interests. The B-Zone's geopolitical uncertainty is a preliminary condition for the investment of so called 'Pan-European' projects focusing on infrastructure and industrial projects realized by international corporations.

As I wrote these lines in mid-2012, the above excerpt appeared to be prophetic (for example, that Greece became the IMF's ground of experimentation in a Europe of 'contagion' and the division of A and B lists in the EU now sounds commonplace). The insight encountered here is not atypical of artistic projects incorporating interdisciplinary research and fast and imaginative exchange of information and ideas. The choice of shared artistic authorship implicitly suggests that mapping this terrain could only be realised collectively and Melitopoulos is a participant/author but primarily an initiator and facilitator of communication among all participant artists/contributors to the video database.

In *Black Sea Files* (2005), Biemann, aided by translators, travels herself to 'the energy geography which connects the landlocked Caspian fossil resources to the world sea system through a giant oil pipeline presently under construction'. She begins in Baku of Ajerbaijan and ends up in Ceyhan, on the coast of South-eastern Turkey. But although the declared aim of the journey is the assemblage of an archive outlining interlocked transformations of ways of life (a biopolitical subjection of land and life to the advance of corporate interests), Biemann's reflections on the nature of her artistic labour incorporated in the video set up a parallel narrative. First, the risks of her work method (the journey) entail instances where her moral integrity is challenged. Biemann lies. She tries to convince two Russian prostitutes – their pimps present and curiously assisting Biemann – to talk to her about their own journeys and what has brought them where they are, at the site of their labour. Biemann responds to the prostitutes' suspicions by saying she is a tourist making a 'home movie'. Her gender makes her believable: what she does is to remain private, diaristic, inconsequential, outside the market and therefore dissemination. Second, the facility with which the artist is identified as a 'she' exists in stark contrast with her crossing of acutely gendered work sites: brothels where women work disciplined by their male pimp, male homosocial oilfields and clandestine construction sites where cheap male workers are imported to slave away. The female voice-over's question, 'what is *she* doing here?' is scripted over a male-dominated scene of an uprising near Ankara – where furious men burn up a garbage site in protest against their condition of unemployment. I have already discussed elsewhere some of the implications of the female voice-over's question whether knowledge produced 'this way' is 'better' than that gained in libraries.[43] Here, I am more interested in that all explicit questions about the nature of artistic labour are deliberately placed in proximity to the world of work, or else of waged labour. They are posed over footage of crisis, of disintegration and collective disidentification, of capital's need for armies of unemployed laid bare. The woman artist's question, to sum it up, accompanies the visual evidence of working-class men going mad at the loss of access to waged labour.

Transcultural Geographies constituted an exemplary site of experimentation for the tactical operation of women artists in the global socio-economic terrain, now providing the site of their labour. Arguably, the concept and form of the 'project', as a fundamental element in the organisation of labour in early twenty-first century capitalism that accords immaterial labour its hegemonic place, is where these journeys are situated. Yet in this case the project became appropriated in a context/work methodology that stressed the materiality of the 'real' theatre of operations of capitalist relations, either by delegating authorship to attend to the specificity of site (Melitopoulos) or by ensuring that authorship is grounded in direct contact with the specificity of the site (Biemann). Experimenting with diverse tactics of subversion, juxtaposing and reading through them was one aim of *Transcultural Geographies*, which posits this dialectic between intersecting methodologies as an alternative to the above/below binary. Crucially, we see here that the lack of an identity-based connection to the route does not amount to a frivolous crossing (the right to speak for others). As a narrative against capital's global imperative, *Transcultural Geographies* has clearly learnt from capital's emphasis on planning, networking and making use of local knowledge. Experimenting with such diverse tactics of subversion depended heavily on the collaboration, exchange of ideas and emotional support among the female artists/researchers. The images of the women's smiling faces and camaraderie of the launching Amsterdam all-female work session, flagged up in the project's public document distributed globally through the Internet, linger on. And yet these images, as a symbolic enactment moment of a female team's journeys (a moment of freedom, of refusal to occupy the domestic and of assessing the risks), are hardly representative of women's social existence today.

Translocal

Jenny Marketou belongs to a growing group of artists, and more generally cultural workers, who are typically described as 'living in between': in this case, between New York, where she came to study in the 1980s, and Athens, where she was born and raised. Mostly known as a new media artist with an

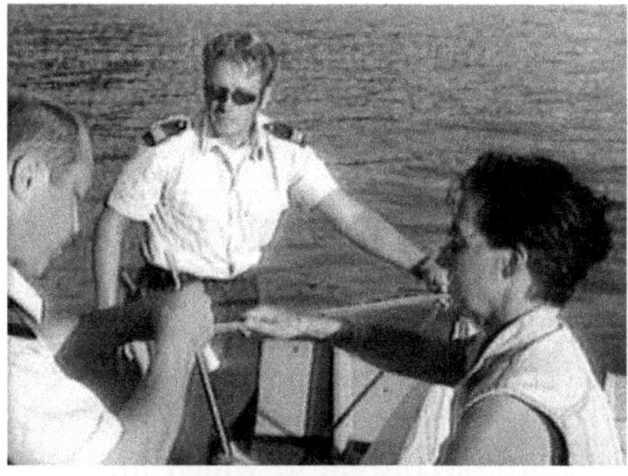

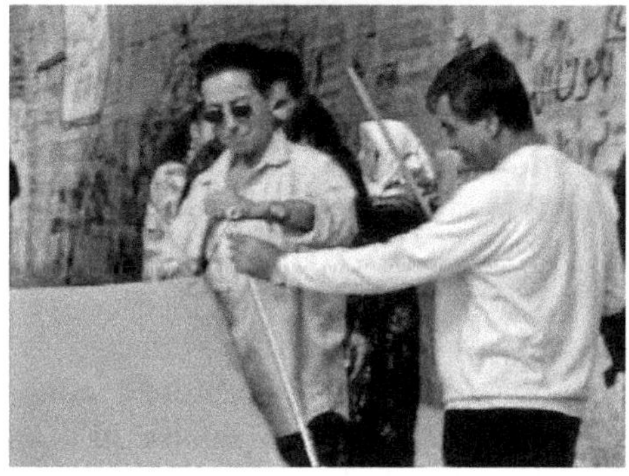

3.4–3.5   Jenny Marketou, *Translocal* (1996–2001). Detail of project. 3.4 (top): Setting up the tent on the Police Boat, Rotterdam, 1996. 3.5 (bottom): Setting up the tent in Ramallah, 1997.

emphasis on digital technology, Marketou has also integrated travel in her work since the early 1990s. *Translocal*, which Marketou realised between 1996 and 2001, was an acknowledgement and exacerbation of this condition, making it too visible as the ground of a contemporary subjectivity. Indeed, *Translocal* was one of the first works to ask how gender becomes relevant to the social articulation of Miwon Kwon's 'itinerant artist', a professional identity made possible through 'an intensive physical mobilization of the artist to create works in various cities throughout the cosmopolitan art world'.[44]

Translocal: Camp in My Tent, as the full title goes, has been described as a 'migratory' project[45] – a performative artwork that both migrated from one place to the next and invited reflection on migration (beginning to be identified as a major issue in the mid-1990s). *Translocal* took the form of a public exercise to be realised at the end of journeys and across locales, most of which became meaningfully connected with one another primarily through the artwork as such. Public action as the outcome of each arrival involved the artist pitching a tent in a public location – parks, squares, border zones, streets – where she would set home for a few days. Marketou would not obtain the formal permission of the authorities. She would be accompanied by a camera-woman (and not a cameraman). And her itinerary – seemingly random or at least inscrutable – would be shaped (and therefore funded) by those cultural institutions that invited her to 'create work' locally, thus actively producing her as an itinerant (woman) artist: Rotterdam (Holland), Mexico City (Mexico), Jerusalem (Israel), Ramallah (Palestinian territories), New London, Connecticut (USA), Düsseldorf (Germany), Snag Harbor, Staten Island, New York (USA), Nicosia (Cyprus), Tijuana (Mexico), Bialystok (Poland) – the exception being her inaugural action, or beginning of the journey, or *prova generale*, in New York where she lived. In many respects, the project parodied a familiar, adventurous tourist ethos, according to which first-hand experience is the optimal way to 'get to know the world' – in quite a different way, that is, from just reading about it in books or watching documentaries on TV – in which case you accept knowledge as the representation of distance.

Yet *Translocal* was not solely an investigation into how a travelling body mediates geographies as subject to multiple processes of appropriation (she never found a 'free spot'). Besides the project's anthropological imperative enabling a comparative approach to public space, *Translocal* interrogated also into the assumed gap separating the 'protected' institutional site and 'the square'. Where possible, the tent positioned outside (the one where the artist would spend her days) had its double in a second tent installed inside, in the material space of the cultural institution the artist would happen to collaborate with. In this second tent, museum visitors were invited to spend their time as they pleased, yet safely, while observing on monitors the artist's occupation of public space. Marketou placed the second (museum) tent emphatically within the logic of leisure travel, producing flyers that advertised the possibility of individual visitors or groups camping in the museum tent and disseminated these flyers across tourist hotspots. The flyers would also get distributed to travel agencies, competing with their other offers.

As Marketou was symbolically initiating *Translocal* in New York's Central Park, following an invitation to participate in Manifesta 1 in Rotterdam in 1996 (the first in the series of roving European biennials), Hal Foster was writing about 'the artist as ethnographer', critiquing how art in the late twentieth century had replaced modernity's artist as producer with the artist as an observer of cultural difference, the artist, that is, whose work method replicates an ethnographic paradigm.[46] Foster's essay does not provide a gendered reading of the ethnographic method, operating perhaps on the assumptions that, first, both male and female artists are equally able and willing to work as ethnographers and, second, that the public spaces male and female artists set out to observe are available to them in the same way. In describing the project as a series of public interventions, rather than inscribing each trip into a singular narrative, Marketou, nevertheless, notes that 'the events which took place' in each trip made her aware of the translocal 'importance of a gendered public space':[47] although she did not set out to test the local manifestations of a globally constituted gendered public space, gender became a binding element of these multiple arrivals in the consciousness of the artist.

In New York, the woman artist and her companion/camera-woman set up their tent in Central Park, but were soon asked to go. Public space was to be crossed, not inhabited, they were told by the police who regarded the pair with curiosity: their place in Central Park lacked evident purpose, therefore meaning, but at least they *were* women and so unlikely to prove violent or cause trouble. One aim of the project was to explore what the 'freedom of access' commonly associated with public space meant in each of the locations visited, and consequently what defined possibly diverse (yet interconnected) processes of material, bureaucratic or ideological enclosure. In Rotterdam's Red Light district, Marketou's exchange with the police was quite different. In that urban space the act of setting up the tent suggested to local pimps and migrant prostitutes from less advanced economies that an 'independent' had arrived: an 'unprotected' (by a male pimp), 'unauthorised' sex worker and unwelcome competitor. In a neighbourhood where prostitutes mainly from impoverished parts of Africa and Eastern Europe walked the streets, the sight of the tent, where the sex–cash exchange was imagined to take place, signified for at least one prostitute, an unbearable sight of privileged 'comfort', as quoted by the artist, denied her.[48] Marketou and her camera-woman were attacked and the police intervened, offering a helping hand. Rather scandalously, the tent was finally pitched on the police boat in a nearby canal.

What did the Rotterdam police really assert by offering their assistance? In the first instance, the police action suggested that public space in Rotterdam is not entirely defined by prescribed gender roles. Women who do not prostitute themselves have an equal right to those who do to inhabit public space. Yet pitching the tent in police property was a compromise, as the safety of the two women making apparent their presence in a public space dominated by prescribed gender roles could not have been guaranteed. But Marketou did not pitch her tent merely as a woman, or for that matter as a homeless foreigner or asylum seeker. She occupied it *as an artist* in the process of realising an ephemeral public action that was ultimately an artwork and supported by an art institution (Manifesta). Traversing the terrain of social relations by creating a delimited private space (the tent) in the occupation of public space was this artwork's 'work', and the police were informed of that. Not asking for a permit to set up a tent in public space was thus counteracted by Marketou revealing to the authorities, should the circumstances present themselves (and they mostly did), that beyond being a woman or a citizen, she was an artist at work.

Arguably, the revelation that she was an artist sooner or later appeared to carry equal weight to her gender with respect to how her action was perceived. This became apparent in Ramallah, the one place where it was not possible to have a camera-woman. It is worth offering the artist's testimony:

Like in all my travels for *Translocal,* I used my Greek passport to travel to Ramallah from Jerusalem. I would have never dreamt making this trip with my American passport, which was likely to get stamped, as I might not be able to be accepted without problems through Tel Aviv on my return. The Greek passport normally does not get stamped. I travelled from Tel Aviv to Ramallah three times for this project, assisted by Jack Persekian.[49] First, to look for the right location to set up my tent, to understand public space there. Second, to give a lecture at the University in Ramallah, at the art school. I had an opportunity to visit the studios. Seeing many female students, I asked if their work addressed gender issues but my question was answered with a question: 'how can you do anything about gender when every day you wake up in the war?' Conflict was embedded in their lives. Us, as Western women, to go there and suggest to them what they should do would be extremely problematic. In my third visit, I set up my tent in Ramallah Square. In this case the camera person was a man, in fact the CNN guy covering Ramallah, because Jack said that one couldn't know what to expect there, and so we needed someone physically very strong and very familiar with the particular public space, and perhaps such a person couldn't have been a woman. I had noticed myself that women mostly crossed public spaces very fast, they didn't take their time. I also knew that the sight of the tent carried certain connotations in Palestine, where displaced people are forced to live in tents. As I was setting up, I realised that all women were actively trying not to look at me, to cover their sight. After I set up, I ended up stopping two women and inviting them to my tent. They refused to join me. Then a man appeared with a megaphone, started calling 'come, come' in Arabic. A long line of men formed outside the tent, in the belief that I was a prostitute. They knew they couldn't have sex in public, but I was still a sight. I was this foreign woman, in trousers, with short hair, setting up home in public, which apparently also aroused the interest of the press. I welcomed each man to the tent. They were friendly and I soon realised that they needed to talk. With many of them I entered deeper discussions. I had to have a translator present. For these men, a tent meant war, conflict, and yet my tent offered a chance to talk openly about this. Some were fascinated with the fact that I was a Greek woman who lived in New York. Having these two men [the camera man and the translator] with me was important though, I had the feeling that their presence lent credibility to what I was doing. When later I gave talks about this project in the US and mentioned 'I pitched the tent in Palestine', some people would ask me afterwards: 'You are not American, are you? An American wouldn't refer to Palestine in this way.' They meant: *as if* Palestine had independent status, *as if* it were a recognised entity, the same as the other countries I visited in the course of the project.[50]

The artist's description of her experience in Ramallah cites all the factors that more or less determined both the process of realising *Translocal* and the encounters it generated, however diverse and context-specific these were. In each case, carrying the right passport – presenting oneself as a citizen of a peripheral, almost but not quite affluent EU country of a Mediterranean life-style and with little influence on global geopolitics (the profile of Greece up until 2010) was important. In each and every case, institutional support was essential. But underwriting all these factors was Marketou's double identification as a woman and an artist.

Predictably, the artist's citizenship played a different role in realising *Translocal* in Cyprus – which is telling about the contextual co-articulation of all the above. There the choice to pitch a tent at the Greek-Cypriot side of the Green Line, the border dividing the Greek and Turkish parts of the capital, Nicosia, upset many in the local art institution.[51] To appease the agitated spirits in Nicosia, known as the last formally divided capital in Europe, Marketou decided to walk the length of the Green Line (that at the time one could not cross) in acknowledgement of the regional trauma that the Green Line stood as the symbol of. Marketou carried her heavy industrial tent and pitched it at the Green Line's end. Institutional scepticism did not prevent the tent from soon becoming a meeting point. The pervasive, stereotypical association of women with peace, seen as an 'extension' of women's biologically-determined life-giving and affective capacities, was the ideological lining in which Marketou's hospitality became possible even in the volatile geopolitical conditions of South-Eastern Mediterranean. And as Marketou herself recalls, visitors to her tent (both women and men), initially curious about the event of a possibly unlawful occupation, felt more relaxed when they realised that she was not a native but a presumably sympathetic foreigner and that her actions were part of an art project – a realisation which raises troubling questions about the implicit association of art with the realm of non-politics as well as about the unstable role that national identity is found to play in the work of itinerant artists. In the case of *Translocal*, the woman artist's positioning as an unthreatening outsider to relations binding an ethnic, national or even urban community generated forms of tolerance that became important for the project's very realisation.

In its consistent engagement of travel as the *sine qua non* of the artist's labour, *Translocal* gives rise to a number of issues pertaining to art's gendered work in, and on, public space. First, *Translocal* constitutes a salient case for grasping the intersectional articulation of the artist's identity across the series of public sites she temporarily occupies. She is never 'just a woman' but rather her gender underwrites the relations of her externality to the conditions that constitute each public site. And such externality is multiply defined: as an artist vis-à-vis the field of pre-existent, 'real' social relations and as a foreigner vis-à-vis the national body or local community. Second, *Translocal* brings into plain view – through hyperbole, one might say – the intricate connection between artistic labour and the institutions of art. The perceived autonomy of the artist's choices (where to go) is apparently predicated on the global availability of institutional mediation that aids each of the project's situated incarnations and permits only a certain degree of unpredictability as regards their outcomes – and does this institutional anchor also promise greater safety for the woman artist?. The material and ideological conventions of social space that *Translocal* renders visible through the artist's presence acquire meaning within the networked activity that sustains the artwork's duration. From the outset, and as the work's title suggests, the meaning of the local is called up only to be tested against a global imperative encapsulated in the connectivity of 'trans' – a widely used prefix in globalisation narratives in art and theory. The random beginning and end dates of *Translocal* mark, however, precisely the *absence* of an event –other, that is, than the inaugural Manifesta invitation in 1996 and the artist's feeling in 2001 that she had made her point, that she could have carried on testing out one gendered terrain after another as licensed by the art institution, that within the artwork every context would be different and yet the same (endpoint). It would therefore be fair, I think, to situate *Translocal* within a cultural ambivalence towards art's presumed capacity to transform – out of thin air, as it were – either space or subjectivity. This ambivalence corresponds to a consciousness of transience, to the need of bringing forth a defined yet arbitrary 'form' (the artwork) where a singular (the artist's) passage can be, finally, connected to the social and become artWork.

Prostitution after the Velvet Revolution

If women's art today privileges a consciousness directed at the experience of transience, of crossing, of journeys, this becomes more pronounced when art becomes explicitly geared towards the extraction of knowledge *from* (rather than experimenting *with*) social space. Strongly connected with a perceived documentary turn in visual aesthetics, such art has been viewed implicitly at least as a form of critical and, according to some, also 'collective pedagogy'.[52] This pedagogy relies on investigative methods, its form (to appeal to this modernist bulwark!) being the passage from the extraction to the processing to the display of information. The artWork is hereby organised as a first-hand experience of social space intended from the outset to transform into a record of a social reality. This is the case with Ann-Sofi Sidén's *Warte Mal! Prostitution*

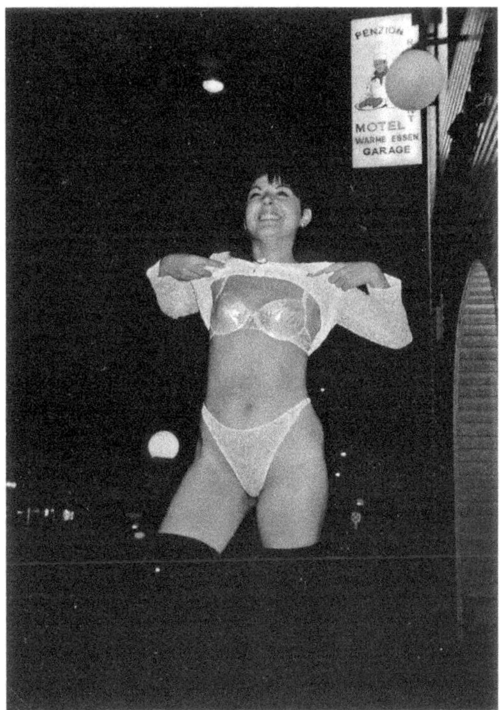
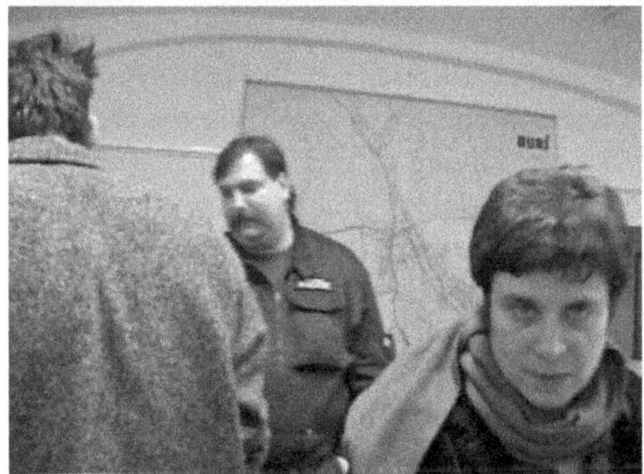

3.6–3.7 Ann-Sofi Siden, *Warte Mal! Prostitution after the Velvet Revolution* (1999). Thirteen-channel video installation with photographs and text. Details.

after the Velvet Revolution from 1999, which could be seen to offer an update on prostitution in post-Iron Curtain or so-called New Europe. Installed as a solo exhibition by the Swedish artist at London's Hayward Gallery in 2002, *Warte Mal!* was described by the Hayward Director as 'a compelling work of art *and* a comprehensive social document'[53] (my emphasis). The disjunction evident in the formulation, the carefully maintained differentiation between the work of art and the document of the social, is not necessarily a gendered condition of contemporary radical art (it does not just concern women's work, for instance). Yet it must be taken seriously by feminist criticism because on the one hand it validates women artists' disidentification with narrating the self and operating instead as productive subjects in a complex field of socio-economic exchanges and interactions. On the other hand, such differentiation is a prerequisite for the institutional ratification and visibility of such art.

The dismantling of the Eastern bloc in the 1990s ushered scores of Eastern European women into poverty and turned a modest sex trade into a burgeoning one. The work's title, Warte mal! or Hey wait! (in German), repeats the cry of the young women whose job is to make a customer out of any man who crosses the border between the Czech Republic and Germany. The women walk, the men are in cars. The slow, 'natural' movement of the first is sharply contrasted with the fast, motorised (hence 'cultural') movement of the second. And so although the women themselves are in motion, they appear as part of the scenery taken in by the male traveller who may well be in motion as part of his job. In this sense, *Warte Mal!* registers a whole economy of intersecting journeys necessary for sustaining the movement of goods across borders. Transposed into an art gallery as an artwork's title, the cry 'Warte mal!' is of course addressed to a public presumed to be distant from the social reality delivered by the artwork.[54] *Warte Mal!* thus makes acutely visible a series of polarisations: between social document and artwork, between Eastern and Western Europe, between the public space of a border town where a social reality is lived and the public space of an art gallery where this social reality is learned, between women who sell sex and men who buy sex as well as those women whose labour can consist of recording the working conditions of the women who sell sex for a living. It is apparent that these polarisations entail not just difference but difference articulated as power and that *Warte Mal!* is, above all, a meditation on the inextricability and continuity of power relations that connect different orders or kinds of space – from the rural borderland all the way to the art gallery. *Warte Mal!* appears to corroborate *and* defy the Foucauldian conceptualisation of power, seen to 'disengage us from simplistic, dualistic accounts' of the latter.[55] The 'dualisms' detected above exist in isolation only analytically whereas when thinking about the material reality to which they correspond, what must be apprehended is their co-articulation.

Warte Mal! Prostitution after the Velvet Revolution is exhibited as a 13-channel DVD installation complemented by photographs and text. Sidén's interviews with a post-socialist cast of small-town characters such as motel proprietors, pimps, pimps' wives, police and, of course, the female prostitutes themselves are complemented, in the Hayward publication, by the excerpts from Sidén's diaries. 'Sleeping here is not like sleeping anywhere else. I just woke up. There is a lot of snow outside. Last night I heard the girls howling "warte mal…warte mal!", over and over into the morning.' And: 'Vlado and his wife, Vasta, are both very short. They own the young, insecure girl, Liba. They push her to be more aggressive with the clients.' And: 'Today I met with the police chief here in Dubi. He believes that the gypsies will make themselves extinct through drugs like heroin.' And: 'I get a big, teddy bear welcome from Eva! Over the summer she had started calling me mama. I was her favourite. In a strange way I was flattered. She warned me that the next time I came to visit she may have a new mama, a new favourite.'[56]

The diaries enhance a peculiar effect of the audio-visual material: despite the latter's explicitness and abundance of information, overall *Warte mal!* induces a feeling of blockage and opacity. The diaries appear as highly fragmented as the audiovisual material, where even interviews come across as snapshots – which may be why the artist collaborated with an architect to achieve a very carefully designed structure of mediation in the Hayward exhibit.[57] This does not challenge the focus of the artwork as a narrative space (there is no ambiguity whatsoever with regard to the 'big issue' exposed). Rather, the work frustrates the spectatorial position as something more than reception, inducing an awareness of exclusion from the daily reality and mess of human bonds that *Warte Mal! became* rather than merely recorded. Simply put, there arises the suspicion that the work's production process *was* the work. And this should be seen as something distinct from the exhibited piece's peculiar commitment to breaking the documentary rules by the artist having put herself in the picture, as an anthropologist commenting on *Warte Mal!* noted.[58] For the 'picture' is not really the work.

Yet 'human bonds' can hardly be invested with positive meaning. *Warte Mal!* leaves no room for the charitable assumption that it made better persons out of those who made it (i.e. the artist, her translator, the prostitutes, the pimps, the police etc). What *Warte Mal!* certainly did was to provide opportunities to those involved to enter a narrative about their place in the world, or else a system of economic relations, as a prostitute, a pimp's wife or even a woman artist. Sidén herself has suggested that her gender was far from an irrelevant factor to the making of *Warte Mal!*: 'being a woman may have made "the girls" more confessional and patient enough to answer many of my "stupid" questions'.[59] Sidén visited the border town of Dubi and its surroundings about seven times during the course of twelve months in the late 1990s, each visit lasting between one and three weeks. She bought a DVD camera and filmed things through a car window or just set a tripod in front of her interlocutors – often at Motel Humbert – or gave the (sex) workers the camera and let them shoot scenes – including footage where she and her male translator, Radek, appear to be immersed in life as usual.

The notebooks (later known as diaries) include notes about things that were happening but could not be filmed. They were secretly read at night by some of the 'participants' (Sidén would often forget the notebooks at the bar) but they were never stolen. Sidén's consecutive visits to the same places, and faces, are marked by her resolute anti-moralising stance, and on the basis of the material made available to the viewer it is unclear whether this has been a conscious decision or a necessary response to the immediacy and urgency of the circumstances. Crucially, Sidén opted not to edit the relentless iteration of ethnic identities by her interviewees: references to 'gypsies' and their cruelty abound, Germans, Austrians and French can be good or bad customers and a prostitute's harrowing testimony about her torture (her punishment for having tried to escape) by means of anal rape by carloads of 'Turkish men' linger on. *Warte Mal!* breaches multiculturalism's etiquette of political correctness, implicitly situating a constellation of Europeans as occupying all positions in the spectrum from victim to perpetrator – although this remains one of the most difficult to digest, and hence least discussed, aspects of *Warte Mal!*'s political work. One can only guess a spectator's relief at the realisation that his ethnicity is spared an appearance in the hellish economy of the border, but it is also for this reason that *Warte Mal!* can claim to, at least, question the pertinence of a representational art paradigm. In its deployment of the documentary mode, *Warte Mal!* hardly attempts to institute a process of self-definition for its many participants, all of who remain locked in their social – that is, economic – roles.

Sidén misses no opportunity to assert the above, and a notable instance is *Warte Mal!*'s sub-narrative of unrequited love. As one of 'the girls' falls in love with Sidén's attractive male interpreter, this reminder of the young woman's humanity is quickly undone as Sidén reveals: 'She flirts with him by crawling around on all fours, popping up from behind the bar or outside the window like a jack-in-the-box.'[60] Radek, the male interpreter is often mentioned in the diaries and appears in the audio-visual material – his mention always a kind of anchor to the affective reality constituting *Warte Mal!*'s production site. Beyond his services as an interpreter, Radek's collaboration with the artist entailed an unspoken for, even subliminal, element of protection – the one without which a woman appears 'unaccompanied' almost anywhere and certainly in a provincial town where many women are openly 'owned'. Gertrud Sandqvist is right to observe that Sidén and 'her interpreter *lived* with a group of prostitutes' [emphasis mine], and it is this dimension of the production process – its main dimension – that is foreclosed to anyone encountering *Warte Mal!* from the position of the 'viewer'. Artist and interpreter had no choice but to accept the psychological and material conditions in which they had to live at the end of each journey to the border zone. Sandqvist's brilliant analysis oscillates between sober citations of Marx's discussion of labour under capitalism as the paradigmatic site of alienation and the awe induced by *Warte Mal!*'s intermittent revelation of the cycle of affect that sustains this particular service economy. The hard work of feminists in support of the recognition of sex workers' agency – the designation sex worker implies a labouring subject, enabling for example unionisation – is undermined as many of the prostitutes seem surprised to find out that what they do could be understood as 'a job'. And so Sandqvist is forced to admit that *this* 'in fact, is worse than [what is described by] the Marxist analysis of capitalism, which assumes a great emotional and class distance between the person who buys the work [labour] and the one who sells it'. Contrary to that, Sandqvist has to refer at length to the entanglement of labour and emotional ties:

> But [the] prostitutes seem to have powerful, close and ambivalent emotional ties to their pimps. Something that is not perhaps so odd, when we hear in the interview with the local policeman that in some cases the pimps are their brothers, fathers or mothers, and in virtually every case, at least at some stage, their lovers. They are dependent in every sense of the word. But these ties to the pimps are not mutual. They are sold on from pimp to pimp, they are regularly mistreated. Katja, a cross between a hotel proprietor and a Madam, talks about how it is not worth helping them, that they have to be beaten regularly so as not to go totally off the rails. At the same time, Katja seems to be 'the girls'' only confidante, since solidarity between 'the girls' seems not to be all that great. They compete with each other for clients, and it is also in the pimps' interest to prevent 'the girls' from working together…thereby depriving them of some of their power…'the girls' were forbidden to talk to each other even when they were walking the street.[61]

Sidén has stressed the importance of various journeys in shaping *Warte Mal!* As a young woman in the 1980s she often hitch-hiked for pleasure around Europe, inevitably becoming 'familiar with the vulnerable situation of being a woman in a stranger's car'. But Sidén's memories of her travels across pre-transition Europe provided a sharp contrast to news she heard about the old continent:

> The strongest visual image of the tragedy was implanted in me by two documentary filmmakers who had been travelling through the Czech republic making a film about Romas in Romania. They told me about these young and old women in colourful miniskirts showing up alone or in groups along forested roads in the middle of nowhere on the border to Poland and in the Czech mountains. I remember these 'primitive' images as if they [showed] some kind of lost exotic birds for anyone to buy in a decaying grey countryside. And that was the image that came to my mind as I passed the very theatrical and staged scenes that play out openly in the Red Light District in Amsterdam, as I was doing my research trip for the exhibition Midnight Walkers and City Sleepers. Recalling what my documentary [filmmaker] friends had told me, I realised then that this was happening in much more odd places. And I began to think

about why and how come?…I wanted to really look into this extended rural red light district in the former eastern bloc instead of looking at the established kind of prostitution that exists in the streets of Amsterdam.[62]

To initiate *Warte Mal!*, Sidén travelled from New York (where she lived at the time) to Prague and from there she travelled extensively in the region with her interpreter already doubling as a bodyguard.[63] She made her own contacts with NGOs and social workers and former prostitutes who had managed to exit the sex trade but ultimately she left this material out. She found herself in an explicitly threatening situation only towards the end of the project, and had this happened earlier she felt that she would have been unable to carry on – the incident not making it to the audiovisual material or the diaries.[64] And what was also edited out was Sidén's intense self-questioning about the mediation she was attempting as an artist and whether there was any point in engaging in anything but charity work in the given social context.[65] Although *Warte mal!* can be misconstrued as an unadulterated document, it is strongly based on personal communication between the artist and the inhabitants of a 'mountain village', whose idea of art made Sidén's presence as an artist in their midst largely incomprehensible. Sidén experienced the other side of this same problem: that as a professional artist, operating within fairly specific structures regulating the supply of galleries and museums with new art and remunerating the artist for such supply, she would have to leave everything behind, conclude the work and prepare for the next project.[66]

What *Warte Mal!* highlights in particular is that artistic labour embedded in global space as a production site (as the site where the production of art meets other forms of production, including that of sex trade) is articulated dialectically with the regime of biopolitical rule, that is, the contexts where power is exercised on social forms of life. Evidently, *Warte Mal!* offers ample evidence about the biopolitical condition of the border prostitute, as a key figure in Europe's advance to a post-socialist era, its larger narrative suggesting that *lives* rather than bodies became the site of the new transnational economy. The other side of this biopolitical condition concerns the woman artist in ways that typically go unacknowledged in the edited material comprising the artwork as a finished text. Sidén was not a mother when working on *Warte mal!*, considering unlikely the realisation of this project, had she been a mother at the time. The requirement of a complete fusion of work and life for the duration of *Warte Mal!* had meant that maternal labour, as a labour of care and safety, would have clashed with the expectations attached to radical forms of artistic labour – those carrying potentially the greater rewards, given the value attached to originality/innovation, autonomy and risk-taking, in opposition to the characteristics of maternal labour.

Leaving a room of one's own: women artists and globalisation as production site

'A woman must have money and a room of her own', Virginia Woolf said famously in 1928, 'if she is to write fiction.'[67] The studio, the mythic space of male creativity in the same modernity that Woolf inhabited, was in many respects the idealised cipher of such a 'room'. Desired by the woman artist as the space of socially valorised non-alienated labour she had been excluded from, the studio stood as the very antithesis of the domestic-maternal spaces of 'natural' reproduction and tasks that did not carry social rewards or generate value. As Griselda Pollock could still observe in the mid-1990s, the studio functioned also as an ideological mechanism for privileging art's attachment to the handmade art object, defined by its ties to representation (of a world external to it) and display, constructed for the purposes of facilitating spectatorship, given to the gaze.[68] In 1996, the year that Pollock's essay was published, Tracey Emin locked herself in a room in a Stockholm gallery for fourteen days. There she tried to paint, making it apparent that she embodied the contradiction of a woman artist creating in the studio: she was naked and the room had holes for the spectator-voyeur who would appreciate her in her double role of object *and* subject.[69] The description of the work, now the 3-D document of creativity past, attenuates the slippage of the studio into the domestic – 'installation including 14 paintings, 78 drawings, 5 body prints, various painted and personal items, furniture, CDs, newspapers, magazines, kitchen and food supplies'.[70] The work's title, *Exorcism of the Last Painting I ever Made*, had some resonance. The works examined in this chapter suggest that at around that time (1996), the symbolic distancing from painting and the studio-kitchen nexus would lead to a wider shift of women's energies to the critical exploration of global space.

The shift is notable especially if placed in a broader paradigm of women's artistic labour. The specific works of Biemann, Melitopoulos, Pippa Bacca, Marketou, Lin+Lam and Sidén discussed here differ in important ways from the work of Ukeles in the 1970s and Janine Antoni in the early 1990s. Helena Reckitt has drawn a connection between Ukeles's *Maintenance* series and Antoni's *Loving Care* (1992) in terms of these works' re-enactment of feminised domestic labour – mopping the floor – in the art institutional site, be it the art museum or a commercial gallery. The recognisability and simultaneous invisibility of feminised domestic labour is an unmissable point of what Ukeles and Antoni delivered. Reckitt is right to highlight Ukeles's and Antoni's work as the 'forgotten relations' of a masculinised relational aesthetics – but perhaps she is *too* right: much like the art classified by Bourriaud as relational aesthetics, Ukeles's and Antoni's specific works posit the art institution as the condition of art's realisation.

This point is also pursued by Julia Bryan-Wilson in her reading of the feminist art critic, personified in Lucy Lippard, as an art worker, much closer to the artist as labourer than previously thought. And like Reckitt, Bryan-Wilson too singles out women artists' work in the 1970s as 'the early roots' of a relational aesthetic eclipsed in Bourriaud's narrative.[71] However, the poster for an important exhibition co-curated by Lippard in 1982 in New York (and discussed by Bryan-Wilson in connection with Lippard's heightened interest in women's labour) features a black female carpenter. Rather than featuring a secretary (and women's contribution to the service sector), the poster prioritised a racialised representation of an unambiguously working-class woman whose labour was all about making tangible objects.[72] This representation of exceptional female creativity (a female carpenter is hardly common) is perhaps suggestive of the continuous attachment, even or especially in the 1980s when the traditional, industrial working class was openly dismantled, to a mixed economy in the feminist art world: one seeking to, first, valorise women's craft, second, express solidarity with the working class, and, third, claim women's right of access to all work, including the terrain of artistic creativity.

This mixed economy depended on the art institution as the regulated environment where a radical experiment with/on representation could be accomplished (however provisionally) and evaluated, that is, displayed. Indeed, Ukeles's famous performances at the Wadsworth Atheneum are regarded as 'early important works of Institutional Critique'.[73] The works examined in this chapter do not really need or depend on the art institution, although they do make use of it in various ways, all converging on one: funding, either to realise travel or to make a living by providing what Boris Groys called 'art documentation' of an art that is 'absent and hidden', absent from the art institution as exhibition site and hidden from those who expect to literally see art there.[74]

My point here, however, is not to detect the degree of attachment to institutional critique but to point to the studio/art institution pair and global social space as two different, if connected, production sites. Let us, for example, also consider this: what is historically dictated, and consequently rendered visible, through the work discussed in this chapter is a remarkable departure from domestic life, and consequently, from the historical association of female labour with the hidden work done at home. Groys's assertion that art in the age of biopolitics is 'hidden', implying that previously it was not, stands awkwardly next to women artists' historical experience and is an expression of the persistent negation of art's gendered context. Feminist art history has researched extensively women artists' lack of access to the 'spaces of modernity'.[75] And the feminist art movement that defined the political consciousness of critical postmodernism in the 1970s could still identify women's domestic isolation as a means of suppressing creativity, and indeed keeping it hidden from view. 'Visibility' became a flagship feminist goal, countering the fate of women's unseen work: repetitive, undervalued, forgotten. In historical terms, for women artists, work not merely outside the home but also performed relationally in the social field is the very antithesis of hidden work, bringing forth the possibility of dis-identifying from the personal as the privileged site of struggle.

Travel, mobility, circulation, the imperative of movement are leaving their mark on contemporary artistic consciousness. But how? Set up in the late 2000s by three important arts associations in Germany united under the title Internationale Gesellschaft der Bildenden Künste (IGBK), the 'a.rtists in transit weblog', subtitled 'a blog about travelling artists and their everyday experiences', is hardly ideologically vacuous, as its title might lead one to believe. 'In terms of professionalization, mobility is seen as being important for the development of the artistic career', its mission statement claims, and so 'the support of mobility of artists and cultural professionals is one priority of the EU cultural agenda and discussions are ongoing on how to better inform people about possibilities and options, on how to overcome obstacles, to strengthen networks, and so on'. In short, travel is deemed to be an inescapable but also desirable aspect of twenty-first century artistic labour, in actual fact essential to professional development as well as placed beyond the gendered division of labour. The reflective or fact-based, diaristic testimonies of the artists who use the blog suggest that mobility – as put by Italian/French, London-based artist Celine Condorelli – is 'a condition, as the circumstances in which some people live and work. Mobility is one of my living and working conditions, like precariousness may be another.'[76] Signalling the bleeding of work into life, the 'condition' of travel is facilitated, regulated and valorised through channels of bureaucratic authority – the same 'plan' that produces insecure and intermittent employment, leaving it up to the individual artist to decide whether they think they can cope with what being an artist means in global capitalism. Despite its symbolic articulation as the refusal of invisibility and containment, travel as artistic labour can hardly be seen as a straightforward empowerment for the woman artist.

Risk, mobility and (at least rudimentary) cooperation are the three essential elements of artistic production – of how art exists as work – in global space. Of these, risk appears to be especially relevant to women's work. Such production requires a form of travel labour that relies on endless negotiations with various configurations of primarily male authority, from the police to the pimp and the factory security. It also involves self-conscious entry into environments so defined by lack of privilege as to heighten (self-)awareness of the limits and limitations of artistic agency. On a symbolic level, the artists discussed in this chapter strive to make apparent the underlying condition of estrangement that work involves for most of us today. But is this estrangement more complicated for the female than male artist (both understood historically)? Arguably, yes. First, post-Fordism (associated with the decline of mass factory-line type production; informatisation and 'knowledge production'; service/experience rather than object-oriented production) has brought forth a new cycle of mind-body hierarchy, a new prioritisation of the immaterial (as in 'immaterial labour') over the material. Experienced by both female and male artists, the regime of production ruled by immaterial labour can only be named as such and claim hegemony if the material ground of its actualisation is accorded secondary position: this can happen when the crossing of the material ground is contained and devalued as 'fieldwork'. This messy, material and merely preparatory 'fieldwork', where gender matters, can then easily become subjugated to the logic of post-production in exchange for an affective moment of (possibly 'gender-neutral') institutional display. Second, for the woman artist bearing a feminist consciousness in the early twenty-first century, embracing a global production space means an 'active estrangement':[77] a wilful departure from the solitary home – a distance from, rejection and refusal of what had been made to feel 'natural' and 'safe', of part-time waged labour so that she can respond to her maternal/care work.

But although art as labour actively produces situations of estrangement for the working subject (the artist), artistic production of the kind described in this chapter contributes to a more elusive network of knowledges, resistances and interactions expressed as 'a common that touches on all aspects of social life'.[78] The surplus of production, often edited out of the completed artwork, is the common experience constructed by the artist and those she interacts with. The work method of travelling often reveals the material specificity of an uneven global space, not only with regard to the rhythms of economic development but also of the desire, as well as opportunity, for struggle. Attending, therefore, to 'women' as the political referent of a radical strand of women's art today requires, and presupposes, travel as a work method. And it is not the other way around: it is not that this radical strand of art making consciously and strategically took up travel as work but rather that the ubiquitous demand for itinerant artists led to the tentative rise of a different art by women. In this different art, travel as work demonstrates the contradictions that globalisation as production site holds for the reconfiguring of the 'woman artist' as a politically invested position.

Notes

1 M. Rosler, *In the Place of the Public: Observations of a Frequent Flyer* (Stuttgart: Hatje Cantz Verlag, 1999 [1993]). The book comprises Rosler's photographs and an essay under the book title. In electronic communication with the author (22 September 2012), Rosler said that the production of the series continues to date.

2 J. Wolff, *Resident Alien: Feminist Cultural Criticism* (New Haven and London: Yale University Press, 1995) 115.

3 For a discussion of this project see 'Brides on Tour by Silvia Moro and Pippa Bacca' (© 2007. Museum of Contemporary Art Republic of Srpska), at http:// msurs.org/en/index.php?sid=content&cid=27 (accessed 1 August 2012). On this site the itinerary given is: 'ITALY • 2008, 8 MARCH: Leaving from Byblos art Gallery, Verona, Italy. Meeting with Francesco Giusti, photographer • Venice, 9 MARCH • Nova Gorica/Gorizia (10–12 MARCH) SLOVENIA (12 MARCH) • Ljubljana CROATIA • Zagabria BOSNIA (13–16 MARCH) • Banja Luka • Sarajevo BULGARIA (17–19 MARCH) • Sofia TURKEY (20–25 MARCH / 26–29 MARCH) • Istanbul • Ankara SYRIA (30–31 MARCH) • Damascus LEBANON – (1–4 APRIL) meeting with photographer JORDAN – (9–15 APRIL) EGYPT (21 APRIL) • Cairo RETURN by air or ship'.

4 Nevertheless, Italy's Associazione Culturale Erodoto assisted in the project by taking over the bureaucratic tasks of organising meetings with foundations and organisations in the various countries of the itinerary.

5 Both quotations from 'Missing Italian Woman Artist Found Dead in Turkey', *Associated Press* (12 April 2008). At: www.foxnews.com/story/0,2933,350970,00 .html (accessed 10 April 2009).

6 A. Saglam, 'Continuing the Journey of Peace Bride Pippa Bacca', *Hürriyet Daily News*, Istanbul (18 February 2010), at: www.asminfilm.com/Basin-detay .aspx?cid=25 (accessed 10 June 2011).

7 C. Doherty (ed.), *Contemporary Art: From Studio to Situation* (London: Black Dog, 2004); N. Bourriaud, 'Altermodern Manifesto: Postmodernism Is Dead' (2009), at: www.tate.org.uk/britain/exhibitions/altermodern/manifesto.shtm (accessed 10 April 2009).

8 J. Pomeroy (ed.), *Intrepid Women: Victorian Women Artists Travel* (Farnham: Ashgate, 2006) and D. Cherry and J. Helmand (eds), *Local/Global: Women Artists in the Nineteenth Century* (Farnham: Ashgate, 2006).

9 D. Cherry and J. Helmand, 'Local Places/Global Spaces: New Narratives of Women's Art in the Nineteenth Century', in Cherry and Helmand, *Local/ Global*, 2.

10 I am referring to Foster's essay, 'The Artist as Ethnographer' in his *Return of the Real*, 1996 and Miwon Kwon, *One Place after Another*. There have been many criticisms of cosmopolitanism as a viable position in the age of capitalist globalisation. See for example I. Chambers and L. Curti (eds), *The Postcolonial Question: Common Skies, Divided Horizons* (London and New York: Routledge, 1996). Numerous reappraisals of cosmopolitanism have taken place beyond the confines of art in the past decade. See J. Nederveen Pieterse, 'Emancipatory Cosmopolitanism: Towards an Agenda', *Development and Change* 37/6 (Nov. 2006), 1247–57.

11 N. Papastergiadis, 'The Cosmopolitan Imaginary of Art: Terror, Fear, Curiosity and Hope', lecture at EMST Athens (20 November 2009), available at: http:// fixit-emst.blogspot.com/2009/11/nikos-papastergiadis-lecture.html (accessed 20 September 2010). See also N. Papastergiadis, *Cosmopolitanism and Culture* (Oxford: Polity Press, 2012).

12 Meskimmon, *Contemporary Art and the Cosmopolitan Imagination*, 6–7.

13 This is the title given to the Introduction of Meskimmon's book, 1. Meskimmon's book structure is in fact based on a departure-arrival metaphor: foundation, threshold, passage, landing.

14 C. Butler, 'Art and Feminism: An Ideology of Shifting Criteria', in *Wack! Art and the Feminist Revolution* (Cambridge Mass.: MIT Press, 2007), 23.

15 A. Liss, *Feminist Art and the Maternal* (Minneapolis: University of Minnesota Press, 2009), 51.

16 Ibid., 53.

17 Ibid., 55.

18 Ibid., 60.

19 See the feature article 'We did it! The rich world's quiet revolution: women are gradually taking over the workplace', *The Economist* (30 December 2009), www.economist.com/node/15174489.

20 Excerpt from 'Introduction', www.cascoprojects.org/gdr/introduction/ (accessed 16 September 2010). 'User's Manual: The Grand Domestic Revolution' was initiated by the collective Casco in Utrecht and as a contribution to Utrecht Manifest – Biennial for Social Design.

21 This information was offered in the exhibition catalogue introduction, South London Gallery 1975 reproduced in J. Mastai (ed.), *Social Project/Collaborative Action, Mary Kelly 1970–1975* (Vancouver: Charles H. Scott Gallery, 1997), 78.

22 Quoted from the artists' presentation during the exhibition and reproduced in Mastai, *Social Project/Collaborative Action*, 89.

23 For a historical contextualisation of these projects, see ibid.

24 S. Malvern, 'Women: Work, Politics and Art – A Chronology of the 1970s', 112.

25 See A. Cramerotti, *Aesthetic Journalism: How to Inform without Informing* (Bristol: Intellect, 2009), 24–8.

26 This emphasis on intersubjectivity as a psychic condition dominates Liss's recent reading of this work, although she notes the formal similarities (the reliance on research and documentation) of 'Post-partum Document' and 'Women's Work'. See Liss, *Feminist Art and the Maternal*, 38.

27 A presentation of the collaborative project *Feministo* can be found in Parker and Pollock, *Framing Feminism*.

28 M. Hardt and A. Negri, *Empire* (Cambridge MA.: Harvard University Press, 2000), 85.

29 S. Mezzadra, 'Taking Care: Migration and the Political Economy of Affective Labor', Lecture, 16 March 2005, Goldsmiths University of London – Center for the Study of Invention and Social Process (CSISP). At: http://caringlabor. wordpress.com/2010/07/29/sandro-mezzadra-taking-care-migration-and-the-political-economy-of-affective-labor/ (accessed online 22 September 2010).

30 Ibid.

31 D. Papadopoulos and V. Tsianos, 'The Autonomy of Migration: The Animals of Undocumented Mobility' (15 September 2008), at: http://translate.eipcp.net/strands/02/papadopoulostsianos-strandso1en#redir (accessed 22 September

2010). Also available in A. Hickey-Moody and P. Malins (eds), *Deleuzian Encounters. Studies in Contemporary Social Issues* (Basingstoke: Palgrave Macmillan, 2007).

32 On one occasion I provided a female curator invited to a conference I had organised with childcare by further exploiting my already low-paid au pair who was looking after my own child so that I would be at the conference. The female curator had to use her honorarium to cover her child's travel fare. On another occasion, I had to ask the (feminist) conference organiser to find funding for an honorarium so that I could pay the travel fare for my child who had to accompany me to a conference abroad. Such cases are not atypical in the art world, though they are rarely acknowledged as part of the political discourse that otherwise unfolds in conference rooms.

33 I. Rogoff, *Terra Infirma: Geography's Visual Cultures* (London and New York: Routledge, 2000).

34 Text sent by Ted Bonin of the Ted Bonin Gallery in New York representing Emily Jacir. Communication with the author, 16 September 2010.

35 See Jones, *Seeing Differently*.

36 Information provided here is based on interview with the author in New York, 6 October 2010.

37 See Jones, *Seeing Differently*.

38 Unless otherwise stated, quotations referring to 'Transcultural Geographies' are taken from the project website www.videophilosophy.de/tc-geographies. net/index.html (accessed 2 October 2010).

39 Ursula Biemann interviewed electronically by the author throughout November 2009.

40 Angela Melitopoulos, Istanbul work session report, quoted online.

41 A. Melitopoulos, 'Before the Representation: Video Images as Agents in "Passing Drama" and "TIMESCAPES"' (May 2003), http://eipcp.net/transversal/1003/melitopoulos/en (accessed 3 October 2010).

42 This designation is given as the work's description on www.videophilosophy.de/ (accessed 20 June 2012).

43 See A. Dimitrakaki, 'The Spectacle and Its Others in Harris, *Globalization and Contemporary Art*', and 'Art, Globalisation and the Exhibition Form'.

44 M. Kwon, 'One Place after Another: Notes on Site Specificity', *October* 80 (Spring, 1997), 85–110. Here 100.

45 From A. Beattie, 'Displacing Identity and Privacy. An analysis of Jenny Marketou's 'Translocal: Camp in My Tent' (2005), at: http://mkpd.home.xs4all.nl/Shelter/Marketou.htm (accessed 10 July 2012).

46 H. Foster, 'The Artist as Ethnographer?' in G. E. Marcus and F. R. Myers (eds), *The Traffic in Culture: Refiguring Art and Anthropology* (Berkeley: University of California Press, 1995). A revised, and more widely known version of the essay, 'The Artist as Ethnographer' is included in Foster 1996. All subsequent references to this text are to the revised version of 1996.

47 Where no other source is cited, the information provided here originates in my first extensive interview with the artist in Athens, 25 September 2012.

48 Ibid.

49 Jack Persekian is a curator and producer, founder and director of Anadiel gallery, the Al-Ma'mal Foundation for Contemporary Art in Jerusalem and XEIN Productions. Marketou collaborated with him for realising *Translocal* both in Israel and in the Palestinian territories. He has also been the artistic director of the Sharjah Biennial's 8th and 9th editions and head curator of its 7th edition, UAE, and has been involved in many exhibitions showcasing Palestinian art all over the world.

50 Interview with Jenny Marketou, Athens, 25 September 2010.

51 The Green Line in Cyprus has a long history tied to the empires claiming the region, with Cyprus ceded to Great Britain in 1878, following the disintegration of the Ottoman Empire. Cyprus gained its independence from Britain in 1960 and experienced serious and deadly inter-communal conflict in the 1960s, which led to the buffer zone, or Green Line, imposed by UN forces. Today it is known as the line that divides the Greek Cypriot Republic occupying the southern part of the island and the Turkish Republic of Northern Cyprus, an unrecognised state instituted after Operation Attila, the Turkish military intervention of the summer of 1974 during which the Turkish Armed Forces attacked and captured part of the island of Cyprus. In 2007, the actual wall dividing Nicosia was demolished by the Greek authorities, asking the Turkish authorities to remove their troops. This was not realised. The city, as much as the island, remains divided.

52 Guerra, 'Negatives of Europe: Video Essays and Collective Pedagogies', in Lind and Steyerl, *The Greenroom: Reconsidering the Documentary and Contemporary Art 1*.

53 S. Ferleger Brades, 'Preface', in *Warte Mal! Prostitution after the Velvet Revolution* (London: Hayward Gallery, 2002), 6.

54 A record of a discussion about *Warte Mal!* involving also a feminist art historian can be found in C. Carolin and C. Haynes (eds), 'The Politics of Display: Ann-Sofi Sidén's *Warte Mal!*, Art History and Social Documentary: A Seminar with Laura Bear, Care Carolin, Griselda Pollock, and Ann-Sofi Sidén', in S. Macdonald and P. Basu (eds), *Exhibition Experiments* (Oxford: Blackwell, 2007).

55 M. Deveaux, 'Feminism and Empowerment: A Critical Reading of Foucault', *Feminist Studies* 20/2, Women's Agency: Empowerment and the Limits of Resistance (Summer, 1994), 223–7. Here 232.

56 Ann-Sofi Sidén quoted in 'Ann-Sofi Sidén's Diary', *Warte Mal! Prostitution after the Velvet Revolution* (London: Hayward Gallery, 1999), 11–14 and 28.

57 This collaboration is recorded in Carolin and Haynes, 'The Politics of Display, 155.

58 Ibid., 159.

59 This information is provided by the artist in an unpublished electronic interview with the author, 12 March 2008 and was also discussed during a face-to-face interview in Stockholm in June 2011.

60 Ann-Sofi Sidén quoted in 'Ann-Sofi Sidén's Diary', *Warte Mal! Prostitution after the Velvet Revolution*, 17.

61 G. Sanqvist, 'Beyond One's Role', *Ann-Sofi Sidén* (Paris: Musee d'Art Moderne de la Ville de Paris, 2001), 15–16.

62 Excerpt from Ann-Sofi Sidén's unpublished electronic interview with the author, 12 March 2008.

63 Sidén had in fact two interpreters, both male but none of them doing this job professionally. Rather they worked in the Czech film industry and could only be with her for some of the time. Excerpt from Ann-Sofi Sidén's unpublished electronic interview with the author, 12 March 2008.

64 In-person interview with the artist, Stockholm, June 2011.

65 Excerpt from Ann-Sofi Sidén's unpublished electronic interview with the author, 12 March 2008.

66 Sidén's repeated attempts to reconnect with some of the girls, to continue a relationship are described by the artist in Carolin and Haynes, 'The Politics of Display', in the 2004 postscript, 168.

67 V. Woolf, *A Room of One's Own* (New York: Harcourt Brace & Co., 1989), 4.

68 G. Pollock, 'Painting, Feminism, History', in Phillips and Barret, *Destabilizing Theory*.

69 Feminist art history has dealt extensively with the difficulty of women artists establishing visual encodings of their femininity as creative subjects while also appearing for the gaze in their own work. See Tamar Garb's analysis in Francis Frascina et al., *Modernity and Modernism: French Painting in the Nineteenth Century* (New Haven: Yale University Press, 1993) and Betterton, *An Intimate Distance*.

70 www.saatchi-gallery.co.uk/artists/artpages/tracey_emin_exorcism2.htm (accessed 3 February 2012).

71 J. Bryan-Wilson, *Art Workers: Radical Practice in the Vietnam Era* (Berkeley: University of California Press, 2009), 170.

72 The exhibition was Working Women/Working Artists/Working Together, co-curated by Lippard and Candace Hill-Montgomery at Gallery 1199 in New York. The poster is reproduced in Bryan-Wilson, *Art Workers*, 170.

73 B. Ryan, 'Manifesto for Maintenance: A Conversation with Mierle Laderman Ukeles' (20 March 2009), at: www.artinamericamagazine.com/news-opinion/conversations/2009-03-20/draft-mierle-interview/ (accessed 27 June 2012).

74 Groys, 'Art in the Age of Biopolitics'.

75 G. Pollock, 'Spaces of Modernity', in G. Pollock, *Vision and Difference: Feminism, Femininity and the Histories of Art* (New York and London: Routledge, 1988).

76 http://blog.igbk.de/igbk/ (accessed 22 June 2012).

77 See F. 'Biffo' Berardi, *The Soul at Work* (Los Angeles: Semiotext(e), 2009), 46.

78 T. N. Hale and A.-M. Slaughter, 'Hardt & Negri's "Multitude": The Worst of both Worlds' (25 May 2005), at www.opendemocracy.net/globalization-vision_reflections/marx_2549.jsp (accessed 15 March 2008).

Gendered economies and knowledge production: Ursula Biemann's video essays and materialist feminism for the twenty-first century

4

Having previously examined the resignification of 'women artists' (as a historical category) in globalisation when the latter is approached in terms of a production site, here I look more closely at the outcomes of this resignification. To make it plain, what does a woman artist produce when her labour is relocated to global space? To say that the consolidation of global capital after 1989 has meant a gradual shift of attention from a politics of representation to a politics of knowledge (of that space) is not enough. To the extent that feminism has played a role in this refocusing of contemporary art's energies, the concepts of 'knowledge' and 'politics' must be at least cursorily delineated. Louis Althusser argued in the 1960s that knowledge 'is not the process of visually registering what comes before us' but must be understood in terms of active production – an observation, Franco Berardi points out, 'rich with implications' even or perhaps especially in the age of capital's global empire.[1]

Such contemporary practice must also be placed within a broader history of art that includes the latter's relation to visual culture. The 'art as documentation' model (proposed by Boris Groys in 2002) does not really address the fate of the moving image across these two terrains. References to a new cinematic regime and the technologies that underpin it hardly ever incite us to think about the political interventions enabled, or even about what moving-image art can offer that 'popular' visual culture cannot, both of which remain crucial for feminist work. As put by a reviewer writing for the non-specialist press and pondering over the early twenty-first-century curatorial mania with overhead projectors: 'Few people from the art world [seem to] watch television or go to the cinema, and that is the problem with video art.'[2] Nor does the invocation of a post-medium condition, in Rosalind Krauss's formulation, serves to safeguard or extend the hard-won right of cultural producers to prioritise the moment of the work's self-conscious social mediation.[3] Social mediation is typically sidelined by the emphasis on the techno-formal innovations that foreground the cinematic as a super-medium – either within or beyond the contemporary art museum.

My intention here is to negotiate critically a practice, the video essay, that can be seen to cut across the problematic of the moving image in terms of social engagement and formal innovation. Ursula Biemann's video essays make manifest what is at stake in the debate over art and documentation; they are a hybrid practice, although their relationship to the post-medium condition is more complex; they see the moving image in the digital age as a historically prioritised mediator of a global condition and try to do with it what popular visual culture does not. And they implicitly reveal what the art world's frequent return to the 'basics' (traditional aesthetic practice) obscures from view. But what makes Biemann's work contemporary in a strong sense is its attempt to move beyond the mainstays of a postmodern idiom. More importantly, in their complex repoliticisation of the feminine subject, brought about by the shift of focus on 'capitalism' rather than 'patriarchy', Biemann's early video essays, around 2000, emerged as a convincing negation of the premises of post-feminism (whether of 'Western' or 'other' origins), if the term describes – as it often did in the 1990s – the advent of a sufficiently transformed social field where feminist politics is redundant. At the same time, the three video essays discussed here demonstrated the need for, as well as scope and potential of, a new materialist feminism in art.

Overall, the video essays' primary concern is to engage critically with the circuits where women find 'their place' in the global capitalist economy. In this project, a major role is reserved for the geographies constituted by, and aligning through, the labour relations (and their 'satellite' identities) required by capital as the twentieth century expired and the ways these refashion both female subjectivity and the consumption of women in spaces ranging from the factory floor and the Internet to the brothel and the desert. The term 'consumption' is purposefully invoked in my analysis to suggest Biemann's departure from an earlier moment of materialist feminism that primarily investigated the production of gendered subjects and that also inflected the theory of the moving image. It was the emphasis on the production of the subject that dictated for many the turn to psychoanalysis. Undeniably, part of this rich and diverse body of theory addressed the consumption of the feminine as well, but this consumption mainly referred to the feminine as image and sign, on the screen. Biemann's practice in the late 1990s, on the other hand, marks a crucial turn while also providing a platform for revisiting the 'aesthetics and politics' debates of the 1960s and 1970s: the (moving) image becomes, in the first instance at least, a tool whereas the actual focus is on the consumption of the materiality of the feminine in its process of being rearticulated through the constant expansion of capital. In the second instance, the image is of course much more than a tool, and so Biemann's projects focus on the dialectic developing between the image and its object (an example of an 'object' in this context would be the global, conspicuously gendered division of labour). Both the image and the video essays' privileged social group (women) are seen as overdetermined by the mode of production and available for consumption in its context. The assertive reintroduction of 'women' as opposed to 'woman' – a dominant referent in second-wave feminist analyses – is the video essays' first insight.

This hardly means that the video essays do not concern themselves with the processes by which history effects the reconfiguration of concepts. But history for Biemann demands examination of, and reflection upon, what we might call a horizontal archive (structured by space rather than time), and a synthesis of synchronicities of diverse orders (say, the tourist gaze in physical space and cyberspace), connected and always somehow in motion. For example, the opening shot of her video essay *Writing Desire* (2000, 26 mins) shows an idyllic beach. The stillness of the landscape along with the elimination of any natural sounds recalls photography: this is the kind of place-image into which the viewer-buyer is invited to project himself and that could function as a travel-agency poster. The camera appears to be hidden in the foliage, making the viewer anticipate the clandestine filming of an intimate scene on the beach, an impression encouraged by the background music. Yet this exotic landscape is not to be animated by human presence but by text. Echoing the gloomy findings of feminist geography, the phrases 'geography is imbued with the notion of passivity', 'feminised national spaces awaiting rescue', 'with the penetration of foreign capital' appear one after the other on the screen. Soon they are replaced by the words 'search engine', then 'sort by' and finally 'country, age, height, weight, education, ID code'. The word 'country' is selected by an invisible hand (that can only possibly belong to the video essayist). An alphabetical list of countries appears and 'Philippines' is chosen. What the viewer sees is a box 'selected' on the screen. Not controlled by the viewer since this is *not* an interactive CD-ROM, this sequence of selections leads to a parade of passport photos of smiling, young Filipina women alternating on a corner of the screen still occupied by the plush landscape. Clearly, the parade of women's photos would have been the inescapable result, no matter which key had been pressed. No choice among those available would have challenged this outcome that ultimately fixes the meaning of the exotic beach as well. This ironic dismissal of postmodern art's (especially digital art's) interactivity and principles of 'choice' forms the introduction to the video essay's main corpus – an introduction interested in manipulating the concept of consumer choice to suggest obliquely that the geographies of capital *are* the only geographies left. It is the political presence of these geographies that necessitates the replacement of 'woman' by 'women'.

Biemann has described her own political formation in terms of a 'Russian doll' with Marxism as its 'hidden' core: she came to feminism via postcolonial theory but her first big project was 'Marxist-feminist' because she 'had been formed by Marxists'.[4] But to say this hardly explains how Marxism may be seen to inform her – or any, for that matter – body of work, especially at this moment in time. A first step would be to say that Biemann's is a practice that unambiguously prioritises the economic as the axis of social subjectivity. The consumption of the materiality of the feminine she seeks to address is organised around that axis. Furthermore, that the ways in which Biemann's video essays work with the moving image (and text) is what anchors them in the contemporary moment in terms of a return to materialism. This return to materialism incorporates, for example, the availability of digital technology to reflect on how capital organises itself as reality and vice versa. Consequently, Biemann's video essays pay equal attention to production (travelling and investigating with a video camera, filming *in situ* and collecting 'footage' from disparate sources) and post-production (the manipulation of the image giving us frames within frames, split-screens, the destabilisation of the 'documentary effect' of a hand-held camera, the wide range of combinations of image and text, or voice-over and image). The opening sequences of *Writing Desire*, described above, already suggest the video essays' investment in post-production techniques. But whereas digital imagery has consistently been allied to the uncertainty and open-endedness principle of dominant strands of postmodernism, thus undermining the belief that the image may bear any secure connections to an external reference, Biemann's video essays strive to achieve the very opposite: the possibility of recombining the data collected points to the existence of an unambiguous terrain of events and processes (external to the image or text) as well as to the desire, ability and right to participate in the struggle for meaning.[5] In effect, the video essays would be unimaginable outside a hegemonic media culture.

Yet the above are not meant to suggest that a materialist strategy is somehow embedded in the formal elements of this work. Rather, I wish to put forward that the materialist strategy of Biemann's work is not reducible to its thematic focus. Historically dictated, the latter is not a matter of (the artist's) choice, of course, which is why so-called content may provide the incentive for imagining and constructing specific spaces of narration (such as the video essay). Biemann's work is thus approached as a case study that makes a strong case for the continual, and possibly increasing, relevance of materialist feminism to developing aesthetic strategies that remain self-consciously political in their head-on confrontation with the dynamism of capital today.

The term 'materialist feminism' and its fuzzy (or even covert) connection to Marxism was critically problematised in the late 1990s.[6] I have, nevertheless, opted to keep 'materialism' as a reference in my argument precisely because of its unstable definition – and this may have been partly why references to materialist, as opposed to Marxist, feminism occur more frequently. Back in 1978 Annette Kuhn and AnnMarie Wolpe implicitly regarded materialist feminism as a more inclusive theoretical direction which *might* provide starting points for a Marxist feminist analysis, admitting that 'Marxist-feminist theoretical work is as yet in its infancy'.[7] The uninterrupted decline of Marxism in the academy, until recently, practically guaranteed that Marxist-feminist theoretical work would remain in its infancy – as indeed happened in art history and criticism. Yet Biemann's video essays concerning women in globalisation have offered an opportunity to rekindle the question of whether 'materialist analyses of women's condition, to the extent that they constitute an attempt to transform Marxism, constitute also a move towards the construction of a Marxist feminism'.[8]

Kuhn and Wolpe adopt Engels's definition of materialism, also cited by others: 'According to the materialist conception, the determining factor in history is, in the final instance, the production and reproduction of immediate life. This, again, is of a twofold character: on the one side, the production of the means of existence, of food, clothing and shelter and the tools necessary for that production; on the other side, the production of human beings themselves, the propagation of the species.'[9] A long string of Marxist feminist theorists have, of course, argued that the 'production of human beings' involves much more than the propagation of the species because the social life of human beings begins and ends in ideology, among other things. With this in mind, Biemann's critical practice departs from the figure of the maternal body, associated in an earlier moment of materialist feminism with the 'propagation of the species', and sets out to map the multiple instances where an expanded feminine, both materially instantiated and ideologically coded, enters the circuits of global capital. My concern is to explore the historicity of Biemann's practice, how it came to be and the discourses that have shaped it. And I aim also to look into how this practice, when linked to a materialist feminist project, intervenes in contemporary discourses and practices that traverse cultural production but are not limited to it. I begin with the latter.

The materialist feminist video essay I: relations in space

Biemann's video essays involve the reappropriation of video from the ideological construct of 'video art' – a construct that, as Martha Rosler has argued, authorised the entry of video in the museum – and its resignification as a tool of social research capable, among other things, of challenging art as an institution condemned perpetually to re-assert its own boundaries.[10] Is the video essay 'art'? Maybe. But it is resolutely *not* 'video art'. A synthesis of a relatively recent moving-image technology (video) and an analytic, positional kind of non-fiction writing (essay), the video essay was particularly attractive to Biemann as it could be shown in art galleries, video and film festivals and activists' meetings, reaching widely diverse constituencies.

Primarily interested in writing into representation the concrete embodiment of abstract economic relations, Biemann understands the video essay as a 'practice that is at the same time artistic, theoretical and political' and 'a distinct aesthetic strategy'.[11] Two things need to be noted: First, the mention of an aesthetic strategy does not designate and deliver 'the artistic' as separate from the social. On the contrary, the video essay acknowledges the aesthetic as a currently privileged dimension both of the social world and of the process by which this social world becomes intelligible. Like Fredric Jameson, Biemann's practice acknowledges that the ubiquity of the image is but a *symptom* of the overt aestheticisation of every aspect of life in contemporary capitalism.[12] Second, the prioritisation of the moving image, and especially video, is far from accidental. To begin with, formalist analyses of the moving image stress the 'spatial density' of video where 'the characteristics of temporal representation…are restructured into forms of the image that spatially represent temporal distance through different layers of images merged with each other into the same image unit'.[13] Biemann's choice of video acquires almost a symbolic significance, since it registers, and works with, simultaneity, compression, inter-layering and opacity, all key attributes of the geographies of global capital. It is, however, worth recalling Raymond Bellour's observation that video, a technology of the image, is best understood as a practice of writing.[14] Despite then Biemann's mention of Chris Marker's film essays of the early 1980s as the ancestry of her practice, her turn to video, especially in its coupling with the essay, is an implicit prioritisation of both textual and spatialising critical cultural practices. Rather than being expressive of a post-medium condition, the video essays propose a strategically-selected intermediality, since 'within one and the same artefact, simultaneously and oscillating, both verbal and iconic signs are present'.[15] Nevertheless, the textuality animating the materialist-feminist video essay hardly abides to the postmodern law of the 'unfixity' of meaning and the 'open-endedness' of the text. Before, however, I move on to consider the reasons for this double negation, I shall attempt a brief description and analysis of Biemann's three major feminist projects to date.

Performing the Border

Performing the Border (1999, 45 mins) takes as its subject Mexican working-class women. Divided into four overlapping 'chapters' ('the plant', 'the settlement' and so on), the video essay is concerned with the *maquiladoras* of the Mexico-USA border where many US corporations had their assembly plants in the 1990s. Among the issues raised in the video essay is why these corporations prefer to hire young women as well as the particular role of working-class femininity in shaping the border.[16] The gendered space of slum

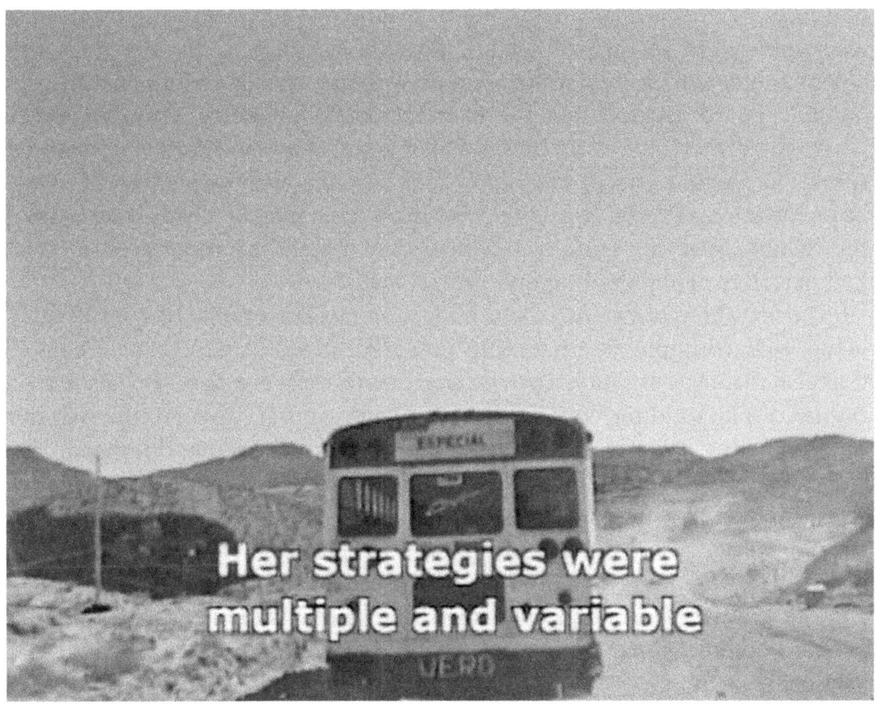

4.1   Ursula Biemann, *Performing the Border*, 1999, 45′. Video still.

neighbourhoods; the male strippers of the Juarez nightclubs, frequented by young female workers; the efforts to revive traditional union politics – all this enters the process of shaping.[17] Long and medium shots of human subjects, factories and neighbourhoods alternate at a rhythm suggested by the commentary in the form of a voice-over or script that appears on the screen. In general, the camera angles may vary, except for interviewed subjects which always appear in the classic head-and-shoulder frame, shot at eye level, occasionally from close up, and often in their natural habitat (which may very well be the street). As the interviewed subject (always female) continues to speak, the frame often changes to images of the border. These images are not necessarily directly connected to what is being said but are intended to highlight some aspect of the material-ideological production of the border that already corresponds to the video essayist's interpretation of the interviewed subject's discourse.

The border's grainy landscapes, animated by the presence of vehicles or humans in various activities, are shot from a moving car. But there is another border, the one that the camera pan reveals for us in the form of impoverished neighbourhoods, the fenced perimeter of 'protected' corporate or institutional buildings, bright company logos, highly technologised assembly lines, archival black-and-white footage of female workers entering or leaving a factory, colour footage of contemporary female workers exiting a company bus, the *maquila* guard approaching the camera to prevent entry, crowded streets where the camera zooms in on groups of young women out for the night (to spend, we are told, part of the money they have made at the plant or to engage in prostitution in order to supplement their basic wages). From time to time, the camera's gaze surveys a two-dimensional map of the wider area in which this narrative of exploitation and protest is located.

The text interacting with these images comprises a range of speech: interviews and testimonies alternate with a theoretically astute critical commentary that also manages to retain a poetic edge. As the title suggests, *Performing the Border* displays a direct transposition of contemporary theory (the mention of 'performing' is emblematic in this sense) on to the video document. The resulting video text retains an organising role: it selects, highlights, synthesises, analyses. For the Western, middle-class subjects assumed to provide the 'art' constituency among the video essay audiences, *Performing the Border* brings about an awareness of *exteriority*, of one's positioning outside the war zone of industrial production by dispelling the illusion of a post-industrial present; but the video essay also engenders an awareness of *interiority*, an awareness of the viewing subject's position within global capital – a position of consumption that involves both the products of these workers' labour (importantly sustaining the re/production of advanced visual technologies)[18] as much as the flow of images and information that mediate the meaning of labour relations to the viewer. The video essay emerges as a self-reflexive piece that draws a distinction between material (extra-discursive) and representational (endo-discursive) spaces while also admitting to an inevitable blurring of their boundaries in its context.

Performing the Border's concluding section, 'The Killings', narrates a situated form of criminality: the abductions, rapes and murders (the notorious 'femicides') of women in the desert by the border, lending the latter a creepier form of biopolitical identity. These are the female workers who have to cross the desert in the early hours to go to the *maquiladoras*. By forging an explicit link between the border-operating serial killer and capitalism, the video essay revisits Donna Haraway's much-hyped figure of the female cyborg from her widely-cited essay of 1985, 'A Cyborg Manifesto: Science, Technology, and Socialist-Feminism in the Late Twentieth Century'.[19] In the mid-1980s it was perhaps possible for a socialist-feminist such as Haraway to posit an 'ironic political myth faithful to feminism, socialism, and materialism' that embraced technology to propose a post-human identity for women of all classes, despite the myth's explicit reference to 'First World women'.[20] The irony, one might think, lay in the fact that the cyborg, the new figure of a global emancipatory politics, realised emancipation precisely as it transcended the 'traditional' gendered body that existed outside technology – and so the ultimate aim of a humanist socialist-feminist politics would be realised through technology but only at the cost of doing away with the female subject as fully/unambiguously human.

Fifteen years later *Performing the Border* suggests that the female cyborg, actualised by the technologies of advanced capitalism, remains a split identity that is most certainly classed – rather conspicuously when attention shifts to women in the developing world.[21] The bodies of the female workers turn into cyborgs on the factory floor, when they enter 'culture', which for these women is the direct consumption of their energies by capital (the video shows these women connected by cables to their benches). The *maquiladora*, the work space, is where the bodies of women are both consumed and protected as they connect with machines to assemble machines.[22] But outside the work space, where this identity collapses, when the link with technology breaks down, the bodies of women return to their pre-cyborgian state: they relapse into vulner-able human biologies and social identities, gendered bodies in the desert where they will be attacked in the most conventional ways. The desert is thus transformed from a purely 'natural' to a 'liminal' space, one superbly absorbed into the fantasies generated by the late-capitalist imaginary. Biemann's narra-tive successfully undermines this fantasised rapture between industrial and pre-industrial space, between culture and nature, by reflecting on the social identity of the serial killer as the embodiment of culture's and nature's interface in the matrix of the border. Significantly, the video essay's 'subjective' outlook chooses to disregard the possible impact of the dissolution of traditional kinship structures (because of labour relations in the border) on the actions of the killer. It emphasises instead that the exchangeability of the working-class women in the *maquiladoras* is symbolically replicated in the desert where, in many cases, the clothes of one female corpse are found to be worn by another.

Writing Desire

Writing Desire (2000, 26 min) takes as its focus the economy of desire of the Internet – an 'economy' in the literal and metaphorical sense, where the boundaries between economics and sexuality further blend.[23] Early in the video essay a woman discusses, indeed *theorises*, the tradition of 'women…writing to far-away, non-existent loves' and 'imaginary interlocu-tors', and at first we are given an opportunity to consider how the dominant ideology in the context of which women learn to think, feel and behave *like women* has paved the way for the fetishisation of the Internet as the twenty-first-century desire machine. Yet Biemann is not concerned with

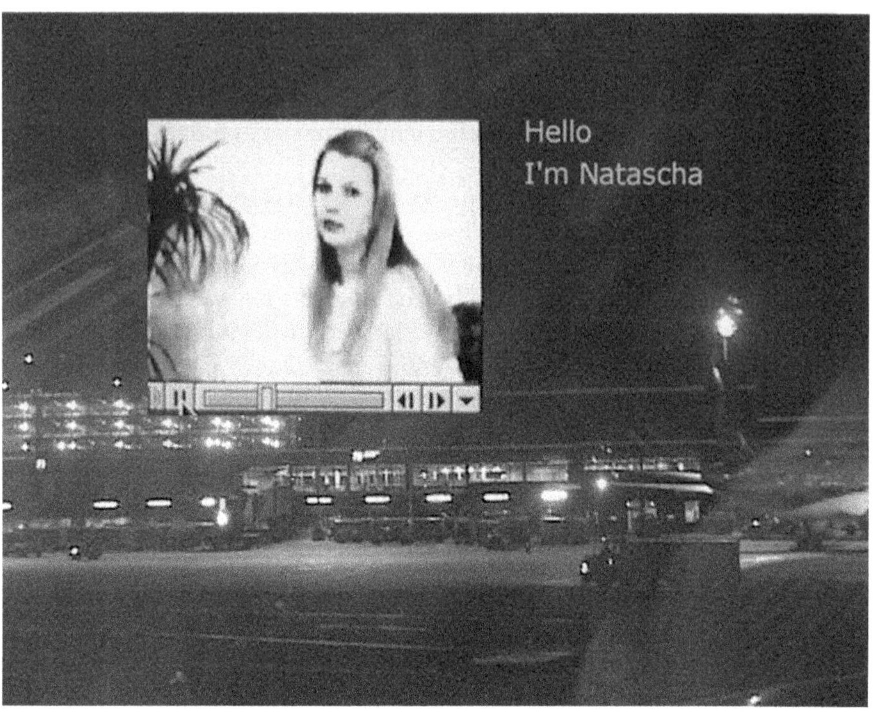

4.2   Ursula Biemann, *Writing Desire*, 2000, 26'. Video still.

pornography as perhaps too obvious a target. Instead, the video essay turns its gaze on women who in seeking 'love on the Net' excel 'at waiting, at fantasising'; women who thrive in mourning and melancholia and who also use the Internet to pursue virtual, and then real, encounters with potential husbands from affluent geographies. *Writing Desire* makes a connection between the middle-class university professor from Mexico who, through the opportunities of cyberspace, learns to forget her left-wing politics and ends up marrying a US Marine, and the Eastern European or Asian (ideologically-coded as 'Oriental') women who 'freely' enter into new forms of arranged marriages with Western men.

Writing Desire is characterised by the use of frames within frames; a dense complementarity between image, speech and text; the wide array of speech and narrative competing for attention (a female philosopher, a female curator, female activists, and the various always-interrupted voices of women introducing their angle on the economy of desire); the use of what appears to be Internet footage from sites where non-Western women present themselves to potential well-off husbands from the West. The images of the women parading for the Western buyers are often deliberately blurry, but the overall impression is that this is happening not in order to protect the women's identities but to expose the possibly unorthodox methods used to produce the video essay as such. One important difference from *Performing the Border* is that here the video essayist does not appear as a voice-over but as text. It is the persistent, if discontinuous, appearance of this text, often highlighting or adding to events and ideas hinted at in the *mise-en-scène*, that holds together the video essay as a coherent whole despite the abrupt cuts and transitions: an airport at night, shot from inside a moving vehicle, is followed by the image of young girls dancing in national costumes as a woman narrates in Spanish her own Internet experience; then the photo of a woman (maybe the one speaking in Spanish) occupies the screen next to that of a man (is it the man she met online?); then footage from Mexico (we assume) shot from a speeding car; the dancing girls make a second appearance, before a family photo (a couple who met online and their children) appears on the screen, to be replaced by the aerial view of a city in a frame within the main frame showing an airport. *Writing Desire* is strongly non-linear, and the sequences of disparate images comprising a 'scene' could appear, one imagines, in whatever order, were it not for the commentary in the form of text. The pace of editing does not correspond to the demands made on the viewer by the sequences of images but to the time one would need to read, but not necessarily reflect on, each fragment of the text that appears on the screen.

Writing Desire concludes with a clip of a young woman in a black gown revealing both her physical beauty and sophisticated taste. The accompanying text on the screen begins as a theoretical meditation on the image of a 'different' femininity (we read: 'she is the copy of the First World's past') until it is surreptitiously replaced by the woman's own 'message' sent to cyberspace (we read: 'I need a man who will fulfill all my needs, who will understand me completely'). Just moments earlier, Socorro Ballesteros from the International Organization for Migration in Manila specifies the Internet as a novel market space where the Western buyer 'can inspect the product before actually buying'. The emphatic self-advertisement of Asian women as making better wives because they espouse 'traditional' values, as opposed to 'emancipated' Western women, or the footage showing Russian women literally offering their vital statistics to russian.bride.com, turn Martha Rosler's celebrated video *Vital Statistics of a Citizen, Simply Obtained* (1977, 39 mins) into a dystopian prophecy that is only beginning to be fully realised under the auspices of global capital.[24] But the theatricality of Rosler's video (exemplified by the appearance of Rosler herself in the role of the woman who offers her body to be measured) has been replaced in Biemann's video essay by the far more disturbing spectacle of reality. In this most alluring spectacle, the video essayist's 'I', in the form of a voice-over or text, competes for airtime (that is, representation) with the multiple first-person narratives.

Writing Desire suggests that women are ultimately good at performing the fetishised object – the commodity – in an economy where, to recall Marx, relationships between things have come to replace relationships between human beings. This is precisely why the video essay is not just concerned with the circulation of women's bodies or images but with the paths of inter-action between femininity and the Internet. Both emerge as mutually supportive structures – of psychology (femininity) and technology (the Internet). In offering an anthology of female social types who, precisely because of their position in a global capitalist economy, are 'wilfully' reified, *Writing Desire* attests to the signifying and material function of femininity on the Internet as a paradigmatic new form of a global capitalist market. This market entails its own gendered parody of 'humans entering the market as free agents': in this instance, the ideology of 'being a woman', combined with 'the femi-nisation of poverty', prompts the free agents entering the market to sell themselves.

But what happens when the distinction between 'agents' and their 'prod-ucts' is lost, as Biemann's video essay suggests, especially since what is now sold is *not* women's labour power? If 'the working class consists of those who own nothing but their labour power',[25] the Internet appears to offer some women a position antagonistic to a working-class identity, since in this case their labour power is not all that they have for sale. *Writing Desire* articulates an intricate narrative incorporating the economic and the ideo-logical: women excluded from the West (as the geography that constitutes the true object of desire because of its dominant position in global economy) enter the Internet market as the sign of the capital of femininity. More importantly, the women themselves seem to believe that if they treat their femininity as a form of capital and invest sensibly, they will be rewarded with profit. And since 'in economies with highly developed financial markets, capital itself becomes a commodity', the Internet facilitates – indeed, makes possible and encourages – the entry of these women into developed econo-mies, and the form of entry is that of the capital-commodity.[26] This advanced form of reification casts the Internet in a double role: in its materiality as technology, enabling the expansion of the market, and in its ideological form through which appearances that are not necessarily false (femininity as capital-commodity) conceal nevertheless real relations (the reification of women in an advanced market place).[27] That this materialist reading is ten-tatively proposed through the analytical structure of *Writing Desire*, rather than authoritatively asserted in the video essayist's own narrative, makes this video essay an exemplary form of intervention in the often elusive social spaces of advanced technology.

Remote Sensing

Remote Sensing (2001, 53 mins) follows the flow of women's movement around the globe, addressing specifically the 'displacement of large numbers of women' either looking for work or entering labour relations despite their will.[28] The video essay observes a contradiction between the encouragement of (women's) movement in cyberspace and the function of the border as the least deregulated space of human activity, through which large numbers of women are nevertheless ushered to the sex industry. *Remote Sensing* integrates and reworks images and data from NASA satellites, among other sources, to rethink the ability of contemporary technology to track movement. The video essay uses this technology to explain movement as a profoundly gendered and classed activity – where indeed whole nations and territories become classed.

This video essay relies more than the ones previously discussed on the reworking of the image and the careful structuring of the screen, which is no longer a unified space. On many occasions the screen is split into three or four concurrent frames and it is virtually impossible to give full attention to all, especially when script providing data of movement (for example, how many

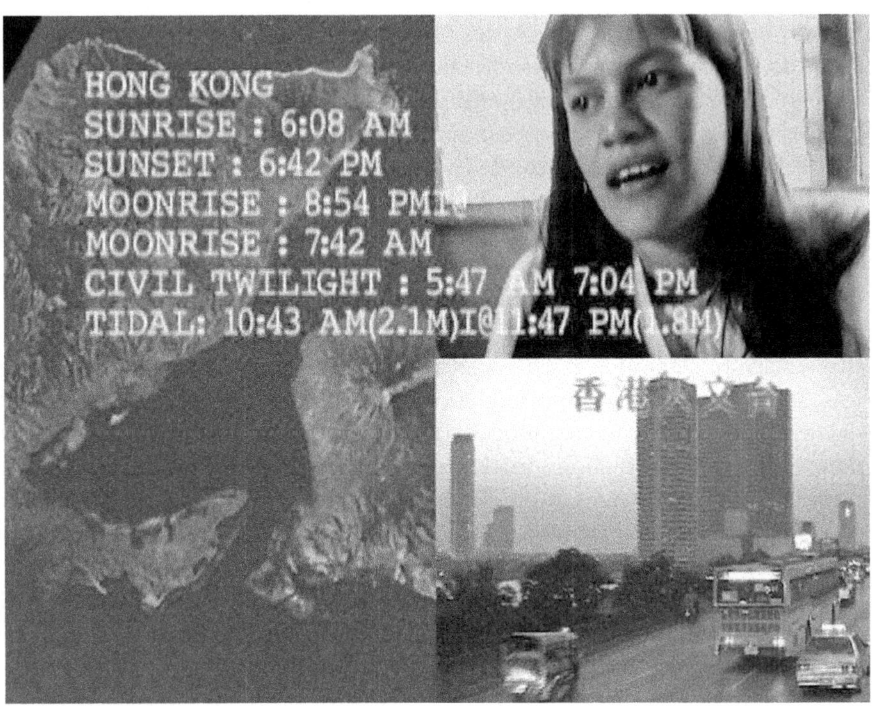

4.3   Ursula Biemann, *Remote Sensing*, 2001, 53′. Video still.

Vietnamese women cross the Thai border or how many Russian women get shipped to the Middle East per year) is superimposed on the images. Often the negative of a woman's passport photo appears as a frame within a frame showing an obscure urban destination. A dizzying description of the woman's complex journey scrolls down the screen. Satellite images of various parts of the globe, fast-moving landscapes or urbanscapes shot from car windows may occupy simultaneously different frames as we also witness excerpts from interviews with women 'entertainers' or anti-trafficking activists. The split-screen sequences get interrupted by single-frame sequences that allow us to focus on one particular visual event. Often, this is a regular street scene shot with a hand-held camera that feigns indifference and maintains a safe (tourist's) distance from the various transactions (among male tourists and local girls, among women, among the police and everyone else). And yet the editing allows us to absorb the information offered, to read the text that intercuts between the various scenes narrating the life of women displaced to bars around US bases, to consider the voice-over reflecting on how and *why* these disparate images are connected.

Despite presenting us with dispassionate images of bulky European males escorted by petite Asian women, there is no glamorisation of non-Western peasant societies exemplifying the doctrine of 'uneven development' that profoundly complicates the trajectories of capitalist migration: in the first half of the video we hear about how certain Chinese farmers abduct Vietnamese women for breeding purposes and as unpaid 'family' labour on farms. A journey across the Czech/German border (the terrain also mapped by Sidén's *Warte Mal!*) where women stand semi-naked in the cold becomes more profoundly melancholic when the voice-over narration informs us that the Eastern European prostitutes 'feel that where they are and what they are is only *temporary*'. 'Where' and 'what': *place* and *the self* become conflated, immersed, disoriented and exchangeable in the abyss of the fleeting. Yet the video essay inscribes the fleeting into a – coherent but not necessarily objective – narrative about a given social truth. The fascination with the fleeting was a staple of a masculinised, European, earlier modernity, articulated through the possessive mapping of urban space performed by the classed *flâneur*. There is no such fascination with the fleeting in *Remote Sensing*, but rather with its contextualisation. Zooming out to survey the interconnectivity of multiple spaces, the technologies deployed, and often purloined, by *Remote Sensing* far exceed the urban. The updated psychogeography of the Situationists' reclamation of urban space that we encounter today in the much-hyped discourse of 'locative media' is merely one reference in the trans-locative connections of *Remote Sensing*.[29]

Biemann's assertion that 'there is a need to investigate the interplay between the symbolization of the feminine and the economic and material reality of women' is informed by her concern over what actually constitutes globalisation in terms of a totality: 'Of course I would like to see the space in which we write our lives, our bodies and sexuality as a heterogeneous one but in the course of creating this space, I am bound to look at the existing technologies and networks of knowledge that operate in delimiting and formalizing it.'[30] We are returned, in unambiguous terms, to the production of global space as a form of technological achievement propagated by capital as a social relation, or a 'pan-capitalist reality' as the female voice states over an image, rotating slowly, frame by frame, of the half-dark, half-illuminated globe. *Remote Sensing* repudiates the postmodern fixation on the 'micro' as an end in itself and reasserts – on historical grounds – the universality of the materialist-feminist project as a response to the dominant 'grand narrative' of capitalist globalisation.

Like the previous two video essays, *Remote Sensing* draws on the resources of feminist research networks and the traditions of feminist activism to explore the *feminine-in-transit* rather than the feminine-in-transition. The work discussed so far affirms the economic significance, and not merely 'existence', of the feminine-in-transit while revealing the feminine in terms of a concept in transition (mutating into the post-human, according to Haraway, for instance) as a premature myth fabricated by liberal feminism. In *Remote Sensing* the feminine is not simply a position in language: military technology reveals it as a position on the planet, conceptualised with the aid of satellite technology. Technology, however, also provides the surface (the moving image) where this position becomes potentially legible – the position, that is, when it crosses into language. Video recaptures something of its former existence as a tool of social intervention, though it would be misleading to project on it this past identity occurring during, but also as an epilogue to, the turbulence of the late 1960s.[31] The messianic role ascribed to video in France, and the West in general, at the end of the 1960s is now absent and the cultural producer's aim is no longer the distribution of video cameras to women (or students, or workers) for the purpose of recording the multiple instances of their oppression and rebellion. Instead, in *Remote Sensing*, video is used to disaffirm and destabilise Geographic Information Systems (GIS). Biemann writes:

> the effect of technology is deeply contradictory and so is my use of technologies in relation to gender and migration in my videos, whereby I'm always particularly interested in addressing optical and visualizing technologies, since this is the field of my artistic intervention. The abstract digital recordings produced by the many image satellites currently in orbit have an impact on how we imagine the Earth and how we relate to its population. Through this lens, the world is viewed as graspable, controllable, and easy to categorize. What I propose in *Remote Sensing* is that satellite visions of globality are producing a

sexual economy in which it has become thinkable to reorganize women geographically on a global scale. These images do not merely document a given situation, they are actively constituting it too. While I critique the technological images and their binary and mutually exclusive categories of interpretation, I'm simultaneously using these very images to enhance the representation of female migration and bring it into this age of visual language.[32]

The above account claims the video essay as an instrument for thinking in relational terms and for making political sense of 'crude' data. This is one reason why the video essay has been gaining momentum since 2000 as an adequate format for extending and renewing the project of materialist feminism in the arts and beyond: The wider scope of Biemann's project is the re-articulation of a comparative methodology that, going against the dominant tendencies of postmodern relativism, proposes the critical observation of space as productive of that which postmodernists despised most: a 'totality'. In her essay on the post-medium condition, Rosalind Krauss writes:

> That nothing could be constituted as pure interiority or self-identity, that this purity was already *invaded by an outside* – indeed, could itself only be constituted through the very introjection of that outside – was the argument mounted to scuttle the supposed autonomy of the aesthetic experience, or the possible purity of an artistic medium, or the presumed separateness of a given intellectual discipline. The self-identical was revealed, and thus dissolved into, the self-different.[33]

Biemann's video essays drop all pretence as to what this 'outside' actually is, revealing it as far less abstract, but also as constitutive of their own existence. Capitalism (the 'outside') provides both the technologies that make the video essays possible and is also the key referent, these technologies' recursive subtext. In this sense, the hybrid form of the video essay is an acknowledgement of a certain failure – the failure of contemporary art to contest what Jameson has called 'the perceptual system of late capitalism' that has made the safeguarding of a 'properly aesthetic sphere…obsolete'.[34] Yet this has not necessarily discouraged the art establishment, often undermining the mobility of the moving image in installation environments where video becomes sculpture, or where fiction is associated with greater artistic skills than non-fiction, or where spirituality, 'beauty', transcendental subjects and enchanting techniques of a neo-surrealist aesthetic mark the loss of distance between art and advertising.[35] Biemann's video essays find themselves at the antipode of these tendencies both in the connections they pursue between gendered subjects and socio-economic forces and in the kind of authorial subject they propose as the narrative's nodal point. What follows is a tentative illustration of the video essay's historically specific modalities of intervention as a materialist feminist practice.

The instrumentality of the author: On a first level, the video essay's intention is to inflect quantitative data with qualitative meaning and introduce them into a common space for activism, art and theory. But to achieve this without resorting to the prescriptive didacticism in the guise of 'objectivity' of which left-wing political discourses have often been accused was the real challenge – or, more accurately, the challenge of a realist method (a point to which I shall return). To counter this threat, the video essays' narrative instantiates a subjective 'I', the video essayist. A video essay is, above all, authored. For some, such an unambiguous return to the author will imply the revival of an older form of pre-Althusserian Marxist humanism, although it might be more accurate to say that the video essays constitute an effort to recast the relationship between 'structure' and 'agency'. Both terms have a double point of reference: 'structure' refers us to the mode of production and the particular configurations of image and text, while 'agency' refers us to the work of the narrator and that of the viewer. The video essays are the platform where the relationship among these four points of reference is negotiated.

To grasp the connection between these four referents, we must consider the video essay's strategic use of the moving image as 'detached display' where the viewing subject's perspective never coincides with the perspective of the monitor.[36] The moving image is thus seen as fundamentally expressive of alienation. And the subjective 'I', to which Biemann ascribes such importance, is an effort to alleviate this alienation effect and propose this detached architecture of the image as the outcome of human action on technology. Typically also, the video essayist's speech (as voice-over and text) does not pose questions: instead, it operates through the statement, which can be either continuous or discontinuous with the image. It is through this unpredictable relationship between statement and image that theory oscillates between a poetic re-inscription and its normative, exegetic capacity. And paradoxically, the constant effort of this speech to rise beyond ideology cannot be characterised as either successful or failing. Hence Biemann stresses that her main interest is in the 'artificial construct'[37] that the video essayist, the subjective 'I', necessarily produces despite her/his emphasis on an objective, extra-discursive reality. In other words, we are faced here with the instrumental revival of the authorial subject that makes explicit the video essayist's own struggle with ideology.

Significantly, the video essays depart from the autobiographical 'I', a key strategy of second-wave feminism in the arts resting on the political articulation of a transformed female subject (a strategy expressed in the slogan 'the personal is political').[38] The video essays thus resist psychoanalysis in an effort to shift attention from the singular to the general, by replacing feminist counter-cinema's emphasis on fiction with counter-geography's emphasis on non-fiction.[39] This resistance to psychoanalysis is indicative of the major 'turn' that the historically precipitated rise of the feminist video essay constitutes in the early twenty-first century. The non-autobiographical 'I' permits the video essayist to be both in the artificial construct of representation (where the shift from the unconscious as a marker of the individual gives way to ideology as the unconscious's equivalent in the arena of political struggle) as much as register the attempt to articulate a speech at the margins of this artificial construct, exemplifying a radical desire to cut through ideology. The non-fictional, subjective 'I' is constantly undermined by the 'objective' but dispersed reality it strives to reach. In the course, then, of rendering visible the process of its making – from the moment of proposing the connections and assembling the information to the moment of screening the edited, manipulated, stratified results – the video essay mimics the position of the alienated spectator, a subject nevertheless keen to resist her alienation. This is the instance of gratification that the video essay constructs for its audiences.

The turn to the multitude of femininity: The video essays write into the increasingly audiovisual language of representation the *movement of the multitude of femininity*. I use 'femininity' to stress the multiplicity of positions occupied by women in capital's global production order because of alleged gender characteristics that go beyond a female anatomy. The 'multitude' refers us to a peculiar form of potentially concerted, if not collective, action: this can emerge provisionally out of networked activity where 'singularities' perform a variety of encounters or arise as unpredictable events. The ascendance of a political theory of the multitude (mainly through thinkers associated with Italian Autonomia, i.e. Negri and Paolo Virno) and the shift of focus witnessed in the practice of the video essay appeared at the same historical conjunction, around 2000, as discrete but historically connected responses to the new conditions of capital.[40] The resurrection of the 'multitude', from Machiavellian political science and Spinoza's philosophy, is witnessed in parallel with the resurrection of the author and both trends testify to the overwhelming demand for *agency* in the face of global capital's aggressive consolidation practices. Biemann's early video essays (1999–2001) appear to share three basic premises with Hardt and Negri's analysis where the multitude is invoked.

First, the view that there is no longer an 'outside' to capital, no remaining space to be conquered: in general terms, this is the historical condition prompting as much as enabling the function of the video essay as a comparative methodology addressing the interpenetration of capitalist spaces; in particular terms, this is, for example, why *Writing Desire* turns to cyberspace as a prime example of new space literally invented by the technologies of capital and used to expand the capitalist market. Second, the view that contemporary, global capital (articulated as 'empire') is not just productive of classed subjects but of a *whole fabric of life*: the multitude of femininity that Biemann traces includes but also exceeds, like Hardt and Negri's 'multitude', a working class proper, shifting instead attention to *the movement of the global poor* – arguably, an anticipated shift given the feminisation of poverty. Third, the view that resistance to the practices of global capital is an important parameter in shaping the geographies of capital: the documentary aspect of the video essays often appears to serve the purpose of balancing the critical melancholy of the video essayist's own reflections, by registering the efforts of dispossessed subjects to name the problem, consider its ramifications and resist its effects.

Yet the video essays refrain from celebrating 'resistance'. Biemann's work does not give in to the temptation (to which Hardt and Negri succumb) of naming a new revolutionary subject because, simply put, the movement (first, in geographical. and second, in political terms) of women on the planet does not permit such leaps of the imagination. The video essays departed from the unwritten rule in much feminist art theory to identify obsessively in women's cultural practices successful 'instances of subversion'. Biemann's turn to social, as opposed to 'cultural', practices enabled her to record slower, in-the-making processes of resistance, but also to present the interplay between coercion and consent that produces the vast majority of feminine subjectivities today. Between 1999 and 2001, then, the video essay signalled the end of liberal (post) feminism and announced the emergence of the feminism of empire, and that is why references to 'patriarchy' were replaced with references to 'global capitalism'.

Overall, at the turn of the twenty-first century, Biemann's video essays performed this double role: on the one hand, they provided concrete evidence that if there was indeed an emergent networked (if not collective) subject of history, this remained profoundly gendered. On the other hand, the gendering (feminisation) of the multitude posed some important questions about the alleged hegemony of 'immaterial labour' – a key concept in Hardt and Negri's analysis.[41] More than ten years later, immaterial labour has been the subject of much debate – except, that is, in feminist art history and theory. Biemann's three early video essays are concerned very much with the intersection of material and immaterial production, should we opt to use these terms. Importantly, Biemann's first video essay, *Performing the Border*, was about female workers on the factory floor, not about women in the service sector. *Writing Desire*, the second video essay, focused much more on the immaterial in terms of the complexity of the Internet as a market, but even then Biemann posed the question: how does the immateriality of desire transform into the circulation of bodies? And in the third essay, *Remote Sensing*, the focus is precisely on the impossibility of immateriality, on women shipped as cargo: it is not enough to transport fantasy, men want to buy flesh.

In the foundational *Performing the Border*, the term 'immaterial labour' appears to describe better the video essayist's work rather than that of the factory workers. The subjective 'I', the resurrected author, brings together information, transvaluates images, denaturalises values. She encases her data in theory and technology and *cooperation* (another key term in *Empire*) is indeed 'completely immanent' to this kind of activity. Yet the data are about the lives of other women as producers in environments of material, if informatised, labour: the cable that connects female Mexican workers to their benches and makes a cyborg out of them leads to the production of material goods in a way that requires the consumption of the body's materiality. Beginning with *Performing the Border*, the video essays cast a long shadow on the assumption that the 'biopolitical production' of the multitude of femininity – operating on a planetary scale – is patterned on immaterial labour (even if the latter is a component of women's labour of intimacy, care and so on). And all three video essays examined here appear to be broadly concerned with the meaning of 'production' when it comes to women: what counts as production bears heavily on any possible 'groupings' and 'collective movement' of contemporary women. Significantly, Biemann's persistent concern with large numbers of women, with transnational 'trends' and 'flows', came well before the post-2008 protest culture took off and screens filled with images of the many. How far a consciousness of power-in-numbers can take women workers today remains to be seen.

The spectacle of reality: Biemann has rightly stressed the distance of her video essays from a documentary practice, arguing that 'the essayist approach is not about documenting realities but about organising complexities'.[42] Her technique is different, for example, even from that encountered in unconventional documentaries of a distinctly political nature that seek to examine critically the passage of life, or better still, history in the making, into the spectacle. An example would be Harun Farocki's *Videograms of a Revolution* (1992, 107 mins), presenting such an unconventional angle on the fall of Ceaușescu in Romania as to depart from standard characterisations of the documentary (despite adhering to linear time of events peaking into drama). But if there is an obvious link connecting the reality of epic moments in history and the spectacle, what about the seemingly uneventful reality identified with the lives of ordinary women? In giving us the big picture of a feminised multitude, the first task of Biemann's video essays has been to suggest that the ordinary women of the post-Cold War era (the great masses of women of the great migration movements) are poor.

Although Biemann has stressed the non-linear logic of the video essay and the strategic disjunction of image and word, the textuality proposed by her work adheres, it seems, to a more complex organising principle. For this disjunction is found to alternate with moments where a *correspondence* between images and words does in fact exist. It is the play between disjunction and correspondence that alerts us to the video essay as a construct which addresses, as much as it manipulates, real space in order to provide an interpretive framework, since 'new image and editing technologies have made it easy to stack an almost unlimited number of audio and video tracks on top of one another…competing for the attention of the audience'.[43] This dialectical tension between 'construct' and 'real space' subtends a move from fiction to reality. The ascendance of the video essay at the end of the twentieth century indicates a more general cultural shift (of which one outcome is the TV 'reality show') by implicitly accepting that the spectacle of reality beats the spectacle of fiction: feminist knowledge production should respond tactically to this – which is what Biemann did.

The subjective but critical 'I' of the authorial voice is an attempt to under-mine the persistent registering of reality as either a free-floating or a regulated spectacle across spaces of representation. Jonathan Crary notes a distinction between Debord's famous formulation in his 'society of the spectacle' and the second era of television where 'with pure flux itself as a commodity, a spec-tacular and ' "contemplative" relation to objects is undermined and supplanted by new kinds of investments'.[44] Yet the video essays make apparent that these new kinds of investments are not altogether 'new', suggesting instead a muta-tion but also an amplification of the spectacle that now supplants 'passive consumption' with this greatly abused concept of 'interactivity' (as, for example, proposed in *Writing Desire*).

However, the attempted deconstruction of the documentary mode through the rejection of an objective vision is never completed, and this possibly is the vulnerable moment of the video essay's criticality. For in embracing contradic-tion, the video essay exploits to a certain extent the illusionism of the moving image to leave open the possibility of traditional 'realism' for those who need it. The video essays anticipate that different audiences will prioritise different registers and effects of the image-text: some will be attracted to the meditative aspects of the video essayist's speech, others to the reciting of hard numbers, factual information or the emotive response invited by the interviewed or observed subjects. Also, the video essays' interest in reaching a wide range of audiences prompts a more populist re-inscription of theory, ranging from a mimesis of poetry to the tropes of advertising. The fragments of text hovering on the screen become intelligible not as a result of their 'objective value' but in the ideologically overdetermined positions foregrounded by the video essayist in her attempt to counter a dominant ideology.

As Wendy Hesford has observed, a video essay such as *Remote Sensing* 'exposes the risks of documentary techniques'. But Hesford rightly, in my view, recognises the deployment of narratives of victimisation interwoven in the video essays. Such narratives play a fundamental role in both negating and affirming the spectacle of reality (to the extent, arguably, that they propose the moving image as necessarily subject to the 'law of the spectacle' in capitalism). While accepting that the 'difficult recording circumstances' (in other words, part of the material conditions of the work's production) places restrictions on the nature of images generated, Hesford argues that the video 'is fragmenting the bodies it seeks to represent' and 'plays upon the cultural expectation that women will be objectified'.[45] The problem then is that the viewer, unless fully versed in deconstruction techniques, may very well be unaware of the processes by which 'an artificial construct' is indeed constructed and forget that the video essay uses data to illustrate a situation on which it takes a 'position'. The eclectic use of documentary techniques may facilitate this misreading. In other words, the video essay has not yet resolved the thorny issue of 'realism'. But to understand this connection we need to turn to the past.

The materialist feminist video essay II: relations in time

The renewed interest in artistic practices that can operate in terms of an alternative pedagogy, of which Biemann's video essays is an example, is not merely an outcome of transnational capitalism but also a response to earlier feminist debates. Crossing from film to visual art, these debates often cited realism as a point of contestation. Undeniably, realism's persistent re-entry into the continuously revised lexicon of art criticism is underscored by realism's relevance to revolutionary politics, counter-revolutionary agendas and the hand-in-hand advancement of capital and technologies of the image. The various Western European feminisms in the arts and beyond inherited the dilemmas of the European left over a somehow ironic object of discourse: the *problematic usefulness* of realism.

The critique of feminist art practices attempting to show what 'real women are really like' is a theme that runs through many of the essays archived in Roszika Parker and Griselda Pollock's *Framing Feminism* in the mid-1980s.[46] The reference to the video essay as an image-text practice echoes Pollock's strategic emphasis on Mary Kelly's 'scripto-visual' work in the 1970s and 1980s – one that paradoxically can also be seen to have resisted psychoanalysis: the appropriation of psychoanalytic discourse as a critical tool *within the artwork* that (contrary to appearances) to an extent pre-empted and hindered the imposition of a psychoanalytic reading from the outside. What Kelly's scripto-visual practice shares with Biemann's video essays is the conscious effort to articulate a space where the image interweaves with its own analysis of 'real (female) subjects' to enable the transgression of conventional modes of pleasure in images of women. But there are important differences between Kelly's and Biemann's work, among which the latter's departure from the politicised autobiographical 'I' is of great importance. Both Kelly and Biemann engage experiential knowledge – suffice to think of Kelly's inscription of her maternal self in her iconic *Post-partum Document* (1973–79). Yet in Biemann's case there is a resolution to disconnect experience from the domain of 'the personal'. The non-autobiographical authorial subject serves to contest what Victor Burgin has called 'the narcissistic fervor with which humanist ideology defends the "individual",[47] asserted in the easiness with which the erstwhile politicised feminist autobiographical subject deteriorated into a profoundly depoliticised confessional mode animating much post-feminist work and fully endorsing the celebrity-artist culture.

But the roots of the materialist feminist video essay should also be traced in cinema, and especially the complex exchanges between Third- and First-World cinemas. The attendance to large numbers of women, and especially to the routes through and by which Third- and Second-World women are allowed to enter First-World spaces, coupled with the explicit imperative to use the video-essay text politically situate the video essay closer to a Third-Cinema modality. Michael Chanan has discussed the mixed ancestry of Third Cinema as such which, he has argued, 'is not restricted to the third world, even in the original conception of the idea', since the authors of the Third Cinema manifesto 'immediately cited examples which come from the first world', including 'Chris Marker in France'.[48] Already in the late 1960s, then, Third Cinema brings together postcolonial critique and new-left subjects to effect politically mobilised experiments with the languages of the moving image. Biemann also cites as her inspiration Chris Marker and specifically Marker's 'film essays', especially *Sans soleil* of 1982–83 (100 mins).[49]

Sans soleil (*Sunless*) opens up to global space in a manner that highlights both its objective reality and its necessarily partial integration into the narrative (the voice-over of a woman reading out letters addressed to an unspecified subject and functioning at the same time as a provisional, poetic commentary on the image). At the other side of the Atlantic in 1980–81 Edin Velez used the term 'video essay' to describe his 'non-linear, poetic documentaries'.[50] Velez's work was of a distinctly anti-colonial ethos and his video essays appeared to provide a solution to what was effectively a problem of language: how to re/present the contradictions suffered in the context of the colonised Mayan society without pretending to be emotionally and intellectually unaffected by them. In the 1980s the moving-image essay became of increasing relevance through works such as John Akomfrah's *Handsworth Songs* (1986, 58 mins), screened also at 'Documenta 11', which took as its subject race and its discontents in Britain. In any case, there is little doubt that the 1980s witnessed a move away from the choice 'art, documentary or theory' and towards a hybrid form of engagement that constitutes nothing less than an attempt to reform a realist method. It was no coincidence that the realist debate in feminist film theory was then at its peak.

Already in the first half of the 1980s both E. Ann Kaplan in *Women & Film* and Annette Kuhn in *Women's Pictures* raised the issue: was realism a politically viable strategy for the feminist filmmaker? Kaplan's and Kuhn's accounts make obvious that although the feminist objective was to change the reality (life) of real women, realism as conventionally defined was not necessarily the most suited means to pursue that goal. In the early 1980s (precisely when we see the rise of the film and video essay) realism was seen to smack of ideology, assuming a 'wholly centred' gendered subject whose reality of oppression could be adequately reflected in the mirror (lens) of technology. Importantly, it was an issue relevant to fiction and documentary film alike, since both these representational practices could seek to reference 'the experience of ordinary people', which was what realism was about.[51]

As Kaplan asserts, European feminist filmmakers and theorists, embracing Althusserian Marxism, were far more opposed to realism as a compromised ideological form, turning instead to 'experimentation' and 'theory'. 'Realism' was thus implicitly identified with 'American pragmatism'.[52] Characteristics of the realist tradition described as problematic included: that the filmmaker 'knows' whereas the spectator passively consumes the knowledge offered; that realist films present their subjects as 'real women' and therefore a realist film does not draw attention to itself as film, that is, as a constructed discourse; that realist films rely on the 'notion of the unified self'.[53] The emergence of feminist counter-cinema in the late 1970s was a direct effort to oppose the mere modification of already tested realist techniques. European counter-cinema and its British expression, identified as 'avant-garde theory cinema' (Claire Johnston, Pam Cook, Laura Mulvey and Peter Wollen), *was* the 1970s answer to the question of realism in the visual field. Doing away with the distinction between theory and practice, avant-garde theory cinema understood the moving image as an extremely complex field for the dismantling of normative visuality, and it involved semiology, structuralism, Marxism and psychoanalysis. Kaplan detected four common characteristics of these films, including the deliberate '*mix[ing of] documentary and fiction*'.[54] Kuhn also turns to an examination of feminist counter-cinema, identifying the two main tendencies of 'deconstruction' and 'feminine writing'.[55] Beginning with Johnston's admonition to articulate the 'female subject in process…by textual practice', Kuhn deploys the notion of 'feminine cinematic writing', a concept adapted from the French term *écriture feminine*. Here, 'narrativity and narrative discourse' along with 'fiction as against non-fiction' and 'openness as against closure' are preferred sites for the inscription of the 'other' voice of the feminine. As for those unrepentant realists, there was a demand for unobtrusive technology, and Kuhn argued: 'If the observer/filmmaker is not to manipulate the profilmic event, then her or his presence on the scene should be as unobtrusive as possible. To this end, film crews would be small and equipment minimal.'[56] Kuhn also detected that the voice-over was absent from feminist documentary – unless it were the voice of the female autobiographical subject – and that such films were largely intended to function as oral history.[57] Kaplan, however, acknowledged the dangers of 'relativism and despair' that accompanied a practice of disaffirmation and deconstruction and accepted 'progress' as a legitimate goal in the theory and practice of film and art. Disaffirmation and deconstruction appear to be a first and necessary stage in the history-to-be of a feminist vision in film. Kaplan admonishes women to begin the job of reconstruction following the knowledge accumulated in the 1970s.

It already becomes obvious that Biemann's video essays converge in many ways with feminist strategies aiming at the politicisation of the moving image as much as they attempt to address the shortcomings of some dominant tendencies. Indeed, they attempt a form of 'reconstruction', as Kaplan suggested, that would not, however, fall back into a naive realism. Biemann's work constitutes an extension of the project of the deliberate 'mixing' of documentary with other forms of narration. However, the intensification of key features of global capital expansion, including the particular roles reserved for women in the visible (legitimate) and hidden (illegitimate) 'networked' economies, dictated a preoccupation with the given modes in which information is collected, processed and analysed rather than the critical disarticulation of dominant gender codes. In practice, this has meant a current preoccupation not with the mixing of documentary and fiction, but of documentary (the empirical) and the *re-articulation of the authorial subject*. The resurrected authorial subject, the subjective, non-fictional 'I' encountered in Biemann's video essays, performs several roles at once: it negates postmodern 'openness' by proposing a coherent locus of meaning; it acknowledges the always 'situated' and embodied viewer whose position the 'I' mimics; it reinstates the relationship of the author to reality as materially stable but discursively unstable, challenging thus the strategic primacy of fiction. Whereas for second-wave feminism, 'fiction' was an attractive option for the self-consciousness it displayed, the institutionalisation and depoliticisation of 'fiction' in the visual arts by the end of the 1990s, and especially in the art embraced by the art museum, had made it a less attractive option to the radical practitioners of the decade.

The mobility, as well as the unobtrusiveness, of video and its potential to fuse with other media also help position Biemann's video essays as a response to specific feminist demands of the 1970s, the same as her emphasis on a synthesis of theory and practice as well as on a deployment of the image as overdetermined by linguistic practice. Despite this, however, her video essays seek to address the split, and hopefully close the gap, between 'theoretically aware deconstruction' and 'accessibility' (a code-name for traditional realism) that characterised feminist interventions in film and the visual arts. They depart from the feminist documentary, at least as defined above, by breaking the rule of the voice-over and by being openly antithetical to a project of oral history in their self-reflexive focus on their own constructedness. And finally, despite Biemann's own preferred moment of origin in Marker's *Sans soleil*, her video essays abandon the figure of the letter-reading 'I' and the style of epistolary narration, which, as Adriana Cerne notes 'is rooted at the nascent site of the literary novel'. Cerne considers Chantal Akerman's *News from Home* (1976) in relation to psychoanalytic criticism – and it is indeed the invocation of a fictional narrator in Akerman's film that makes this possible. Biemann's work, however, effects a shift from psychoanalysis to geography (dictated by the move from fiction to non-fiction) to expose and reflect on the consumption of the materially-defined multitude of femininity as opposed to the sign of the feminine or 'Woman-as-absence'.[58] The materialist feminist video essay displaces the circulation of signs to focus on the circulation of embodied subjects as the true marker of a contemporary modernity.

In conclusion then, the materialist-feminist video essay retains a multi-sided, yet not infinitely flexible and negotiated, identity. It takes as its broader subject the intersection of globalisation, labour, migration, capital, consumption but above all production and the feminine. Biemann singles out the performative aspect at the core of the video essay's *modus operandi*.

> My videos tackle *topics which are typically associated with a documentary practice* – topics over which feminists have articulated clear positions in the past decades – only to break open speculative spaces by making unusual associations and juxtapositions which defy causal explanations or the simple affirmation of facts. The process *from the imaginary to representation* is not a smooth, linear one. How can you document this process? You cannot. All you can do is perform it.[59] [my emphasis]

Her position is very close indeed to John Roberts's reading of Henri Lefebvre's 'model of critical practice based on art and theory as *practical* forms of knowledge and activity'. Roberts explains: 'Lefebvre wants to drive home the point that artistic and theoretical activity is actually *performed out* of the contradictions of everyday life.'[60] But of course, Biemann's video essays are not strictly speaking concerned with 'the everyday', a concept central to the discourse of an earlier phase of modernity. That 'the everyday', along with 'the autobiographical', was recuperated within second-wave feminism and thus extended its life-span all the way to the 'post-feminist' 1990s, testifies to the essentially *modern* discourse of second-wave feminism – which provided its fundamental contradiction in the context of hegemonic postmodern demands, leading to the dissolution of Western women's movements in general and the women's art movement in particular. Yet materialist feminism of the twenty-first century makes a critical departure from the everyday to large-scale processes where autobiographical devices fade away and where the return of the authorial subject becomes a condition for the gaze turning outwards. By tracing the movement of large numbers of women, *always exceeding the analytical capabilities of a subjective, narrative 'I'*, the video essay tests the realised power of a mode of production against the unrealised power of the subjects formed through this very mode of production. The emphasis on this precarious, dialectical asymmetry is an acknowledgement of the fact, to quote David Harvey, 'that elements, things, structures and systems do not exist outside of or prior to the processes, flows and relations that create, sustain and undermine them'.[61] Conscious of its material and ideological overdeterminations, the video essay becomes a filtering mechanism where discourses and practices converge to pull together an enquiry into representation and a plane of mediation for a reality that, until the moment of the video essay's realisation, exists independently of it. For all these reasons, the materialist feminist video essay makes manifest the possibilities of a politically aware practice, more radically irreverent than predictably ironic in its crossing through art, activism and theory.

Notes

1   Berardi, *The Soul at Work*, 54. Berardi quotes from L. Althusser and E. Balibar, *Reading Capital*, transl. Ben Brewster (London: NLB, 1977).
2   B. Lewis, 'Private View', *Prospect* (October 2005), 68.
3   R. Krauss, *A Voyage on the North Sea: Art in the Age of the Post-Medium Condition* (London: Thames & Hudson, 2000).
4   Electronic interview with the author (December 2004). Biemann has stated: 'I came to feminism via postcolonial criticism. And the first major research project I did after art school was about the border of Mexico as a place of international labor division, a Marxist-feminist project, probably because I had been formed by Marxists I was of the opinion that power relations between men and women could only change if the capitalist conditions of production changed.' Biemann has also stated that her major concern is 'how to transpose old labor questions into a contemporary aesthetic and theoretical discourse in a globalized context'. Biemann, 'Performing the Border: The Transnational Video', in Ursula Biemann (ed.), *Stuff It! The Video Essay in the Digital Age* (Institute for Theory of Art and Design, Wien: Zurich and Springer, 2003), 89.
5   In that respect, the video essays' form of mediation prefigures an important recent phenomenon that may seriously challenge a notion of public space relying on delegation and representation: the rise of the blog where individuals take it upon themselves to make sense of the labyrinth of signs that surrounds us and thus assert their right to make sense of reality.
6   See M. E. Gimenez, 'Marxist Feminism/Materialist Feminism' (copyright 1998), www.cddc.vt.edu/feminism/mar.html (accessed 4 June 2005). See

also M. Gimenez, 'What's Material about Materialist Feminism? A Marxist-feminist Critique', *Radical Philosophy* 101 (May/June 2000), 18–28.

7 See their introductory essay 'Feminism and Materialism', in A. Kuhn and A.-M. Wolpe (eds), *Feminism and Materialism: Women and Modes of Production* (London: Routledge, 1978), 7.

8 Ibid., 8–9.

9 Engels [1883] quoted in Kuhn and Wolpe, *Feminism and Materialism*, 7.

10 M. Rosler, 'Video: Shedding the Utopian Moment', in D. Hall and S. Jo Fifer (eds), *Illuminating Video: An Essential Guide to Video Art* (New York: Aperture and Bay Area: BAVC, 1990).

11 Biemann, *Stuff It!*, 8.

12 F. Jameson, *The Cultural Turn: Selected Writings on the Postmodern, 1983–1998* (London: Verso, 1998), 109–12.

13 My emphasis. Y. Spielmann, 'Expanding Film into Digital Media', *Screen* 40/2 (Summer 1999), 131–45. Here 138.

14 R. Bellour, 'Video Writing', in Hall and Fifer, *Illuminating Video*, 421.

15 A. Hansen-Löve quoted in Spielmann, 'Expanding Film', 136.

16 'From the settlement of the first maquiladora, gender has been a major employment criterion for assembly workers in the industrial parks. Why this is so has been widely discussed: nimble fingers make for better and faster precision work in electronic assemblage operations; adolescent girls have no experience in the public sphere and are thus less likely to organize into unions; young girls can be paid much lower wages because they count as secondary income to a household; and they are generally the most vulnerable segment of the population because they have the least autonomy within their families but high responsibilities towards their members. The industrial complexes have relied on all these factors and on patriarchal family structures in the region, which have the effect of pressuring daughters to comply with any working conditions because they bring home the only income to a family in which father, uncles and brothers are unemployed. Even though the male share of employees has increased in recent years, the great majority of the population of Ciudad Juarez is female – there are large desert areas where only women live. Adolescent girls and young women have moved into these vast areas on the edge of the city to set up a shack right on the desert sand because there is no housing made available for workers. They build their own houses with wood and cardboard scraps from the factories.' I. Szeman, 'Remote Sensing: An Interview with Ursula Biemann', *Review of Education/Pedagogy/Cultural Studies* 24 1/2 (January–June 2002), 91–109. Here 94–5.

17 See M. Davis, 'Planet of Slums: Urban Revolution and the Informal Proletariat', *New Left Review* 26 (March–April 2004), 5–26. Here 17.

18 'These workers [at the maquilas] don't just pay with their time. There is another, more disturbing side to this contract. A good part of the equipment produced in the maquiladoras are optical technologies: medical and cyber optics, surveillance instruments, X-ray satellite technologies, micro- and telescoping, audio-visual media, identification, scanning, digitizing, controlling and simulating electronics. They all improve our optical range from entering the tiniest

particles to peeking into deep space. One of the major hiring criteria is excellent eyesight in order to be able to perform precision tasks.' Biemann, in Szeman, 'Remote Sensing', 99.

19 D. Haraway, 'A Cyborg Manifesto: Science, Technology, and Socialist-Feminism in the Late Twentieth Century', in *Simians, Cyborgs and Women: The Reinvention of Nature* (New York: Routledge, 1991), 149–81. Originally published as 'Manifesto for Cyborgs: Science, Technology, and Socialist Feminism in the 1980s', *Socialist Review* 80 (1985): 65–108.

20 Haraway, *Simians, Cyborgs and Women*.

21 'It is not the jet-setting, palm-using business elite nor the skate-boarder computer nerd who retires at age 30, it is the Mexican female cyborg who is linked to her workbench by an electric discharge cable and returns to her shack without electricity at night.' Biemann, 'Performing Borders: The Transnational Video', in Biemann, *Stuff It!*, 86.

22 'Experience shows that the average eyesight is sharp enough for about eight years, then she will have to be replaced by a fresh young worker. This means that her organic vision is consumed in the making of the visualization technologies our society relies on. These female bodies need to be continuously recycled.' Biemann in Szeman, 'Remote Sensing', 99.

23 The artist's website introduces this video essay as an investigation into 'the new dream screen of the Internet and how it impacts on the global circulation of women's bodies from the third world to the first world'. Quoted from http://www.geobodies.org/art-and-videos/writing-desire (accessed 10 July 2013).

24 Nothing shows the contemporaneity of *Writing Desire*'s subject as the immense popularity of Michel Houellebecq's novel *The Platform* negotiating through its overstated misogyny western men's desperate search for 'Third-World' women still eager to please (France 2001, English translation 2003).

25 T. Bottomore (ed.), *A Dictionary of Marxist Thought* (Blackwell: Oxford, 1985), 473.

26 Ibid., 87.

27 'The simplicity of commodity fetishism makes it a starting point for analyzing non-economic relations. It establishes a dichotomy between appearance and concealed reality (without the former being necessarily false) which can be taken up in the analysis of ideology', Ibid., 87.

28 See www.geobodies.org/video/sensing/sensing_descript.html (accessed 5 May 2005).

29 See Simon Pope's essay on locative media in *M29: The Precarious Issue* (February 2005) from *Mute Magazine*, www.metamute.org (accessed 6 May 2005).

30 U. Biemann, 'Remotely Sensed: A Topography of the Global Sex Trade', *Feminist Review* 80 (2005), 180–93. Here 185.

31 See S. Cubitt, *Timeshift: On Video Culture* (London: Routledge, 1991).

32 Biemann in Szeman, 'Remote Sensing', 108.

33 My emphasis. Krauss, *A Voyage on the North Sea*, 32.

34 Jameson, *The Cultural Turn: Selected Writings on the Postmodern*, 110–12.

35 Noting 'an institutional drive to compete with spectacle rather than offer an alternative to it', James Meyer asserts a return to beauty and neo-spiritualism

in the film and video art endorsed by the contemporary museum, arguing that 'in many if not all of today's video and film projections, the viewer experiences a soothing bath of images and sound'. J. Meyer, '"The Strong and the Weak": Andrea Fraser and the Conceptual Legacy', *Grey Room* 17 (Fall 2004), 82–107. Here 92. The moving-image art that Meyer critiques includes, for example, Bill Viola's projection of 'diaphanous, floating 'angels' (ibid., 92) in the surrealist space of his *Angels for the Millennium*, bought, as Meyer asserts, by not least than three major art museums in the USA, Britain and France.

36 'A necessary condition of the cinematic image: all photographic and cinematic images are detached displays…Something is a motion image only if it is a detached display. Such an image presents us with a visual array whose source is such that on the basis of the image alone we are unable to orient ourselves toward it in the space that is continuous with our own bodies. We are necessarily 'alienated' from the space of detached displays whether those displays are photographs or cinematic images.' N. Carroll, *Theorizing the Moving Image* (Cambridge: Cambridge University Press, 1996) 63.

37 Biemann, 'Performing Borders: The Transnational Video', 85.

38 My argument here does not intend to underplay the complex function of 'autobiography' within feminist criticism and practice. As a feminist art strategy, autobiography has often been radically different from traditional, linear autobiographical narratives proposing a mythically complete subject, and psychoanalytic criticism, as practised by feminist scholars and some artists, greatly contributed to subverting politically reactionary notions of autobiography. Rosemary Betterton argues that the 'feminist writing of the self…resembles unfinished business' and aims 'towards the production of an identity that is still '"in process"', reminding us of the critical exchanges between postmodernism, post-structuralism and feminism in the last quarter of the twentieth century. See Betterton, *An Intimate Distance*, 173. Also, an emphasis on the collective coexisted with the politicisation of the personal within the feminist art movement (see, for instance, Parker and Pollock, *Framing Feminism*), even if by the end of the 1970s it was no longer clear precisely *how* the personal was political (see M. Rosler, 'Well, *Is* the Personal Political?' in Robinson, *Feminism-Art-Theory: An Anthology 1968–2000*, 95–6). The feminist emphasis on the collective in the first half of the 1970s, often associated with working-class identities, did not necessarily carry on; in any event, the new conditions of globalisation today necessitate the articulation of a *redefined* concept of the collective in contemporary art and theory.

39 Biemann draws on geographer Saskia Sassen's definition of the latter term to undermine the positivism currently embedded in the discourse of networks: whereas women's counter-cinema was a practice of subversion directed against the normative. See Biemann in Szeman, 'Remote Sensing', 101.

40 For a concise and useful account of the differences between Negri's and Virno's approaches, see C. Mouffe, 'Critique as Counter-Hegemonic Intervention' (April 2008) at http://eipcp.net/transversal/0808/mouffe/en (accessed 5 April 2010). Mouffe contrasts these thinkers' position, summarised as 'withdrawal' to her own, summarised as 'engagement'.

41 'Since the production of services results in no material and durable good, we define the labor involved in this production as immaterial labor – that is, labor that produces an immaterial good, such a service, a cultural product, knowledge or communication.' Hardt and Negri, *Empire*, 290. '[…] three types of immaterial labor … [a] an industrial production that has been informationalised … [b] the immaterial labor of analytical and symbolic tasks … [c] immaterial labor [that] involves the production and manipulation of affect and requires (virtual or actual) human contact, labor in the bodily mode', in Hardt and Negri, *Empire*, 293.

42 Biemann, 'Performing Borders: The Transnational Video', 83.

43 Biemann, 'The Video Essay in the Digital Age', 9.

44 J. Crary, 'Eclipse of the Spectacle', in Wallis, *Art after Modernism: Rethinking Representation*, 287.

45 See W. S. Hesford, '*Kairos*, Global Sex Work, Video Advocacy', in W. S. Hesford and W. Kozol (eds), *Just Advocacy? Women's Human Rights, Transnational Feminisms, and the Politics of Representation* (Rutgers University Press: Piscataway, NJ, 2005), 160.

46 Parker and Pollock, *Framing Feminism*.

47 V. Burgin, *In/Different Spaces: Place and Memory in Visual Culture* (Berkeley: University of California Press, 1996) 211.

48 M. Chanan, 'The Changing Geography of Third Cinema', *Screen* 38/4 (Winter 1997), 372–88. Here 374.

49 Biemann, 'The Video Essay in the Digital Era', in Biemann, *Stuff It!*, 8.

50 D. Boyle, 'A Brief History of American Documentary Video', in Fifer and Hall, *Illuminating Video*, 65.

51 A. E. Kaplan, *Women & Film: Both Sides of the Camera* (Routledge: London, 1988 [1983]), 126.

52 Ibid., 125.

53 Interestingly, she notes: 'The use of both home movies and old photographs is crucial as a device that establishes continuity through time and that reflects the fiction-making urge that … pervades even the documentary', Ibid., 128.

54 My emphasis. Ibid., 138.

55 A. Kuhn, *Women's Pictures: Feminism and Cinema* (London: Verso, 1993 [1982]), 160.

56 Ibid., 147.

57 Artists did take part in the making of feminist documentary cinema and Kuhn examines *Women of the Rhondda* (1973), co-directed by Mary Kelly, the main exponent of the deconstructive approach in the British feminist art scene. Ibid., 148.

58 A. Cerne, 'Chantal Akerman's *News from Home*', in G. Pollock (ed.), *Psycho-analysis and the Image* (Oxford: Blackwell, 2006), 200.
59 Electronic interview with the author (December 2004).
60 Emphasis in the text. J. Roberts, *Realism, Photography and the Everyday* (Manchester: Manchester University Press, 1998), 8–9.
61 D. Harvey, *Justice, Nature & the Geography of Difference* (Oxford: Blackwell, 1996), 49.

Masculinity and the economic subject in contemporary art   5

Masculinity has been a relatively underrepresented subject in feminist art history, despite the occasional publication and exhibition for which it has provided a focus. Published in the 1990s, Amelia Jones' essays on masculinity and twentieth-century performance art and Abigail Solomon-Godeau's on neo-classical masculinity as the site of a crisis in representation remain canonical, without however having been associated with a shift of focus within feminist analysis (which remained preoccupied with femininity).[1] 'Women's Images of Men', an exhibition based on role reversal, that is, on women artists exploring something akin to the enigma of masculinity, was one of the three feminist shows hosted by London's ICA in the early 1980s and it remains the most memorable feminist curatorial approach to the subject.[2] Remarkably, the role reversal approach was revived in California thirty years later, in 2011, for the exhibition 'Man as Object – Reversing the Gaze'. The curatorial statement promised that in the show, to which women and transgender artists would contribute, 'the male figure will assume the historically "female" role with the male body and its gender expression shown as spectacle for a woman's viewing and contemplation.'[3] Overall, to the extent that group exhibitions have attempted to introduce multiple angles in relation to, and negotiations of, masculinity, they have mostly registered the awkwardness of a curatorial discourse that persists in its attachment to a politics of representation habitually transcribed as a politics of identity. The focus on the black male, masculinity in sports, masculinity as masquerade and masculinity and desire exemplify the reiteration of familiar themes, and specifically the transposition of postmodern feminism's approach to femininity onto more recent approaches to masculinity.[4]

The indicative thematic foci given above refer to group shows from the mid-1990s to the end of the 2000s, and what is indeed striking is the absence of curatorial and theoretical endeavours that might self-consciously connect capital, and by extension globalisation, and masculinity through contemporary art. Such a concern emerges only indirectly in projects such as Helen Molesworth's landmark exhibition 'Work Ethic' from 2003, where attention to the entanglements of art and labour reveals the undiminished relevance of gender to art as a form of productivity that transforms along with the economy.[5] Molesworth considered, in particular, how changes in artistic labour in the 1960s were linked to changes in capitalist production, further arguing that a recent 'return to artistic strategies of the 1960s' owed much to the fact that the early twenty-first century was also 'marked by radical transformations of the global labour force'.[6] Molesworth's principal categories of artistic labour – 'the artist as manager and worker', 'the artist as manager', 'the artist as experience maker', 'quitting time' – the artist's refusal to work – point to the rise of a managerial ethos and a service-and-experience economy but miss the gendering of global space and an explicit interrogation of masculinity in that context. The exhibition's concluding section on the artist's refusal to work brings into clearer focus the work vs. leisure distinction running through all sections. A few years later, in 2006, masculinity would be unambiguously connected with the rebellious potential of art as an exodus from work in David Hopkins' 'Dada's Boys: Identity and Play in Contemporary Art', an exhibition he curated in Edinburgh. This connection between subversive play and masculinity as rebellious creativity, passing through an anti-bourgeois and yet occasionally misogynistic modernism (Dada), has shaped the vision of contemporary masculinity through art.[7] Katarzyna Kosmala's 2013 study of masculinity offers a more holistic approach to the subject, where art is, however, affirmed as the privileged, sophisticated site of a critique addressed to the vicissitudes of a 'low' visual culture.[8]

Yet a new feminist politics in art history cannot afford to remain uninterested in the social production and, indeed, consumption or use of masculinity in globalisation. Precisely because of feminism's impact, contemporary art appears to be a sound terrain for exploring how the twentieth-century masculinity script fares in the early twenty-first-century world of global capital. Yet the persistent deconstruction of the heroic, male modern artist by feminist art history in the 1970s and 1980s hardly meant a less male-dominated paradigm in the 1990s. If Nicolas Bourriaud included a sprinkle of women artists in his salutary *Relational Aesthetics*, his critic, Claire Bishop (credited also with spotting contemporary art's 'social turn'), included just male artists in her alternative relational art paradigm.[9] Feminist responses were slow to emerge. As noted in previous chapters, in 2009 Julia Bryan-Wilson observed succinctly that contemporary participatory work associated with relational aesthetics finds an unacknowledged precursor in the feminist interventions of the 1960s and 1970s.[10] In 2013 Helena Reckitt is the first to discuss at length this 'forgotten' relation. In considering the suppression of feminism's legacy in Bourriaud's fleshing out of a theoretical framework for art in the 1990s and after, Reckitt implicitly at least posited relational aesthetics as a thesis that re-masculinises contemporary art from the 1990s onwards.[11]

The above (Reckitt's analysis especially) prompted me to start thinking about how indeed men and masculinity featured specifically in radical/emergent art paradigms around 2000. Negotiating the place of men and masculinity could be another way for affirming the need for feminist analysis in contemporary art history. This chapter outlines two related, and yet distinct, lines of enquiry in this area, by looking, first, at the renewed interest of art in the traditional – that is, 'material' as opposed to 'immaterial' – male worker and even a male working class and, second, the advent of a generation of 'bad boys' (as opposed to the 'bad girls' of the 1990s) whose provocative artWork methods cater what we might call moral titillation to the audience.

The spectral (male) working class

Materialist feminism cannot accept masculinity as a cross-class category, seeing it rather just as situated and class-bound as femininity. Globalisation's impact on the organisation of labour now permits, and makes even imperative, a revisiting of the male labouring subject and a re-engagement with the material-ideological terms of this subject's constitution. In the early 1980s, Richard Dyer could assert in a *Screen* article on masculinity:

> White men are more likely to be class differentiated, but this does overlap with the work/leisure distinction. Work is in fact almost suppressed from dominant imagery in this society – it is mainly in socialist imagery that its images occur. In nineteenth-century socialist and trade union art and in Soviet socialist realism the notions of dignity and heroism of labour are expressed through dynamically muscular male bodies.[12]

The above passage is a concise account of what has changed since the peak of postmodern sensibilities, when it was written. But although I cannot begin to address here all the issues raised in Dyer's text, I must point out that 'dynamically muscular bodies' rarely now compete for our attention in the flood of work images to the museums and biennials of 'this society'. It is a fact that a number of artists and filmmakers today address labour processes in their work – this is a crucial change: the subject of work has become global and certainly 'Western'. But what kind of work? The post-2000 artwork typically documents labouring subjects that have been rendered invisible, or are presumed to be obsolete, in so-called post-industrial societies – that is, labour subjects identified with an allegedly disappearing working class engaged in old-fashioned material/manual/physical labour. Often such labour subjects are identified as male.

Contemporary art's turn to the manual worker is one of the least discussed aspects of artistic production since the 1990s, and one closely connected with artists' experimentation with a documentary method. In film,

Michael Glawogger's epic *Working Man's Death: Heroes* (2004) offers a harrowing portrayal of male workers slaving away in globalisation's industries from Pakistan and the Ukraine to Indonesia, Nigeria and China. In his equally epic *The Lottery of the Sea* (2006), Allan Sekula inscribes the male dockers into contemporary capital's operations at sea, putting together pieces of a global tale that runs from Greece to Spain, China and beyond. The (male) miner has acquired nearly symbolic value in the past ten years, featuring in the work of artists from Europe to Asia – Steve McQueen's *Western Deep* (2002) and Jeremy Deller's *Battle of Orgreave* (2001) tell the different sides of this story of labour in South Africa and Britain respectively, while Yang Shaobin, himself born to a coal-mining family, in collaboration with the Long March group has done the same for coal miners in China in his long-term Coal Mining Project (2004–8) comprising a number of sub-projects and anything from paintings to diaristic material to photography to documentaries.[13] As the previous list of artists and dates suggests, art featuring male workers invested in physical toil is no longer associated with the Socialist Realism of the Soviet era (or its equivalent in pre-1989 China).[14] Far from peripheral, the image of a rediscovered male working class claims instead a high degree of visibility in mainstream art institutions – from museums to commercial galleries and to biennials (note, for example, that the latest edition of Manifesta, the roving European biennial, in the summer of 2012, and just before this book goes to press, is about the coal mining industry and installed in the coal-mining city of Genk in Belgium).

This visibility in the art institution exists in sharp contrast with this labour's invisibility everywhere else, and especially in the social imaginary of the informatised First World. The subtitle 'heroes', of Glawogger's documentary, is however representative of a more general outlook:[15] where portrayals of male workers converge is in the extraordinary bravery and self-effacement of the subjects involved in this kind of labour. Despite these men working outside of home, they are as invisible as homebound housewives, mothers and their low-paid female substitutes. Alongside maternal labour, the manual workers' labour offers a view of social space in terms of privatised enclaves – rather than the familiar private versus public division. But that's where the similarity between the male proletarian's production and the mother's reproduction ends. The male workers appear to battle, or at least grapple, with great powers – the earth, the sea, the police, capitalism. A notable feature in these works' narratives is the persistent entanglement of natural and social forces, standing at odds with the popular belief that production has become thoroughly technological. If considered together, the above artworks present a global economy sustained by male proletariats' hands. Moving goods and digging out materials, these men are invested in forms of labour so basic and primary as to result in the workers' absorption into an inanimate infrastructure, taken for granted and eclipsed from view. The heroism of these men is, in some respects, tied to informatised capital's denigration of manual labour as well as to global capital's sheer and awe-inspiring magnitude.

McQueen's and Deller's diverse take on the male miner is of particular interest precisely because what they present is shaped by a specific (British) experience and its links to globalisation. Deller's *The Battle of Orgreave* addresses the violent contraction of Britain's white, 'indigenous' male working class during the Thatcher regime. Following extensive and collaborative research, the work inaugurated the twenty-first century by recreating a violent confrontation between the striking miners and the police from the 1980s. It was a 'blockbuster' participatory art project, its production process described in detail on the website of its principal production agency, London's Artangel.[16] The British (not just English) miners' defeat in the mid-1980s could only be interpreted in one way in the twenty-first century: as a symbol for a dawning era in capitalist development, one of outsourcing manufacture to the Third World and of turning Britain – a 'core' Western country and birthplace of the industrial revolution – into a primarily service-and-finance sector economy, in what has been recently described as the 'greatest de-industrialisation of any major nation'.[17] Significantly, *The Battle of Orgreave* was not an analytical artwork, observing coolly and interpreting, for instance, the division among working-class men as expressed in the very act of low-paid police literally working against the interests of the striking miners. Rather, the emphasis was on a physical re-enactment, the hopefully cathartic but certainly painful and spectacular re-creation of an emotional moment resulting in (male) violence. The 'disappeared' white miner of Europe appears however to have re-materialised elsewhere on the globe, as a black African miner in McQueen's *Western Deep* (2002) and *Gravesend* (2007).

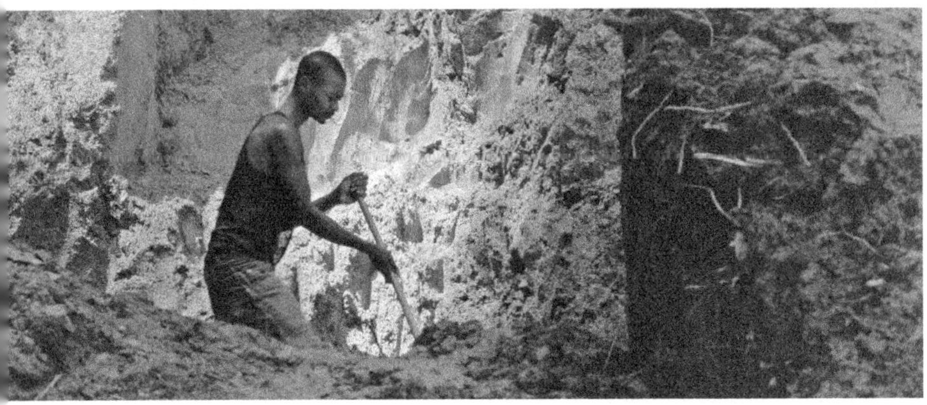

5.1 Steve McQueen, *Gravesend* (2007), 35 mm film transferred to high definition, 17′58″. Still.

I have argued elsewhere that the institutional embracing of images present-ing material labour, witnessed since 2000, may well provide a way for making newly productive the 'obsolete' (material) worker in the production sites of immaterial labour – including museums, biennials and other sites prioritising communication and affect – defining post-Fordism as globalisation.[18] At the same time, this particular incorporation of labour into the institutions of art calls attention to rather complex, and possibly unintended, inscriptions of masculinity, in the sense that such inscriptions cannot be adequately con-densed to the 'feminisation of work'. As Keti Chukhrov notes:

> In the social space of developed countries, physical labor is invisible; and if it comes into view, it is seen as something hovering between the exotic and the obscene. In the works of artists such as Artur Żmijewski, Michael Glawogger, or Mika Rottenberg, material labor testifies to the fatal division between routine, mechanical labor, and the intellectual-creative and cultural space of middle-class life and activity. In Artur Żmijewski's 'Selected Works', an indus-trial worker's 24-hour cycle appears as bare life, akin to that of an animal, split between existential survival and the material-physical labor necessary for that survival. The cultural, creative, or cognitive dimension of the worker's life is entirely out of the question here.[19]

Such an observation brings forth politically engaged art's fundamental contradiction: the division of labour between artists and their subjects. This becomes obvious if attention shifts to, as Hito Steyerl's admonishes, 'what art does – not what it shows'.[20] And yet, what art shows is a crucial guide to figur-ing out what it does. Steyerl's remark that 'if contemporary art is the answer, the question: How can capitalism be made more beautiful?' acquires a possibly unintended meaning if we think about it as we watch, in an art gallery's immersive black box, McQueen's beautifully shot scenes of black men's physi-cal toil leading to outright exploitation in the darkness of mines.

The response of art critics is illuminating. Writing in 2002 about *Western Deep*, British Adrian Searle notes positively that 'the periods of silence, the intermittent light, the camera burrowing into near-dark and illuminating glimpses of things that are very close, seen only partially, is itself close to what the workers in this mine experience every minute of every shift'.[21] The naivety of this statement, resting on art's assumed capacity to generate empathy when wilfully detached from its conditions of production and consumption, marks the gap between a black male subject involved in immaterial labour in the West (McQueen/the artist) and a black male subject involved in more tradi-tional, physical labour in the Third World (the miners filmed). Chrukhrov is right to note that immaterial labourers or ' "the cognitariat" do not constitute a class', being 'a social group that can include top managers of the higher echelon, white-collar workers, and service industry workers on short-term contracts.'[22] But given that she herself acknowledges the excision of any creative or cognitive 'dimension' from the lives of contemporary material labourers, the gap between physical and immaterial labour remains simply unnameable (and unbridgeable, in this case).

This excision, producing the stereotype of a debased, working-class masculinity limited to brainless, muscular force and open to all sorts of political manipulations, has been an important and gradual development in the history of nineteenth and twentieth-century capitalism, brilliantly described by Harry Braverman in his 1974 classic *Labor and Monopoly Capital: The Degradation of Work in the Twentieth Century*. Braverman notes capital's great and long-term efforts to limit workers' access to the production and possession of both techno-scientific knowledge and critical thinking associated with the humanities.[23] It is this long process that has partly enabled a racially and geopolitically enhanced version of this stereotype to be put to work in *Western Deep* – although the unity of the stereotype's racial axis is undermined by the male artist's 'blackness'. This is indeed where the platitudes of postmodernist identity politics break down. Is this a black male artist making art about black men or is it an institutionally rewarded, male immaterial labourer in the West appropriating men's material labour in Africa? Institutionally rewarded art is an emblematic form of immaterial labour at present as it offers ample opportunities for the extraction of a different kind of surplus value: first, corporations directly appropriating the workers' production extract surplus value; then the artist/the curator/ the collector appropriating the workers' production as image extracts surplus value. It is hardly surprising then that writing in 2007 about McQueen's film *Gravesend* (2007), Puerto Rican Pedro Vélez is far less impressed when he notes that this is a film 'about savage capitalism, neo-imperialism and the ways that multinationals mine riches from war-ridden, corrupted and otherwise ravaged countries around the globe. Sound familiar? A huge production, the film backfires conceptually and sadly makes oppression seem fashionably exotic.'[24] But what is fashionably exotic here?

By 2007 art institutions had made the scenario familiar indeed – even to those members of the art community who had managed to miss the ubiquitous critique of global capital's enterprise. Included in 'Uneven Geographies' in 2010, a Nottingham Contemporary exhibit showcasing art about globalisation, *Gravesend* interspersed images of black men extracting coltan (used in consumer products such as mobile phones), visions of hi-tech labs processing the precious metal and a slow-motion sunset over an industrial landscape. The roomy, soundproofed black box where the film was screened and the large scale of projection as such provided the proverbial (or rather Derridean) 'frame', reconstructing a spectatorship based on enforced isolation and contemplation of the artwork in terms of a sequence of carefully edited images. Given that organising spectatorship in this immersive fashion has been the norm since moving-image art became entrenched in the museum, a political negotiation of the artwork required the re-establishment of the old conceptual gap between image content (representation of labour) and form (of, and around, the artwork). An exhibition reviewer who wondered 'but if not urging us to take to the streets, then what is the exhibition actually for?' posed an important question.[25] The question had received a provisional answer by Vélez three years earlier in his review of *Gravesend*:

> Unfortunately, the art experience doesn't last long, as we are presented once again with sweaty anonymous workers in trenches. Real people, used first as disposable labor and now as an esthetic excuse. The workers are presumably completely and utterly alienated from the economic or intellectual value this piece finds through its exhibition in the glamorous and academic confines of art institutions.[26]

In globalisation's techno-savvy art worlds, impoverished male workers, manual labourers embodying a prevalent economic other, are literally and metaphorically drawn into visibility from their dark, subterranean tunnels. Their transient appearance on art's screens literalises the distance between the viewer's affective response to the image from the utopian prospect of viewers and miners entering a common struggle. The miners have become a spectral working class, when, to quote Tim Fisken, 'the specter has an ambiguous relationship to appearance, because it seems to be an appearance without the proper relationship to a reality of which it is the appearance.'[27] Distilled into 'appearance' and introduced into an aesthetic context, the miners are put to work. Eventually they will join the reclining women-signs of the twentieth century in museum collections, having become 'feminised' in the critical aspirations of contemporary art. Vélez's criticism cited above cannot be limited to the particular artwork: rather, it is an observation about how art, as a particular kind of labour, recontextualised within the institutions of global capital, attempts to carry on with its representational work, having lost touch with how it itself (art) operates, as Walter Benjamin once asked, within a historically specific regime of production.[28]

Finally, Vélez's formulation implies that, in contrast to the doubly-exploited black male miner, the black male artist is *not* alienated from 'his' art/work. Labour is privileged over race as the key parameter. And it matters little whether the black artist is a token or at best an 'exceptional' presence in a white male-dominated art world: the black miner's and the black artist's work are perceived as fundamentally different – an observation in support of an intersectional reframing of the male subject and against an understanding of race in terms of class. The profession of the artist has not been coveted as the sole form of non-alienated labour but as a specific form of non-alienated labour that can, nevertheless, attract social and economic rewards within the capitalist organisation of labour. The particular ways of realising artistic labour have hardly managed to challenge this. As expressed by Miwon Kwon, 'clearly, dealers have figured out how to sell art-as-idea or art-as-action'.[29] And the art world has managed to sustain and reproduce hordes of 'failed' artists that provide its variety of low-cost labour, armies of creative types assigned to various roles in the art economy.[30] In fact, whether art constitutes a form of alienated labour or not is getting to be less of an exciting issue, precisely because the ranks of artists as immaterial labourers – to follow Chukhrov – are class divided in obvious ways. In this context, class divisions are tied to explications of 'success' moulded in a celebrity culture (fame plus market value), and predictably the top-of-the-list artists are white men: in 2010 Damien Hirst and Jeff Koons as No. 1 and No. 2 respectively.[31]

'A long hard look at the man in the mirror': globalisation's bad boys

Hirst and Koons are male artists – and specifically male artists strongly associated with daring, controversial, provocative work (in an architectural metaphor about the division of labour, 'planned' rather than 'built' by the artists) and super-wealthy collectors who appreciate and support this kind of work. In a competitive art market, the choice of what an artwork shows can hardly be distinguished from how it shows it as a factor determining the artist's success or 'failure', always in a highly specific historical context. This is what the case of so many institutionally endorsed male artists making art about the invisible (outsourced) or defeated (Western) manual worker suggests. But is there something more to say here than articulating the mere fact that contemporary, post-1989 art is a good place for observing the intersection of masculinity, class and geography?

Yes, is the short answer. Artists' turn to manual labour has meant that there are now more images of men in the contemporary art museum and biennial. These images – including, or especially, those of workers – are not celebratory but partake of a critical paradigm. However, beyond the intended criticality, what kind of social metaphor does their aggregate bring forth? Hito Steyerl captures this anxious mood perfectly when arguing that contemporary art 'is involved in mining for raw materials for dual-core processors....From the deserts of Mongolia to the high plains of Peru, contemporary art is everywhere. And when it is finally dragged into Gagosian dripping from head to toe with blood and dirt, it triggers off rounds and rounds of rapturous applause.'[32] It sounds like Steyerl has been looking at art featuring male labour and thinking about where it is being produced and for whom. Steyerl's reference to contemporary art as a whole is daring, precisely because feminist readings of art as an inherently gendered production regime have fallen so out of grace. Steyerl is among the very few to have sought an explicit connection between contemporary art's usefulness to a globally dominant capitalism and a generic Western masculinity as contemporary art's dominant ideology.

> Why and for whom is contemporary art so attractive? One guess: the production of art presents a mirror image of postdemocratic forms of hyper-capitalism that look set to become the dominant political post-Cold War paradigm. It seems unpredictable, unaccountable, brilliant, mercurial, moody, guided by inspiration and genius. Just as any oligarch aspiring to dictatorship might want to see himself. The traditional conception of the artist's role corresponds all too well with the self-image of wannabe autocrats, who see government potentially – and dangerously – as an art form. Postdemocratic government is very much related to this erratic type of male-genius-artist behavior. It is opaque, corrupt, and completely unaccountable. Both models operate within male bonding structures that are as democratic as your local mafia chapter. Rule of law? Why don't we just leave it to taste? Checks and balances? Cheques and balances! Good governance? Bad curating! You see why the contemporary oligarch loves contemporary art: it's just what works for *him*.[33] [my emphasis]

This is an important observation for answering, however provisionally, the question posed in this book's Introduction – what is the political work (the articulation of and intervention into power relations) that art realises today as a gendered practice? Steyerl detects something more than masculinity's structural presence in recent art (in which depicting a 'what' is intimately connected with a 'where'). In crossing from Europe to Africa and back, running the distance from the strongholds of immaterial labour all the way to where affordable cups of brain-stimulating coffee or healthy green tea begin their journeys (in plantations employing cheap coloured muscle), masculinity emerges as class-divided on a global scale, its 'meaning' deciphered as situated economic effect.

But according to Steyerl, in certain contexts this economic effect is inextricably linked with the end of an important alliance: that between democracy and the capitalist market. Can contemporary, post-1989 art be seen as expressive of a new, authoritarian, macho spirit of capital? This possibility was already visible in Eastern Europe in the 1990s. Zaneta Vangeli's *The Inner Circle*, one of the three elements of her installation *Social Plastic of Macedonia* (1996) gained iconic status by demonstrating the masculinisation of the post-socialist regime in the fragmented Yugoslavia. The inner triangle, rather than circle, of power in the violently reconstituted post-socialist Balkans comprised three larger-than-life (over two metres high) black-and-white photographic portraits: the male leader of the Macedonian Orthodox Church, a so called 'underground guru' and a male minister (of foreign affairs). Capitalism would not thwart but revivify gender stereotypes, pushing forward a dominating

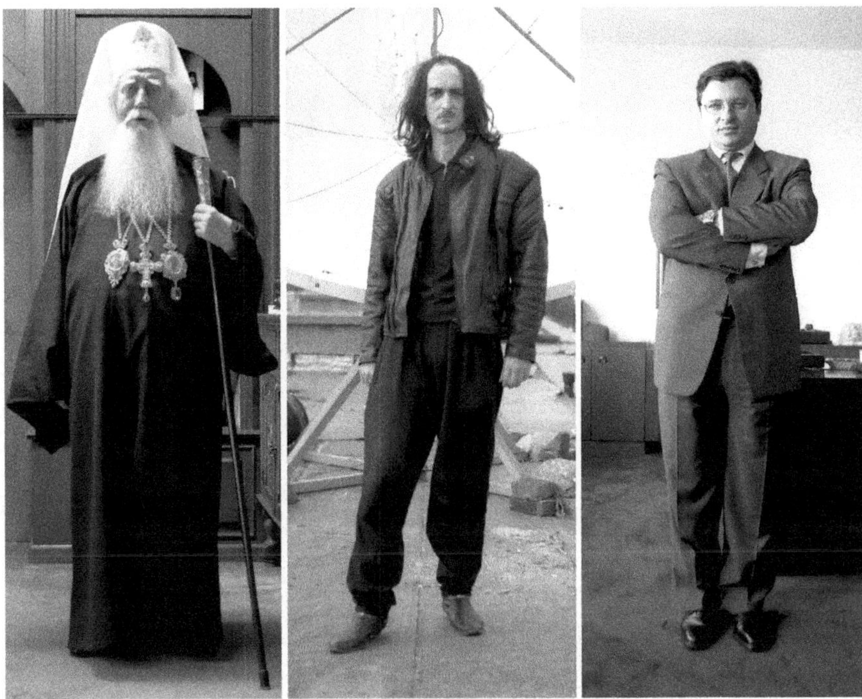

5.2   Zaneta Vangeli, *The Social Plastic of Macedonia/The Inner Circle* (1996). 2 triptychs, b/w photo/wood, each 100 × 210 cm. Installation detail. Left: The Archbishop of the Macedonian Orthodox Church, Gospodin Gospodin Mihail. Middle: Baškim Ademi, underground guru. Right: The Minister of Foreign Affairs, Ljubomir Danailov Frčkoski.

rogue male as a legitimate and desired political subjectivity geared to the challenges of both the new century and (new) capitalism. A new breed of male artists, thriving on provocation and explicitly challenging the link of democracy to participation was to conquer the biennials-and-museums galaxy.

Published in *The New York Times*, Ken Johnson's review of two Artur Żmijewski's shows in New York in 2009 ends with this piece of advice offered to the artist: 'he [the artist] should take a long, hard look at the man in the mirror'.[34] Johnson's review testified to the speedy popularisation of a new art-history terminology, as the Polish artist is said to practice 'a form of relational aesthetics in which ordinary people are invited to participate in artificially constructed situations as a way of revealing deep social problems' – a description that concurs with Claire Bishop's positive appraisal of an art paradigm that highlights antagonism rather than consensus and which, as noted earlier, is dominated by male artists. Interestingly, this exuberant revival of the male artist as the cipher of aesthetic experimentation, bold confrontation and moral

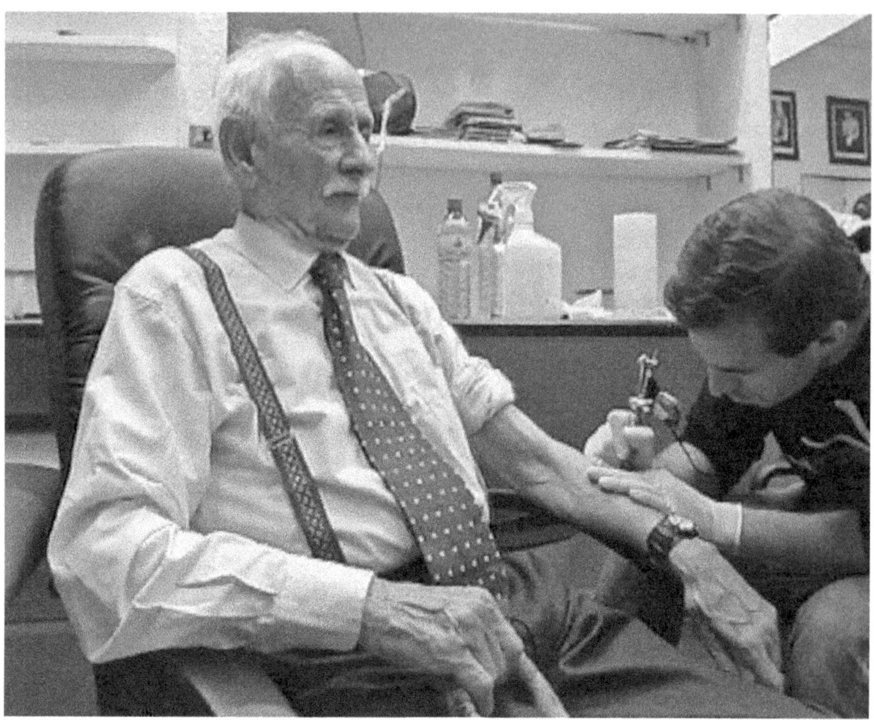

5.3   Artur Żmijewski, *80064* (2004), video, 11′. Video still.

controversy occurred at the cusp of the new century, following the overcoming of postmodernism. Although Bishop is careful to avoid references to postmodernism in her 2004 discussion of relational aesthetics, she does consider art since the 1960s, highlighting the relationship between Hans Haacke and a 'subsequent generation of artists'. This subsequent generation, that came of age in the late 1970s and 1980s, much like postmodernism in the visual arts, is implicitly identified with women artists – Cindy Sherman, Barbara Kruger and Sherrie Levine – all using photography and two of them (Sherman and Kruger) strongly identified with feminist critique.[35] We may then wonder: what happened between the 1980s and the 2000s? How and why did this female cast of art-world stars come to be replaced by an all-male cast?

The above shift from female to male artists is complemented with a shift from America to Europe. With the exception of Rirkrit Tiravanija, who as the son of a diplomat lived in so many places as to embody globalisation's idealised cosmopolitan individual, Bishop's male cast (Liam Gillick, Santiago Sierra and Thomas Hirschhorn) is European born and bred, much like Żmijewski. Europe, as noted throughout this book, became particularly exciting after the demise of Soviet culture and economy. War, reconfigured borders, diminished democratic rights, antagonistic economies, booming migration, structural adjustment programmes, corruption, emerging social movements have all generated a volatile space – and Steyerl's insightful remarks of 2010 concerning the male autocrat's narcissistic and flattering reflection in the mirror of contemporary art appear to have been inspired by flamboyant male European leaders such as Berlusconi (Italy), Putin (Russia), Sarkozy (France), Cameron (Britain) and Papandreou (Greece), who either claimed popularity on dismissive attitudes towards unmanly 'political correctness' or ruled undeterred by their unpopularity. This sort of masculine leadership is part of a new *zeitgeist* where democratic values, as known since the 1960s, are questioned at best – when not debunked by a new and explicitly fascistic masculinity represented by the 'political' mass murderer Anders Breivik in Norway and the male thugs of Greece's neo-Nazi party Golden Dawn appealing to a stunning 11 per cent of voters in 2012.[36] The new *zeitgeist* requires and promotes this kind of 'masculine' leadership – even when performed by the occasional iron lady such as German chancellor Angela Merkel and French IMF Director Christine Lagarde – because globalisation as twenty-first-century capitalism can ultimately be realised through a speedy and heavy-handed operation targeting a long-standing social consensus on the necessity of labour rights and a welfare state. The 'persuasive' tactics of shock and awe, as described by Naomi Klein, are indeed no longer marginal aberrations but central to neoliberal governance[37] – as is the increasing acceptance of torture in military and so-called anti-terrorist operations. To make a long story short, at the time of writing, in 2012, capitalism does not seem to need democracy any longer or for the time being. And so this early twenty-first century 'breach of pact' between capitalist markets and democracy is the wider political framework where masculinity meets experimental artistic labour to spectacular results. Żmijewski was included in the group show 'Ethics of Encounter', Parts I and II, held in Edinburgh in 2010. Curated by Kirsten Lloyd, the exhibition sought to bring together artworks that were symptomatic of a disregard towards 'accepted conventions and frameworks'.[38] Pertinently, the exhibition included only male artists.

Żmijewski's work in the show was his notorious video *80064* (2004) showing a young man, the artist, trying to persuade 92-year-old Józef Tarnawa, to have re-tattooed on his forearm his fading identification number from his days in the Nazi concentration camp of Auschwitz-Birkenau. One presumes that had the old man been an old woman, or the young man been a young woman, the relationship of pointless manipulation (in the sense of 'art for art's sake') would have been tainted by gender politics. In this confrontation between an old and a young man, what remains is purely the young man's generational arrogance versus the old man's vulnerability: the artist had hoped that refreshing the tattoo would make the old man regain his memory of the horrific past.[39] The old man is implicitly at least presented as having lost touch with his formative trauma! Indeed, the young male artist's claim of entry to history (the history of art) by way of ridiculing an older man represents a tragic moment in history (world history). In this game, it is important that the elderly man appears to be proud of the fact that he is a 'survivor', as he says in the video, that despite everyone around him succumbing to death, he managed to keep himself alive. This confidence in his own strength, and even power over circumstance, is what the young man seeks to undermine. A third (young) man in the scene, the tattoo artist, plays a more disturbing role, as his 'function' is to do as instructed, to execute, to imprint no-questions-asked the outcome of a master plan of manipulation and humiliation on a human body already too near to death (at the age of 92, the new tattoo is bound to last until the end).

Dani Marti's *Bacon's Dog* (2010), also in the exhibition, similarly engaged a young man (the artist) and an older man (an art collector). The creative young man filmed his sexual encounter with an old man who never had sex before. Yet sex in this case was introduced in a tale about intimacy as a deep human need, perhaps even an inalienable 'right' that the elderly man had been deprived of through circumstance. The elderly man is thus painfully vulnerable as the recipient of human touch and a warmth formerly denied him. The common feature of this and Żmijewski's piece is arguably the implication of the life of others, in its undiminished materiality, in the production process of the work of art. Exactly as in Żmijewski's art, the person is named. Here it is Peter Fay, an Australian curator and collector in his mid-60s, whom the viewer is offered the opportunity to observe in a situation of sexual intimacy with the artist. Positive responses to Andrea Fraser's *Untitled*, discussed in Chapter 1, had suggested that the work had devised a context of intimacy, thus

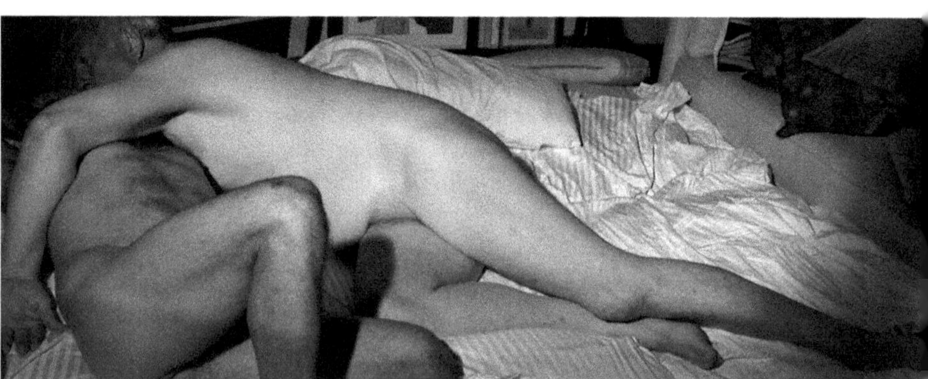

5.4   Dani Marti, *Bacon's Dog* (2010), video still. HDV, 2:55, two-channel projection. Duration 11'30".

're-humanising' the relationship between artist and collector.[40] It is important that Marti's video deliberately elides the distinction between sex (possibly identified as work) and intimacy (mostly identified as life). As a biopolitical artwork, *Bacon's Dog* articulates a full-blown parody of art as social work. When it comes to the provision of affect, art can boldly go where other care professions cannot. In its provision of a record for the extreme care work it provides (the documentary video taken to the gallery), art can demand access to income. And it can also demonstrate that incorporating sexual and love labour into how one makes a living is no longer just limited to prostitution. Rather, and this is the point, making a living becomes indistinguishable from living – in fact of living with, and thanks to, others.

It is perhaps easy to see that the abolition of such a distinction is the first step towards conflating different orders of power. A more Foucauldian operation of power takes hold: liquid, cloud-like and naturalised, it becomes as hard to grasp as the process of resisting it. This is one of the issues raised by contemporary art's fascination with, and investment in, young men who transgress accepted morals. The question, of course, is who holds the mirror into which – the critic says – Żmijewski should take a long hard look. Twenty years ago Kaja Silverman had already given this answer: 'Ideology holds out the mirror within which that [exemplary male] subjectivity is constructed.'[41]

Men, poverty and (post)colonialism: Renzo Martens' *Episode 3*

Renzo Martens' *Episode 3: Enjoy Poverty* (2008) was also included in 'The Ethics of Encounter' exhibition, which was appropriate given that this artwork stages a personified version of the problematic encounter of the West (the male artist) and Africa (the poor people of the Congo). Many other characters associated with various agencies and corporations become at times part of a harrowing exploitation plot, in essence a hands-on enquiry into what constitutes extraction of value in the image economies of global capitalism. For the purposes of my analysis, it is significant that *Episode 3* defies categorisation, its production process drawing on two salient radical trends in post-1989 art: the documentary turn and participatory action involving the artist. In that respect, *Episode 3* is markedly different from Olaf Breuning's *Home 2* (2007), also featuring a young, white male traveller and his encounters: the Swiss artist's contribution to the Whitney Biennale of 2008 included this film, described on the Biennial site in rather parochial terms: 'The viewer is left with the distinct notion that neither the traveler nor the world he has left is enriched by the experience. Contextualizing the helplessness of today's global citizen, Breuning examines a basic human quest for commonality in an increasingly global, but ever more fragmented, world.'[42]

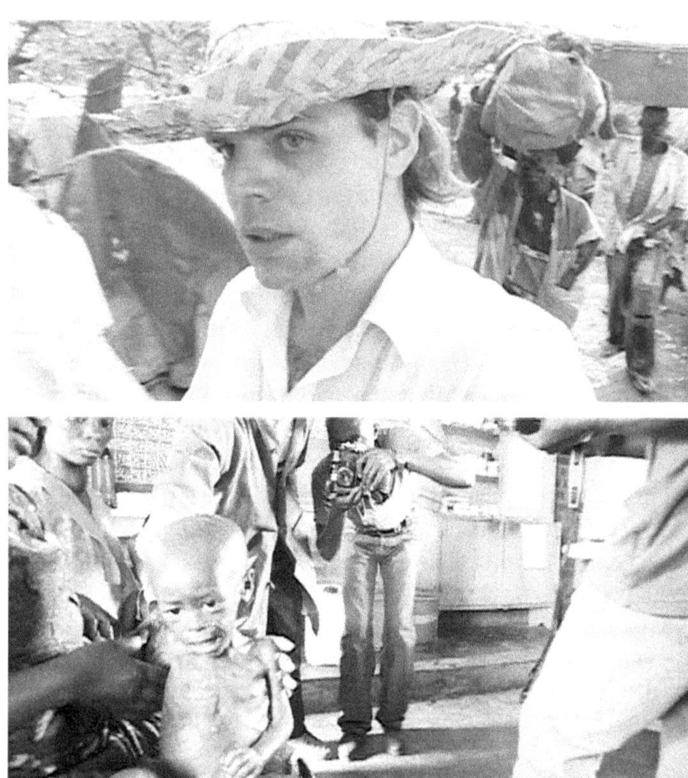

5.5–5.6   Renzo Martens, *Episode 3: Enjoy Poverty* (2009), 90'. Stills.

Yet Breuning hired a male actor to be filmed travelling the non-Western world as a tourist and interacting in often jackass ways with the 'natives' and everyone else. The same actor in Breuning's first instalment of his meditation on the conflict between the need for home and the imperative to travel, *Home* (2009), had said (in the guise of his character): 'I am not an intellectual but a little thought never hurt anyone.' Although the same boyish anti-intellectualism (infused with self-irony) permeates *Home 2* as well as Martens' *Episode 3*, the fact that we are witnessing the artist's own journey, efforts and failures in the latter enhances the provocation of the confrontation. In some respects, *Episode 3* provides a typical example of the video/film essay, as it constructs a positional narrative on the artist's passage through a socio-economic geography, the Congo (standing also for Africa), where the impact of capital's global imperative, extending and building on a colonial logic registers as an unmitigated disaster in humanitarian terms. Recent work where the conquering White Man is replaced by the conquering China-man, as the axis of power is slowly shifting from the West to Asia, is notable for not challenging the image of men as 'those who conquer': this is shockingly portrayed in Paolo Wood's photographic series *Chinafrica* (2007), where African men hold umbrellas over the heads of Chinese men or clean their swimming pools. Yet *Episode 3* achieves much more than a positional narrative, as the artist systematically rehearses, through his recorded actions in the field, a broad spectrum of encounters between Europe and Africa, only to demonstrate their political, rather than merely ethical, deficit.

The film's 'Renzo Martens', actually travelling through the Congo, first tries to teach the indigenous population to stand on their own feet exploiting their own resources. Following the failure of this attempt he tries to convince the indigenous population to come to terms with their predicament, to be happy in spite of being poor, explaining how knowledge of 'their' suffering enriches 'his' life. Following this second failure, exacerbated by the devastation generated by the death of a malnourished child (who, the viewer knows, stands for millions of others), Martens resorts to a one-off charity act, feeding a local family of plantation workers their first decent meal in ages (if not ever). The materiality of food and full stomachs finds its immaterial, ideological counter-narrative in the bitter acknowledgement of the transient effects of this philanthropic gesture. And the narrative concludes with a scene where Martens confronts another white man who – like the artist's image visiting him from the future – emerges out of the Congo river's 'black waters', infested with dangerous, untameable nature. In terms of both the second man's monologue and the mise-en-scène, the closing sequence suggests that the perverse enjoyment of this 'other' wild nature is what remains of the Western individual's inability to help Africa, as market-leader China is taking over! *Episode 3* constitutes a bold exploration of the causes determining such serial failure as it pretends to explore the sites of Africa's misery and mystique. Els Roelandt, who had several conversations with the artist while the film was in the making, writes about *Episode 3*:

Martens has once again set out with his camera for a region scarred by war and poverty. This time, it is Congo. He has travelled both on his own and with two porters, in the latter case letting himself be directed to various locations where NGOs were at work. Martens joined a group of journalists and photographers, and were duly confronted with the food relief activities of Unicef, infirmaries supervised by Doctors Without Borders and such events as the Congolese presidential elections. In other segments of the film, we see Martens engaged with local people. He tries to make the mechanisms of their exploitation clear to them. He moreover teaches them to photograph their own circumstances, just the way the white 'relief workers' appear to be doing. He teaches them to enjoy their poverty: the words, "Enjoy Poverty," are spelled out in big neon lights mounted on a raft with which he travels along the Congo River. The locals, who speak French, are given a translation and remain behind, bewildered and uncomprehending. Once Martens has summoned these mechanisms of abuse for the viewer (and for the local people), he goes a step further, confronting Western relief workers, journalists, art photographers and collectors with their own activities. He tries to show them (using a kind of Socratic Method) that what they are doing can be seen as patently unethical. As a result, Martens is repeatedly forbidden to film and at more than one point, the situation in which he finds himself looks downright dangerous.[43]

Roelandt's description captures a peculiar aspect of the work's production: although it involves a number of people in close interaction with each other, and engaged in dialogue, it is not really collaborative, if this term points to someone's willing participation. Rather, the people encountered appear to be trapped in situations which they help perpetuate but are not ultimately responsible for. The narrative as such offers a slightly different view on this same work in progress, both marking the artist's effort to produce a cooperative approach to the issue at hand – defying poverty in Africa – and rendering visible the substantial, possibly insurmountable, obstacles along the artist's path. These obstacles represent a complex outcome of interrelated factors: first, the hypocrisy of Western agents in Africa, including plantation owners, NGOs and the documentary photographers who act as delegates of a visual culture feeding off the exoticisation of misery; second, the indigenous population's internalisation of a position of disempowerment – although the film's narrative, to its credit, makes apparent that such self-identification with destitution and received or denied 'help' (the indigenous population patently addresses the artist as someone who has come to help them) is predicated on the institutionalised exclusion of this population from resources; third, the ideological and material framework in which the Western artist's role is inscribed as an encounter with economic others, irrespective of the artist's intentions.

The artist's intentions play a significant role in the action and narrative, not least because they appear to be openly part of the artwork's concept and process of realisation. *Episode 3* can be summarised as the artist's explicit attempt to teach the indigenous population how to turn their extreme poverty into a potentially profitable resource. In brief, this potential transmission of knowledge takes place as an encounter among men; specifically, one white man who is the heir of Europe's colonial project and guilt and many black men who represent the heirs of communities of dispossessed. The youthfulness of both the white man and the black men is important, disrupting a familiar patriarchal narrative where the patriarch (ruling father) controls both women and boys. In belonging to the same generation, the white man and the black men's relationship becomes a parody of an exchange between equals. This is because the white man's youth makes him the perfect representative of a privileged, geographically bound generation that has assimilated a key lesson of advanced post-Fordist economy: that everything can become productive and hence profitable, including one's poverty. If poverty is the end-product of a certain economic process, this end-product can also be recycled, sold to the appropriate market (visual culture) and re-enter the economic process. This is something that the young male black photographers of African villages do not grasp in the first instance, and something that the young male white image-maker has to teach them in a classroom context complete with white board and animated by what Roelandt calls 'Socratic method': questions and answers.

This Socratic method becomes, nevertheless, credible and persuasive through the preferred, or arguably sole, methodology of orthodox, neoliberal economics: arithmetic. The young white man scribbles calculations on the white board that demonstrate convincingly the rate of profit, should the black men switch from photographing the positive aspects of community life to photographing raped women and starving children. Uttering their concern about lacking access to the market for humanitarian disaster pho-tography, the black men are, nevertheless, convinced to explore this option and the men begin touring the medical units where black children can be found dying and black women weeping. The white artist teaches the black photographers what to look for and how to take pictures guaranteed to achieve the maximum affect-impact on those who view them. But such apprentice time will not ultimately lead to a successful (profit-making) career for the young black men. This awareness emerges dramatically when master and apprentices visit a white male doctor who scolds them for their ethically condemnable intentions, as he also tells them that only designated Western photographers are formally allowed to take and sell pictures. Following this encounter that reveals who is entitled to free trade and who is not, the white young man is only left with the option of charity. In one of the film essay's most ethically shocking moments, he offers a fulfilling meal to a black plantation worker and his starving family, which is received with desperate gratitude.

We see then how the artist's intentions, as declared within the film narra-tive, gradually transform: the frustrated intention to teach ends up as the intention to be philanthropic, in full awareness of the ineffectiveness and transience of this last-resort action. One can be a lot more speculative about the artist's intentions as they do not appear in the film narrative. For Paul O'Kane, the artist's intentions are summarised as 'provocations', with the plural here functioning as an homage to the diversity of moral and political concerns that the narrative brings forth. But O'Kane also argues that 'what Martens (like a born-again Joseph Beuys) seems to offer the Congolese is the possibility of determining and constructing their own reality directly from their own needs by following the model – not of the politician, journalist or priest – but of the *modern artist*'[44] (my emphasis). O'Kane is led to this assessment by referencing both the act of placing a 'disruptive sign', the words 'Enjoy Poverty', in the midst of the normal circle of signs referencing reality and the modern artist's bohemian lifestyle where a necessary evil (poverty) was appropriated as a 'virtue'.[45] O'Kane hardly intends this invocation of the modern artist as a criticism. Instead, he corroborates the plausibility of this reference by placing Martens in a lineage familiar to feminist and anti-feminist art historians alike: Beuys, Manet, Courbet, Mondrian, Malevich, Picasso – in order of appearance in his review article. The first names of these grandfathers are redundant, we all know who the grandfathers are and what they signify – they are not a Frida Kahlo, a Lee Krasner or a Louise Bourgeois but just a 'Picasso'. These are the only artists' names framing Martens' work and the complex positioning of *Episode 3* in the history of art. That said, the film's complexity is enhanced by, and yet not exhausted in, the revenge of history: in 2008–9, when the film was released, the beginning of 'the first systemic crisis of the neoliberal stage of capitalism' turned the sign 'Enjoy Poverty', transported in the luggage of a European artist visiting Africa with a mission, into a cynical message transmitted from Africa back to Europe.[46]

One particularly complex aspect of the work, as much as of the human relationships it documents, is how it relates to women. Women are mostly absent. They appear only sporadically as black mothers bent over dead or dying children, black war widows whose inability to act hurts, stupid white gallery-goers made (by the male artist) to admit that they are in fact gazing at images of poor black people, clueless, white press or NGO members. What makes this approach to women complex is the impossibility of passing a judgement over whether women have been marginalised consciously or not by, and through, the artist's choices or whether this is the salient moment of the film functioning as a social document, merely presenting what the white male explorer encountered. But to say this means that the film is placed squarely within a politics of representation – either women are misrepresented in images that display a variety of positions of disempowerment, victimisation and politically correct naivety or they are realistically represented. Yet what is hard to dispute is that the artist enters dialogical situations nearly exclusively with men: plantation owners, plantation workers, doctors, soldiers, photographers, the fellow (well-intended) white man. If one of the video's opening scenes focuses on two black men wrestling each other in a publicly set ring, cheered by a male crowd, the narrative overall appears to provide countless variations of this theme, expanding the remit of confrontations among men and weaving into them the economic significance of race.

O'Kane's invocation of modern art's Old Canon, by which I mean the lineage of forefathers who claimed and won – through work and lifestyle – modern art's autonomy, acquires particular relevance in light of the film's particular portrayal of men and women. In claiming that the bohemian (male) modern artist provides the model of emancipation offered to twenty-first-century Africa, O'Kane imputes to *Episode 3*'s homosocial environments the meaning of a return path to a heroic masculinity. Feminist art history in the West has produced highly focused critiques of this heroic masculinity, including corrective narratives that present a more complex constitution of the story of modern art. But when the appeal to the Old Canon achieves a connection between art's one-dimensional, masculinist history and the encounter between Europe and Africa in the context of capitalist globalisation, ironies proliferate. In narrating the white man's serial failure in this new context, *Episode 3* appears to be structured through an antinomy: it both dispels and revives the myth of a singular masculinity. I say antinomy and not contradiction because masculinity is typically found to be defined through the 'law' of male dominance and the visibility of male action (as the other side to female subordination and passivity). On the one hand, *Episode 3* narrates the un-translatability of the European modern artist's glorification of poverty into the life of the African male subject today. This happens for the same historical reasons that produce both the African man's poverty and the West's class of precarious cultural workers, on which so much has been recently said. The mere possibility of such a link, as proposed by O'Kane, would introduce a new mythification of Africa as falling outside global capital's time – the time that has made it impossible for Western cultural workers to misrecognise their precarity as some kind of freedom but makes it possible for African photographers and plantation workers alike to do just that.

On the other hand, *Episode 3* appears to lend some credibility to a project of a singular, transcontinental masculinity by simply presenting men as agents of all action. *Episode 3* performs its antinomy by staging an inflated image of male narcissism centred, quite literally, on the face of the artist-essayist. Going through the film in pristine white shirts, Martens comments towards the end: 'and I know I am capable of vanity', having the camera function as a reflective surface of the artist's purposefully exaggerated self-admiration. Registering the details of the artist's facial expression, the camera manages to deliver the ideological aspect of the filmed Renzo Martens' vanity: his belief that he, the solitary, heroic male individual will save Africa as a victimised continent. In this sense, *Episode 3* exposes the entire idea of modern art – as the effect of creative genius on the world – as a by-product of a delusional, atomised bourgeois masculinity. Could Hito Steyrel be right? Is contemporary art at large premised on a renewal of the pact between capital and masculinity as dominant ideology?

Notes

1 See A. Jones, 'Dis/playing the Phallus: Male Artists Perform their Masculinities', *Art History* 17/4 (Dec 1994), 546–84; A. Jones ''Clothes Make the Man': The Male Artist as a Performative Function', *Oxford Art Journal* 18/2 (1995), 18–32; and specific chapters in A. Jones, *Body Art: Performing the Subject* (Minneapolis: University of Minnesota, 1998). See also A. Solomon Godeau, *Male Trouble: A Crisis in Representation* (London: Thames & Hudson, 1997).

2 The exhibition was accompanied by the volume S. Kent and J. Moreau (eds), *Women's Images of Men* (London: The ICA/Writers & Readers, 1985).

3 See T. Augsburg, 'Man as Object – Reversing the Gaze' at: http://manasobject. weebly.com/index.html (accessed 10 March 2012). 'Man as Object: Reversing the Gaze' was at SOMArts Cultural Center, 934 Brannan Street, San Francisco, CA, 4–30 November 2011.

4 'Black Male: Representations of Masculinity in Contemporary American Art' was at the Whitney Museum of American Art in New York in 1994–95, just before 'Masculin-Féminin, le sexe de l'art' at Centre Goerges Pompidou from 19 October 1995 to 8 January 1996. In connection with the last show, a reviewer noted at the time that 'since most of the works shown were made by men (overwhelmingly the case for pre-1970 pieces), there was a crushing preponderance of the masculine or, rather, of the phallic. Not to mention that the works themselves, with but a few exceptions, were manifestly focused on heterosexuality'. See E. Lebovici, 'French Lessons', *Artforum* (March 1996), at: http://findarticles.com/p/articles/mi_m0268/is_n7_v34/ai_18403695/ (accessed 14 December 2010). 'Masculinities' took place at Kunsthallen Nikolaj – Nikolaj Copenhagen Contemporary Art Center from 3 November to 30 December 2001. As noted in the press release, 'an important theme of the exhibition was to show masculine figures of desire as they come across in the Western culture of both homosexuality and heterosexuality. A number of artists focused on masculinity as it relates to sexuality and power, and desire and aggression', at: www.kunstaspekte.de/index.php?tid=24578&action=termin (accessed 13 December 2010). 'Masquerades: Femininity, Masculinity and Other Certainties' was at the State Museum of Contemporary Art in Thessaloniki from 6 December to 18 February 2007. 'Hard Targets: Masculinity and American Sports' was at the Los Angeles County Museum of Art in fall 2008. 'Thread Baring: A Portrait of Masculinity One Thread at the Time', at the Milwakee Union Art Gallery (19 November to 18 December 2009), presented male artists working in so-called traditionally female media, such as weaving and knitting.

5 Helen Molesworth's 'Work Ethic' was on view at The Baltimore Museum of Art from 12 October 2003 to 4 January 2004.

6 H. Molesworth, 'Introduction', in H. Molesworth (ed.), *Work Ethic* (Pennsylvania: The Baltimore Museum of Art/Pennsylvania State University Press, 2003), 18.

7 This is not a purely curatorial project, as the exhibition shares its title with Hopkins' book of 2008. The exhibition, which despite its title also included two women artists (Sarah Lucas and Lee Miller), was at the Fruitmarket

Gallery, Edinburgh, from 27 May to 16 July 2006. See D. Hopkins, *Dada's Boys: Masculinity after Duchamp* (New Haven: Yale University Press, 2008).

8 K. Kosmala, *Imagining Masculinities Spatial and Temporal Representation and Visual Culture* (London: Taylor & Francis, 2013).

9 C. Bishop, 'Antagonism and Relational Aesthetics', *October* 110 (2004), 51–79; and 'The Social Turn: Collaboration and Its Discontents'.

10 Bryan-Wilson, *Art Workers*, 170.

11 H. Reckitt, 'Forgotten Relations: Feminist Artists and Relational Aesthetics', in Dimitrakaki and Perry, *Politics in a Glass Case*, 131–152.

12 R. Dyer, 'Don't Look Now: The Male Pin-Up', in *The Sexual Subject: A Screen Reader in Sexuality* (London and New York: Routledge 1992).

13 Lu Jie curated the exhibition 'Yang Shaobin: The X Blind Spot – A Long March Project' at Long March Foundation in Peking, from 4 September to 18 October 2008. The press release mentions that 'in 'X-Blind Spot' Yang Shaobin delves into the psychology of those who endure, enact, and persist with the toil of coal mining life. This exhibition presents a complete body of new work which reflects an introspective, and at times disturbing cruelty and exploitation observed in the social transformation of farmer to laborer – the reality of many coal miners today in China.' Available in English at: www.kunstaspekte.de/index.php?tid=44764&action=termin (accessed 15 December 2009).

14 For a Chinese art focused on the worker but divided into a pre- and post-1989 period see Lu Jie '800 Metres' on an exhibition of the same title held at Long March in Beijing from 2 September to 15 October 2006, at: www.artlinkart .com/en/space/exh_yr/ee1etw/6ofaxzr (accessed 3 April 2012).

15 Glawogger's triptych on global labour includes *Megacities* (1998), *Working-man's Death: Heroes* (2005), *Whores* (2011).

16 www.artangel.org.uk//projects/2001/the_battle_of_orgreave/background/ the_english_civil_war_part_ii (accessed 14 November 2011).

17 A concise presentation of such developments can be found in A. Chakrabortty, 'Why Doesn't Britain Make Things Any More?', *The Guardian* (16 November 2011), at: www.guardian.co.uk/business/2011/nov/16/why-britain-doesnt-make-things-manufacturing?INTCMP=SRCH (accessed 16 November 2011).

18 See Dimitrakaki, 'The Spectacle and Its Others', in Harris, *Globalization and Contemporary Art*.

19 K. Chukhrov, 'Towards the Space of the General: On Labor beyond Materiality and Immateriality', *e-flux journal* 20 (November 2010), at: www.e-flux.com/ journal/view/180 (accessed 14 December 2010).

20 H. Steyerl, 'Politics of Art: Contemporary Art and the Transition to Postde-mocracy', *e-flux journal* 21 (December 2010), at: www.e-flux.com/journal/ view/181 (accessed 16 December 2010).

21 A. Searle, 'Into the Unknown', *The Guardian* (8 October 2002), at: www. guardian.co.uk/film/2002/oct/08/artsfeatures.art (accessed 16 December 2010).

22 Chukhrov, 'Towards the Space of the General'.

23 H. Braverman, *Labor and Monopoly Capital: The Degradation of Work in the Twentieth Century* (New York: Monthly Review Press, 1974).

24 P. Vélez, 'Hearts of Darkness', *Artnet magazine* (14 December 2007), at: www
   .artnet.com/magazineus/reviews/velez/velez12-14-07.asp (accessed 16 December 2010).
25 R. Matthews, 'Art: Uneven Geographies, Nottingham Contemporary', *Nottingham Post* (14 May 2010), at: www.thisisnottingham.co.uk/news/Art-Uneven-
   Geographies-Nottingham-Contemporary/article-2149196–detail/article.html
   (accessed 16 December 2010).
26 Vélez, 'Hearts of Darkness'.
27 T. Fisken, 'The Spectral Proletariat: The Politics of Hauntology in *The
   Communist Manifesto*', *Global Discourse* [Online], 2: II (2011), at: http://
   global-discourse.com/contents.
28 W. Benjamin, 'The Author as Producer' (1936), widely reproduced in print and
   online.
29 M. Kwon, 'Exchange Rate: On Obligation and Reciprocity in Some Art of the
   1960s and after', in Molesworth, *Work Ethic*, 84.
30 Sholette, *Dark Matter*.
31 In 2010 these were: Damien Hirst, Jeff Koons, Takashi Murakami, Brice
   Marden, Julian Schnabel, Anish Kapoor, Jasper Johns. See 'The World's
   Wealthiest Artists?' (23 February 2010), at: www.artinfo.com/news/story/33945/
   the-worlds-wealthiest-artists/ (accessed 3 March 2011).
32 Steyerl, 'Politics of Art: Contemporary Art and the Transition to Post-
   Democracy'.
33 Ibid.
34 K. Johnson, 'An Artist Turns People into His Marionettes', *The New York
   Times* (29 November 2009), at: www.nytimes.com/2009/11/30/arts/design/
   30zmijewski.html (accessed 16 December 2010). At the time Artur Żmijewski
   had a show at X Initiative in Chelsea while 'Projects 91: Artur Żmijewski' was
   on at the Museum of Modern Art.
35 Bishop, 'Antagonism and Relational Aesthetics', 63. Bishop writes: 'It was not
   enough to show that the artwork's meaning is subordinate to its framing (be
   this in a museum or magazine); the viewer's own identification with the
   image was deemed to be equally important. Rosalyn Deutsche usefully sum-
   marizes this shift in her book *Evictions: Art and Spatial Politics* (1996) when
   she compares Hans Haacke to the subsequent generation of artists that
   included Cindy Sherman, Barbara Kruger, and Sherrie Levine. Haacke's work,
   she writes, 'invited viewers to decipher relations and find content already
   inscribed in images but did not ask them to examine their own role and
   investments in producing images.' By contrast, the subsequent generation of
   artists 'treated the image itself as a social relationship and the viewer as a
   subject constructed by the very object from which it formerly claimed
   detachment.'
36 Both Breivik and Golden Dawn are connected with the astonishing rise and
   diverse forms of fascism in early twenty-first-century Europe and were often
   headlines in 2012, as I was completing this book.
37 N. Klein, *The Shock Doctrine: The Rise of Disaster Capitalism* (New York:
   Penguin, 2008 [2007]).

38 Press Release, www.stills.org/exhibition/past/social-documents-ethics -encounter-part-i (accessed 12 April 2012).

39 See description of artwork at www.digitalartlab.org.il/ArchiveVideo.asp?id=16 (accessed 23 September 2012).

40 See S. E. Cahan, 'Regarding Andrea Fraser's Untitled', *Social Semiotics* 16/1 (April 2006), 7–15.

41 K. Silverman, *Male Masculinity at the Margins* (New York and London: Routledge, 1992), 15.

42 S. Goergen, 'Olaf Bruning: About the Artist', at: http://whitney.org/www/ 2008biennial/www/?section=artists&page=artist_breuning (accessed 10 April 2012).

43 E. Roelandt, 'Renzo Martens' Episode 3: Analysis of a Film Process in Three Conversations', at: http://squarevzw.be/picturethis/renzoapm16.htm (accessed 8 December 2010). First published in *A Prior Magazine* 16 (February 2008).

44 P. O'Kane, 'Renzo Martens' Episode 3', *Third Text* 23/6 (November 2009), 813–20. Here 816.

45 Ibid., 816.

46 D. Mcnally, *Global Slump: The Economics and Politics of Crisis and Resistance* (Oakland Calif.: PM Press, 2010).

Acting on power: critical collectives, curatorial visions and art as life

Telling the problem differently: from women artists to feminism, power
and the art institution

'I sometimes wonder if I know what the problem really is', Griselda Pollock
says in a 2010 essay tracing the entanglement of historiographical and curatorial practices as constitutive of a 'living' feminist history of art. She continues
as follows: '…or if the terms in which we have told it [the problem] to ourselves, using the language of modern feminism, has not failed in some ways
to enable us to make the change we desire'.[1] Pollock wonders how what appears
as truth to her as a feminist – women's creativity as a fundamental motor for
culture – is not held as a general social truth, which has been one way of
defining the problem. There is evidence that the problem persists. Pollock
quotes critic Jerry Saltz for whom New York MOMA's long and ongoing exclusion of women artists amounts to an 'apartheid'.[2] Press releases of women-
friendly private galleries (a most rare breed anyway) convincingly place their
projects in a cultural climate where women artists do not win enough prizes
or are scarce in museum collections.[3] In 2008, Joanne Heath was able to cite
activist art research dispelling the myth that women artists are necessarily
better represented in museum displays forty years after the emergence of the
feminist art movement. But more depressingly, Heath poses the question
whether the recent phenomenon of blockbuster retrospectives featuring
women artists 'can in fact be characterized by a near-total negation of feminism'.[4] Heath's comments imply something important for a contemporary
feminist politics in, and about, the art world: that what the institution of art
persistently seeks to curb, abort, diffuse is not so much women's creativity as
its imminent or potential political power – and even selective, populist show-
cases of women artists can be marshalled to this cause.

Beginning from the position that the relationship between radical feminist
politics and the art institution can no longer be centred on the question of
women artists' inclusion, in this chapter I seek to explore different paths connecting women artists and curators with action, with activism, with power,
with subversion even. The discussion turns to channels and contexts through

which feminist doing is realised and feminist desire for doing is transmitted in ways that perhaps allow for a range of responses to this issue: how do feminist politics relate to the art institution, if it is not just about entering the latter but also about negating or simply crossing through it but hoping to get across to some other social reality?

In the 1960s and 1970s women artists' absence from the art institution transformed from a lesson in feminine humility taught to women to a cause for militant politics. Women's absence generated a feminist counter-public that researched the causes of this exclusion and actively protested against it. Yet this counter-public, where it existed (it was not universal), was ideologically divided and never grew to the point where the art institution would find it impossible to resist its pressure. Instead of getting structurally reformed, the art institution was able to get away by accepting the least painful feminist demands – which is how the woman artist blockbuster show devoid of feminism became possible.

Critiques of second-wave feminism around 2000, already discussed in previous chapters, suggest that whatever gains feminism made from the 1960s onwards, these were not the triumphant outcome of feminist protest in any straightforward way. More work is required to help us address the dialectic between radical politics and the conditions of their realisation. For example, in projects such as *Feministo: The Portrait of the Artist as Housewife* (1975–77, Britain) we see that some women took collective action to function as artists on the basis of extra-institutional networks. This does not of course equal a rejection of the art institution, but it is telling that *Feministo* involved both professional, if struggling, female artists as well as 'amateur' full-time housewives.[5] In twenty years' time any such projects would be overshadowed by the media and market success of 'exceptional' women in Cool Britannia's art world, which managed to combine an aesthetic of 'cool' (normally ascribed to the social margins) and a 'celebrity' culture (normally ascribed to mainstream sensibilities). Angela McRobbie has argued that in post-feminist Britain, a gender 'equality of sorts' was in fact 'undermined by subtle forces of patriarchal retrenchment implemented through the seemingly harmless but in fact ruthless and tyrannical deployment of 'cool' as a disciplinary regime in work and leisure'[6] – and it is too easy to see how the 'ladette' generation of Tracey Emin, Sarah Lucas and Sam Taylor-Wood successfully exploited their own subjection to such a disciplinary regime.

Of course, not everyone did. Loraine Leeson, whose exemplary collaborative and community-oriented projects were informed by feminist politics in the 1990s, admits to the difficulty of working as a feminist in a British context defined by post-feminism: the issues she tackled, concerning maternal labour, women's health and the rise of religious fundamentalism that put women's life at risk, entered (to the extent that they did) public consciousness much later, as globalisation was spiralling into conflict and crisis, demanding a return to politics.[7] Such issues had remained intensely marginal in the 'cool' British art world that had every interest in closing the chapter 'feminism'. Leeson crucially implicates the institutionalisation of feminism in the 1990s as occurring also in the academic context where theory production had effectively disengaged 'with issues on the ground'.[8] This was still a time, however, when art making rather than curating was widely perceived as the chief site for (feminist) politics.

It would not be until 2006 when UK-based feminist art journal *n.paradoxa* would get Renee Baert to edit a very special issue, the one launching a more systematic enquiry into the intersection of feminism and curating. Baert's assessment that 'feminist practices today are often "folded in" with other issues and positions' would be hard to disprove.[9] In hindsight, it is evident that 'folded in' could be defined across a spectrum of meanings – ranging from an oppositional politics of alliance to feminism's absorption into the brand museum of the twenty-first century and its populist mega-shows. For example, there has been much concern about the museum manufacturing 'feminist art': once the outcome of a living movement, now packaged as a genre belonging to the past (and mostly to the West). As Lara Perry has argued in her examination of Tate Modern, such 'feminist art' gets to be productively appropriated to modernise art collections integral to the policies of the neoliberal museum.[10] The widely cited group of pioneer feminist art-world activists Guerrilla Girls, that formed in the USA in 1985, now list on their website the museum collections that have acquired their agit-prop posters and other 'visualised' interventions explicitly targeting the art institution.[11] It is not then just feminist art but also feminist critique that has been 'folded in' in that sense – but then there has been a thin line between the demand to transform the art institution and the desire to do so by being accommodated in this very institution.

My aim in this chapter, however, is not to explain women's desire to be in the institutions of art of the late twentieth century. For what is persistently explicated as a demand for visibility can invite a different interpretation if we turn to the issue of remunerated labour: the institution of art is also, and primarily, an employer or an income source – especially as the state cuts welfare, withdraws arts funding and could not be further for considering a basic income for artists. Such conditions force artists to make a necessary connection with the market through any means possible. Women, often burdened with 'dependants', can have income once they enter the institution of art (either as artists or curators and increasingly in recent years as also researchers) – which makes it obvious why the institutional pull has been virtually impossible to resist. Instead, this chapter is concerned with how women in the past decade have acted in relation to the institution of art and its command of power, in acknowledgement of the fact that such action may take place both within and beyond the institution. This is also why I attempt to read across art making and curating, temporarily at least suspending the barriers between these practices to arrive at an understanding of where and how a contemporary feminist politics, an acting on power, is articulated.

Since 2000 women and, indeed, feminist curators have even succeeded in organising blockbuster shows – from 'Wack! Art and the Feminist Revolution' (2007) to 'Global Feminisms' (2007) in the USA to 'Gender Check' (2009) in Europe. But as already suggested above, most such curatorial ventures have been criticised by the feminist community, which has seen such initiatives as never quite managing to not exclude, to not historicise, to not compromise – for example, see the criticisms of 'Gender Check' in Chapter 2. Although this chapter does not provide an analysis of such curatorial projects and their critical reception (that would require a chapter in its own right), their passing mention here serves to sketch a background for understanding perhaps less visible, or at least so far less discussed, confrontations with power in the art world. Feminism as a modality of doing can take place in and through art, curating, activism or, perhaps increasingly in a more fluid service-and-entrepreneurialism economy, through various combinations of the above. Discourse is not absent from these practices but tends to be incorporated into purposeful action. The examples of practice presented here bespeak of very complex trajectories and may well constitute ideological positions in their own right. I believe that by placing them together, we can begin to think about both the *historical grounding* as well as the *flexibility of resistance*, that feminism can engage after 2000. Collectivism and/or collaboration are central here, though they may not always assume the forms one might have imagined.

On curatorial power and the artist's power: a gendered view

I begin with art as a practice of power, and specifically art that takes as its focus the relationship between curator and artist. Tanja Ostojić completed several such durational, participatory artworks under the general title 'Strategies of Success/Curators Series' between 2001 and 2003. That is, this series of works was conceptualised and executed while the curator was becoming consolidated as a figure of power. Indeed, a few years later the curator had displaced the artist, the collector and certainly the critic as the global art world's most powerful figure.[12] Even if the veracity of such an appraisal could be contested, the rhetoric concerning the alleged or real power of the curator around, and since, 2000 was enough to suggest a broader ideological shift whereby curatorial labour moved from care to (creative) management. 'Creative' appears here bracketed – as somehow superfluous – in order to highlight that, in the economic system where the shift occurred, management is rewarded as a socially necessary and highly productive form of creativity. The rise of a (creative) managerial class is one of the foremost features of the post-Fordist economy sustaining global capital. And so, around 2000, it was evident that the celebrity artist was matched by the celebrity curator, when 'celebrity' connoted 'success'. Unsurprisingly then, Ostojić gave her series a title that addresses success both playfully and seriously – since her artwork is intended as a parody of the art world's best-kept public secret: that for an artist to succeed, networking with, and preferably, befriending the curator is essential.

'Strategies of Success/Curators Series' encompasses no fewer than twelve works, and the titles of some are revealing: *I'll Be Your Angel* (2001), *Be My Guest* (2001), *Sofa for Curator* (2002), *Vacation with Curator* (2003). The titles reveal an inverted relationship. Instead of the curator facilitating the artist, the artist now facilitates the curator: accommodation, hospitality and care provided by the artist to the curator are the behavioural modes that hide behind these titles. A second theme running through the series is that of referencing the histories of art, as in *Black Square on White* (2001) and the rather mysteriously titled *Politics of Queer Curatorial Positions: After Rosa von Praunheim, Fassbinder and Bridge Markland* (2003). Finally, a third theme can be established in an engagement with the confessional mode in *Venice Diary* (2002) and *Venice Diary Reading* (2002 and 2003). The list of works offered in a volume that documents the series includes mention of all principal collaborators. There are many relations between the pieces – for example, in *Venice Diary Reading* the artist perfomatively reads to the public her emotionally loaded personal record of *I'll Be Your Angel* – whereas in many cases the audiovisual record of an originally live, participatory piece is classified as a separate piece of work. What unites all the works, however, is the acknowledgement of the artist–curator bond in terms of a gendered dynamic organised by power and disempowerment (much like Ostojić's major biopolitical work, the orchestration of her own marriage to a male EU citizen, which she was living through at the time).

I'll Be Your Angel was performed at the 49th Venice Biennale. The performance, which lasted four days, consisted in the young female artist appearing elegantly and expensively dressed on the side of the senior male curator of the Venice Biennale, Harald Szeemann. She appeared smiling, reticent, patiently waiting for him to speak at press conferences or at dinners and brought him cups of coffee. Szeemann was hardly a random choice. Post-2000, the appraisal of his work, seen to mark a crucial shift in a global refocus of the curatorial field as one of power (over others), suggests that the forms of artistic labour witnessed in the output of Ostojić can hardly be decoupled from responses to this shift.[13] Ostojić's insight was to launch a critique of the latter in ways that brought to the fore the continuous purchase of a feminine/masculine polarity:

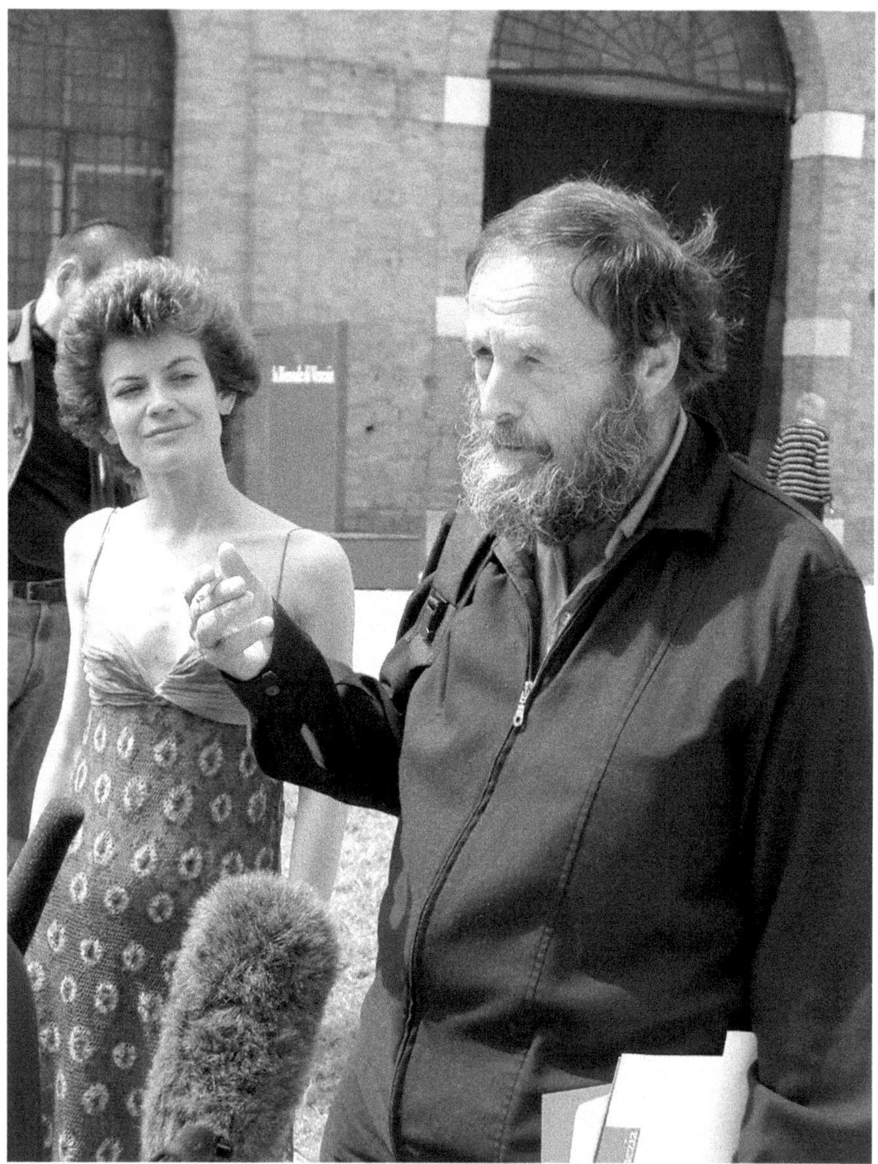

6.1   Tanja Ostojić, 'Strategies of Success/Curators Series' (2001–3). *I'll Be Your Angel* (2001), four-day performance with Harald Szeemann, Plato of Humankind, 49th Venice Biennale.

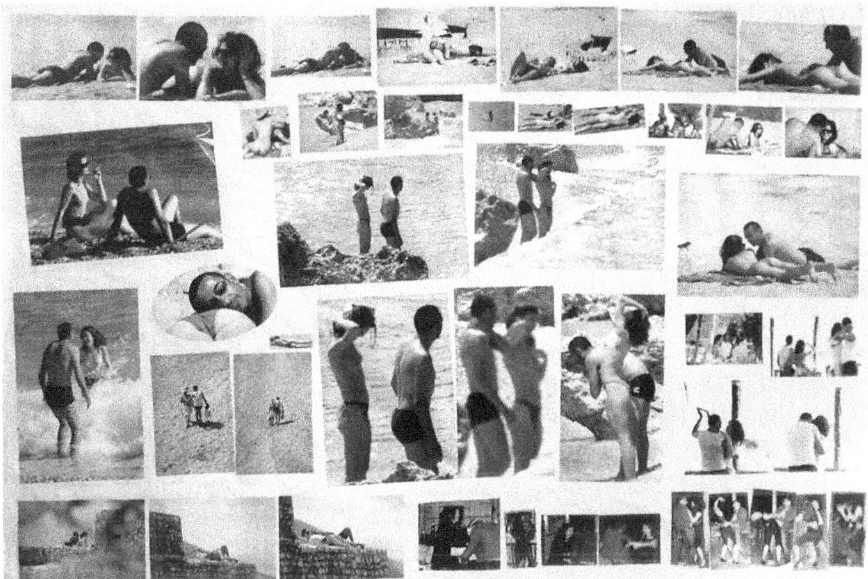

6.2 Tanja Ostojić, 'Strategies of Success/Curators Series' (2001–3). *Vacation with Curator* (2003). Photo Collage, 62.5 × 93 cm. From: the project at 2nd Tirana Biennale, Albania, with curator Edi Muka.

the artist is coded feminine (decorative, exchangeable and submissive) whereas the curator is coded masculine (serious, individualised and leading). The tentative success of the 'feminine' artist in managing to do her radical work is achieved at the cost of public humiliation or, put more mildly, in accepting the terms of the game. Yet Ostojić has suggested – upon reading an earlier draft of this text, and this is perhaps important- that recording such 'ephemeral' events in publications was a way of asserting her 'right to speak about what happened after'. 'That's the reason', Ostojić says, that 'the works are 'extended in time'… Some reactions came only later, and some were too bizarre to [even] include in the book'.[14] So, making apparent the general rule of accepting the terms of the game, yes; leaving it at that, no: putting effort into creating micro-environments where the terms of power continue to be questioned, beyond the exhibition/biennial time framework, is important. This is another example where the work done by art, the artWork, merely begins with the formal, regulated piece.

Be My Guest is the title of both a participatory artwork and an edited film based on its recording. When invited by curator Bartolomeo Pietromarchi to have a performance at Rome's Palazzo delle Esposizioni, Ostojić invited the curator by letter to join her for drinks, dinner and an informal conversation.

As a bourgeois pastime, this dinner party would also involve light conversation subjects, such as art and gossip (focused on the participants' personal lives). The letter further detailed that the artist would then have a bath in the Jacuzzi installed in the gallery. Arrangements proceeded according to plan, and on this evening of the performance, observed by a live audience, the artist entered the Jacuzzi naked. She was soon joined by a male critic (Ludovico Pratesi) who had also dined with the artist and, as arranged in advance, would take the place of the curator in the Jacuzzi, happy to participate in champagne drinking, chatting and flirting.[15] All this actually took place as operatic music filled the space, adding to the 'refined, civilized' atmosphere that the artist intended as a necessary aspect of a collaborative piece offering a metaphor of the sociality associated with the Western art world (which, as noted, the artist was seeking at the time to join through her long-term piece *Looking for a Husband with EU Passport*).[16]

In *Sofa for Curator*, Ostojić washed the feet of a rather reluctant and puzzled Belgrade curator, Stevan Vukovic, as a performance at the opening of a show in Graz, Austria entitled 'The Balkan Consulate Proudly Presents: Belgrade. For Vacation with Curator' (2003) the artist went on holiday with Edi Muka, at that time art director and chief curator of the Tirana Biennial, and instructed a photographer to take paparazzi-style snapshots of the two of them on the beach (with Muka's knowledge). The revealing paparazzi photos never made it to the Albanian press, as the artist intended them to, where they'd be 'adorned' with yellow-press and possibly career-damaging stories; nor were they included in the Tirana Biennial catalogue (the work was made as part of the Tirana Biennial in 2003). *Black Square on White* consisted in the artist offering exclusive access to the corporeally realised (upon her own body) reconstruction of the famous modern-master work of the same title to the Biennale Director Harald Szeemann, 'in order for him to declare the 'hidden Malevich' in between Ostojić's legs to officially be part of the Biennale'.[17] *The Politics of Queer Curatorial Positions: After Rosa von Praunheim, Fassbinder and Bridge Markland* is a performative photograph where the curator-theorist-artist Marina Gržinić and Ostojić reference the sixteenth-century painting *Gabriele d'Estrees and one of her Sisters* (1595) and a portrait of Andy Warhol from the Christopher Makos's series 'The Altered Image' (1981). The two women appear naked from the waist up with Ostojić pressing lightly on Gržinić's right nipple while Gržinić's right hand is suspended mid-air. Her thumb and finger create a circle – the symbol of zero and nothing as well as of a binding engagement ring, alluding to the complexity of a possible (imagined or real) erotic encounter between the two women, here personifying two positions (curator and artist) in the art world.

Finally, the three installations grouped under 'Strategies of Success' (in Cacak, Berlin, Bourges, 2001–3) present environments based either on female vanity and beautification rituals or objects and text openly referring to the art world as the site of a gendered sexual trade. In Berlin, a mountain of 3,520 unused condoms pushed to a corner, as if spilling out of a crack in the red walls, was accompanied by a hand-written message (with misspellings as if hastily scribbled on a toilet door): 'This is the exact amount of condoms that I used during my career in order to serve curators who helped me become famous.' An arrow drawn on the wall and pointing to the pile of condoms shot out from the phrase. Given that the artist is a woman, the condom is here contextualised as a protective mediator of heterosexual sex. Although Suzana Milevska argues that 'the revelation of truth is obviously not what is at stake here', referring to the exaggerated number of the condoms, the assumption is precisely that the viewer is not faced with a certain kind of lie.[18] Rather, the viewer is faced with the exaggerated form that a certain kind of truth can assume: that the contemporary art world as the site of trade is not so much the place of sexual permissiveness as of relationships replicating sexual domi-nation. Milevska reads this condition as one exemplifying a master/slave dia-lectic where 'the artist/slave works positively with the objects, puts a specific form to them, so that while working on them, he/she becomes aware of his/her independence'.[19]

But the point is precisely that the artist is a 'she'. If the artist were a 'he', Mr Ostojić would not, and could not, have reserved references to queer politics for the title of one particular work. The performative photograph *The Politics of Queer Curatorial Positions*, where female artist Ostojić is touching the breast of female curator/theorist/artist Gržinić, is indeed an anomaly in a series otherwise exclusively inscribing the dynamics between a female artist and male curators. And yet, even here, it is the artist that appears in profile, staring longingly into the curator's face whose gaze is turned outwards, towards an assumed viewer. Even here, the feminine 'rituals of seduction' that Milevska speaks about in her essay are deployed by the artist to appeal to the curator, who expects to be seduced *by the artist* rather than the work. If the curator is not seduced, it is unlikely that the artist shall be invited to exhibit work. And Ostojić takes a shortcut to fulfilling this requirement of seduction by offering herself as 'the work'. In the series as a whole, the seduction requirement entails more than an overt sexualisation of the artist's body, playing up to the popular fantasy of success as achieving the lifestyle of the rich and famous. It is a fantasy sold by capital East and West, North and South. This is why Ostojić is presented in expensive, haute couture outfits and has her paparazzi-style photos taken. 'The work' is also (if not especially) an elegant young woman who can go smoothly through dinner, chatting about art and 'passing' while side by side with a renowned, middle-aged, male curator during his four days of previewing the world's queen of biennials. Far from displaying the possibil-ity of a democratic art world, the strong collaborative impulse of the series illuminates complex and deeply rooted hierarchies chiefly by reproducing them to an extreme.

But why begin this examination of feminist action with a series of works that *succeed through failing* to extricate the woman artist from gendered environments of acute humiliation? There are good reasons. First, Ostojić's series operates in many dimensions, its sociality never quite remaining confined to the space and time initially allocated to the artwork. In the publication on the series, edited by the artist herself, it is not clear where the Venice diaries excerpts end and where their evaluative dissection begins. It is unclear whether *I'll Be Your Angel* and *Black Square on White* concluded during the Venice Biennale or whether they were extended through the documents of their aftermath – for example, a postcard sent by Szeemann to Ostojić in Belgrade that read: 'Dear Tanja, how is my angel? I would like to thank you for your participation and for having brought to Venice the "Black Square". Best, Harald Szeemann.'[20] It is unclear how long *Be My Guest* actually lasted, given that Ostojić writes three years after the performance: 'At some point I asked Pratesi: – How do you like this artwork? He said that it is the most enjoyable artwork he has experienced his entire life. [...] Some time later [...] he described me as a "a specialista di scandali d'arte" (specialist in art scandals) and missed to mention again that he was the one who joined me in the bath.'[21]

The relations traversed, reproduced and enacted are simply impossible to disentangle, and devising a start and end date for an artwork seems arbitrary, maintained mostly by a force of habit to which artists, curators and art historians succumb. This sociality, beyond conceivable confines, carries the stamp of gendering as a process so connected with power that it becomes an important impetus for action. The facility with which this process is reproduced goes far beyond any intentions of those involved in its reproduction. The question 'how is my angel?', as an intimate, affectionate and humorous appellation, could only have been addressed to a woman (artist), much like from a parent to a child. The sexual nature of an art scandal (an artist and a curator or critic touching each other in a publicly installed Jacuzzi) must be the responsibility of the perennial female temptress. Ostojić's 'Strategies of Success/Curators Series' thus suggests that the age of the curator (or the age of global capital) is rife with complicated and co-implicated antagonisms. The invocation of 'strategies' in the series title, as the prevalent political concern of second-wave feminism in the arts dividing its ranks, is now turned on its head: what takes the place of a successful political, collective cause (feminism) is individual professional success. Isn't this after all what feminism wished for each and every woman artist?

Second, the series negotiates a vision of a contemporary art world where the thought of uncurated art is simply unthinkable, as if art not somehow mediated and managed were an impossibility (and this despite the argument that participatory models of art have challenged the mediating work of the critic).[22] And it matters little if the outcome of managerial (curatorial) creativity is a more conventional exhibition or a project. What matters is that most artists who either defy a curatorial economy or cannot enter it are destined to provide Gregory Sholette's 'dark matter', that is 'the obscure mass of 'failed' artists' without whom 'the small cadre of successful artists would find it difficult, if not impossible, to sustain the global art world as it appears today'.[23] The power of the curator is accrued and exercised in this divided terrain of 'failed' and 'successful' artists, and by extension human beings – both producing the art world economy. Ostojić addresses and exposes the gendered dynamics of the success–failure relationship – in actual and symbolic terms. In actual terms, the series inscribes the complicity of female artists and male curators in sustaining the sexualisation and paternalism of their encounter. In symbolic terms, the series introduces into debates concerning the enmeshment of art and post-Fordist economy something akin to a feminisation of the artist and a masculinisation of the curator, irrespective of their actual gender or even sexual orientation (as *The Politics of Queer Curating* suggests). In this sense, 'Strategies of Success/Curators Series' sets up a practised critique of the early twenty-first-century art world, placing symbolic and actual gender hierarchies at its core.

The 'woman (or feminist) question' and more: collectives in the curatorial field

Ostojić's 'Strategies of Success/Curators Series' was realised at a time when some women curators were exploring curatorship as a field of strategic action, in the sense that the 'measures' proposed to combat realities of discontent could be seen to sustain broadly oppositional visions. Where such oppositional visions could be more clearly grasped was in the emergence of female curatorial collectives – and yet attributing such an emergence to some romanticised revolutionary feminist spirit would be profoundly misleading – as misleading as failing to consider the tradition of feminist collectivism in thinking about these groups' formation. Overall, the return to collectivism has been noted as an important feature of a contemporary art scene, with Blake Stimson and Gregory Sholette arguing that a periodisation (that is, an art history) of collectivism is in order.[24] It would indeed be possible to write an alternative, or at least different, history of art by looking at emerging and dissolving forms of collectivism. One of the most immediate issues then is that collectivism no longer describes just art practice but becomes a more general principle of creativity, moving with ease from the artist(s) to the curator(s). This general principle of creativity is multifariously connected to the contemporary organisation of labour, and often so-called immaterial labour: it spurs and accelerates innovation based on 'think thank' get-togetherness while sharing tasks permits the realisation of difficult, deadline-tight and even risky projects. Curating today is very much about all this. But also the encounter of curating, collectivism and feminism after 2000 vindicates Stimson and Sholette's observation that whereas during the Cold War 'the ideal of collectivism was to realize itself not in the social model or plan but in the to-and-fro of cultural exchange', now it is about 'engaging with social life as production'.[25] Indeed, one sees no good reason why and how in these new conditions shaping forces and relations of production art-making and curating would not come impossibly close as forms of cultural labour. The rise of female curatorial collectives compels us to think at least about how the curatorial field of labour is not crowded with Harald Szeemanns but has opened up to the energies of precarisation, flexibilisation and feminisation. Unsurprisingly perhaps, Europe, as a continent divided into zones of imagined or real affluence, perceived growth or stagnation, and lately crisis, zones defined by reshuffled borders bound to generate a consciousness of 'inclusion', 'exclusion', opportunism and militancy, has provided a fertile ground for such a turn.

Significantly, the emergence of female curatorial collectives is witnessed in both Eastern and Western Europe, which makes the question of such groups' ancestries a truly complicated one while it is also suggestive of the possibly diverse socio-economic and political realities such groups address. It is worth citing some dates and cities. In the former East, the collective WHW (abbreviated form of Why, How and For Whom?) was formed in Zagreb in 1999 while The City of Women Association for Promotion of Women in Culture was established as a non-governmental organisation in Ljubljana in 1996. Moving west and north, the B+B female 'curatorial partnership' was founded in London in 2000, the all-women curatorial collective The Office formed in Berlin in 2004 and Kuratorisk Aktion in Copenhagen in 2005. All these curatorial collectives have engaged in a wide range of activities, sustained varied levels of relationships with institutional contexts from museums to biennials and identified to equally varying degrees with feminism as a radical set of ideas and social praxis.[26] It is, however, instructive how salient issues of mobility and access remain in the work of all the above: from B+B seeking to raise awareness of the gendered experience of migration to The Office collaborating through their platform 'Salon populaire' as an antidote to institutional contexts where 'the audience operates as a mere witness to the production of cultural surplus value'.[27] Indeed, not all these curatorial collectives self-identify as feminist, preferring to flag up their all-women camaraderie, while some incorporate a feminist problematic into a broader agenda of an oppositional stance enabled through curatorial activity. The 'contemporaneity' of these collectives' constitution is exemplified in programmatic work that is often, and openly, directed against capitalism, in recognition of the need for an intersectional struggle or forms of integrated social struggle that would benefit women (among others).

Here I concentrate on two collectives, WHW from Croatia (not a member of the European Union until July 2013) and Kuratorisk Aktion from Denmark (member of the European Union since 1973). This choice is based as much on their different regional provenance as on the groups' different relationship to the institution of contemporary art. In respect to geographical provenance, the fact that WHW are based in post-socialist Eastern Europe and Kuratorisk Aktion originate in Scandinavia can initially tempt one to draw facile conclusions with regard to the social contexts in which these collectives operate, the issues they target and the interventions they forge. To state the obvious, Scandinavia has been seen as a haven of gender equality in a context free from social upheavals and economic instability. Emerging out of a cut-up socialist Yugoslavia, most of Croatia is situated in the Balkan peninsula, a land of mythified conflict and unrepentant machismo, its populations enjoying all the 'privileges' of a textbook case in the 'semi-developed' European periphery. (Blending love – mostly heterosexual – with political disappointment, Zagreb's new, award-winning, sleek Museum of Broken Relationships, situated in the Croatian capital's well-kept tourist zone stands as an allegory for the painful 'transition' process that the country has been going through.) The first questions that arise is why indeed we witness this turn to female collectivism in the curatorial field in such diametrically opposed social realities and what this turn reveals about how these social contexts partake in the larger reality constructed globally by capital.

Kuratorisk Aktion (KA) have given a clear enough answer to the above question:[28] the collective was formed as a response to the gap that its two members, Tone Olaf Nielsen and Frederikke Hansen, perceived between the image of Scandinavian, and specifically Danish, society and the wider social truth of capitalist globalisation in which Scandinavia has been a privileged First-world participant. KA have implicitly at least drawn a parallel between the self-image of their native country as a society with little need for politics ('even post-political', in KA's words) and the stereotype of the allegedly liberated (possibly therefore post-feminist) Danish woman, whose life and choices are nevertheless moulded in, and by, a heteronormative context of prescribed gender roles in the service of capitalist development. But such a revisiting of a national/regional context was the outcome of an existent mobility culture and of leaving Denmark: in the late 1990s, Nielsen went to study in a California of acute socio-economic and racial divisions while Hansen moved to Berlin, a city of less streamlined sub-cultures affording opportunities for exploring the synergies of queer and feminist politics. In addition to experiencing the diversity of social antagonisms of less insular western societies, the acceleration of history – from the Seattle uprising to the wars in Afghanistan and Iraq- after 2000 suggested to Nielsen and Hansen that the time had come 'to take sides', and that self-proclaimed national bubbles of comfort were in fact narratives of complacency when observed from within a global context.

Indeed, KA's curatorial oeuvre appears to include at least one great experiment of transposed politics, in their opting to focus much of their energy to the exposure of what they have called 'Nordic colonialism'. The project was realised in Iceland, Greenland and Finland in 2005–6, in collaboration with the Nordic Institute for Contemporary Art (NIFCA) in Helsinki, where – as part of the New Institutionalism breed of progressive cultural institutions in Europe –it facilitated radical curating.[29] Developing a programme of activities and exhibitions around this subject, KA's main impetus has been both a form of historical pragmatism – that is, to bring to view what had been hidden from a factual history of oppression that could matter locally and globally – but also a symbolic declaration: that ultimately no affluent society could boast for its state of exception from the driving force – colonisation – which had made global capitalism possible. The ideological cornerstone of KA's curatorial methodology, defined as 'curating across capitalist divides', appears thus to rely on a reworked approach to colonisation, amounting to a queering of postcolonial discourses in the greater sense. This emphasis on queering is central to KA's tactical self-positioning as a feminist and anti-capitalist curatorial collective, methodologically committed to an opening up and testing of intersectionality. In this case, 'queering' is not exhausted in asserting the revolutionary role that gay and lesbian subjectivities can play in subverting normative social realities of oppression, though it certainly encompasses such positions. For KA, queering becomes part of a feminist anti-capitalist practice in the knowledge that capital's biopolitical grip is exerted across each and every locus and moment of intimacy and subject constitution.

Their statement that they 'curate critique' – rather than, for example, art – demonstrates a curatorial vision that possibly achieves a significant break with institutionally based curating. In the case of KA, curating is not registered as a service to art history or even art, being instead affirmed as an *autonomous* platform from which to undertake or, better, coordinate socially transformative action. Curating becomes a critical interventionist pedagogy or, more accurately, is realised as an intervention in the form of public pedagogy. A characteristic of this pedagogy is not so much that it is available (potentially) to all, or that it is always issue-based, but that it claims its right to be openly positional – to be openly feminist, anti-colonialist, anti-capitalist and queer – irrespective of the existence of a social movement that could provide its ideological safety net. It is therefore significant that KA was formed prior to the eruption of the global financial crisis in 2008 and the avalanche of protest movements this generated in many parts of the world, and certainly in Europe. What we begin to get a glimpse of here is that, in the early twenty-first century, the legacy of feminism as political discourse and social activism that once registered as a social movement can inspire initiatives that, even as they espouse collectivism, largely rely on singularity. By 'singularity' I do not mean individual consciousness. Rather, I mean a formation that is exceptional within the social context where it is located, in that it relies on the encounter and enmeshment of desires, motives and aspirations that can at first be temporary, unstable or shared by a very small number of people (here, just two). It is this that permits the formation of feminist collectives in the absence of a major feminist movement in the early twenty-first century.

KA maintain what might be called a necessary relationship with the institution of art, in the sense that they either approach specific organisations as possible hosts of events and exhibitions or accept invitations to work with, or for, such organisations. Yet in all cases they prioritise their own political narratives. The collective's formation appears to be rooted to a great extent in the DIY ethos of a feminist revival which, around 2000, had emerged as the negation of the depoliticisation of post-feminism in the 1990s. This DIY or 'third-wave' feminism has not so far evolved into a movement with a large social basis. Instead, it has thrived on community spirit and micro-interventions. DIY feminism, not limited to art-related initiatives, shares a lot with the anti-capitalist movements that came to the fore at that time, when the values of Autonomia, originally a political project in Italy in the 1970s, were gaining ground globally: 'autonomy' from state structures tied to capitalist and patriarchal oppression and work from below was a value that rang unsurprisingly attractive to millions of disenchanted voters in the West's capitalist democracies. Encapsulated in Hardt and Negri's *Empire* and John Holloway's *Change the World without Taking Power*, Autonomia values were turning into powerful arguments about forging a political culture away and beyond formal political parties. The distrust of both traditional platforms for politics and the state as the arbiter of political culture were palpable at that point, only to mobilise greater constituencies towards autonomous action and 'direct democracy' throughout the past decade.

It is important, therefore, to acknowledge that DIY feminism, including its expression as a novel curatorial culture, does not just entail a return to the early stages of second-wave activism but is eminently contemporary. Red Chidgey explains the rise of DIY feminism as a 'micro-political feminist response to consumer capitalism and state authority', seeing such rise as 'symptomatic of a broader political malaise with mainstream politicians and government actions'.[30] Interestingly, Chidgey does not explicitly cite in the first instance the movement's roots in second-wave feminism, asserting instead: 'Drawing on genealogies of punk cultures, grass-roots movements, and the technologies of late capitalism, this movement meshes lifestyle politics with counter-cultural networking.' Such networking has been incredibly important for the realisation of KA's curatorial vision, often enabling the conceptualisation and realisation of projects free from institutional demands, in the first instance. However, it would be a serious omission of this analysis to not mention what this distance from the institution has meant for KA. As Nielsen and Hansen explain, even if based in affluent Scandinavia, the collective has not escaped precarity as the endemic condition of art workers in globalisation. Using the 'technologies of capitalism' – technologies of long-distance communication – has often meant working from home, in conditions of an atomised production process that require immense commitment, self-motivation and energy. The collective's comment that they support their 'families by doing odd jobs after Kuratorisk Aktion "office hours", but are painstakingly aware that being in our early forties [in 2010], we may not "have the muscle" to keep up Kuratorisk Aktion for another ten years while attending to two-three "day jobs" on the side' is illuminating: it offers a sobering perspective on the less glamorous side of freelancing and on the complex forms of productivity sustaining so-called creative economies at their interface with activism. The ideology of art workers 'owning' the work process and being among its principal beneficiaries ensures the required levels of commitment. Moreover, KA's statement helps us grasp the connection between such initiatives and the mandate of voluntary labour associated with women and the young.

Founded by Ivet Ćurlin, Ana Dević, NataŠa Ilić and Sabina Sabolović, WHW maintain a different approach to the institution of art, one necessitated by the particular demands of post-Yugoslav social space and facilitated to an extent by a burgeoning and, significantly, global biennial culture.[31] In 2009, WHW curated the 11th Istanbul Biennial, one of the most established art biennials in the world, and in 2011 the Croatian pavilion of the 54th edition of the Venice Biennale. Also in 2009 they taught at the prestigious Curatorial Studies programme of Bard College in the USA. WHW have given numerous talks internationally, including in strongholds of institutionalised art and curating such as MOMA in New York, which were compelled to join other art museums' belated feminist 'turn' after 2000 (in 2010 MOMA organised a series of public talks and symposia entitled 'Art Institutions and Feminist Politics Now', inviting WHW among others).[32] Yet WHW's relationship to the institution of art entails a more permanent element: in 2003, only four years after the collective's formation in 1999, WHW were appointed directors of the programme of Nova Galerjia, a non-profit city-owned gallery in Zagreb. This space has been important for the realisation of the collective's curatorial projects, though it is perhaps not as important as the independent office they keep in a rented, modest Zagreb apartment, where they also store their extensive archive.

The distance from the nomadic platform of KA, cemented by the latter's decision to not share an office, is startling. Operating from a permanent, material, publicly funded institutional space apparently afforded opportunities for

WHW to establish themselves both locally and internationally. Arguably, they are the most internationally visible all-female curatorial ensemble to have emerged from Eastern Europe and possibly the most prominent curatorial collective in Europe overall. What contributed to such impact was the implementation of a programme of 'expanded' curating, incorporating exhibitions, events and publishing projects persistently addressing the relationship of art and politics. The publications programme notably includes (though it is not limited to) collaborations with well-known, western, anti-capitalist thinkers writing on art, such as Brian Holmes (USA) and Stephen Wright (France), and celebrity male curators such as Hans Ulrich Obrist. These names immediately suggest the scope of operations and collaborations that WHW have pursued as a parameter in their regional, continental and global recognition.[33] A question that must be posed is to what extent WHW's self-identification as an all-female rather than feminist collective has been a (determining) factor in their success. I shall return to this question but first it is important to stress that this success is not conventionally defined as one may at first assume.

To begin with, appointing a four-member curatorial collective does not mean that funding bodies or institutions issuing invitations have necessarily multiplied individual wages by four – rather the opposite (sharing the curatorial fee) has been the case. Like KA, WHW have not been exempt from the structural condition of precarity plaguing radical curating. The issue of how and where to fundraise without compromising curating as an intervention in political consciousness has been constant and yet coupled with a pragmatism generated by the absence of viable alternatives – either to institutional collaborations or to the culture of permanent fundraising. Here, the distrust of the state acquires a more specific form: when the government's role is to ensure that a population turns into human resources for the successful implementation of a profiteering production regime, a collective such as WHW could see little, if any, difference from being funded by a private organisation or by a right-wing government. The turbulence of regional politics and humanitarian disasters in the 1990s and the Croatian state's attempts to promote processes of 'normalisation' (meaning, the normalisation imposed by global capitalism and access to capitalist markets) were of paramount importance to the collective's ideological positioning and practical decisions. Unlike KA, WHW did not have to face a local culture of apathy but rather one where questions about the economy were purposefully sidelined by rampant nationalism and the return to religion (and specifically the Catholic Church), a process of disidentification with the Balkans (seen as the problem-ridden, 'primitive' East).

Yet the spirit of self-organisation and subcultural forms of opposition did inform the genesis of the group, with an urgency lacking in less turbulent societies. WHW were much inspired by the anti-war fanzine ArkZine (1992–98), which provided a platform also for feminist voices and succeeded in bringing together intellectuals and activists on the left. Maintaining that 'we are all feminists, emancipation on the left includes feminism as well', WHW began their broader curatorial project with an exhibition on the 152th anniversary of the *Communist Manifesto* in 2000. Visitors were, nevertheless, surprised to see not images of Marx and Engels or old editions of the *Communist Manifesto* but works of art addressing the terrifying distance of a contemporary, global economy from the *Communist Manifesto*'s teleological vision of a just world. The publication accompanying the show includes two illustrations that make apparent the project's 'new interpretation' of the *Communist Manifesto*'s significance in neoliberal times: first, an illustration of the globe cut into two, a northern and a southern hemisphere; second, a female-coded silhouette posing behind a loaded supermarket trolley under the famous title of the Brecht/Weill song 'What keeps mankind alive?' The North/South divide and woman as a symbol of 'the right to consume' complement each other in a narrative that brings forth the unrealisable promise of common (that is, global) affluence. Having received the bleak answer 'bestial acts' by Brecht in 1928, the question 'what keeps mankind alive?' haunted WHW, who returned to it throughout the decade, finally appropriating it as the title of the Istanbul Biennial they headed in 2009.

The *11th Istanbul Biennial Exhibition Guide* conveys a sense of the scale of institutional intervention that WHW have attempted: the guide opens with several pages of exhibition 'facts' (data), concerning anything from funding sources to the gender, age ratio and geographical provenance of selected artists.[34] The exhibition facts reflect an internalisation of the threads of critique that have been shaping an alternative art world for decades and certainly from the 1970s onwards. This is not a 'regional' Eastern European art world, as the data provided reflect anything from feminist to postcolonial enquiries and interventions (largely developed at the intersection of former empires and former colonies, yet certainly a 'Western' discourse as far as Eastern European scholarship was concerned until recently). This is in addition to issues pertaining to flows of humans, goods, communication, migratory routes and not least the economy. All these issues became prevalent after 1990. Here is how WHW describe their emergence in connection with accepting to curate a major biennial:

> In our exhibitions we are often making references and dedications, but as in the case of our first exhibition 'What, how and for whom', dedicated to the 150th anniversary of the Communist Manifesto, around which we came together as a collective in the late '90s, the Manifesto itself was not the subject of the exhibition, but a trigger to initiate a public debate on recent history. The biennial, called 'What Keeps Mankind Alive?' after the protest song from *The Threepenny opera* written by Bertolt Brecht in 1928, does not directly thematise

Brecht's heritage. Brecht's assertion that 'a criminal is a bourgeois and a bourgeois is a criminal' from *The Threepenny Opera* is as true as ever. The parallels of the rapid expansion of the liberal economy and the disintegration of the existing social consensus in 1928, a year before the Great Depression, and the contexts of the contemporary global crisis are striking. Thus 'what keeps mankind alive' also links us back to the *economic concerns* of 'what, how and for whom'. In that sense, the three basic questions of every economic organisation – what, how & for whom – that have continuously and repeatedly been shaping our work, remain constant concerns.[35] [my emphasis]

Much like the ubiquitous statement concerning the collective's formation (available on many websites), the above quote suggests that WHW's evolving curatorial agenda recognised from early on the shift from culture to economy in the terrains of contemporary art, discussed in previous chapters. And WHW opted to prioritise this shift, tactically underplaying, but not excluding, feminism as a contributing narrative to the story of the collective's formation and most ensuing projects.

Significantly, the 11th Istanbul Biennial's return to Brecht under the directorship of an all-female collective appears to bear little resemblance to Western feminism's turn to Brecht in the 1970s and 1980s, as for example witnessed in the work of UK-based Griselda Pollock who argued about the need to incorporate Brechtian distanciation in feminist artistic strategies.[36] In that case, 'distanciation' amounted to a new feminist realism, whereby the feminist work substituted a seamless representational fiction with the purposeful glimpse of the actual conditions of entry to gendered social/psychic space. In WHW's attendance to Brecht, 'distanciation' was hardly absent. Yet this time distanciation registered as alienation from the seamless fiction of 'equal participation', identified with a global art world and its proliferating biennials. WHW were confronted with much criticism because of their use of Brecht in the context of a biennial, by 2009 a sure symbol of global capital's ideological domination of the contemporary art field. In a comprehensive review article of the show, Gail Day, Steve Edwards and David Mabb asserted that 'the correlation of Brecht with the corporate sponsors seems to have especially upset the critics' – especially on the Turkish left.[37] The same authors discuss the Istanbul Biennial as Turkey's calling card, intended to advance the cause of the country's access to the European Union and its values (somehow disputed from 2010 to date because of the turmoil in the Eurozone!). And although the issue is not raised, offering the biennial directorship to a politicised female collective from Europe's internal other (Eastern Europe still in 2008–9) was consistent with cultivating a façade of tolerance and gender equality as the values nominally promoted by a neoliberal European Union. The participation in the show of Eastern European feminist veteran artist Sanja Iveković with crumpled red sheets left on the floor of biennial venues 'condemn[ing] the fate of abused Turkish women via shock statistics and angry demands from anonymous NGOs (Turkish Report 09, 2009)', noted by Tirdad Zolghadr, certainly corroborates this.[38]

Gender, and even feminist critique, then, can evidently be instrumentalised in the intricate bids for power comprising globalisation's geopolitics – but it is unthinkable that WHW would have been unaware of this. Instead, their choices are underwritten by the lack of choice (the 'no outside' thesis) when it comes to thinking seriously about the material conditions of curating politically and from the left. How can we, however, position women's turn to collectivism in this context, beyond Marxist critics' appraisal that in WHW's re-mobilisation of the Brecht method, 'we may be witnessing a significant puncturing to capital's hegemony of ideas within significant sections of the growing creative and cultural workforce'?[39] Notably, WHW received invitations from direct-action anti-capitalist platforms to exit the 'white cube' biennial and its arms-dealer sponsor and assist resistance in the streets of Istanbul.[40] In WHW's response that 'Brecht is ours, we want to protect Brecht from Koç [sponsor]', what stands out is the striking deployment of the 'we', its meaning oscillating between describing the intentions of the collective and a broader, transnational oppositional community. In either case, the act of setting up a collective offers an implicit acknowledgement of the value of a less atomised political culture, and emerges here as the desire, and mechanism, for sharing responsibility (of success and failure) rather than constituting some form of radical strategy by default. Bearing this in mind, women's curatorial collectives signify an emphatic acknowledgement of women's participation in emerging political cultures and the commitment to practising everyday solidarity in balancing and managing the encounter of grass-roots experience with institutional formats.

WHW's left politics, as articulated in the choice of themes and approach to exhibitions, coexist with their close attendance to the lessons of capitalism learned in a transitional Eastern Europe. The collective's emphasis on the three questions of 'every economic organisation' hardly points to the difference between a former socialist and a current capitalist and entrepreneurial economy, as having shaped the collective's political choices. 'What, How and for Whom' can equally well be applied to capitalist enterprise, especially of the kind that espouses an ethical form of capitalist development. That WHW's mission statement highlights that the three questions, or perhaps principles, 'concern the planning, concept and realisation of exhibitions as well as the production and distribution of artworks and the artist's position in the labor market' is indicative of the collective's awareness that the market is the condition underlying their curatorial practice, no matter how far left the latter is positioned.[41] Such awareness could certainly be gained in the transition period following the break-up of Yugoslavia: the planned and expedient transformation of the economy rendered more visible the form of institutions-to-be. In effect, the formation of WHW rested on a split between the group's ideological self-positioning (what we might call 'beliefs') predicated on a vision of human emancipation that encompassed feminism and the pragmatism forced by the transition. Such pragmatism created a very different 'what is to be done' from that raised by the group's beliefs. If the latter entailed a macro dimension, the former concerned the channels of acting on power, responded to the immediacy of circumstances, decoded the remit of the possible and, on occasion, translated the latter into a 'how'. This 'how' has been the prevalent concern of female collectivism engaging feminism from 2000 onwards – a 'how' with which women experimented both as curators and artists.

Feminist artist collectives: pedagogical and street activism from Argentina to Sweden

In 2003 Mujeres Públicas was formed in Buenos Aires, two years after the collapse of Argentina's economy, which resulted in many taking to the streets in protest. Hard perhaps to imagine at the time, street protest cultures generated during national economy meltdowns (as witnessed in Argentina) or otherwise connected with economic inequality (such as the transnational Occupy movement), were to become a hallmark of early twenty-first-century crisis capitalism. The impact of such turmoil on art and feminist activism is only beginning to raise lines of enquiry in art history. Mujeres Públicas admit that forming a collective was also intended to challenge the view that 'political art addresses the state and that feminism is not politics'.[42] In the Argentinean context this has been indeed a dominant outlook: the 2001 event of the economy-turning-into-politics was preceded by decades of the Argentinian people being intermittently persecuted by the state (the most recent military dictatorship was from 1976 to 1983 when about 30,000 people 'disappeared') or demanding justice for its victims (Mothers of the Plaza de Mayo in the 1980s and 1990s). On the one hand, this legacy of confrontation nurtured women's militancy but on the other, the intense focus on the state as the source of power (to be battled) rendered feminism, with its assumed focus on the everyday and the 'personal', into a second-class oppositional politics – if accepted as such at all. In the first published self-introduction of the collective's activities in English in a feminist art journal, Mujeres Públicas offered, however, an account of their ancestry, noting the project of an interrupted feminist art politics from the 1960s onwards in Argentina.[43] Yet, picking up the thread does not just mean entering, but rather re-inventing, a feminist continuum.

In 2008 Mujeres Públicas delivered a paper at the feminist symposium Privilege Walk (where I met them) and the roving anti-capitalist European

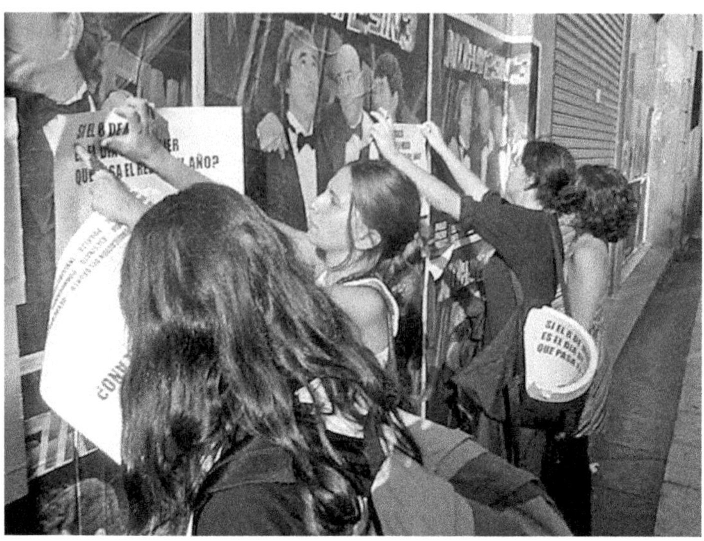

6.3   Mujeres Públicas, public action, 8 March 2004, Buenos Aires.

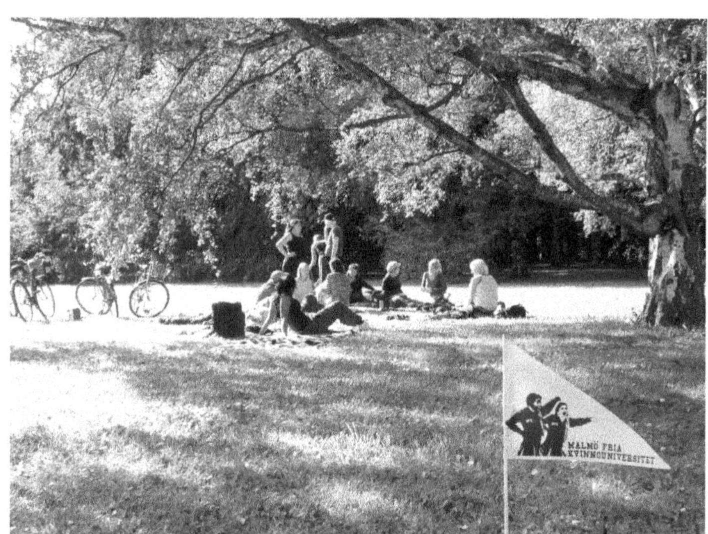

6.4   MFK, Picnic Poetry in Pildammsparken, 10 September 2006, Malmö.

Social Forum, both in Malmö, giving as the collective's *raison d'être* a feeling of 'discordance' with the social reality. Mujeres Públicas, whose name in Spanish is hardly ambiguous ('public women' registers immediately as 'prostitutes'), named the street as their site of action – action that they sought to distance from feminism's image as a theoretical practice and a reformist discourse of ethical (rather than political) correctness. They wrote: 'We went out to the streets to destroy.' Naming religion (the Catholic Church in particular since Argentina is a Catholic country) along with the state as agents operating against women's control over their lives, naming themselves 'women' and 'lesbians', they also declared: 'we went out in the streets to construct'. This was to admit to a feminist cause fraught with contradictions and without obvious and easy answers. But more importantly, they clarified:

> Mujeres Públicas is defined as a feminist (not a lesbian) group, because we understand that feminism implies the defense of the rights of all women without making any distinctions. We believe that from this position we contribute to [bringing] the lesbian movement closer to the feminist movement, but also to mak[ing] non-activist lesbians come together and get to know the feminist thought, as well as making heterosexual women [come] closer to the experiences of [...] lesbians.[44]

The above offers the key operating principle of a new form of feminist art activism: subject positions are not invoked to safeguard difference but to justify the social demand of acting with others (lesbians and heterosexual women). Identity, including self-identity, is mobilised to enable alliances rather than question their desirability or viability. The consciousness of addressing and fighting for the rights of all women, stated both by Mujeres Públicas and other feminist collectives, is a prevalent feature of a new feminism in the arts, critically antithetical to postmodern feminism.[45]

However, despite their open self-identification as feminists, Mujeres Públicas share, with much anti-capitalist theory, a suspicion towards practices and contexts of representation. In the Malmö text, they reject the museum as the 'space of the legitimated word', 'the nameable' and 'the showable.' Delegitimation of the obvious – often engaging tactics of parody where a concept is re-signified against its dominant meaning – is central to the collective's activism. In 2004, they realised *The Museum of Torture*, an arrangement of glass cases holding a stunning array of contemporary beauty equipment, implicated in women's normalisation as beautification as feminisation. *The Museum of Torture* is one of the very few 'installations' put together by the collective with the purpose of being exhibited in an enclosed space rather than in the street. Having been first shown in an alternative downtown gallery owned by the mother of a Mujeres Públicas member, it was then installed in a feminist and lesbian cultural centre, and in 2010 it was assembled for the last time in a building (Escuela de Mecánica de la Armada – ESMA) originally used as a clandestine detention centre and torture prison between 1976 and 1983, but later home to cultural centres, research units and TV stations.[46] To actually show a work about a long-standing feminist issue in a space so strongly associated with national trauma was a bold and daring action-statement, one typical perhaps of Mujeres Públicas' persistent juxtaposition of the particular (women's rights) and the assumed general (human rights).

Yet most of the collective's work takes the form of provocative text and drawings made public as posters or confrontational and unsolicited dialogical situations – when, for example, they burst into a public gathering, asking people what they think about heterosexuality. The questionnaire included questions normally asked about homosexuality: Do you consider yourself heterosexual? How did you realise that? What do you consider to be the cause of your heterosexuality? Do you think that your heterosexuality has a cure? What would you do if your daughter tells you that she's heterosexual? Were you ever discriminated because of your heterosexual condition? Do they know it at your job? Are you afraid of getting fired? Mujeres Públicas consider the act of asking questions a consciousness-raising activity where didacticism has been replaced with confrontation, but beyond this they consider their very presence in the street as a means of 'questioning bourgeois morals', describing such morals as experiments on how to keep 'us away from the street'. In the Malmö essay, who this 'us' refers to is left purposefully ambiguous: it can refer to the domestication of women in non-secular societies but also to all those who succumb to domestication as an effect of technologies (computers, television) creating private (if interactive) individuals. And like KA, Mujeres Públicas make much use of the concept of colonisation, drawn in this case from the continent's history as having shaped a social imaginary. Indeed, Mujeres Públicas have argued that in Latin American societies, and specifically that of Argentina, the concerns and ideas prevalent in Western feminism appear so irrelevant as to be perceived in terms of an attempt to colonise local struggles.[47] By which one might understand that academic feminism's alliance with post-structuralism and the critique of 'truth politics' were unlikely to serve the feminist cause in a social context defined by the truths of, first, fascistic rule and, a bit later, economic terror.

On the other hand, 'colonisation' was a familiar concept in this same context. Charges against colonising powers appear often in the collective's work – for example, *Colonised Women* (2004) consisted of publicly placed posters presenting instances of women's bodies and minds occupied by patriarchal religion. A year later, the poster *Home Work* (2005) brought to the street the issue of women's support of the economy as unpaid and super-exploited home workers. Like most of the group's posters, this one also made use of an accessible image-text style, combining figurative cartoon-like illustrations and short textual descriptions to offer a cumulative 'visual effect' of a more ethereal economic reality: if time is money, here's the time that women spend serving others for free. In 2009 Mujeres Públicas wrote – collaboratively – the book *Choose Your Own Dis-adventure: The Incredible and Sad Story of Any One of Us*, as a different format for exposing how women's lives are typically produced through consecutive pseudo-choices ('available' only to that one gender).[48] The narrative satirised the postmodern literary trope of the reader being invited to choose her own turn of events/fiction/ending. Written in Spanish, the book narrated and interwove the lives of the collective's five original members (since 2009 only the three core members remain in the group: Magdalena Pagano, Lorena Bossi and Fernanda Carrizo) in an effort to expose the myth of individual achievements, failures and life courses. And in 2010, following a public campaign against the rights of gay and lesbian marriages, Mujeres Públicas placed in city streets the poster '*Revol*ution'. Highlighting in red the inverted 'love' hidden in the longer word in bold black fonts, they created a family-tree type of drawing to provide examples of non-traditional encounters, get-togethers, sustained forms of living 'with' rather than couples: in their own words, it was an effort 'to think of something beyond the principle of equal rights, which refers to the ability to think broader and more diverse unions'.[49]

Each of Mujeres Públicas' interventionist actions addresses a specific issue, and moreover an issue that, even if of global relevance, arises from the close observation and inhabiting of a local and primarily urban reality where class divisions, religion and militancy generate and cross-fertilise various forms of radicalisation. It is notable that on their website Mujeres Públicas introduce themselves as a 'feminist group of political action', though the Spanish version of their introductory text defines them as 'a feminist group of visual activism [grupo feminista de activismo visual]'. In either case, what is undermined is any straightforward self-identification with being an artist group, despite one of the collective's members working in an art school. The collective's work arises out of the diverse interests, skills and knowledge that each member can contribute: 'The three members of the group are very different and have different interests, Fernanda adds much in terms of communication, Lorena is always attentive to issues of class and does drawing, I [Magdalena] seek out visual strategies and always bring new readings for us to think about as a group.' The collective's aims are defined as doing 'politics from a creative perspective', emphasising their use of cheap materials distributed 'in great quantities'. The public is always invited to take ownership of the work and 're-edit it', as a strategy that has created 'an important distribution and re appropiation network…in different provinces of the country and throughout other countries of Latin America'.[50] Mujeres Públicas' existence in a global context comes primarily from networking with collectives from various parts of the world but more perhaps from Latin America and Europe (Spain and Scandinavia). The collective's debut global art-world appearance came only in 2012 – and that was on an invitation from Cuba's Havana Biennial, which has traditionally not enjoyed large-scale corporate sponsorship and has supported artists, mostly from Latin America and the non-Western world. The decision to accept the invitation came after much discussion, in the assumption of the specific biennial's alternative character but also out of the need to look outward and expand the sites of struggle.[51]

Crucially, the acceptance that creative work may not be a source of income, so prevalent in a post-Fordist regime of generalised production, is in this instance an enabling factor in sustaining a relationship between art and activism. All three members make a living in education and publishing. Mujeres Públicas' project of transforming public consciousness while seeking to maintain such distance from the art market and the exhibition as distribution mechanisms (with a price to pay, as we have seen so far) implies the deployment of different criteria for evaluating a successful feminist practice: here, strategic separatism is directed against the institutionalisation of feminism, its containment as pure theory, as bureaucratic mandate or museum-installed art. Mujeres Públicas strive to keep apart from all such diminished versions of feminism, apprehending the latter in terms of a unifying political force in the process of bringing a public space into existence. That said, their *Home Work* campaign already reveals the contradictions facing their interventionist practice. On the one hand, to call attention to this persistent problem of women's domestication is rather bold, expressing the willingness to act beyond the timeline of a Western feminism and post-feminism and start from scratch, if necessary. This 'from scratch' implies an understanding of the non-repeatability of history: Mujeres Públicas are not there to repeat, with feminist objectives, the great Argentinian interventionist work of *Tucumán Arde* (1968) but to respond to the urgent demands of their own circumstances.[52] On the other hand, they appear aware that in their specific urban reality, many women, whom Mujeres Públicas wish to address, remain domesticated. Subjugated to the undervalued work of care and reproduction, these women may be crossing the urban space where Mujeres Públicas place their action but may be less inclined to occupy it politically. The relationship between private and public, flagged up by second-wave feminism, features, then, very strongly in Mujeres Públicas' street-based activist art, its centrality apparently unchallenged by the shift of focus from representation to participation. Are Mujeres Públicas in the street as the site of women's symbolic time-outside-the-home? Or are they there because like all activists, and unlike advertisers and IKEA designers, they have no access to the still private space where women are drawn back to becoming women? Posing these questions hardly dissolves the impact of their activist art in a socio-cultural context (extending in fact from Latin America to Europe) where the configuration of art and politics is still likely to exclude feminism as, precisely, a political project.

Swedish collective MFK, or Malmö Free University for Women, existed from 2006 to 2011 and was described by its two founding members, artists Lisa Nyberg and Johanna Gustavsson, as 'an ongoing participatory art project and a feminist organisation for critical knowledge production'. In 2011 MFK published a bilingual (Swedish–English) manual explaining their practice and aspirations. It was published months before MFK ceased to exist and the narrative – including detailed descriptions of events or the process of making choices and passages of reflection on failures – succeeds not just in offering a record but on conveying an experience: the experience of experimenting with what the feminist artWork as grass-roots action might mean today. The website Radical Pedagogy, set up also after the collective's disbanding, aims to facilitate the further dissemination of this experience.[53] MFK's intensively collaborative practice was highly structured and played out on two fronts, both on the level of collaboration among the two founders of their collective and through collaborating with a broader and, in hindsight, not necessarily cohesive or even highly motivated community. Entitled *Do the Right Thing!*, The MFK manual is a rare kind of document where the difficulties of fostering a collaborative practice crossing through art, feminist politics and activism can be observed. Before focusing on MFK's understanding of radical pedagogy, I shall attempt a brief outline of their double focus on collaboration, starting with why it was deemed necessary.

In many respects, MFK was both an outcome of the Swedish state's liberal-egalitarian policies, including its declared emphasis on gender equality, and a response to these policies' inadequacy, to not being radical 'enough'. Setting up MFK was the decision of two young women artists who did not feel nervous about being identified as feminist. MFK was an implicit acknowledgement that education (that is, its absence) is at the heart of women's oppression globally and an explicit acknowledgement of the 'academisation' of feminist knowledge (a premise they share with Mujeres Públicas). MFK was meant to provide a framework where feminist theory could reconnect with the challenges of the everyday, including lack of consensus on what an ideal society might be, limited time for, or interest in, issues relating to gender discrimination, precarity and so on. In the chapter 'Start', MFK manage to demolish the myth of Sweden as a feminist (let alone women's) haven by referring to the country's political life, which MFK was able to link to 'personal' experiences, thus renewing the relevance of the second-wave feminist thesis on politicising the personal. The course of action and targets are explicit: to 'merge art/culture, activism and academia, and fight back against the neoliberal and racist developments'.[54]

Existing within the broader pedagogy turn sweeping contemporary radical art, MFK have described their intense desire for a 'space' and a 'place' in which to exist as feminists and artists, having rejected an expressive, if socially minded, practice centred on the studio. The studio would have to be replaced by a more fluid and yet always already active context in which the two MFK founders would place their own collaboration. It was decided that what they needed was a university – one dedicated to feminist practices of knowledge production and dissemination, with women as its main beneficiaries and at a distance from the 'industrialisation' of education advanced in neoliberal Europe, and evident even in Sweden. From its inception, MFK seemed aware that sustaining a public, democratic platform for radical pedagogy required a rather pragmatic approach to homebred trust. Instead of seeking to achieve consensus, the two MFK founders started from a position of mutual support and encouragement of each other's vision: 'if my colleague finds this [an idea] important, I support her'.[55] Disagreements on practical matters, such as the 'looks' of a poster to be placed in the public domain, would often be resolved by accepting both proposals, in a context of what MFK called its 'yes policy'. But the founders' commitment to the project required that radical decisions were made and often revised. They started without funding, establishing a nomadic counter-institution free to congregate wherever it was possible; moved on to a joint bank account, applied and received grants which allowed them to 'spend less time on…day-jobs and more on MFK' and, crucially, accepted full responsibility for their failure to ultimately sustain a steady stream of public funding. This in particular was a result of MFK being assessed by funding bodies as not 'enough art/culture oriented', and 'not democratic', implementing instead 'different forms of separatism'.[56] Accepting that 'our respective personal finances have affected how much work we could do together', MFK was even able to accommodate its two founders' widely divergent approaches to economic survival, with one of the two artists (Gustavsson) enhancing her personal links to the art world while the other (Nyberg) returned to a day job – a return deemed necessary for sustaining her ideological independence.

As a framework for an expanded collaboration, MFK implemented a carefully articulated approach prioritising the following: an expansion of the group's 'yes policy' (accepting and encouraging the realisation of proposals), active seeking of participants, reflection and planning on how to engage participants and turning any such failure into a lesson from which MFK's programmatic vision could progress. Significantly, MFK found artists the most difficult to engage in collaborative projects, citing as a reason for this scepticism MFK's commitment to activism: in effect, artists associated with MFK would risk being blacklisted in an art world still bent on policing the boundaries between pure art and its lesser others.[57] However, the pervasive ideology of project ownership – that is, initiating one's own projects rather than appearing as a follower of another artist's initiative was also a factor contributing to this ambivalence. MFK also discuss at length their response to the art institution, offering examples where such collaboration was undertaken only when the group was able to answer the question, 'how can we use this situation?', which meant that the art world as such was to be used as a 'resource'.[58] This 'resource' had to enable both the collective's political intervention but, crucially, also their visibility within 'art history'. This is then another instance where the objectives of second-wave feminism were reactivated – with the firm desire to be part of an art historical narrative, necessarily entailing relationships with the art institution. And finally, MFK focused on 'strategic separatism', 'intersectionality', 'collective dependency' and 'utopia' – concepts seen to inform both the ways that the collective sought to collaborate with others and its philosophy of radical pedagogy.

The focus on radical pedagogy places MFK within a broader trend in contemporary art throughout the past decade – one where we encounter initiatives ranging from Edinburgh's Proto-academy to Copenhagen Free University to travelling projects such as Martha Rosler's Library. The trend intersects with, but is hardly reducible to, initiatives corresponding to the potential of a radicalisation of art education specifically.[59] Or at least it could be said that initiatives such as Copenhagen Free University and MFK attempted a repositioning of art education into a more or less autonomous context of pedagogy about the social field. What such collectives have been interested in is a pedagogical context that not only educates people in how to subvert capital as a dominant ideology but also where the values of neoliberalism (competition, ranking, measure, hierarchy etc.) are left outside the counter-institution's door. MFK's appropriation of the contemporary capitalist university's familiar parlance of 'knowledge exchange and knowledge production', which emerged in the past decade, exists within a framework of highly specified ways of working as an artist today. For example, setting up MFK as a durational, long-term feminist artwork was also a way of defeating the fragmentation inherent in the short-term 'project' as the currently dominant form of artistic production. Projects lead, of course, to other projects and the proliferation of networks, as a staple of immaterial labour. Claiming MFK as an artwork extending and evolving over time, and not just as an enabling framework, betrayed at least the desire to commit to stable values, sustain a move from aesthetics to poetics (or else from the sensorial realm to that of interventionist action) and defy the principle of constant transformation that lies at the heart of capitalism. This alternative art-making prioritised longevity, interdisciplinarity (in this case, of feminist and politically engaged research) and the commitment to generating feminist responses to contemporary problems – MFK's workshop 'Culture, Labour and Neoliberalism – How do we respond?' is an indicative example.

In practical terms, MFK have stressed that 'it wasn't until we got a place of our own that we realised how important it was to have a physical place'.[60] A physical place permitted MFK to borrow technical equipment when needed, to receive donated books and journals. Their pedagogical practice has been very coherent and involved 'learning by doing', sharing ideas and rejecting competition, 'mak[ing] what you can from what you have' rather than waiting for funding to arrive, refusing to promote consensus but embrace conflict instead, a commitment to experimentation with different formats for activating a learning process, and, as already seen, the implementation of a 'yes-policy' (always say yes to submitted proposals) but where 'a yes is followed by a how?'[61] The publication of a 'manual', where self-reflection and analysis, organised into discrete chapters each of which concludes with bullet points offering structured advice based on the collective's experience, is, in its own right, an answer to this 'how?'

Overall, this 'how?' has not been exclusive to feminist collectivism of the present but has permeated ongoing debates in the global justice movement following Holloway's 2002 proposal to 'change the world without taking power'.[62] MFK discovered early on that power was a nebulous concept, especially when approached from a platform of oppositional politics. To begin with, the founders' attempt to step down and let others lead MFK did not prove fruitful. In some respects, this was a turning point, as MFK came to realise that direct democracy was not necessarily the best means to sustain an alternative pedagogy with a highly specific political agenda. Their approach to separatism, intersectionality and 'collective dependency' can be understood with this in mind. In a paper delivered at the University of Gothenburg titled 'Essentially Experimental?', MFK described 'intersectionalty as a theoretical tool deployed to formulate critical knowledge production and strategic separatism as a way to practice intersectionality.'[63] Soon enough, and as a response to external enquiries about the right to participate in MFK activities, the MFK 'all women welcome' policy was rescripted: first, as 'open to anyone who identifies as woman', and soon after 'for and by any persons who now or at some point identify as a woman'.[64] Practising other forms of separatism, and most notably class separatism, threw up similar kind of issues, as the MFK class sub-group pondered over imaginary scenarios where a choice would have to be made between admitting a working-class man or a middle-class woman to the collective.

It is, indeed, hard to articulate an ideological context for MFK's strategic separatism, apart from reiterating the Swedish state's partial success at implementing gender equality or ameliorating class and racial forms of inequality. On the one hand, MFK's holding on to the identity 'woman' made apparent the will to keep women central to a problematic addressing an aggressive, viral contemporary capitalism. Yet separatism entailed also, in this case, a strong pull towards identity, and despite the impulse to actively queer processes of self-identification as 'woman' and to encourage self-identification, it is questionable whether MFK managed to avoid the pitfalls of identity politics. Re-scripting the definition 'woman' to foster inclusivity could expand indefinitely in a social context of liberal politics (such as Sweden), but as the MFK class group dilemmas made apparent, it was unimaginable that participation could be scripted along the lines of 'open to anyone who feels or has felt working-class'. In this imaginary scenario, a solidarity based on some-one's material conditions, and poverty, would have been seriously challenged by the presence of those whose class privilege was an outcome of making other people poor. This means that in striving for solidarity through identity, as a pedagogical project in its own right, MFK overlooked the connection between difference, power and exploitation. Indeed, 'exploitation' does not appear in the English version of their text and their commitment to frequently revising the very meaning and usefulness of separatism did not implicate this term.

MFK's discussion of intersectionality is at the core of their radical peda-gogy, drawing both on Chandra Mohanty's emphasis on shared 'political con-viction' rather than the endless articulation of difference and Gayatri Spivak's process of 'unlearning' in order to see social relations through privilege offered on the basis of aspects of our identity. Yet a tension can be observed between practising identity-based separatism and MFK's commitment not to 'rate some oppressions invisible in order to highlight others' – for this is exactly what separatism is about as a political strategy that keeps resurfacing in the long history of feminism.[65] MFK emphasises the use of 'each other's temporary power advantages' in seeking to understand what 'makes it possible as a white person to engage in the fight against racism', but the issue is that power advan-tages are not primarily temporary but structurally embedded and reproduced: this is, for instance, what maintains the North/South divide in terms of class, race and gender privileges.[66] It can be in fact easier for a white person to join the struggle against racism, if such struggle becomes decoupled from ques-tions about class and structural exploitation and is turned into a matter of ethical-behavioral choices. Overall, it is easier to advocate 'new and unholy alliances' by practising a pragmatism that seeks to challenge access to privilege than undo relations of structural economic exploitation.

Yet to say all this hardly evacuates MFK of its value as a political interven-tion realised through, and as, radical pedagogy. Perhaps where this appears more clearly is in MFK's emphasis on utopia and especially in connection with the need to engage the concept not as a distant, fuzzy possibility but 'as a tool for change' and 'as a method'. For MFK, this method involved a projection into the future – indeed a future imagined as a positive outcome of current struggles. Addressing how it will be 'when we win', as put by MFK, is an anti-dote to the immense energy that goes into maintaining a present as the pro-tracted crisis of capitalism and sweeping through politics and art[67] – though in fact, MFK talk about politicians and artists. In its focus on actively imagin-ing a future now, MFK's pedagogy resonates with Cicero's alleged insight that education is about freeing the student from the tyranny of the present. To enable an active imagining of what this 'feminist future' might be like, MFK would do lock-ins: abandoning all other commitments for a few days, a small group of people would move in together to achieve 'total participation'. However, MFK did away with the requirement that an output 'be presented to the outside world' at the end of this process, refusing to subject their pedagogy to the imposition of measure so favoured by contemporary capitalism in institutionally controlled education. And it is telling perhaps that MFK did not document and make publicly available the content of discussions pertaining to the imagining of a feminist utopia. What MFK recorded instead was a commitment to a feminist *method*: a constant probing of the meaning of democracy and inclusivity, an active engagement with the values of feminisms past, a valorisation of purpose, directionality and imagination.

Feminism, terrains of action, capitalism

How then can we make sense of the threads of feminist action directed at regimes of power presented in this chapter? What connects Ostojić's anatomy of the artist-curator relation to reveal its gendered encoding with KA's emphasis on curating across capitalist divides and WHW's politically motivated pragmatism that permits the use of capitalist structures? How can we speak of Mujeres Públicas' strategic anti-separatism and MFK's critical encompassing of strategic separatism as choices informed by the discontent generated through a shared historical moment? Can we detect a common feminist goal across these women's divergent responses to power?

In some ways, the answer to the last question is yes. What all practices discussed in this chapter share is a commitment to reconnect feminism with doing as a continuous process rather than an explosive event. Seen together, the forms of action pursued by curators and artists betray that such 'doing' crosses through the everyday, affecting the way that women art workers live their lives rather than 'do their jobs' and requires resilience and contexts enabling day-to-day support and the sharing of responsibility. This is what all-female collectives appear to offer alongside the opportunity to practise democracy on the ground (WHW) or to probe an understanding of how, and first if, democracy and political action meet or not (MFK). Such 'doing' acknowledges the necessity of the cooperation of others for realising action – from the curators who collaborated with Ostojić to the constituencies that responded to MFK's calls to explore the possibility of feminist knowledge production. And such 'doing' is apparently fraught with difficulties, evident perhaps in the kind of choices curators and artists face. These may range from implicating your person and identity as a woman artist in exposing the art world as the aggregate of power relations, to seeking visibility for the oppositional stance of contemporary art by placing it in the capitalist art institution, to accepting precarity as the structural condition of questioning, through practice, where, when and how things get done.

Where, when and how things should get done is an implicit or explicit question in all the practices encountered in this chapter. And the answer is apparently: everywhere, now, and with whatever means available. There seems to be no patience on the part of women art workers to first sort things out on a conceptual or theoretical level. Questions such as 'is our practice feminist and in what way?' or 'do our practices differ from the action taken by second-wave feminists?' do not arise. Indeed, a cursory examination of the issues brought forth by second-wave feminism suffice to establish a continuity of concerns. Hilary Robinson's headings that serve to organise the section 'Activism and Institutions' in the voluminous reader *Feminism-Art-Theory* charting the field from 1968 to 2000 are telling: 'Challenging Patriarchal structures', 'Building Feminist Structures', 'Activism in Practice, Practices of Activism', 'Education', 'Censorship'. Of these categories, only censorship appears to be absent from current feminist action in the art world. This, in turn, can be explained as an outcome of reconfiguring feminist politics today away from concerns with practices of signification. What is witnessed instead is the greater relevance of embodied, lived struggle. There is an acknowledgement of the urgency of the circumstances or, as put by KA, of the need to take sides and, at the same time, to use the art world and its very manipulation of political desires as an opportunity for redressing power. Feminist politics appear less heroic in such contexts but also less solitary. The work examined here exploits the massive discontent unleashed by the crisis of confidence in global capitalism, witnessed well before 2008, and claims the right of feminism and of women to contribute to transformative processes of direct, resolute resistance.

Notes

1 G. Pollock, 'Encounters in the Virtual Feminism Museum: Time, Space and the Archive' in Hedlin Hayden and Sjöholm Skrubbe, *Feminisms Is Still Our Name*, 32.
2 Jerry Saltz quoted by Pollock, ibid.
3 Indicatively, the press release for the show *The Body in Women's Art Now: Part 3 – ReCreation* in Cambridge and London states: 'The exhibition series also aims to redress the imbalance of representation of women artists by highlighting the groundbreaking theoretically engaged work being made by women artists about the body today – at a time in the UK where only 37 of the 118 artists short-listed for the Turner Prize since its origins in 1984 have been women artists – and only three women have ever won the Prize, and as noted by *The Guardian*: of the 2,300 works on show in the British National Gallery just four of these are paintings by two women artists.' The exhibition was curated by Philippa Found and was at ROLLO Contemporary Art, 27

November 2011–6 January 2012 and at the New Hall Art Collection, Cambridge, 20 January–2 March 2012.

4 J. Heath, 'Women Artists, Feminism and the Museum: Beyond the Blockbuster Retrospective', in A. Kokoli (ed.), *Feminism Reframed: Reflections on Art and Difference* (Newcastle: Cambridge Scholars, 2008), 22.

5 On this intervention, see A. Kokoli, 'Undoing 'Homeliness' in Feminist Art: Feministo – Portrait of the Artist as a Housewife (1975–7)', *n.paradoxa: international feminist art journal* 13, Domestic Politics (January 2004), 75–83. See also N. Mulholland, *The Cultural Devolution: Art in Britain in the Late Twentieth Century* (Aldershot: Ashgate, 2003).

6 A. McRobbie, 'Reflections on Feminism, Immaterial Labour and the Post-Fordist Regime', *New Formations* 70 (Autumn 2010), 60-76. Here 74.

7 See N. Lüth, 'Between Family Lines – Talking about Art and Feminism with Loraine Leeson', in C. Mörsch (ed.), *Art for Change – Loraine Lesson, Works from 1975–2005* (Berlin: NGBK, 2005).

8 Leeson quoted in Mörsch, *Leeson*, 124.

9 R. Baert, 'Editorial', *n.paradoxa: international feminist art journal* 18 (2006), issue on curatorial strategies, 4.

10 See L. Perry, 'A Great Time to Be a Woman?', in Dimitrakaki and Perry, *Politics in a Glass Case*.

11 See www.guerrillagirls.com/ (accessed 8 November 2010).

12 *Art Review* Power 100 for 2009, available on www.artreview100.com/power-100–lists-from-2002–through-2008/2009/ (accesses 8 November 2010).

13 See for example D. Levi Strauss, 'The Bias of the World: Curating after Szeeman and Hopps', in S. Rand and H. Kouris (eds), *Cautionary Tales: Critical Curating* (New York: Apexart, 2007).

14 Ostojić in electronic communication with the author, 13 September 2012.

15 The curator explained to the artist that marital commitments prevented him from participating in the Jacuzzi part of the performance. Confirmed in electronic communication with the artist, 13 September 2012.

16 For the full letter see Tanja Ostojić (ed.), *Strategies of Success – Curators Series 2001–2003* (Belgrade: SKC, 2004), 66.

17 M. Gržinić, 'Tanja Ostojić: 'Yes, It's Fucking Political' – Skunk Anansie', in T. Ostojić (ed.), *Strategies of Success – Curators Series 2001–2003* (Belgrade: SKC 2004), 15.

18 Milevska in Ostojić, *Strategies of Success*, 38.

19 Ibid., 39.

20 Reproduced in Ostojić, *Strategies of Success*, 62.

21 T. Ostojić, 'Be My Guest', in Ostojić, *Strategies of Success Curators Series*, p. 67.

22 See G. H. Kester, *Conversation Pieces* (Berkeley: University of California Press, 2004).

23 Sholette, *Dark Matter*, 3.

24 B. Stimson and G. Sholette, 'Introduction: Periodizing Collectivism', in B. Stimson and G. Sholette (eds), *Collectivism after Modernism: The Art of*

Social Imagination after 1945 (Minneapolis: University of Minnesota Press, 2007).

25 Stimson and Sholette, *Collectivism after Modernism*, 10 and 13.

26 In 2011 the B+B website explains that 'aspects of B+B remain active' despite its two members, Sarah Carrington and Sophie Hope, working independently at present. B+B have placed great emphasis on providing an accessible and expanding archive of the collective's curatorial action stretching from activist projects to the publication of theoretical writings. See www.welcomebb.org. uk/ (accessed 25 October 2011).

27 See S. Carrington, 'Traded Places', *Feminist Review* 77 (2004), 162–6. Identified in the author biography as 'one half of B+B', Carrington describes the collective's activities as 'residencies and community-based projects to acts of consultation and activism'. Salon populaire is a project realised collaboratively by THE OFFICE (Ellen Blumenstein, Fiona Geuß) and Arthur Berlin (Tanja Schomaker) and raumlaborberlin (Markus Bader). See www.salonpopulaire.de/ (accessed 25 October 2011).

28 Interviews with Kuratorisk Aktion in Malmö in 2008 and 2010. A long version of the final text can be found on the site of the research network, 'Transnational Perspectives on Women's Art, Feminism and Curating', at: http://arts.brighton. ac.uk/research/irn. A shorter version is included in Dimitrakaki and Perry, *Politics in a Glass Case*. My discussion here draws on the published texts of the interview.

29 'Rethinking Nordic Colonialism: A Postcolonial Exhibition Project in Five Acts' was realised in Reykjavik, Iceland; Nuuk, Greenland; Tórshavn, The Faroe Islands; and Rovaniemi, Finnish Sápmi. NIFCA, which played a key role in facilitating the project, ceased to exist in 2006, having started its activities in 1997. See www.nifca.org/2006/ (26 November 2011).

30 R. Chidgey, 'DIY Feminist Networks in Europe', *Journal Transform!* Europe 5 (2009), at: www.transform-network.net/en/home/journal-transformeurope/ display-journal-transform/article//DIY-Feminist-Networks-in-Europe-Personal-and-Collective-Acts-of-Resistance.html (accessed 9 June 2011).

31 I interviewed WHW in their Zagreb office on 3 July 2011.

32 In 2011 the WHW website listed the following institutions and cities where the Collective gave public talks, extending from China and Australia to Israel and the US: 'ULLENS Center for Contemporary Art, Beijing; Goldsmiths University, London; PhotoCairo, Cairo; Center for Contemporary Art, Tel Aviv; Nuova Accademia di Belle Arti, Milano; Art History Department of the School of Philosophy, University of Zagreb; HomeWorks, Beirut; Museum of Modern Art, New York; Van Abbemuseum, Eindhoven; Museum of Modern Art, Warsaw; Center Georges Pompidou, Paris, Museum of Contemporary Art, Belgrade, and Artspace, Sydney.' From http://whw.posterous.com/pages/ about-what-how-and-for-whom-whw (accessed 23 June 2011).

33 As noted on the WHW website, 'in 2008 WHW was the first recipient of Igor Zabel Award for Culture and Theory, awarded in recognition of cultural activities related to the Central and South Eastern European region.' Ibid.

34 *11th Istanbul Biennial Exhibition Guide.*

35 WHW quoted in N. Garín, 'Curatorial Practices: Interview with WHW Collective' 01/01/10, *LatinArt.com: An Online Journal of Art and Culture*, www.latinart.com/aiview.cfm?id=420 (accessed 21 June 2011).

36 See the essay 'Screening the 1970s: Sexuality and Representation in Feminist Practice', in Pollock, *Vision and Difference.*

37 G. Day, S. Edwards, D. Mabb, 'What Keeps Mankind Alive?': The Eleventh International Istanbul Biennial. Once More on Aesthetics and Politics', *HM: Research in Critical Marxist Theory* 18 (2010), 135–71. Here 153.

38 T. Zolghadr, '11th Istanbul Biennial', *frieze* 127 (November–December 2009) www.frieze.com/issue/review/11th_istanbul_biennial/ (accessed 26 October 2011).

39 Day, Edwards and Mabb, 'What Keeps Mankind Alive?': The Eleventh International Istanbul Biennial. Once More on Aesthetics and Politics', 148.

40 Ibid., 152–3.

41 ' 'What?' 'How?' and 'For whom?' the three basic questions of every economic organization, and are fundamental to the planning, conception, and realization of exhibitions and the production and distribution of artworks and the artist's position in the labor market. These questions formed the title of WHW's first project, in 2000 in Zagreb, dedicated to the 152nd anniversary of the Communist Manifesto, and became the motto of WHW's work and the name of their collective.' At: http://curatorsintl.org/collaborators/whw (accessed 8 March 2013).

42 Mujeres Públicas in electronic interview with the author, 7 December 2011.

43 See María Laura Rosa, 'Our Bodies, Our History: Mujeres Públicas's Activism in the City of Buenos Aires', *n.paradoxa: international feminist art journal* 30 (July 2012), 5–11.

44 Quotes taken from 'Paper read at the European Social Forum, Malmö and Privilege Walk Symposium, organised by the Malmö, Sweden 2008, The YES! Association and Lilith Performance Studio', www.mujerespublicas.com.ar/ (accessed 23 June 2011).

45 See For example the papers presented at the Common Differences symposium held in Tallinn in May 2010 and especially Katja Kobolt's paper 'Feminist Curatorial Practices and Feminist Canon-Building Strategies as Political Actions.' Kobolt was co-director and programmer of the City of Women Festival in Ljubljana and is at the time of writing co-coordinator of the Cross Border Experience project at the Peace Institute Ljubljana. On the symposium see http://common-differences.artun.ee (accessed 8 December 2011).

46 Mujeres Públicas in electronic interview with the author, 7 December 2011.

47 Ibid.

48 An engaging review of the book appeared on the blog of Just Seeds: Artists' Co-operative, bringing together artists from North America and Mexico. Just Seeds stresses the significance of a feminist art collective appropriating the novel motif to produce a consciousness-raising narrative. See www.justseeds.org/blog/2009/02/choose_your_own_dis_adventure.html (accessed 8 December 2011).

49 Commentary drawn from the collective's website: www.mujerespublicas.com.
ar/ (accessed 26 November 2011).

50 Ibid.

51 This issue is discussed in more detail in Rosa, 'Our Bodies, Our History: Mujeres Públicas's Activism in the City of Buenos Aires', published when the Havana Biennial was already over.

52 *Tucumán Arde*, executed by Grupo de Artistas de Vanguardia, is perhaps the best-known instance of radical socially engaged Argentinian and indeed Latin American art, discussed recently in a number of contexts, including the feminist journal *n.paradoxa*. See also the discussion of this work in W. Bradley and C. Esche (eds), *Art and Social Change: A Critical Reader* (London: Afterall and Tate Publishing, 2008).

53 Following the dissolution of the collective/artwork, its two founding members set up a website to keep its legacy alive and to continue collaborations with the public and the academy. See www.radikalpedagogik.blogspot.com/#!/p/in-english.html (accessed 28 November 2011).

54 MFK, *Do the Right Thing! A Manual from MFK* (Malmö 2011), 7.

55 Ibid, 15.

56 Ibid, 22.

57 Ibid, 27.

58 Ibid. 27.

59 On this see S. H. Madoff (ed.), *Art School (Propositions for the 21st Century)* (Cambridge, Mass: The MIT Press, 2009).

60 Ibid, 10.

61 Ibid, 14.

62 M. De Angelis, 'How?!?! An Essay on John Holloway's *Change the World without Taking Power*', *HM: Research in Critical Marxist Theory* 13/4 (2005), 233–49.

63 MFK, *Do the Right Thing!*, 41.

64 Ibid., 33–4.

65 On the history of feminism's use of strategic separatism see Estelle Freedman, 'Separatism as a Strategy': Female Institution Building and American Feminism, 1870–1930', in P. A. Weiss and M. Friedman (eds), *Feminism and Community* (Philadelphia: Temple University Press, 1995). The essay first appeared in *Feminist Studies* 5/3 (Fall 1979), 512–29.

66 MFK, *Do the Right Thing!*, 39.

67 Ibid., 57.

Postscript: what is a feminist beginning?

In the six to seven years it took me to complete this study (2007–13), my sense of where this investigation into contemporary art, gender and globalisation was leading changed in a way that I had not anticipated. Whereas I had originally assumed that I would be narrating a closure, or more accurately, a break and an *ending* (feminism's disaffiliation from a postmodernist art world), I ended up feeling that I had been researching and trying to give discursive shape to a *beginning* (the emergence of a feminist anti-capitalist paradigm in art). No doubt the landmark year 2008, when the global financial crisis began spinning a spectacular range of economic others overtaking postmodernism's cultural others as the ground of political protest, put things into perspective: what had started as an interrogation into the possibility of a feminist continuum that had survived internal fragmentation and depoliticisation mutated into a search for feminist practices at the forefront of a global opposition to perpetuating a diminished human lifeworld.

And yet art, much like art history, had been relegated to the margins of feminist political thinking, as if somehow being condemned to merely signify. Even as such ability and willingness to define opposition on a symbolic level remained important, it ultimately marked the distance from the ground of 'real' struggles. From a point on, feminist critique in the realm of art was seen as trapped in this no-woman's land – that is, feminist art and theory became mired in self-doubt about their contribution to changing the world. What I have tried to ask in this book is: is this still the case, and if so, does it have to be? Or does a greater, historically dictated awareness of the current organisation of labour (divided and yet collectively sustaining a global empire of capitalist production) make the gendered terrain of art and its contexts more implicated into understanding the overwhelming grip of capital over social life? My answer to this question has been positive. I now conclude my thoughts by revisiting certain aspects of my argument, in light of this perceived change in the broader framework where feminism must do its radical work as we are getting well into the twenty-first century.

This is my first thought: I am no longer worried about the survival of feminism, the survival of art or the survival of feminism in art and vice versa. In the networks of global capital coordinated by immaterial (and yet material!) labour, 'feminism and art' taken together amount to something more than a sum of parts. Yet this does not apply to just any interpretation of feminism or to a generic notion of art. The moment to think strategically has come again, as was the case in the 1970s. In this study therefore, 'feminism' has often been interpreted as materialist feminist politics; and as for 'art', it has not been so much the selection of specific practices but rather paradigms of art production that I found myself returning to time and again. The paradigms I prioritised posit art as less tied to the senses, that is, to our *aisthiseis* and therefore aesthetics – let alone an aesthetics of the visual. It is not simply that, as Marx had assumed, our senses are not immutable but transform alongside the (*sic*) man-made environment, that the senses, much like gender and labour, have a history. This is of course critical, pointing to the need to keep revising a feminist aesthetics: there could never be a terminal collapse of the feminine into the tactile or of the masculine into the visual. More than that, though, given that the impetus for this study has been that our moment in history, the *right now everywhere*, has remained largely unarticulated in feminist art history, this is the time to ask: should feminist practices located in the art world and claiming experiential rather than representational knowledge of the social be tactically prioritised over the possibly radical pleasures of (making or disseminating) a feminist aesthetics? It is not a very original question for those who remember that Laura Mulvey, in her foundational essay 'Visual Pleasure and Narrative Cinema' of 1975, admonishes us to 'destroy' the pleasure of normative identification and replace it with 'the thrill that comes from leaving the past behind without rejecting it'.[1] Rather, what is original and new is the horizon created since 1989 out of global capital's efforts to further contain the radical possibilities that arise in the world of labour. It is this recalibrated horizon – revealed to be a glass dome in 2008! – that forces a rethinking of the meanings of the still gendered and classed division of labour. And this is the case even, or perhaps especially, with labour encountered in the art world (its fringes and mainstream).

What has motivated this book has been the possibility of offering a perspective on a historical moment for which feminism in the world of (and created by) art can be deployed as an oppositional force. To sum it up, the book makes three points in connection with this. All three have to do with comprehending the terrain of power that feminism is now called to bring into view and break free from. Feminism is understood as a political project seeking to end the oppression of women – it is in this sense that the term is deployed here. But what configurations of power actually create women's oppression – which women, and where, remains an important question to that end. Broadly speaking, I have argued that capitalist globalisation, in its geopolitical and biopolitical dimensions, is the overdetermining factor in the contemporary struggles of feminism. It is the dialectic between capitalist globalisation and feminism that provides the wider context where my narrative about art unfolds, delineating its more precise political focus. The three points through which we can grasp the latter are: (a) the need for rethinking the priorities of feminist art history: (b) the need to prioritise, in analysis, gendered labour and/in global space: and (c) the need to reinvestigate women's and feminists' relationship to the art institution, power and resistance.

Why rethink feminist art history?

Feminist art history came into existence and achieved its path-breaking critique between the defeat of May 1968 and the capitulation of the 'alternative systems' in Chinese and Soviet territories to the markets (symbolically expressed with the fall of the Berlin Wall). It was an era that opened with Jean Buadrillard's *The Mirror of Production* (1973), as a rejection of Marxist thought on production, and ended with Francis Fukuyama's *The End of History and the Last Man* (1992), as a reduction of Marxist thought into a disastrous experiment in production that had finally folded. It was a complex twenty years, the second and final half of a Cold War between two allegedly antithetical systems of organising production and human life locked into positions of battle. The end of the story, the escalation of a crisis, is too well-known – although less so when it comes to understanding how such a historic shift has shaped women's production as well as the systems where this is evaluated. (This question of value is something to which I will return.)

Not only did Fukuyama's dream of the world staying still after overcoming the Soviet experiment not materialise, but rather history became accelerated. The reason for this acceleration was, rather ironically, the impossibility of enacting globally Fukuyama's endpoint of history: capitalist liberal democracy as the ideal state for atomised self-fulfilment. This was *not* after all going to be the context where feminist art history would have to operate in the emerging global paradigm – something which feminist art history came to apprehend only recently. For example, in *Seeing Differently*, Amelia Jones pays heed to a 'post-secular subject' to an extent that would have been unthinkable (and perhaps unnecessary) in the heyday of feminist art history's first wave. As she says, 'the world is riven by differences'.[2] But why indeed be interested in this at all unless you (the historian) have not been afforded a world-perspective through the very historical conditions in which you write?

Although Jones' concerns in her 2012 study are very different to my own here, our explications of cultural phenomena are both inflected by the material premise of a world-view, by a universalism peculiar to globalisation as *precisely the articulation of a totality that cannot be fully known.* Let us then say that my prevalent concern is what happens when feminist art history encounters, and needs to operate within, this totalising process (preformed globally every day) – which, conceptually, is very different from what happened to feminism in postmodern times. If then feminism was instrumentalised as a political platform working convincingly towards smaller and more identifiable interest groups, in 2013 feminism's strength is expressive of quite the opposite: in the identification of 'women' as its plural, *queered* subject of emancipation ('anyone who ever identified as a woman', as put by Swedish art collective MFK) we can recognise the possibility of a growing community of protest action or a transgressive coalitional politics. This feminist beginning is for women *and* 'feminised' male workers. The question, to paraphrase Chandra Mohanty, is 'what do we have in common?' rather than 'how do we differ?' Yet alongside Mohanty, my invocation of historical materialism, is necessary in order to avert the risk of a void answer being given to the first question. In short, what 'we' have in common cannot be asserted discursively in a world where women are locked into circuits of exploitation. How can we avoid placing this question of commonality and of the common, and this questionable 'we', as an ethical counter-paradigm to an economy dividing sharply women as well as a feminised workforce? 'We' do not know how to avoid that – so far. Yet the validity of the question can be test-driven in a reconfigured feminist writing of contemporary art history. And this happens for many reasons, but especially because feminist thinking can articulate the complex positioning of gendered labour in art – a terrain of production connected in various ways to the dynamism and rejuvenation of capitalism.

Why focus on labour and artWork?

Such an enquiry into contemporary art as a site of gendered labour, and indeed labour that constructs a peculiar form of social work – as *artWork* – occupies the best part of the book. Inevitably, it is approached eclectically, by highlighting and analysing highly specific forms of artistic and (to an extent) curatorial engagement. The latter fall into two broad categories: biopolitical and post-documentary work (with the video essay as a salient example). What both these practices – which may well overlap – have in common is their radical relationship to global space as a site of production claimed as such by the woman artist.[3] The examples discussed here, across several chapters, suggest that 'global space' is far more than geographical territory, far more than a topography, for the female creative subject. And although recent studies have emphasised the urban contextualisation of gendered creative work (see, for example, Angela McRobbie), the identification of woman's work with knowledge production in the friction zones of the global economy is a novelty in the history of art. By focusing extensively on travel, on crossing, on the journey as a critical work method adopted by the woman artist around 2000, there emerges an anti-domestic ethos, a refutation of being incorporated into nuclear family structures and the undervalued work of care. But this hardly means an exodus from capitalist relations of production. Miwon Kwon's itinerant artist must caution us against any simplified reading of what women artists do outside the home – exactly when the very existence of an 'outside' to capitalist relations of production is vigorously contested (as impossible) or idealised (as already available). Quite simply, leaving home does *not* equal leaving capitalism as the very system where gender is appropriated in terms of 'gender specific human resources'.[4]

The preceding chapter on masculinity, where travel also features as an essential aspect in the relationship of man to the materiality and ideological constitution of global space, suggests both that there is a distinction to be made between how female and male artists travel and that any such designation (i.e. 'itinerant artist') must be differentiated along gender lines. The distinction I claim to see between male and female artists relying on the work method of travel has to do specifically with the relocating of art-making from the regime of signification to that of materially embedded social relations. Although the post-structuralist impulse takes over, the materiality of the social context where art does its work indicates the possibility of reaching a social truth. It is a gendered social truth: the woman artist is likely to encounter risk of the kind that the male artist will not (which does not mean that the male artist's journey is necessarily risk-free). In the late 1990s, Ursula Biemann's interest in female workers getting murdered while crossing the desert, in her first video essay about women and global capital (*Performing the Border*), can also function successfully as a metaphor for an internalised fear, an anxiety about being a female artist and the anticipation of dangerous crossings. Travel as a work method proved steeped in power relations defining gendered access to global space, which is why it occupies a central place in this study. Danger does not of course valorise the work done – nor should it, within feminist analysis. For feminist analysis, the value of the work is in its material(ist) engagement with the lives of other women (and feminised non-subjects), the acknowledgement that difference is always sown into socio-economic privilege, or lack thereof, and the direct confrontation with the current inadequacy of our being-together in struggle. Ann-Sofi Sidén's *Warte Mal!* demonstrates, both to the artist herself and hopefully to her female viewers at least (much more likely to be exposed to sexual violence than male viewers) precisely that crossing is not inhabiting, and what those of us identifying as feminists choose to do or not do with that knowledge is *not* the responsibility of art.

Besides this, there should be no doubt that in the capitalist art world, the sign of the female border prostitute, as much as the sign of the male miner, is put to work, generating affect in the expanded exhibition space.[5] The more we feel pressured under the labour of the sign on our condition of spectatorship, the more symbolic capital we (the 'affected' viewers) generate for the artwork as an object on display, and the more the prostitute and the miner are drawn into the extraction of surplus value. *This*, on the other hand, falls within the remit of artistic responsibility: it has to do with how and where the artist works and what he pulls into Gagosian. And at this point we can only hope that the artist as the producer of social documents will keep reflecting on the political implications of such artistic labour.

Can feminism change the world without taking power?

Although the book's final chapter is the one most clearly focused on power, this study as a whole has been preoccupied with a feminist charting of globalisation as a web of power relations. Power has been commonly associated with the art institution – that is, with the defined, legitimated contexts where art is ratified as such. Women artists' exclusion from the art institution was partly what generated the feminist art movement of the 1970s and 1980s, primarily in the West. But why should this kind of power be revisited in the first place? This can receive a rather straightforward answer: expressed concerns about the accommodation of feminist struggles in the art institution as well as the alleged re-constitution of power in the art institution (through, for example, the New Institutionalism of the 1990s) had a role to play. Clearly, feminist subversion in the capitalist art world can no longer be limited to ensuring that more women artists have access to the market and its support mechanisms.

The work performed by feminist collectives since 2000 emerges out of such awareness. Significantly, however, there is no single source inspiring such awareness. Feminist activism, less concerned with remaking the contemporary art world and more with connecting the latter with the real world, takes many routes and is defined by diverse traditions. Apparently, anything – from Mohanty's turn to historical materialism to a country's troubled history (Argentina, Croatia) to feminist legacies – can congeal into springboards for action in the 'right' historical moment. This is one way to say that feminist histories are necessarily embedded into broader paradigms of opposition – and to acknowledge that does not detract from the uniqueness of feminist demands but rather helps us identify, strategically, opportunities for coordinated action. In many ways, the revival of feminist and female collectivism demonstrates an understanding that the art institution cannot remain the privileged arbiter of change. Of course, if we take Europe as an example, thanks to funding cuts and capital's recent attack on anything that can be identified with critique, the art institution can no longer be seen as a site of unilateral privilege. The rise of women's collectivism is also a response to the newly precarious position of the museum and the contemporary art centre. It is a form of organising teams sharing a political vision but not dependent on institutional resources – or at least, not as dependent on them. Broadly speaking, female collectivism is a way of expressing the willingness to both defy power and be empowered. In paraphrasing John Holloway's hopeful admonition of the early 2000s, to change the world without taking power, I have also sought to qualify it for an emergent contemporary feminism. Hell, no, it is *not* possible to change the world without taking power – but the sites where power is claimed and who the allies are, need not be as predictable. Rather, choosing or discovering such sites and allies can be part of claiming intersubjective agency, which is the form of power we need.

In the age of global capital (or capitalism after postmodernism), modern feminism needs to be reappraised and reconnected with a fast transforming political landscape. This can be the next task and step for a contemporary materialist feminist theory taking on both its own historical conditions of being and the fate of women in the gulags of capitalist accumulation of the twenty-first century (in which I have to include my university office extending all the way to the desk in my bedroom in a mortgaged apartment which I may not *work-live* long enough to pay off). If Virginia Woolf once said 'as a woman I have no country, as a woman I want no country, as a woman my country is the whole world', how can her refusal be turned into a meaningful *practice* of solidarity against capital's achieved objective of world domination? Following Woolf, can contemporary feminism generate a global imperative intended to subvert globalisation's rule as a form of biopower where gender divisions are harnessed into ever more complex regimes of production for profit, and where 'women's rights' can be appropriated in the racist speech of neo-fascistic formations flourishing in conditions of economic despair? If we can envisage an affirmative answer to this question, persisting with the feminist analysis of a gendered paradigm of artWork in terms of its political articulation can perhaps contribute to making real the long-standing dream of labour's liberation from capitalist patriarchy.

Notes

1 L. Mulvey, 'Visual Pleasure and Narrative Cinema', *Screen* 16/3 (Autumn 1975), 6–18.
2 Jones, *Seeing Differently*, 222.
3 On global space as production site see Dimitrakaki, 'Art, Globalisation and the Exhibition Form'.

4 Frey et al., 'Gender Manifesto', quoted in A. McRobbie, *The Aftermath of Feminism: Gender, Culture and Social Change* (London: Sage, 2009).
5 In the summer of 2012 *Manifesta 13* in the (former) mining region of Genk in Belgium, provided a wealth of information about the masculinisation of the miner in the course of the twentieth century as well as included exciting archival material concerning legislation that banned women and minors from working as miners in the West (women were assigned side roles, such as washing coal).

Bibliography

Alberro, A. and S. Buchman (eds), *Art after Conceptual Art* (Cambridge Mass.: The MIT Press and Vienna: Generali Foundation, 2006).

Allara, P., 'Geo-Bodies: Feminist Activists Crossing Borders', in M. Gržinić and T. Ostojić (eds), *Integration Impossible? The Politics of Migration in the Artwork of Tanja Ostojić* (Berlin: Argobooks, 2009).

Althusser, L. and E. Balibar, *Reading Capital*, trans. B. Brewster (London: NLB, 1977).

Araeen, R., 'A New Beginning: Beyond Postcolonial Cultural Theory and Identity Politics', *Third Text* 50 (Spring 2000), 3–20.

Aranda, J., B. Kuan Wood and A. Vidokle (eds), *Are You Working Too Much? Post-Fordism, Precarity, and the Labour of Art* (Berlin: Sternberg Press, 2011).

Ashcroft, B., G. Griffiths and H. Tiffin (eds), *The Postcolonial Studies Reader* (London and New York: Routledge, 1995).

Baert, R., 'Editorial', *n.paradoxa: international feminist art journal* 18 (2006), 4.

Benhabib, S., 'Feminism and Postmodernism: An Uneasy Alliance', *Praxis International* 11/2 (1991), 137–50.

Bellour, R., 'Video Writing', in D. Hall and S. J. Fifer (eds), *Illuminating Video: An Essential Guide to Video Art* (New York: Aperture and Bay Area: BAVC, 1990).

Berardi, F., 'Biffo', *The Soul at Work*, trans. F. Cadel and G. Mecchia (Los Angeles: Semiotext(e), 2009).

Betterton, R., *An Intimate Distance: Women, Artists and the Body* (New York and London: Routledge, 1996).

Biemann, U., 'Remotely Sensed: A Topography of the Global Sex Trade', *Feminist Review* 80 (2005), 180–93.

Biemann, U., 'Performing the Border: The Transnational Video', in U. Biemann (ed.), *Stuff It! The Video Essay in the Digital Age* (Zurich: Institute for Theory of Art and Design and Vienna: Springer, 2003).

Billig, J., M. Lind and L. Nilsson (eds), *Taking the Matter into Common Hands* (London: Black Dog, 2007).

Binkley, S. and J. Capetillo (eds), *A Foucault for the 21st Century: Governmentality, Biopolitics and Discipline in the New Millennium* (Newcastle: Cambridge Scholars, 2010).

Birkeland, I., *Making Place, Making Self: Travel, Subjectivity and Sexual Difference* (Aldershot: Ashgate, 2005).

Bishop, C., *Artificial Hells: Participatory Art and the Politics of Spectatorship* (London: Verso, 2012).

Bishop, C., 'Antagonism and Relational Aesthetics', *October* 110 (2004), 51–79.

Bishop, C., 'The Social Turn: Collaboration and Its Discontents', *Artforum* (February 2006), 179–85.

Blunt, A. and G. Rose (eds), *Writing Women and Space: Colonial and Postcolonial Geographies* (New York: The Guilford Press, 1994).

Bottomore, T. (ed.), *A Dictionary of Marxist Thought* (Oxford: Blackwell, 1985).

Bourriaud, N., 'Altermodern', in N. Bourriaud (ed.), *Altermodern Tate Triennial* (London: Tate Publishing, 2009) unpaginated exhibition catalogue.

Bourriaud, N., *Relational Aesthetics* (Dijon: Les presses du réel, 2002).

Boyle, D., 'A Brief History of American Documentary Video', in S.J. Fifer and D. Hall (eds), *Illuminating Video: An Essential Guide to Video Art* (New York: Aperture and Bay Area: BAVC, 1990).

Bradley, W. and C. Esche (eds), *Art and Social Change: A Critical Reader* (London: Afterall and Tate Publishing, 2008).

Braidotti, R., *Transpositions: On Nomadic Ethics* (Cambridge: Polity, 2006).

Braverman, H., *Labor and Monopoly Capital: The Degradation of Work in the Twentieth Century* (New York: Monthly Review Press, 1974).

Brody, J. D. V., *Punctuation: Art, Politics and Play* (Durham: Duke University Press, 2008).

Broude N. and M. D. Garrard, 'Introduction: Reclaiming Female Agency', in N. Broude and M. D. Garrard (eds), *Reclaiming Female Agency: Feminist Art History after Postmodernism* (Berkeley: University of California Press, 2005).

Bryan-Wilson, J., *Art Workers: Radical Practice in the Vietnam Era* (Berkeley: University of California Press, 2009).

Buck-Morss, S., 'The Post-Soviet Condition', in IRWIN (eds), *East Art Map: Contemporary Art and Eastern Europe* (London: Afterall, 2006).

Bull, M., 'Globalization and Biopolitics: Introduction to New Left Review 45', *New Left Review* 45 (May–June 2007), 1–2.

Burgin, V., *In/Different Spaces: Place and Memory in Visual Culture* (Berkeley: University of California Press, 1996).

Buskirk, M., *The Contingent Object of Contemporary Art* (Cambridge Mass.: The MIT Press, 2003).

Butler, C., 'Art and Feminism: An Ideology of Shifting Criteria', in C. Butler and L. G. Mark (eds), *Wack! Art and the Feminist Revolution* (Cambridge, Mass.: The MIT Press, 2007).

Butler, J., *Excitable Speech: A Politics of the Performative* (London and New York: Routledge, 1997).

Butler, J., *Bodies that Matter: On the Discursive Limits of Sex* (London and New York: Routledge, 1993).

Butler, J., *Gender Trouble: Feminism and the Subversion of Identity* (London and New York: Routledge, 1990).

Cahan, S. E., 'Regarding Andrea Fraser's Untitled', *Social Semiotics* 16/1 (April 2006), 7–15.

Carrington, S., 'Traded Places', *Feminist Review* 77 (2004), 162–6.

Carolin, C. and C. Haynes (eds), 'The Politics of Display: Ann-Sofi Sidén's Warte Mal!, Art History and Social Documentary: A Seminar with Laura Bear, Care Carolin,

Griselda Pollock, and Ann-Sofi Sidén', in S. Macdonald and P. Basu, (eds), *Exhibition Experiments* (Oxford: Blackwell, 2007).

Carroll, N., *Theorizing the Moving Image* (Cambridge: Cambridge University Press, 1996).

Castells, M., *The Rise of the Network Society, The Information Age: Economy, Society and Culture Vol. I* (Hoboken: Wiley-Blackwell, 2011 [1996]).

Cerne, A., 'Chantal Akerman's *News from Home*', in G. Pollock (ed.), *Psychoanalysis and the Image* (Oxford: Blackwell, 2006).

Chambers, I. and L. Curti (eds), *The Postcolonial Question: Common Skies, Divided Horizons* (London and New York: Routledge, 1996).

Chanan, M., 'The Changing Geography of Third Cinema', *Screen* 38/4 (Winter 1997), 372–88.

Cheah, P., 'The Cosmopolitical', in M. Rovisco and M. Nowicka (eds), *The Ashgate Research Companion to Cosmopolitanism* (Farnham: Ashgate, 2011).

Cherry, D. and J. Helmand (eds), *Local/Global: Women Artists in the Nineteenth Century* (Farnham: Ashgate, 2006).

Clegg, S., 'The Problem of Agency in Feminism: A Critical Realist Approach', *Gender and Education* 18/3 (May 2006), 309–24.

Connor, M. and K. Deepwell, 'Working Notes: Conversation with Katy Deepwell', *Art Journal* 61/2 (Summer 2002), 32–43.

Copjec, J., *Imagine There's No Woman: Ethics and Sublimation* (Cambridge Mass.: The MIT Press, 2004).

Cramerotti, A., *Aesthetic Journalism: How to Inform without Informing* (Bristol: Intellect, 2009).

Crary, J., 'Eclipse of the Spectacle', in B. Wallis (ed.), *Art after Modernism: Rethinking Representation* (New York: New Museum of Contemporary Art, 1984).

Crenshaw, K., 'Demarginalising the Intersection of Sex and Race: A Black Feminist Critique of Anti-discrimination Doctrine, Feminist Theory and Anti-Racist Politics', *University of Chicago Legal Forum* (1989), 138–67.

Critchley, S., *Ethics, Politics, Subjectivity* (London: Verso, 1999).

Cubitt, S., *Timeshift: On Video Culture* (London: Routledge, 1991).

Czegledy N. and A. Szekeres, 'Agents for Change: The Contemporary Art Centres of the Soros Foundation and C3', *Third Text* 23/3 (2009), 251–9.

Davies, A., 'Basic Instinct: Trauma and Retrenchment 2000–4', *Mute: Culture and Politics after the Net* 29 (February 2005), 1–14.

Davis, M., 'Planet of Slums: Urban Revolution and the Informal Proletariat', *New Left Review* 26 (March–April 2004), 5–26.

Day, G., S. Edwards and D. Mabb, 'What Keeps Mankind Alive?': The Eleventh International Istanbul Biennial. Once More on Aesthetics and Politics', *HM: Research in Critical Marxist Theory* 18 (2010), 135–71.

De Angelis, M., 'How?!?! An Essay on John Holloway's *Change the World without Taking Power*', *HM: Research in Critical Marxist Theory* 13/4 (2005), 233–49.

De Haan, F., K. Daskalova and A. Loutfi (eds), *Biographical Dictionary of Women's Movements and Feminisms in Central, Eastern, and South Eastern Europe: 19th and 20th Centuries* (Budapest: Central European University Press, 2006).

Demos, T. J., 'Moving Images of Globalization', *Grey Room* 37 (Fall 2009), 6–29.

Deveaux, M., 'Feminism and Empowerment: A Critical Reading of Foucault', *Feminist Studies* 20/2. *Women's Agency: Empowerment and the Limits of Resistance* (Summer 1994), 223–47.

Dimitrakaki, A., 'The Lessons of Sexual Politics: From the 1970s to *Empire*, an interview with Amelia Jones', in A. Dimitrakaki and L. Perry (eds), *Politics in a Glass Case: Feminism, Exhibition Cultures and Curatorial Transgressions* (Liverpool: Liverpool University Press, 2013).

Dimitrakaki, A., 'Art, Globalization and the Exhibition Form: What Is the Case, What Is the Challenge?' *Third Text* 26/3 (May 2012), 305–19.

Dimitrakaki, A., 'The Spectacle and Its Others: Art, Conflict and Labour in the Age of Global Capital', in J. Harris (ed.), *Globalization and Contemporary Art* (Hoboken: Wiley-Blackwell, 2011).

Dimitrakaki, A., 'Labour, Ethics, Sex and Capital: On Biopolitical Production in Contemporary Art', *n.paradoxa: international feminist art journal* 28 (July 2011), 5–15.

Dimitrakaki, A., 'Researching Cultures and the Omitted Footnote: Questions on the Practice of Feminist Art History' in A. Jones (ed.), *The Feminism and Visual Culture Reader*, 2nd edn (London and New York: Routledge, 2009 [2000]).

Dimitrakaki, A., P. Skelton and M. Tralla (eds), *Private Views: Spaces and Gender in Contemporary Art from Britain and Estonia* (London: The Women's Art Library, 2000).

Djuric D. and M. Suvakovic (eds), *Impossible Histories: Historical Avant-gardes, Neo-Avant-Gardes and Post-Avant-Gardes in Yugoslavia* (Cambridge Mass: The MIT Press, 2003).

Doherty, C. (ed.), *Contemporary Art: From Studio to Situation* (London: Black Dog, 2004).

Douzinas, C. and S. Žižek (eds), *The Idea of Communism* (London: Verso, 2011).

Doy, G., *Materializing Art History* (Oxford: Berg, 1998).

Dyer, R., 'Don't Look Now: The Male Pin-Up', in *The Sexual Subject: A* Screen *Reader in Sexuality* (London and New York: Routledge 1992).

Dyer-Witheford, N., 'Cognitive Capitalism and the Contested Campus', *European Journal of Higher Arts Education* 2 (February 2005), 71–93.

Ebert, T. L., 'Ludic Feminism, the Body, Performance, and Labor: Bringing 'Materialism' Back into Feminist Cultural Studies', *Cultural Critique* 23 (Winter 1992–93), 5–50.

Eisenstein, H., *Feminism Seduced: How Global Elites Use Women's Labor and Ideas to Exploit the World* (Boulder and London: Paradigm Publishers, 2009).

Eisenstein, Z. (ed.), *Capitalist Patriarchy and the Case for Socialist Feminism* (New York: Monthly University Press, 1979).

Enwezor, O., et al. (eds), *Documenta 11_Platform 5: Exhibition* (Ostfildern-Ruit: Hatje Kantz Publishers, 2002).

Federici, S., *Revolution at Point Zero: Housework, Reproduction and Feminist Struggle* (New York: Autonomedia, 2012).

Federici, S., 'Precarious Labour: A Feminist Viewpoint', *Variant* 37 (Spring/Summer 2010).

Federici, S., *Caliban and the Witch: Women, the Body, and Primitive Accumulation* (New York: Autonomedia, 2004).

Ferleger Brades, S., 'Preface', in *Warte Mal! Prostitution after the Velvet Revolution* (London: Hayward Gallery, 2002).

Foster, H., 'The Artist as Ethnographer?', in G. E. Marcus and F. R. Myers (eds), *The Traffic in Culture: Refiguring Art and Anthropology* (Berkeley: University of California Press, 1995).

Foster, H., *The Return of the Real* (Cambridge, Mass.: The MIT Press, 1996).

Foster, H., (ed) *Postmodern Culture* (London: Pluto Press 1985).

Foster Gage, M. (ed.), *Aesthetic Theory: Essential Texts for Architecture and Design* (New York: W.W. Norton, 2011).

Frascina, F., et al., *Modernity and Modernism: French Painting in the Nineteenth Century* (New Haven: Yale University Press, 1993).

Fraser, A., 'How to Provide an Artistic Service: An Introduction', in S. Leung and Z. Kocur (eds), *Theory in Contemporary Art since 1985* (Oxford: Blackwell, 2005).

Fraser, N., 'Feminism, Capitalism and the Cunning of History', *New Left Review* 56 (March/April 2009), 97–117.

Freedman, E., 'Separatism as a Strategy': Female Institution Building and American Feminism, 1870–1930', in P. A. Weiss and M. Friedman (eds), *Feminism and Community* (Philadelphia: Temple University Press, 1995).

Gade, R., 'Making Real: Strategies of Performing Performativity in Tanja Ostojić's Looking for a Husband with EU Passport', in M. Gržinić and T. Ostojić (eds), *Integration Impossible? The Politics of Migration in the Artwork of Tanja Ostojić* (Berlin: Argobooks, 2009).

Gimenez, M., 'What's Material about Materialist Feminism? A Marxist-feminist Critique', *Radical Philosophy* 101 (May/June 2000), 18–28.

Gonzalez, M. A., 'Communisation and the Abolition of Gender', in B. Noys (ed.), *Communisation and Its Discontents: Contestation, Critique, and Contemporary Struggles* (New York: Minor Compositions/Autonomedia, 2011).

Groys, B., 'Art in the Age of Biopolitics: From Artwork to Art Documentation', in *Documenta 11_Platform 5: Exhibition* (Ostfildern-Ruit: Hatje Cantz Publishers, 2002).

Gržinić, M., 'Decoloniality of Knowledge', in M. Gržinić and T. Ostojić (eds), *Integration Impossible? The Politics of Migration in the Artwork of Tanja Ostojić* (Berlin: Argobooks, 2009).

Gržinić, M., 'From Transitional Postsocialist Spaces to Neoliberal Global Capitalism', *Third Text* 21/5 (2007), 563–75.

Gržinić, M., 'On the Re-politicisation of Art through Contamination', in IRWIN (eds), *East Art Map: Contemporary Art and Eastern Europe* (London: Afterall, 2006).

Gržinić, M., 'Tanja Ostojić: 'Yes, It's Fucking Political' – Skunk Anansie', in T. Ostojić (ed.), *Strategies of Success – Curators Series 2001–2003* (Belgrade: SKC, 2004).

Gouma-Peterson T. and P. Mathews, 'The Feminist Critique of Art History', *The Art Bulletin* 69/3 (September 1987), 326–57.

Guerra, C., 'Negatives of Europe: Video Essays and Collective Pedagogies', in M. Lind and H. Steyerl (eds); *The Greenroom: Reconsidering the Documentary and Contemporary Art 1* (Berlin: Sternberg Press, 2008).

Habermas, J., 'Why Europe Needs a Constitution', *New Left Review* 11 (Sept.–Oct. 2001), 5–26.

Haraway, D., *Simians, Cyborgs and Women: The Reinvention of Nature* (New York: Routledge, 1991).

Hardt, M. and A. Negri, *Commonwealth* (Cambridge Mass.: Harvard University Press, 2009).

Hardt, M. and A. Negri, *Multitude* (New York: Penguin Books, 2004).

Hardt, M. and A. Negri, *Empire* (Cambridge Mass.: Harvard University Press, 2000).

Harris, J. (ed.), *Contemporary Art and Globalization* (Hoboken: Wiley-Blackwell, 2011).

Harvey, D., *Spaces of Hope* (Berkeley: University of California Press, 2000).

Harvey, D., *Justice, Nature & the Geography of Difference* (Oxford: Blackwell, 1996).

Harvey, D., *The Condition of Postmodernity: An Enquiry into the Origins of Cultural Change* (Oxford: Blackwell, 1989).

Hawkesworth, M. E., *Globalization and Feminist Activism* (Maryland: Rowman & Littlefield Publishers, 2006).

Heath, J., 'Women Artists, Feminism and the Museum: Beyond the Blockbuster Retrospective', in A. Kokoli (ed.), *Feminism Reframed: Reflections on Art and Difference* (Newcastle: Cambridge Scholars, 2008).

Hennesy, R. and C. Ingraham (eds), *Materialist Feminism: A Reader in Class, Difference and Women's Lives* (New York and London: Routledge, 1997).

Hesford, W. S., '*Kairos*, Global Sex Work, Video Advocacy', in W. S. Hesford and W. Kozol (eds), *Just Advocacy? Women's Human Rights, Transnational Feminisms, and the Politics of Representation* (Piscataway, NJ: Rutgers University Press, 2005).

Hill Collins, P., 'Gender, Black Feminism, and Black Political Economy', *Annals of the American Academy of Political and Social Science* 568 (2000), 41–53.

Hock, B., 'Gendered Artistic Positions and Social Voices: Politics, Cinema, and the Visual Arts in State-Socialist and Post-Socialist Hungary', unpublished PhD thesis (Budapest: Central European University, 2009).

Holloway, J., *How to Change the World without Taking Power* (London: Pluto Press, 2002).

Holmes, B., *Escape the Overcode: Activist Art in the Control Society* (Zagreb: WHW; Eindhoven: Van Abbemuseum, 2009).

Holmes, B., *Unleashing the Collective Phantoms: Essays in Reverse Imagineering* (New York: Autonomedia, 2008).

Hopkins, D., *Dada's Boys: Masculinity after Duchamp* (New Haven: Yale University Press, 2008).

Hyde, L., *The Gift: Creativity and the Artist in the Modern World* (London: Vintage Books, 2007 [1983]).

Jablonskiene, L., '"Just an Artist?": An Imaginary Exhibition Project', in M. Helin Hayden and J. Sjöhlm Skrubbe (eds), *Feminisms Is still Our Name: Seven Essays on Historiography and Curatorial Practices* (Newcastle: Cambridge Scholars, 2010).

Jackson, S., *Social Works: Performing Art, Supporting Publics* (London and New York: Routledge, 2011).

Jameson, F., *Postmodernism, or the Cultural Logic of Late Capitalism* (London: Verso, 1990).

Jameson, F., *The Cultural Turn: Selected Writings on the Postmodern, 1983–1998* (London: Verso, 1998).

Jones, A., *Seeing Differently: A History and Theory of Identification and the Visual Arts* (London: Routledge, 2012).

Jones, A., 'The Return of Feminism(s) and the Visual Arts, 1970/2009', in M. Hedlin Hayden and J. Sjöholm Skrubbe (eds), *Feminisms Is still Our Name: Seven Essays on Historiography and Curatorial Practices* (Newcastle: Cambridge Scholars, 2010).

Jones, A., 'Introduction: Conceiving the Intersection of Feminism and Visual Culture, Again', in A. Jones (ed.), *The Feminism and Visual Culture Reader*, 2nd edn (London and New York: Routledge, 2009 [2000]).

Jones, A. and J. Doyle, 'New Feminist Theories of Visual Culture', a special issue of *Signs: A Journal of Women in Culture and Society* 31/3 (Spring 2006).

Jones, A., ' "Post-feminism": A Re-masculinisation of Culture?', in H. Robinson (ed.) *Art-Theory-Feminism* (Oxford: Blackwell, 2000).

Jones, A., *Body Art: Performing the Subject* (Minneapolis: University of Minnesota, 1998).

Jones, A., ' "Clothes Make the Man": The Male Artist as a Performative Function', *Oxford Art Journal* 18/2 (1995), 18–32.

Jones A., 'Dis/playing the Phallus: Male Artists Perform Their Masculinities', *Art History*, 17/4 (December 1994), 546–84.

Kaplan, A. E., *Women & Film: Both Sides of the Camera* (Routledge: London, 1988 [1983]).

Karlholm, D., 'Surveying Contemporary Art: Post-War, Postmodern, and Then What?', *Art History* 32/4 (September 2009), 712–33.

Karlholm, D., 'Reality Art: The Case of Oda Projesi', *Leitmotiv* 5 (2005–6), 115–24.

Kelly, M., 'Re-viewing Modernist Criticism', in B. Wallis (ed.), *Art after Modernism: Rethinking Representation* (New York: New Museum of Contemporary Art, 1984).

Kennedy, J. and L. Linden, 'Making Ourselves Visible', *Alphabet Prime* 1 (Fall 2009), 16–24.

Kent S. and J. Moreau (eds), *Women's Images of Men* (London: The ICA/Writers & Readers, 1985).

Kester, G. H., *Conversation Pieces: Community and Communication in Modern Art* (Berkeley: University of California Press, 2004).

Kipnis, L., 'Feminism: The Political Conscience of Postmodernism?', *Social Text* 21, Universal Abandon? The Politics of Postmodernism (1989), 149–66.

Klein, N., *The Shock Doctrine: The Rise of Disaster Capitalism* (New York: Penguin, 2008 [2007]).

Kokoli, A., 'The Woman Artist as Curatorial Effect', in A. Dimitrakaki and L. Perry (eds), *Politics in a Glass Case: Feminism, Exhibition Cultures and Curatorial Transgressions* (Liverpool: Liverpool University Press, 2013).

Kokoli, A., 'Undoing "Homeliness" in Feminist Art: Feministo – Portrait of the Artist as a Housewife (1975–7)', *n.paradoxa: international feminist art journal* 13 (January 2004), 75–83.

Kosmala, K., *Imagining Masculinities: Spatial and Temporal Representation and Visual Culture* (London: Taylor & Francis, 2013).

Krauss, R., *A Voyage on the North Sea': Art in the Age of the Post-Medium Condition* (London: Thames & Hudson, 1999).

Kristeva, J., 'Women's Time', *Signs* 7/1 (Autumn, 1981), 13–35.

Kuhn, A., *Women's Pictures: Feminism and Cinema* (Verso: London 1993 [1982]).

Kuhn, A. and A. M. Wolpe (eds), *Feminism and Materialism: Women and Modes of Production* (London: Routledge, 1978).

Kwon, M., *One Place after Another: Site-Specific Art and Locational Identity* (Cambridge Mass.: The MIT Press, 2004).

Kwon, M., 'Exchange Rate: On Obligation and Reciprocity in Some Art of the 1960s and after', in H. Molesworth (ed.), *Work Ethic* (The Baltimore Museum of Art and Penn State University Press, 2003).

Kwon, M., 'One Place after Another: Notes on Site Specificity', *October* 80 (Spring, 1997), 85–110.

Madoff, S. H. (ed.), *Art School (Propositions for the 21st Century)* (Cambridge, Mass: The MIT Press, 2009).

Malos, E. (ed.), *The Politics of Housework*, 2nd edn (Cheltenham: New Clarion Press, 1995).

Malvern, S., 'Women: Work, Politics and Art – A Chronology of the 1970s', in J. Mastai (ed.), *Social Project/Collaborative Action, Mary Kelly 1970–1975* (Vancouver: Charles H. Scott Gallery, 1997).

McNally, D., *Global Slump: The Economics and Politics of Crisis and Resistance* (Oakland: PM Press, CA., 2010).

McRobbie, A., 'Reflections on Feminism, Immaterial Labour and the Post-Fordist Regime', *New Formations* 70 (Autumn 2010), 60–76.

McRobbie, A., *The Aftermath of Feminism: Gender, Culture and Social Change* (London: Sage, 2009).

Meskimmon, M., *Contemporary Art and the Cosmopolitan Imagination* (London and New York: Routledge, 2011).

Meskimmon, M., 'Chronology through Cartography: Mapping 1970s Feminist Art Globally', in C. Butler and L. G. Mark (eds), *Wack! Art and the Feminist Revolution* (Cambridge, Mass.: The MIT Press, 2007).

Meyer, J., '"The Strong and the Weak": Andrea Fraser and the Conceptual Legacy', *Grey Room* 17 (Fall 2004), 82–107.

MFK, *Do the Right Thing!: A Manual from MFK* (Malmö: Malmö Free University for Women, 2011).

Mies, M., *Patriarchy and Accumulation on a World Scale* (London and New York: Zed Books, 1986).

Milevska, S., 'Femina Sacra: Bio-Power and Paradoxes of Humanity in the Art of Tanja Ostojić', in M. Gržinić and T. Ostojić (eds), *Integration Impossible? The Politics of Migration in the Artwork of Tanja Ostojić* (Berlin: Argobooks, 2009).

Milevska, S., 'Master/Slave', in Tanja Ostojić (ed.), *Strategies of Success – Curators Series 2001–2003* (Belgrade: SKC, 2004).

Milevska, S., 'Introduction', in S. Milevska (ed.), *Gender & Capital* (Skopje, 2001).

Mohanty, C. T., *Feminism without Borders: Decolonizing Theory, Practicing Solidarity* (Durham: Duke University Press, 2003).

Mohanty, C. T., 'Under Western Eyes: Feminist Scholarship and Colonial Discourses', *Boundary* 2 12/13 (1–3) (Spring-Autumn 1984), 333–58.

Molesworth, H. (ed.), *Work Ethic* (Pennsylvania: The Baltimore Museum of Art/The Pennsylvania State University Press, 2003).

Močnik, R., 'East!', in IRWIN (eds), *East Art Map: Contemporary Art and Eastern Europe* (London: Afterall, 2006).

Mouffe, C., *On the Political* (New York and London: Routledge, 2005).

Mulholland, N., *The Cultural Devolution: Art in Britain in the Late Twentieth Century* (Aldershot: Ashgate, 2003).

Mulvey, L., 'Visual Pleasure and Narrative Cinema', *Screen* 16/3 (Autumn 1975), 6–18.

Nagar, R., V. Lawson, L. McDowell and S. Hanson, 'Locating Globalization: Feminist (Re)readings of the Subjects and Spaces of Globalization', *Economic Geography* 78/3 (July 2002), 257–84.

Nederveen Pieterse, J., 'Emancipatory Cosmopolitanism: Towards an Agenda', *Development and Change* 37/6 (Nov. 2006), 1247–57.

Negri, A., 'Communism: Some Thoughts on the Concept and Practice' in C. Douzinas and S. Zizek (eds), *The Idea of Communism* (London: Verso 2011).

Nielson, B. and N. Rossiter, 'Precarity as a Political Concept: New Forms of Connection, Subjectivation and Organization', *Open* 17 (2009), 49–50.

Novakov, A., *Veiled Histories: The Body, Place and Public Art* (New York: Critical Press, 1997).

Nussbaum, M. C., *Not for Profit: Why Democracy Needs the Humanities* (Princeton: Princeton University Press, 2010).

Levi Strauss, D., 'The Bias of the World: Curating after Szeeman and Hopps', in S. Rand and H. Kouris (eds), *Cautionary Tales: Critical Curating* (New York: Apexart, 2007).

Lewis, B., 'Private View', *Prospect* (October 2005).

Liss, A., *Feminist Art and the Maternal* (Minneapolis: University of Minnesota Press, 2009).

Lotringer, S. and C. Marazzi (eds), *Autonomia: Post-Political Politics* (New York: Semiotext(e), 2007).

Lüth, N., 'Between Family Lines – Talking about Art and Feminism with Loraine Leeson', in C. Mörsch (ed.), *Art for Change – Loraine Lesson, Works from 1975–2005* (Berlin: NGBK, 2005).

O'Kane, P., 'Renzo Martens' Episode III', *Third Text* 23/6 (November 2009), 813–20.

Owens, G., 'Feminists and Postmodernism', in H. Foster (ed.), *Postmodern Culture* (London: Pluto, 1985).

Ostojić, T. (ed.), *Strategies of Success – Curators Series 2001–2003* (Belgrade: SKC, 2004).

Ostojić, T. 'Be My Guest', in Ostojić, (ed.), *Strategies of Success – Curators Series 2001–2003* (Belgrade: SKC, 2004).

Pachmanova, M., 'In? Out? In Between? Some Notes on the Invisibility of a Nascent Eastern European Feminist and Gender Discourse in Contemporary Art Theory' (2009) in B. Peji (ed.), *Gender Check – A Reader: Art and Theory in Eastern Europe* (Cologne: W. König, 2010).

Papadopoulos, D. and V. Tsianos, 'The Autonomy of Migration: The Animals of Undocumented Mobility', in A. Hickey-Moody and P. Malins (eds), *Deleuzian Encounters. Studies in Contemporary Social Issues* (Basingstoke: Palgrave Macmillan, 2007).

Papastergiadis, N., *Cosmopolitanism and Culture* (Cambridge: Polity, 2012).

Parker, R. and G. Pollock (eds), *Framing Feminism: Art and the Women's Movement 1970–1985* (London: Pandora, 1987).

Pearce, D. M., 'The Feminization of Poverty: Women, Work, and Welfare', *Urban and Social Change Review* 11 (1978), 28–36.

Pejić, B., 'Proletarians of All Countries, Who Washes Your Socks? Equality, Dominance and Difference in Eastern European Art', in B. Pejić (ed.), *Gender Check: Femininity and Masculinity in the Art of Eastern Europe* (Vienna: MUMOK Museum, 2011).

Perchuk, A. and H. Posner (eds), *The Masculine Masquerade: Masculinity and Representation* (Cambridge, Mass: The MIT Press 1995), exhibition catalogue.

Perry, L., 'A Great Time to Be a Woman?', in A. Dimitrakaki and L. Perry (eds), *Politics in a Glass Case: Feminism, Exhibition Cultures and Curatorial Transgressions* (Liverpool: Liverpool University Press, 2012).

Pomeroy, J. (ed.), *Intrepid Women: Victorian Women Artists Travel* (Farnham: Ashgate, 2006).

Pollock, G., 'Encounters in the Virtual Feminism Museum: Time, Space and the Archive', in M. Hedlin Hayden and J. Sjöholm Skrubbe (eds), *Feminism Is still Our Name: Seven Essays on Feminisms, Historiography and Curatorial Practices* (Newcastle: Cambridge Scholars, 2010).

Pollock, G., *Differencing the Canon: Feminist Desire the Writing of Art's Histories* (London and New York: Routledge, 1999).

Pollock, G., 'Painting, Feminism, History', in M. Barrett and A. Phillips (eds), *Destabilizing Theory: Contemporary Feminist Debates* (Stanford University Press, 1992).

Pollock, G., 'Women, Art and Ideology', in R. Parker and G. Pollock, *Old Mistresses: Women, Art and Ideology* (London: Pandora Press 1991).

Pollock, G., 'What's Wrong with 'Images of Women'?', in R. Parker and G. Pollock (eds), *Framing Feminism: Art and the Women's Movement 1970–1985* (London: Pandora, 1987).

Pollock, G., *Vision and Difference: Feminism, Femininity and the Histories of Art* (New York and London: Routledge, 1986).

Power, N., *One Dimensional Woman* (Winchester and Washington DC: Zone Books, 2009).

Rancière, J., *The Emancipated Spectator*, trans. G. Elliott (London: Verso, 2009).

Reckitt, N., 'Forgotten Relations', in A. Dimitrakaki and L. Perry (eds), *Politics in a Glass Case: Feminism, Exhibition Cultures and Curatorial Transgressions* (Liverpool: Liverpool University Press, 2012).

Richards, M., *Marina Abramovic* (Abingdon and New York: Routledge, 2010).

Roberts, J., *The Intangibilities of Form: Art after Deskilling* (London: Verso, 2008).

Roberts, J., *Realism, Photography and the Everyday* (Manchester: Manchester University Press, 1998).

Rogoff, I., *Terra Infirma: Geography's Visual Cultures* (London and New York: Routledge, 2000).

Rosa, M. L., 'Our Bodies, Our History: Mujeres Públicas's Activism in the City of Buenos Aires', *n.paradoxa: international feminist art journal* 30 (July 2012), 5–11.

Rosler, M., *In the Place of the Public: Observations of a Frequent Art Flyer* (Cantz 1999 [1993]).

Rosler, M., 'Video: Shedding the Utopian Moment', in D. Hall and S. J. Fifer (eds), *Illuminating Video: An Essential Guide to Video Art* (New York: Aperture and Bay Area: BAVC, 1990).

Rosler, M., 'Well, *Is* the Personal Political?', in H. Robinson (ed.), *Feminism-Art-Theory: An Anthology 1968–2000* (Oxford: Blackwell, 2001 [1980]).

Sanqvist, G., 'Beyond One's Role', in *Ann-Sofi Sidén* (Paris: Musee d'Art Moderne de la Ville de Paris, 2001).

Shaw, J. and P. Weibel (eds), *Future Cinema: The Cinematic Imaginary after Film* (Cambridge Mass: The MIT Press, 2003).

Sholette, G., *Dark Matter: Art and Politics in the Age of Enterprise Culture* (London: Pluto Press, 2011).

Shukaitis, S., *Imaginal Machines: Autonomy and Self-Organization in the Revolutions of Everyday Life* (New York: Minor Compositions and Autonomedia, 2009).

Silverman, K., *Male Subjectivity at the Margins* (New York and London: Routledge 1992).

Solomon Godeau, A., *Male Trouble: A Crisis in Representation* (London: Thames and Hudson, 1997).

Solomon-Godeau, A., 'The Legs of the Countess', *October* 39 (Winter, 1986), 65–108.

Spielmann, Y., 'Expanding Film into Digital Media', *Screen* 40/2 (Summer 1999), 131–45.

Stallabrass, J., *Art Incorporated: The Story of Contemporary Art* (Oxford: Oxford University Press, 2004).

Stallabrass, J., *High Art Lite: British Art in the 1990s* (London: Verso, 2001).

Stimson, B. and G. Sholette, 'Introduction: Periodizing Collectivism', in B. Stimson and G. Sholette (eds), *Collectivism after Modernism: The Art of Social Imagination after 1945* (Minneapolis: University of Minnesota Press, 2007).

Surkis, Judith, 'Tanja Ostojić's European Border Work', in M. Gržinić and T. Ostojić (eds), *Integration Impossible? The Politics of Migration in the Artwork of Tanja Ostojić* (Berlin: Argobooks, 2009).

Szeman, I., 'Remote Sensing: An Interview with Ursula Biemann', *Review of Education/Pedagogy/Cultural Studies* 24, 1/2 (January–June 2002), 91–109.

Tatlic, S., 'The Truth Machine: The Relationship between Life and Sovereign Power', in M. Gržinić and T. Ostojić (eds), *Integration Impossible? The Politics of Migration in the Artwork of Tanja Ostojić* (Berlin: Argobooks, 2009).

Taylor, S., 'Negotiating Oppositions and Uncertainties: Gendered Conflicts in Creative Identity Work', *Feminism & Psychology* (2010), 1–18.

Van Mourik-Broekman, P., 'State of Play: An Interview with Mare Tralla', in A. Dimitrakaki, P. Skelton and M. Tralla (eds), *Private Views Spaces and Gender in Contemporary Art from Britain and Estonia* (London: Women's Art Library, 2000).

Vanhaesebrouck, K. 'Dead as a Dodo? Commitment beyond Postmodernism', in L. De Cauter, R. De Roo and K. Vanhaesebrouck (eds), *Art and Activism in the Age of Globalization* (Rotterdam: NAi Publishers, 2011).

Virno, P. and Hardt, M. (eds), *Radical Thought in Italy: A Potential Politics*, trans. M. Hardt (Minneapolis: University of Minnesota Press, 1996).

Vogel, L., *Essays for a Materialist Feminism* (London: Pluto Press, 1995).

Von Osten, M. *et al.*, "She Now Works Flexible...", in J. Billing, M. Lind and L. Nilsson (eds), *Taking the Matter into Common Hands* (London: Black Dog, 2007).

Walby, S., *The Future of Feminism* (Cambridge: Polity Press, 2011).

Walby, S., *Globalization and Inequalities: Complexity and Contested Modernities* (London: Sage, 2009).

Weeks, K., *The Problem with Work: Feminism, Marxism, Antiwork Politics and Post-work Imaginaries* (Durham, NC: Duke University, 2011).

Williams, R., 'Beyond Actually Existing Socialism', *New Left Review* I, 120 (March–April 1980).

Wolff, J., *Resident Alien: Feminist Cultural Criticism* (New Haven and London: Yale University Press, 1995).

Wolff, J., 'On the Road Again: Metaphors of Travel in Cultural Criticism', *Cultural Studies* 7 (1993), 224–39.

Woolf, V., *A Room of One's Own* (New York: Harcourt Brace & Co., 1989 [1929]).

Zerilli, L., *Feminism and the Abyss of Freedom* (Chicago: University of Chicago Press, 2005).

Internet sources

Anonymous, 'The Price of Being Female' (20 May 2012), at: www.economist.com/blogs/prospero/

Tanya Augsburg, 'Man as Object – Reversing the Gaze', at: http://manasobject.weebly.com/index.html

'We did it! The rich world's quiet revolution: women are gradually taking over the workplace', *The Economist* (30 December 2009), at: www.economist.com/node/15174489

Ursula Biemann's website, at: www.geobodies.org/video/sensing/sensing_descript.html

Francesca Boenzi, 'Do you speak Spamsoc?', *Mousse* 23, at: www.moussemagazine.it/articolo.mm?id=540

Nicolas Bourriaud, 'Altermodern Manifesto – Postmodernism Is Dead', at: www.tate.org.uk/britain/exhibitions/altermodern/manifesto.shtm

Aditya Chakrabortty, 'Why Doesn't Britain Make Things Any More?', *The Guardian* (16 November 2011), at: www.guardian.co.uk/business/2011/nov/16/why-britain-doesnt-make-things-manufacturing?INTCMP=SRCH

Red Chidgey, 'DIY Feminist Networks in Europe', *Journal Transform!* Europe 5 (2009), at: www.transform-network.net/en/home/journal-transformeurope/display-journal-transform/article//DIY-Feminist-Networks-in-Europe-Personal-and-Collective-Acts-of-Resistance.html

Keti Chukhrov, 'Towards the Space of the General: On Labor beyond Materiality and Immateriality', *e-flux journal* 20 (November 2010), at: www.e-flux.com/journal/view/180

Peter Cuninghame, 'Italian Feminism, Workerism and Autonomy in the 1970s: The Struggle against Unpaid Reproductive Labour and Violence' (2008), at: http://libcom.org/history/italian-feminism-workerism-autonomy-1970s-struggle-against-unpaid-reproductive-labour-vi

Nick Dyer-Witherford, 'Autonomist Marxism and the Information Society', *Multitudes Web* at: http://multitudes.samizdat.net/Autonomist-Marxism-and-the.html. Original publication of article in Capital & Class 52 (1994).

Tracey Emin, 'What Price Art?' (documentary, Channel 4, 15 March 2006), at: www.bbc.co.uk/radio4/womanshour/01/2006_11_wed.shtml

www.saatchi-gallery.co.uk/artists/tracey_emin.htm

www.whitecube.com/artists/emin/

Silvia Federici, 'Precarious Labour: A Feminist Viewpoint' (2008), at: http://inthemiddleofthewhirlwind.wordpress.com/precarious-labor-a-feminist-viewpoint/

Tim Fisken (2011), 'The Spectral Proletariat: The Politics of Hauntology in *The Communist Manifesto*', *Global Discourse* [Online], 2: II (2011), at: http://global-discourse.com/contents

Maja and Reuben Fowkes, 'Contemporary East European Art in the Era of Globalization: From Identity Politics to Cosmopolitan Solidarity', *ARTMargins Online* (29 September 2010), at: www.artmargins.com/index.php/2-articles/598-contemporary-east-european-art-era-globalization-identity-politics-cosmopolitan-solidarity#ftn_artnotes1_1

Nancy Garín, 'Curatorial Practices: Interview with WHW Collective' 01/01/10, *Latin-Art.com: An Online Journal of Art and Culture*, at: www.latinart.com/aiview.cfm?id=420

Martha E. Gimenez, 'Marxist Feminism/Materialist Feminism' (copyright 1998), at: www.cddc.vt.edu/feminism/mar.html

Stacey Goergen, 'Olaf Bruning: About the Artist', at: http://whitney.org/www/2008biennial/www/?section=artists&page=artist_breuning

Marina Gržinić, 'Analysis of the Exhibition "Gender Check – Femininity and Masculinity in the Art of Eastern Europe", Museum of Modern Art (MUMOK), Vienna, November 2009/February 2010' (December 2009), at: http://eipcp.net/policies/grzinic/en

Thomas N. Hale and Anne-Marie Slaughter, 'Hardt & Negri's 'Multitude': The Worst of Both Worlds' (25 May 2005), at: www.opendemocracy.net/globalization-vision_reflections/marx_2549.jsp

Beata Hock, 'Agency Gendered: Deconstructed Marriages and Migration Narratives in Contemporary Art', *ArtMargins* (8 July 2011), at: www.artmargins.com/index.php/2-articles/636--marriages-and-migration-in-art

Lu Jie '800 Metres' on an exhibition of the same name held at Long March in Beijing (2 September to 15 October 2006), at: www.artlinkart.com/en/space/exh_yr/ee1etw/6ofaxzr

Ken Johnson, 'An Artist Turns People into His Marionettes', *The New York Times* (29 November 2009), at: www.nytimes.com/2009/11/30/arts/design/30zmijewski.html

Maurizio Lazzarato, 'Biopolitics/Bioeconomics: A Politics of Multiplicity', *Multitudes* (April 2006), at: http://multitudes.samizdat.net/Biopolitics-Bioeconomics-a

Elisabeth Lebovici, 'French Lessons', *Artforum* (March 1996), at: http://findarticles.com/p/articles/mi_m0268/is_n7_v34/ai_18403695/

Izabela Kowalczyk, Dorota Łagodzka and Edyta Zierkiewic, 'Anger of Bojana Peji: An Interview', Warsaw (23 February 2010), *Obieg*, at: www.obieg.pl/artmix/18402

'Masculinities' Kunsthallen Nikolaj (3 November to 30 December 2001), at: www.kunstaspekte.de/index.php?tid=24578&action=termin (accessed 13 December 2010).

Riah Matthews, 'Art: Uneven Geographies, Nottingham Contemporary', *Nottingham Post* 14 May 2010, at: www.thisisnottingham.co.uk/news/Art-Uneven-Geographies-

Nottingham-Contemporary/article-2149196-detail/article.html (accessed 16 December 2010).

Angela Melitopoulos, 'Before the Representation: Video Images as Agents in "Passing Drama" and "TIMESCAPES"' (May 2003), at: http://eipcp.net/transversal/1003/melitopoulos/en

Sandro Mezzadra, 'Taking Care: Migration and the Political Economy of Affective Labor', Lecture, March 16th 2005 Goldsmiths University of London – Center for the Study of Invention and Social Process (CSISP). http://caringlabor.wordpress.com/2010/07/29/sandro-mezzadra-taking-care-migration-and-the-political-economy-of-affective-labor/

'Missing Italian Woman Artist Found Dead in Turkey', Associated Press (12 April 2008), at: www.foxnews.com/story/0,2933,350970,00.html

Linda Nochlin in 'Feminism & Art (9 views)', *Artforum* (October 2003), at: http//findarticles.com

Jessica Lack, 'Artist of the Week 22: Hito Steyerl', *The Guardian* (31 December 2008), at: www.guardian.co.uk/culture/2008/dec/30/contemporary-artist-hito-steyerl-new-wave

Elisabeth Lebovici, 'French Lessons' *Artforum* (March 1996), at: http://findarticles.com/p/articles/mi_m0268/is_n7_v34/ai_18403695/

Lies: A Journal of Materialist Feminism, Volume 1 (2012), at: http://liesjournal.info/index.php?/volumes/volume-1/

Dimitris Papadopoulos and Vassilis Tsianos, 'The Autonomy of Migration: The Animals of Undocumented Mobility' (15 September 2008) , at: http://translate.eipcp.net/strands/02/papadopoulostsianos-strands01en#redir

Nikos Papastergiadis, 'The Cosmopolitan Imaginary of Art: Terror, Fear, Curiosity and Hope', lecture at EMST Athens, 20 November 2009, at: http://fixit-emst.blogspot.com/2009/11/nikos-papastergiadis-lecture.html

Simon Pope, 'The Shape of Locative Media', *Mute*, M29: The Precarious Issue (February 2005), www.metamute.org

Els Roelandt, 'Renzo Martens' Episode 3: Analysis of a Film Process in Three Conversations', at: http://squarevzw.be/picturethis/renzoapm16.htm (accessed 8 December 2010). First published in *A Prior Magazine* 16 (February 2008).

Bartholomew Ryan, 'Manifesto for Maintenance: A Conversation with Mierle Laderman Ukeles' (20 March 2009), at: www.artinamericamagazine.com/news-opinion/conversations/2009-03-20/draft-mierle-interview/

Asli Saglam, 'Continuing the Journey of Peace Bride Pippa Bacca', *Hürriyet Daily News*, Istanbul (18 February 2010), at: www.asminfilm.com/Basin-detay.aspx?cid=25

'Adrian Searle, 'Into the Unknown', *The Guardian* (8 October 2002), at: www.guardian.co.uk/film/2002/oct/08/artsfeatures.art

Yang Shaobin: The X Blind Spot – A Long March Project' at Long March Foundation in Peking (4 September to 18 October 2008). Available in English at: www.kunstaspekte.de/index.php?tid=44764&action=termin (accessed 15 December 2009).

Hito Steyerl, 'Politics of Art: Contemporary Art and the Transition to Postdemocracy', *e-flux journal* 21 (December 2010), at: http://e-flux.com/journal/view/181

Marion von Osten, 'de-, dis-, ex- on Immaterial Labour: An Interview with Marina Vishmidt', at: http://republicart.net/disc/precariat/vishmidt-osten01_en.htm

User's Manual: The Grand Domestic Revolution. Excerpt from 'Introduction', http://www.cascoprojects.org/gdr/introduction/

'Transcultural Geographies', at: http://www.videophilosophy.de/tc-geographies.net/index.html

Tirdad Zolghadr, '11th Istanbul Biennial', *frieze* 127 (November–December 2009) www.frieze.com/issue/review/11th_istanbul_biennial/

www.jennymarketou.com/projects/translocal.shtml

Pedro Vélez, 'Hearts of Darkness', *Artnet magazine* (14 December 2007), at: www.artnet.com/magazineus/reviews/velez/velez12-14-07.asp

The Commoner 15 (Winter 2012), special issue Care Work and the Commons, at: www.commoner.org.uk/2012/05/post-war-artists-auction, at: www.justseedsorg/blog/2009/02/choose_your_own_dis_adventure.html www.radikalpedagogik.blogspot.com/#!/p/in-english.html Sam Taylor Wood *'Fuck, suck, spank, wank'* (1993) sale at Christie's, at: www.christies.com/lotFinder/lot_details.aspx?intObjectID=1478109

Tsianos, V. and D. Papadopoulos, 'Who's Afraid of Immaterial Workers? Embodied Capitalism, Precarity, Imperceptibility' (2006), at: http://preclab.net/text/06–TsianosPapadopoulos.pdf.

Conferences

'Global Cultures', Centre of Modern Studies, University of York, 20 June 2009.

'Work, Work, Work: A Series of Seminars on Art and Labour' IASPIS, November–December 2010.

'"Mashing Up": Art + Labour, A Public Conversation' organised by *Variant*, Glasgow (9 November 2010).

Angela Dimitrakaki, 'Beyond the Global Flâneuse: Travelling Women and the Politics of Art as Labour', in the session 'Dis-Locations: Movements and Migrations', organised by Rosemary Betterton and Dorothy Rowe, *Location: the Museum, the Academy and the Studio* AAH Annual Conference, held at Tate Britain and Tate Modern, London (2–4 April 2008).

'Whither Feminist Art History?', organised by Francesca Berry and Amy Mechowski, 32nd AAH Annual Conference *Contents, Discontents, Malcontents*, University of Leeds (5–7 April 2006).

INDEX

Note: Exhibition titles appear in italics.

EU authorised representative for GPSR:
Easy Access System Europe, Mustamäe tee 50,
10621 Tallinn, Estonia
gpsr.requests@easproject.com

www.ingramcontent.com/pod-product-compliance
Ingram Content Group UK Ltd.
Pitfield, Milton Keynes, MK11 3LW, UK
UKHW021826150726
7214IPUK00017B/340